The
Information Broker's
Handbook

Other books by Alfred Glossbrenner

Making Money on the Internet by Alfred and Emily Glossbrenner, 1995

Finding a Job on the Internet by Alfred and Emily Glossbrenner, 1995

The Little Online Book, 1995

The Complete Modem Handbook, 1995

How to Look it Up Online, 2nd Ed. by Alfred Glossbrenner and John Rosenberg, 1995

Internet 101: A College Student's Guide, 1995

Internet Slick Tricks by Alfred and Emily Glossbrenner, 1994

DOS 6, 1993

Power DOS!, 1993

File & Disk Management: From Chaos to Control, 1993

Glossbrenner's Guide to Shareware for Small Businesses, 1992

DOS 5, 1992

Glossbrenner's Master Guide to GEnie, 1991

Glossbrenner's Complete Hard Disk Handbook, 1990

The Complete Handbook of Personal Computer Communications—3rd Edition, 1990

Glossbrenner's Master Guide to FREE Software for IBMs and Compatible Computers, 1989

Glossbrenner's Master Guide to CompuServe, 1987

How to Look It Up Online, 1987

The Complete Handbook of Personal Computer Communications—Second Edition, 1985

How to Get FREE Software, 1984

How to Buy Software, 1984

The Winning Hitter by Charley Lau with Alfred Glossbrenner, 1984

The Complete Handbook of Personal Computer Communications—First Edition, 1983

Word Processing for Executives, Managers, and Professionals by Timothy R. V. Foster and Alfred Glossbrenner, 1983

The Information Broker's Handbook

second edition

Sue Rugge
Alfred Glossbrenner

McGraw-Hill, Inc.

New York San Francisco Washington, D.C. Auckland Bogotá
Caracas Lisbon London Madrid Mexico City Milan
Montreal New Delhi San Juan Singapore
Sydney Tokyo Toronto

pbk 1 2 3 4 5 6 7 8 9 DOC/DOC 9 9 8 7 6 5
hc 1 2 3 4 5 6 7 8 9 DOC/DOC 9 9 8 7 6 5

Library of Congress Cataloging-in-Publication Data

Rugge, Sue.
    The information broker's handbook / by Sue Rugge, Alfred Glossbrenner. —2nd ed.
        p.   cm.
    Includes index.
    ISBN 0-07-911877-1 (h)   ISBN 0-07-911878-X (pbk)
    1. Information services industry—Management. 2. Information services. 3. Information scientists. I. Glossbrenner, Alfred. II. Title.
    HD9999.I492R84   1994   94-45359
    025.5'2'068—dc20   CIP

Acquisitions editor: Brad Schepp
Editorial team: Emily Glossbrenner, Book Editor
                David M. McCandless, Managing Editor
                Joanne Slike, Executive Editor
Production team: Katherine G. Brown, Director
                Donna K. Harlacher, Coding
                Lisa M. Mellott, Coding
                Joann Woy, Indexer
Designer: Jaclyn J. Boone

EPC1
911878X

Contents

Appendices

Foreword

The first words I ever heard from Sue Rugge's office were "You're talking to a desperate woman! When can you start?"

Actually, the words were those of Sue's Director of Research, Barbara Newlin Bernstein. I'd just moved back to California after a stint as an engineering company librarian in Reading, Pennsylvania, and I was looking for work. I'd heard of Sue Rugge and her pioneering efforts in what was then called the fee-based information business. So when I came across the ad for a research associate at her firm, Information on Demand, I leaped for the phone.

IOD, in turn, leaped for me. They were short two researchers, it turned out, and had more work than they could handle. What I'd assumed would be a one-hour job interview turned out to be the first day of almost six years with Information on Demand. No resume or references changed hands that day; Sue and Barbara had a warm body and a passable intellect in their grasp, and they weren't about to let go. I was given a desk, a telephone, and a few simple guidelines. Seven hours later, I could tell you anything you wanted to know about water-pumping windmills.

Those words of Barbara's proved to be prophetic. The demand for information, and for knowledgeable people to retrieve, manage, and massage it, has continued to accelerate. Hundreds of new entrepreneurs have entered the business since 1981, the year I was semikidnapped into it. Some of their ventures have succeeded, but the majority, I suspect, have failed.

Why? One major reason is a lack of solid, straight-from-the-shoulder information about the information industry in general and the information brokering profession in particular.

That's why a book like this is so refreshing and so essential. Sue Rugge has no illusions about the independent research business. She has no vested interest other than helping to maintain the profession's high standards and making the world aware of all that it has to offer.

Sue's concern for the profession led to her early involvement in the Association of Independent Information Professionals (AIIP), an organization she headed as president in 1988–89. Her pragmatic view of the industry has been invaluable to me, to other AIIP officers, to hundreds of seasoned information brokers, and to thousands who aspire to enter the profession.

When people ask me for advice on becoming an information broker, I recommend Sue's seminars, telling them that the registration fee is a small price to pay for a reality check—for insurance against making a career move that might *not* be in their best interest.

Sue knows what kind of training, experience, and personality traits make a good information broker. As an industry pioneer, she is passionate about getting good people more involved. She is equally passionate about dissuading those who see the opportunity to make a quick buck, or for whom the fit just doesn't seem right.

Sue Rugge knows, in short, what *you* need to know. And she and Alfred Glossbrenner have captured in this book as much of that expertise as it is possible to transfer from human brain cells to the printed page.

Alfred has been writing books about computers and computer communications since 1981. We met through Sue several years ago, when we all "performed" at the same small information-oriented conference. We hit it off instantly, and I know that much of the chemistry among the three of us lay in Alfred's ability to become totally engrossed in the concerns and interests of the people he is conversing with. He asks intelligent questions, absorbs what you know about the subject, draws you out, and internalizes the knowledge that you have to offer. The result is a detailed conceptual map of a subject, presented with crystalline clarity in easy, conversational tones.

Information brokering has come a long way since the early days at IOD. As in the past, most successful practitioners today have a library background, but that's changing. We're seeing more people with years of experience in a particular industry, or with a background in marketing or business management, who are willing to *learn* to do research, or to partner with someone who knows how. This increasing diversity of experience and perspective is a good thing; we can all learn from each other.

From what I've seen, there's plenty of business out there. The information profession can *always* use good people. If you are good, and if you work hard, you have an excellent chance of carving out a tidy market niche for yourself, especially if you have expertise in a hot industry or technology, or access to unique resources.

One thing that has characterized this profession from its inception is a spirit of cooperation, rather than competition, among its members. This has its roots, I think, in the library world, where the thrill of the hunt, and of *finding* what you're looking for, is something to be shared with your colleagues. If this excitement—this love of research for its own sake—resonates with you, you're already ahead of the game. Now it's time for you to listen to Sue and Alfred.

Reva Basch

A past president of the Association of Independent Information Professionals, Reva Basch's most recent book is *Secrets of the Super Searchers: The Accumulated Wisdom of 23 of the World's Top Online Searchers*, published by Online, Inc. She can be reached at Aubergine Information Services in Berkeley, California, and at REVA@WELL.SF.CA.US.

Introduction
TANSTAAFL

There's a lot of misinformation around about the information brokering profession. So we owe it to you to set the record straight right from the start.

You've all seen those pie-in-the-sky ads, the ones that promise to let you in on the "secrets" of how to make a good living working for yourself, in your spare time, at home. No bosses, no time cards, no worries. Nothing much to do, apparently, but trundle on down to the mailbox each day and pick up those fat checks your customers are so eager to send.

And all this from what? Stuffing envelopes? Selling magazine subscriptions over the phone? Enlisting people as soap salespeople in your "multi-level marketing" pyramid?

Well, maybe. It's possible that some people really have discovered a magic formula. But we've never known anyone like that. We've certainly never known any information brokers who've managed to make money so effortlessly. Our experience, in fact, tracks more with the philosophy stated by the late science fiction writer Robert A. Heinlein. Heinlein summed up his opinion in a nine-character expression: TANSTAAFL.

Translated, this means "There ain't no such thing as a free lunch!" And, of course, it's true. If it weren't, the world's taverns, pubs, and assorted watering holes—the originators of the "free lunch" concept—would soon go out of business. Somebody *always* pays. And unless you happen to own a savings and loan or other government-backed institution, that someone is almost always you.

No free lunch!

We bring this up because for the last several years the old get-rich-quick offers of the past have been updated for the '90s. The pitch today is not so much to the desire we all have to make a ton of money, though that is still a strong undercurrent. The main focus now is on Personal independence, entrepreneurship, working for yourself, making your own hours, and working from home.

Unfortunately, the profession that has long been called information brokering has received greater attention in these ads than ever before. After all, it offers everything a con artist could want, starting with a very plausible story. Here's the pitch:

An information broker is someone who finds answers for money, right? And as we all know, lots of people need answers—doctors, lawyers, Fortune 500 companies, investors—you name it. Best of all, we live in the Information Age, where answers can be found virtually lying on the ground, like apples fallen from a tree.

All you have to do is fire up your computer and your "telephone modem" and swing onto the Information Superhighway. The stuff's just lying there waiting for you to pick it up and deliver it to your client, who will then pay you a hefty fee. Anyone can do it! Best of all, you can work for yourself, at home, setting your own hours.

The idea is irresistible. And, aside from the part about the insatiable demand, the hefty fees, and the ease with which answers can be found, it's all true. Mostly. Of course, all it takes is a computer and a modem, which the pitchman may be willing to sell you for a modest fee. Plus the pitchman's "exclusive" kit and home study guide, offered for a distinctly immodest fee.

Raking in the big bucks

But, hey, you're worth it. Besides, this is your career we're talking about here. In a few weeks, the cost won't matter because after that, you'll be raking in the big bucks.

Best of all, the promoter has the perfect out: "What? You say you've followed the program for six months and haven't gotten a single client? Well, you're probably not doing it right. There must be something you've missed. Maybe you should buy the Phase II kit and home study guide to *sharpen up your skills.*"

You know the routine. What you probably don't know is that in this country of over 250 million people, there are *at most* a thousand or so full-time information brokers—men and women who earn enough money finding and delivering information for clients that they don't have to do anything else. There are a few hundred more who work at the profession part-time. Many of these folks hold down full-time jobs as professional librarians and corporate information center managers and do their information brokering after normal working hours.

Whether full-time or part-time, many of the people working as information brokers today have advanced degrees, often in information and library science. They are very, very good at finding answers. Yet, as noted, only a fraction of them can make a living as full-time information brokers.

That should tell you something.

It should tell you that the world is not beating a path to the information broker's door. On the contrary, while most people pay lip service to the Information Age, when it comes to actually *paying* for information or the services of an information professional, most people and companies are extremely reluctant to part with their dollars.

Typically, they'll find a way to do without or, worse, try to do it themselves. And the thing of it is, most manage to get by. At least for a while. The fact is, they never know what they're missing and would almost certainly have had even greater success had they used the services of an information professional. But that's difficult to prove.

We know it's true. We know that day in and day out, the business that has the best information is going to out-perform those that are merely getting by. But often, in this era of mediocrity, getting by is more than sufficient.

Not until Company A is repeatedly beaten by Company B on bids, on contracts, and on sales will Company A begin to ask "Why?" Hopefully some bright bulb at Company A will realize that the reason the firm is getting its hind quarters kicked from here to November is that Company B has superior information. Only then will Company A eagerly seek out the information broker.

The long climb to enlightenment

As for those companies who value information but think that all they need is a Dialog account and a clutch of databases on CD-ROM, wait until the paralegal, college intern, mid-level executive, or whatever other amateur is doing the searching misses something. Wait until the company makes a decision based on this incomplete information and ends up losing its investment or being sued. Then they may see the value of hiring an information professional.

In the meantime, if you want to make a living as an information broker, you are going to have to spend a great deal of your time marketing your services. Or you are going to have to team up with someone who can do it for you. You do *not* have to have a computer and a modem. That kind of equipment is extremely helpful, to be sure, but it is not absolutely essential. What you really need is a telephone and the imagination and tenacity of a crack investigative reporter.

You'll also need a good head for business. And you will need patience, for what we have told you so far is the bad news. The good news is that information consciousness is growing. More and more people are beginning to realize how much information is available and how useful it can be.

The opportunities are definitely there. But you have to know how and where to look for them. You have to be willing to master a set of new skills and patiently, tirelessly build your business. But then, that's true of any business or profession.

Money to be made

Though our evidence is only anecdotal, it does appear that the opportunities for professional information services are growing. Once you know more about the incredible depth and diversity of information that *is* available—either through the skilled use of a computer and modem or through the imaginative use of the telephone—you will agree that the rise of the professional information consultant is inevitable.

There is money to be made. And there is a growing demand for professional information services. But there's still no such thing as a free lunch.

If you want the freedom and independence that information brokering can provide, you can have it. You'll have to have a certain aptitude, and, like all self-employed people, you'll have to be willing to work like hell—in learning your trade, in marketing your services, and in delivering what you promise.

This book will show you how to accomplish all of these tasks. We'll show you what the profession of information broker is all about. We'll give you the tips and techniques you need to market your services. And we'll show you how and where to look for the answers to your clients' questions. We'll also tell you how to run an information consulting business.

Finding your niche

The rest is up to you. If you enjoy information, but take no pleasure in the hunt—in the process of throwing your mind, imagination, and skills against a problem—then you may want to team up with someone who does. You could be the marketing arm, and your partner could be the search arm of an excellent business.

If you don't see yourself as a marketer and have no special *love* for information, then you should probably investigate other self-employment opportunities. Of course, we're biased. But then, we also know a thing or two about what it takes to be a *successful* information broker. It's not the same as selling soap, three-penny nails, or accounting services.

These are all honorable pursuits, and most of them are better paying. And in those jobs, you don't have to love the product to be a success. In contrast, if you don't love information and have a profound respect for its value, its power, and the thrill of finding answers, you'll never be happy as an information broker.

On the other hand, if you have a natural curiosity about things, if you are willing to work, and if you're willing to sell or team up with someone who can, then you really can become a self-employed information professional. And you really can make a living at it.

This book will show you how.

How to use this book

This book is designed to give you everything you need to know to become a successful information broker, regardless of your previous level of information-related experience. We are very much aware, however, that the distance separating the most experienced reader from the least experienced is likely to be very great indeed.

If you are a trained librarian or information professional, or if you have a strong information background, you have one set of needs. If you have no formal training but have a strong interest in the profession, you have a different set of needs.

As we all know, no single book can be precisely tuned to every requirement every reader may have. So let us tell you what we have done, show you how the book is arranged, and offer some suggestions on how to make the most of it.

In our opinion, there is a certain quantum of knowledge anyone must have to become a successful information broker. Therefore, we begin at the beginning with a discussion of the current market for information, and then offer some insights on how an intelligent, curious, *motivated* person can seize the opportunities that exist in this field. The book continues straight through this continuum of essential information.

If you are new to the information field, we strongly suggest that you begin by surveying all of the chapters in this book, pausing now and again to read passages that catch your eye, and then return to the Introduction and read straight through. In general, each chapter assumes that you have read all of the chapters that precede it on the "continuum."

On the other hand, if you have had some experience in an information-related field, you may want to approach things a bit differently. You may want to review the Table of Contents, select a chapter of interest, and read it in toto. You may wish to jump around. We would like to suggest, however, that you at least skim every chapter, even those that appear to cover topics long familiar to you. You never know where or when you might pick up some useful tip, technique, or tidbit.

The Table of Contents is largely self-explanatory, so we will not preview each chapter here. As you will notice, however, the book is divided into four main parts. Part one discusses the information business in general. It offers a no-holds-barred, straight-from-the-shoulder analysis of the market, the pluses and minuses, and your chances for success.

Part two assumes that, despite our best attempts in the first six chapters to scare you off, you really do have what it takes to become a successful information broker. (Or at least you think you do.) That's why Part two focuses on the basic techniques of information gathering every information broker needs to master, including an entire chapter, new in this second edition, devoted to public records searching.

Part three continues the tutorial by discussing the incredible array of electronic databases and online systems that are yours to mine for the raw material you need. It covers the databases and other traditional sources, as well as the Internet, bulletin board systems, and online special interest groups. Part three concludes with a chapter on CD-ROM (Compact Disk—Read Only Memory), a technology that promises to revolutionize the information business.

With Part four, we really get down to business. Here you will find the most thorough, comprehensive, and downright useful compilation of information available anywhere about what it *really* takes to establish and run a successful information brokering firm. You can be the most skilled online searcher in the world . . . you can have an armload of advanced degrees . . . but if you fail to project an image of credibility, if you neglect marketing and sales, you will *not* succeed as an independent information professional.

We're simplifying greatly here, but in a nutshell, Sue Rugge's message to all prospective information brokers is this:

If you can search, join forces with someone who can sell, and if you can sell, team up with someone who can search.

Either way, you will find the chapters in Part four invaluable.

The book concludes with six appendices designed to provide you with the tools you need to get off to a good start. There are addresses, contacts, information sources, reference works and directories, and "free" business-related programs to know about.

There is also the disk that accompanies this book. As Appendix F explains, this disk can be used by *everyone*, whether you own an IBM-compatible DOS/Windows machine or an Apple Macintosh or Power PC. The disk contains clean ASCII text files designed to be imported into your favorite word-processing program. The files include forms, contacts, and addresses printed in the book. But—and this is very important—the disk also includes information not found in these pages, including a sample services contract, an actual information broker report, and a variety of actual cover letters sent to information broker clients.

Our goal with the accompanying disk was to come as close as possible to providing you with a "turnkey" information broker operation. Print out the forms. Mark them up and customize them to your own needs. Then load the appropriate file into your favorite word-processing program and make the modifications. What might have taken hours if you had to start from scratch can be done in minutes when you use the files on the accompanying disk as your starting point.

In conclusion, we think you will be fascinated by the dynamic profession of information brokering. It's exciting, frustrating, demanding, and immensely rewarding, all at the same time. It's definitely not for everyone. But, by the time you finish this book, you will know whether or not it's for you.

1 The market for information

Can *you* make a living as an information broker? We can't tell you that. But one thing is certain: you'll never even get off the ground until you have an appreciation of just what it is you're dealing with. So let's talk for a moment about the commodity we're supposedly in the business of finding, packaging, selling, or otherwise "brokering." Let's talk about *information*.

President Clinton and Vice President Gore have done us all a tremendous favor by promoting the notion of the Information Superhighway. Regardless of your politics, no one can deny that not only was George Bush baffled by supermarket scanners, he didn't even know how to turn on his computer. He said so himself. Clinton and Gore, in contrast, each have CompuServe mailboxes.

Whether they personally pick up their e-mail or not is beside the point. As is the fact that, for all the hoopla, the Information Superhighway does not really exist yet. Indeed, there are about as many definitions of what it will eventually be and do as there are experts on the subject. What's significant about the Clinton/Gore Administration is how it has dramatically raised the "information consciousness" of the American public. The Internet was even a *Time* magazine cover story (25 July 1994), for heaven's sake!

Clearly information is hot, and the information industry is the place to be. Which makes it all the more important to emphasize the fact that successful information brokers do not sell information. Let us say it again for emphasis: Although we deliver facts, figures, reports, transcripts, reprints of magazine and newspaper articles, and the like to our clients, it is not the information itself that we're selling.

It is our *expertise* in searching for information. That may seem like a subtle distinction, but it's crucial. A client who believes that what he or she is buying from you is information is likely to gauge your worth on the gross tonnage you deliver, not on its quality or relevance to the question at hand. If you know anything about information retrieval, you know how short-sighted that is on the client's part. But if you know anything about human nature, you know that it is inevitable—if you position yourself as a seller of information.

Educating the client

Thus, one of the first jobs of every information broker is to educate the client about information and the "Information Age." The "Information Age" is a phrase used so frequently that it has become a cliché even more tiresome than "Information Superhighway." In fact, it's worse than a cliché, for as tired and shopworn as even the most common cliché may be, at least everyone knows what it means.

We all know what the phrases "Closing the barn door after the horses have escaped" or "As scarce as hen's teeth" mean, even though very few of us have ever owned a horse or peered into the open beak of a chicken. The Information Age is far less clear and far more nebulous. Most of the time, as with Lewis Carroll's Alice, we make the words mean whatever we want them to mean at the time.

And that's the point. The Information Age may mean cable television, with more channels than ever before and round-the-clock, up-to-the-minute news, weather, sports, and financial reports. It may mean the explosion of magazines and paperback books stuffed into store shelves, supermarket racks, and even vending machines. It may also mean the increased use of electronics—computers, fax machines, cellular telephones, databases, and satellite dishes—in nearly every industry or profession.

There is simply no clear definition of what constitutes the Information Age. Yet the Information Age itself defines these as we must all swim in as information professionals. The Information Age *is* today's reality.

Fortunately, while no one can agree on its details, nearly everyone would agree that the two most important characteristics of the Information Age are quantity and availability. It is those two features we will consider next, especially as they relate to the information profession and the market for information-related services.

Quantity: Miles & miles of pretty files

The breadth and scope of the information that exists today on virtually any topic, person, or place is simply staggering. If you are new to the information business, you probably accept that statement the way one accepts the statement that the planet Jupiter is 1,300 times the size of Earth. Your intellect acknowledges its accuracy, but your gut doesn't feel its truth.

As a prospective information broker, however, it is essential to truly experience this fact, to feel it in your soul. A stroll through your local library won't do it. As impressive as they are, most public libraries hold only a tiny fraction of all that's available on any subject.

To even glimpse the kind of quantity we're talking about, you would have to spend a couple of days prowling the stacks at a major metropolitan or university library: floor after floor containing mile after mile of books, racks of microfilm, and entire rooms piled high with back issues of magazines, journals, and newsletters.

Yet this isn't even the tip of the iceberg. After all, most metropolitan and university libraries not only have a main building but many subsidiary buildings as well, each of which houses a separate collection. At one university we know of, for example, there is not only a huge main library—three floors of which are underground—but also separate buildings for materials on art and architecture, chemistry, engineering, and psychology, to say nothing of the little niche libraries tucked away in smaller buildings on campus. Each one of these buildings houses more subject-specific books and publications than you'll find in all the branches of many county library systems.

We don't want to belabor the point. But until you've felt your heart pounding and your breath grow short when confronting the vast quantities of information available—until you have been *overwhelmed*—you'll never be a full-fledged information consultant.

On being overwhelmed!

This is not some macho rite of passage. It is pure practicality. After all, if you were a king, who would you rather send to slay the fire-breathing dragon? An over-confident new recruit who has never actually seen the beast? Or a seasoned warrior who in the past has been toasted by its flames? Which of these individuals is likely to give you the most accurate advice on just what can be accomplished and how long it will take? More to the point, which is likely to make the more credible presentation?

Throughout this book you'll find numerous ways to expose yourself to the dragon's fire. If you follow our advice, you'll come away with a healthy respect for what you're up against. Equally important, you'll come away with confidence. Confidence in your ability to do what others cannot do. Indeed, what most people have no idea *how* to do—retrieve information. You must never forget that what you're selling as an information broker is not really the information itself; you're selling your skill and ability to retrieve it.

The other major characteristic of the Information Age is the availability of information. It is important to realize that, judged by the standards of the times, a great deal of information about a great many things has *always* existed. Record-keeping has long been a human habit.

Availability: All you have to do is ask

Government bureaucracy, to take but one example, did not start with the invention of the typewriter. Even today, archaeologists continue to turn up literally mounds of contracts, property transaction records, bills of sale, and other mundane "documents" dating back more than a thousand years B.C.

Many of these ancient documents were punched into soft clay tablets with the wedge-shaped implement that is the hallmark of cuneiform. The tablets were then baked into stone, yielding what one must naturally refer to as the world's first "hard copy."

Or the records were scratched on sheep guts (vellum) with a stylus and ink of carbon black and olive oil. Or written with a quill pen on parchment, with a dollop of hot sealing wax embossed with the signer's personal crest to testify to authenticity. But they were "information" all the same.

Today, in keeping with the "bigger, better, faster, more complete, more complex" orientation of modern civilization, documents are more detailed, and there are many, many more of them. But today, the documents are also *available*. And that makes all the difference.

Today, you don't have to book passage across the Mediterranean to consult the scrolls tucked inside the leather cylinders of the library at Alexandria. You don't have to be a noble or a scholar to gain access to your county's file of deeds or property transactions.

Easier access to public records

Democracy, the great leveler, gives every citizen access to vast quantities of government information. Indeed, in some states, if you have a personal computer and a modem and know what numbers to dial, you may not even have to leave your home or office to obtain the local government information you want or need. A number of counties, for example, have made their databases of real estate transactions available in this way.

But that's only the beginning. As you will see in Chapter 9, Public Records Searching, local governments have gotten into online information in a big way. Whether it's vital statistics (birth, death, marriage, etc.) or voter registration, fishing licenses, and court records, our states, counties, and municipalities have begun to make it much easier to obtain public records information online.

And this is just government information. Even more information is published by commercial sources, much of it available by personal computer, at libraries, through the inter-library loan network, and via the many other systems that have been created for the sole purpose of making information available.

More & more on CD-ROM

The forms are changing as well. For example, Alfred uses a CD-ROM product sold by the Ziff-Davis Publishing Company to instantly access the full text of literally hundreds of computer magazines and newsletters. The product is called Computer Select, and subscriptions run about $1,200 a year.

That's a stiff price, to be sure. But consider the alternative: box after box of printed magazines in the attic, all of which take up space and none of which are easily accessible due to poor or nonexistent indexes. Add to this the fact that the CD-ROM product includes publications of interest that one might not normally subscribe to, and the price begins to look much more reasonable.

Ziff-Davis's Computer Select has only been available since 1988. But it is part of a trend toward making more and more information more easily available to an ever widening audience. We'll have much more to say on this in Chapter 17. But here it is important to point out that the information industry itself has not yet worked out a procedure for dealing with CD-ROMs.

On the one hand, companies want the profits from selling CD-ROM products to writers and end users like Alfred. On the other, they want to preserve their income stream from information brokers like Sue who heretofore have paid to search these databases online. So far, the solution has been a wacky pricing structure that requires professional information brokers to pay more for the identical CD-ROM product than end users who are part of the general public.

What is information?

This, then, is the Information Age: an incredible amount of information on an infinite variety of topics readily available to virtually everyone. This is the realm in which every prospective information broker must make a living. It is a realm that needs an information broker's services because, while all of this information is indeed available, in reality, considerable skill and expertise are required to retrieve it.

There's just one thing missing from this broad definition—a more concrete idea of just what is meant by "information." The term, like the "Age," has prodigious elasticity. Which is to say, it is used to cover nearly everything.

When RNA molecules pass on a cell's genetic code, they are said to be transferring "information." Television commercials for everything from pain killers to breakfast cereal often claim they are providing "important information" about the products they were designed to sell. Not for them the crass sales pitches of the competition. They're providing you with *information*.

And presumably the half-hour "infomercials" for everything from stain removers to Chinese woks or vegetable juicers are of an even higher caliber since they are providing you with even more "information."

The list goes on and on, and of course it includes "relative value" type data. To you, a scrap of paper bearing a sequence of digits may be about as valuable as a gum wrapper. But to someone who knows that the numbers are the combination to the office safe, the password to a secure database, or a government official's private phone number, that paper could be priceless.

Even a lack of information is significant

In some instances, even the fact that there is *no* information on a particular topic is in itself valuable information. Imagine you're an inventor who wants to patent an invention, or a marketer interested in establishing a new brand name, or a personnel officer interested in making sure that a candidate you plan to recommend for a high-level position has never been indicted.

Police arrest records are not publicly available, but newspaper accounts and court transcripts certainly are, as are records of convictions. In all of these cases, the fact that there is no similar patent or brand name or record of a run-in with the law is in itself valuable information.

Clearly, it is impossible to come up with a universal definition of what constitutes information. But for our purposes as information brokers, we can define it quite precisely:

Information is whatever someone wants to know—and is willing to pay to find out.

Anything. Anything at *all*.

Your role as an information broker is to find whatever it is your client wants to know, using whatever *legal* means are available and working within whatever the client's budget will allow. Information brokers may offer other services as well, but fundamentally, information brokering is about finding information.

As such, you have a great deal going for you right off the bat. In the United States, an individual with the proper skills and unwavering dedication can find out nearly anything he or she wants to know. This is an awesome prospect: anything at all that you or your client wants to know can be discovered, given sufficient time and sufficient financial resources.

Of course there are limits. You can't break the law. You must respect a person's right to privacy. You must maintain the highest ethical standard at all times—even if it means turning down assignments because you know they would force you to sail close to the wind. And undoubtedly, there are some things you cannot legally discover. But before you assume that the exceptions are large and significant, consider the case of Tom Clancy, best-selling author.

The case of Red October

Consider what happened after the publication of *The Hunt for Red October*—Clancy's novel about a Soviet submarine commander who defects and takes his submarine with him. The author was summoned by the CIA and asked in no uncertain terms to name his sources. Who, the Agency wanted to know, had leaked the classified information that enabled him to give his book such authoritative and accurate descriptions of secret submarine weapons systems?

Clancy replied that, far from having a mole in the Pentagon, he had found all the information he needed in the public record. And not just in obscure government studies and documents. Clancy freely admitted to reading *Aviation Week and Space Technology*, for example, a widely available technical and trade journal.

Yes, he had extrapolated. Yes, he had made some educated guesses. But there's no escaping the fact that here was a former insurance executive—not even an engineer—who had come uncomfortably close to some of the Navy's most closely guarded secrets. All from paying careful attention to publicly available documents. It gave our military people pause, to say the least.

The point is simply this: In the Information Age, for all intents and purposes, the information your client wants *is* available. The money may not be there to pay the costs of obtaining all of it, but it both exists and is available.

Complete confidence

As an information professional you are not selling a bag of hot air. You are selling something very real and very valuable—your ability to find information that you have every reason to believe does indeed exist. (And if the information does not exist, you have every reason to be confident that you will discover that fact as well, which in itself is often valuable information.)

It's like being a nuclear physicist probing the innards of an atom. You may never have seen a particular particle, but through knowledge and experience you *know* it must exist, and you know that it must have certain well-defined properties. When, after a good deal of effort and the smashing of a few billion atoms, the particle one day leaves its unmistakable signature in the cloud chamber, no one is less surprised than you. You knew it was there all the time, it was simply a matter of bringing it to light.

How can you profit from your skills?

With this brief introduction to today's world of information as background, let us now look more closely at the market for information. Or more precisely, the market for *information retrieval skills*.

Let's think about how someone with information retrieval skills can make money from those skills. We start by asking the basic question, the question anyone in our position would ask: what is the demand for information? Who is likely to be interested in our services?

The answer is that the demand for information is limitless. There is hardly anyone who wouldn't like to know more about a topic of personal, professional, or business interest. People will be glad to accept anything you can provide.

But don't ask them to pay for it.

Clueless clients

To give them the benefit of the doubt—never call anyone "cheap" if you can avoid it—most people haven't a clue about what information costs. They don't know about online database subscriptions and connect time charges or the search training you have paid for. They have no idea how to "work a library," nor do they understand the time, effort, and sheer running around that can be involved in locating the right books and documents. They don't know about copyright clearance fees, or the unbilled time you must spend reading journals and manuals to keep current in your profession.

All they know is that you have told them there is a good chance you can find the information they want, and that you want them to pay you for this service. It is at this point that the lip service most people pay to the Information Age stops and we really get down to cases. The fact is that when the subject is dollars and cents instead of smart-sounding but vague generalities like "the information economy," most people find a way to do without.

In fairness, you really can't blame them. Information resource awareness is today at about the same level that environmentalism was prior to the publication of Rachel Carson's *Silent Spring*. It is all but nonexistent. Combine this lack of awareness with the nebulous nature of information, and you're looking at a very tough sales job. People who have gotten along for years quite nicely without the kind of services you can provide will be inclined to continue to do so. Particularly if they can see no tangible benefit stemming from this most intangible of products.

Follow the money, find the market

Our problem here is that we've asked the wrong question. Demand alone doesn't make a market. Money makes a market. Follow the money and you'll find your market.

Thus the question every prospective information broker should start with is: Who is willing to pay for information and the retrieval skills I can bring to bear? You may encounter an occasional client willing to hire you to settle a bet or merely to satisfy his or her curiosity. But most people, businesses, and professionals will spend money on information only if they believe that the information will help them make *more* money.

What is the market for information? The market consists of anyone in a position to materially benefit from that information. The corollary follows naturally: The more a client can expect to make from the information you provide, the more he or she will be willing to pay you for your services.

Who wants to know?

Now we're getting somewhere. Instead of looking at who would be interested in the information you can provide, you're zeroing in on those who can make money from that information.

Consider a simplistic example. An investment banking firm involved in corporate takeovers where hundreds of millions of dollars change hands with the stroke of a pen would think nothing of paying thousands of dollars for an in-depth report on the target company. Yet you could spend the same amount of time researching the love life of Jonathan Swift for a college English professor whose entire grant might not even be enough to cover your expenses.

The lesson once again is this: everyone wants information, but not everyone is willing or able to pay for it. So go where the money is. Focus your efforts on those people, professions, and companies that are in a position to profit from the information you can provide.

We've already identified one promising category—investment banking. Unfortunately, though it's hard to believe if you lived through the 1980s, investment bankers are relatively few and far between. And the successful ones either have an in-house research staff or long-standing relationships with established information consultants or both.

Insurance & investment companies

So who else stands to make more money from the money they invest in you? The ideal client is someone who constantly needs information on a constantly changing list of topics. Insurance companies are a possibility— think of all the different risks they cover. But unless you live in Hartford, Connecticut, or are otherwise close to an insurance company's home office, your local opportunities here may be limited. It isn't likely that your neighborhood Prudential representative will have the authority to hire someone like yourself. But then again, it could be worth checking.

The same goes for your town's stockbrokers. Stockbrokers and investment advisers are constantly looking at new companies, entire industries, corporate executives, SEC data, and more. As you might suspect, however, most are well supplied with information. But there may be a niche they've overlooked or something you can do for them faster and better than it is currently being done. It doesn't hurt to check. And, of course, we're limiting ourselves here to *local* concerns. Always remember that as an information broker, your clients can be physically located all over the globe.

Stockbrokers and insurance agents have something obvious in common: both can materially benefit from the information you can supply. In addition, both professions often deal with a wide range of ever-changing subjects. But they have something else in common as well, something that is not immediately evident. The insurance and financial industries depend for their very existence on computers and computerized information.

For the people who work in these professions, a modicum of computer literacy is virtually a condition of employment. Even in the smallest of towns. In fact, *especially* in the smallest of towns where computer communication offers the only link to the markets, the home office, and their fellow employees.

Later in this book you will find two complete chapters devoted to marketing and sales. But even at this early stage it's a good idea to begin thinking about where you will sell your services. Start following the money—literally—by focusing on companies involved in investment and finance.

Advertising, public relations, & attorneys

Of course, financial people aren't the only good prospects. Two of the professions at the top of our list, for example, are attorneys and advertising or public relations agencies.

In any given month, an attorney in general practice might need information on half a dozen corporations (balance sheet, income statement, profiles of top executives, etc.); personal biographies of assorted plaintiffs and defendants; a year's worth of magazine articles on a particular drug, industrial process, or social phenomenon; background for prior art in a patent litigation; and a list of expert witnesses on auto safety, combined with copies of all the articles each one has ever written on the subject.

An advertising agency always needs to know what a client's competition is doing. Agencies also need background information for ad campaigns or for their own marketing purposes. The more clients the agency has, the more reports it will need. It needs marketing studies and surveys for a wide range of products and services. It needs government data and reports. It might even need to know the personal preferences and prejudices of a key executive at a company it hopes to win as an account.

The Rugge Group has always found ad agencies to be an excellent source of business. For example, a leading agency once asked for a report on the origins of wine corks. The final report included not only text but pictures of traditional cork makers hand carving their products in Portugal. The research was later used in a series of commercials promoting Gallo's line of "better" wines. The Rugge Group also developed crucial information used in campaigns for PIP printing, and has supplied ad agencies with pictures of such things as the sinking of the Titanic, an erupting volcano, and an exploding atomic bomb.

Public relations firms or the PR departments of small ad agencies have a similarly varied list of needs. They must know about local issues and angles, individuals, movers and shakers, and buttonmen. And all of them desperately need reports on how their press releases or publicity campaigns are playing.

Companies in general

We've talked so far about some of the more obvious opportunities for information brokers. There are many others that are less obvious. Large companies, for example, rarely rely exclusively on their advertising agencies for market research and competitor analysis. Most have departments to address these needs, and all of them are potential clients.

At small companies, the need for information retrieval services is even more acute. (Though often it is not recognized.) Most small firms cannot afford to maintain a well-equipped, fully staffed corporate library or "information center," as such facilities may be called. Yet most could benefit greatly from the services an information consultant can provide.

So much information is available that at the very least, your services could put even a small company on a nearly equal footing with a corporate giant. The fact that such services are available on a freelance, independent-contractor basis is ideally suited to a tight budget.

In short, even if you do as we suggest and rule out all those clients who are unable or unwilling to pay you what you are worth, even if you only "follow the money," the potential market for information and the services of an information consultant is huge.

The one thing the market definitely is not, however, is well-defined. Information is such a nebulous commodity, and client needs can be so incredibly varied, that nothing is cut and dried. Every time you go in to sell yourself, you are, in effect, selling a highly customized, one-of-a-kind service. You can't just open your samples case and say "I've got this, this, and this. Would you like them in blue or green?"

A nebulous commodity

Similarly, every prospective information broker's situation is different. If you were selling dental office supplies or auto mechanic tools, we could easily tell you how to develop a list of prime prospects, and we could offer some reasonably accurate assessments of the extent of the market.

But information and information consulting services, as we have been at pains to emphasize in this chapter, are different. It is entirely possible, for example, that there simply is no market for information consulting in your area. Some brokers have been able to overcome this because their particular skills—like chemical patent researching—are in such demand. Others have brought with them a client base developed through some other endeavor.

In general, you should begin by at least trying to establish a local base. That may or may not be possible. It may be that your particular area is rife with opportunities. Or it may be that there is simply no one within a 50-mile radius of you who is willing to pay for information brokering services. There's just no way to tell until you go look for yourself.

A local base?

Don't be discouraged, though, if you find that your local area is less than fertile for an information business. When Sue ran Information On Demand (IOD), people always assumed that the company had lots of clients in the Berkeley area. After all, Berkeley is one of the main sites for the University of California. The truth is, however, that in the eight years that Sue was associated with IOD, the company had only two clients from the University. By far the majority of its clients were geographically located well beyond the Bay Area.

Ultimately, the best anyone can do is to guide you in the right general direction and hopefully keep you from making the same mistakes we have made. We will go into more detail later in this book. But one thing we can tell you for certain: It *is* possible to make a living as an information broker.

There *is* a market for what we all offer, and it is growing. But it is not rocketing through the roof. This is not at all like the early days of the fast-food business when anyone able to raise the capital to buy a McDonald's franchise was guaranteed to make a fortune.

Also, regardless of where you live, information brokering is hard work. To be successful, you must be of above average intelligence, you must have a healthy amount of innate curiosity, and you must have the creativity and imagination of the finest investigative journalist or consulting detective.

It's a tall order. Yet the way things are today, even these skills and abilities aren't enough to *ensure* your success. To have a chance, you must also be able to overcome the disadvantage suffered by all information consultants. This is the previously mentioned lack of "information consciousness" on the part of the vast majority of people.

You will find, for example, that prospective clients don't ask you for data they think is impossible to obtain. They don't understand the depth of information that is available or the sophistication of the tools an information broker uses. So they can't conceive of asking someone to do something they think is impossible.

Educating the client, again

Earlier we compared the staggering amount of information available today to a fire-breathing dragon, and we postulated two knights, one who knew about the dragon but had never confronted it and one who could personally testify to its ferocity and strength. The plain, unvarnished truth is that most of your potential clients don't even know there *is* a dragon, let alone appreciate the skills required to bring it to heel. To say nothing of understanding the costs involved.

This means that you are going to have to spend the first precious minutes of a 25-minute sales call educating your potential client. You'll have to spend even more time sensing what it is the client is trying to accomplish. Then you'll have to draw on your knowledge and skill to propose on the spot an information "product" customized to answer those needs. And, oh, yes, you'll also have to figure out what to charge for delivering this product and when it will be ready.

Clearly, it takes a special kind of person to be a successful information broker. No one has yet come up with a slogan to match "The few. The proud. The Marines." But if our profession had a slogan, it would be along those lines. (Though somehow "The few. The proud. The Informed." doesn't quite do it.) If you've got what it takes, there's a job for you as an information professional. You probably won't get rich, but you'll never be bored. And, as we'll see in the next chapter, the avenues open to you are as limitless as the Information Age itself.

2 What is an information broker?

In this chapter we'll introduce you to the wide world of practicing information brokers. You'll get a glimpse of the kinds of projects successful practitioners take on and the challenges they accept. You will be amazed at the depth and variety of the information specialist's world. But search as you may, you won't find any activity that can legitimately be called "brokering."

This leads to an important point that must be addressed before we go any further. The term "information broker" is one of the great misnomers of the age. This is particularly ironic since, if any profession prides itself on accuracy, it is ours.

Defining the terms

The general press and even some professional journals can use the term all they want. That won't change the fact that the men and women commonly referred to as "information brokers" don't broker anything. A broker, after all (according to *Merriam Webster's Collegiate Dictionary*), is someone who "acts as an intermediary," who serves as "an agent who arranges marriages," or "negotiates contracts of purchase and sale (as of real estate, commodities, or securities)."

It is certainly true that today's information brokers act as intermediaries between information resources and the people who need the information. But as it is used today, the term *broker* really applies to someone who is actively sought out by both buyers and sellers and who profits by taking a commission on the sales he or she arranges.

An information broker actually has far more in common with an attorney or a doctor than with brokers who deal in securities, real estate, or pork bellies. As you will see, the people whose hard work and success have defined the profession are consultants, or specialists, or professional searchers. They don't sell information, and they don't take a commission for arranging such a "sale." Like doctors, lawyers, and certified public accountants, they charge a fee for professional services. They are not "brokers" of anything.

Co-author Sue Rugge used to describe Information On Demand, the firm she founded, as "a fee-based information gathering company." Others have suggested the term "information intermediary." Helen Burwell, publisher of the only directory of information specialists, began by referring to the profession as "fee-based information services." (The word "fee" was included in both cases to emphasize the distinction between the services provided by free public libraries and money-making information firms.)

One could debate the proper terminology for hours. But in the end, you would inevitably conclude that the activities and job descriptions of information brokers are so varied that no single term will ever be totally accurate. Yet the public—and your potential clients—demand a quick handle. And "information broker" is fast becoming the recognized tag. Even the latest edition of Ms. Burwell's famous directory is called *The Burwell Directory of Information Brokers.*

Parenthetically, it is worth noting that the term "fee-based" service is being used extensively in Europe, and increasingly in the United States, to distinguish corporate, public, and academic information services from the independent, entrepreneurial professionals we normally think of as information brokers.

But we are also finding that many private investigators and others who specialize in searching public records have begun calling themselves "information brokers." These men and women are generally good folks— indeed, many of them are good clients—who can locate a tax lien, a judgment, or a Uniform Commercial Code (UCC) filing at any county courthouse in the country. But they couldn't search DIALOG or NEXIS to save their lives.

The terminology, in short, is a mess. In general, the momentum behind "information broker" appears to be too strong for it to be derailed in favor of a more accurate term. That's the term the public is coming to associate with the kind of activities discussed in this book, so that's the term we will use.

Incidentally, since we can now talk one-on-one, from here on we'll refer to ourselves as Sue and Alfred. No point in standing on formality.

Now let's look at the job of the information broker. Let's look at the kinds of things you'll be doing to earn your bread once you enter the profession.

If this were an ordinary book about an ordinary profession—like being a lawyer, accountant, or salesperson—we could click off in short order the duties, tasks, responsibilities, rate of pay, types of assignments, and skills that would be required. Presenting you with an accurate and fairly complete job description would be no problem.

Alfred has done this many times in the past with pieces like "How to Get a Job in Construction," "Reserving Your Seat in the Travel Industry," and the unforgettable "Food Service and You," all written for a career encyclopedia published by the Baker & Taylor Companies in the 1970s. If nothing else, being able to tick off a definitive description of the job of information broker would appeal to Alfred's sense of organization.

But Alfred and everyone else who likes things tied up in neat little packages is forever doomed to be disappointed when describing the job of information broker. Because frankly, there *is* no job description. You've heard about those positions in corporate America where you're told "Joan/John, you can make this job anything you want"? Well, being an information broker is exactly like that and then some.

The reason for this isn't hard to understand. As we said in Chapter 1, information itself is nebulous, and the needs of clients for information services are incredibly varied. Under the circumstances, it would be impossible for the information broker's job not to be equally nebulous and varied. Consequently, no two information brokers' jobs are exactly alike.

Information retrieval & a database thumbnail

Fortunately, while specific projects and assignments vary widely, it *is* possible to classify virtually all information broker activities under two major headings: information retrieval and information organization. By information retrieval we mean any activity involved in finding out what the client wants to know. Many times, the activity involved will be searching an online electronic database.

At this point we should take time out for just a moment in deference to those of you who have only the vaguest notion of what an online database is and how to access it. You'll find lots of hands-on details later in the book, but since we are going to be referring to online databases quite frequently, a quick thumbnail sketch is crucial to those who have never used one.

Vast stores of information exist today in electronic form, either because they were keyed in at a computer when they were created or because someone has paid to have them keyed in or electronically scanned after publication. A number of companies have collected information of this sort and put it into their mainframe computers. These computers are connected to special phone networks that make it possible for you to dial into them with your own personal computer.

To do so, you will need communications software and a modem, a black box that connects your computer to the phone lines. You will also need an account number and password to get into the system you want to call. The systems have names like DIALOG, The Knowledge Index, LEXIS/NEXIS, NewsNet, DataTimes, and Dow Jones News/Retrieval. All of them charge you for the time you spend online and most charge for the information you retrieve as well.

The two final points you need to know for now are, first, that the online industry as a whole consists of some 5,300 databases available through some 800 online systems. The industry covers *everything*. Patents and trademarks; information from Dun & Bradstreet, Standard and Poor's, and Moody's; all the leading newswires; almost every magazine, journal, newspaper or newsletter (available either as a citation or as the full text of the publication); chemical formulas; engineering specifications; doctoral dissertations; the entire Library of Congress; and on, and on, and on.

Second, in most cases, these online systems are not designed for use by the general public. Even those that claim to be "user friendly" aren't. Tapping an online database requires practice, skill, and often, special training, which most database vendors will be only too happy to provide—for a fee. (To be fair, some online systems like D&B, Predicasts, and Information Access Corporation do offer free classes and seminars.)

Returning to retrieval

To the information broker, an online database often offers the fastest, cheapest, and sometimes, only way to fulfill a client's request. But though online database searching gets most of the press coverage, it is only part of the job. After all, huge amounts of information still are not recorded or indexed in databases. Indeed, at any given moment, the most current information doesn't exist in print—it exists inside the brains of experts in the field. Interviewing these experts and other authorities on the phone also constitutes information retrieval. So, too, are market research assignments in which both multiple online searches and multiple interviews may be conducted.

There is also "document delivery," the most basic form of information retrieval. Information brokers are frequently asked to supply either photocopies or originals of magazine and newspaper articles, government reports, oversight agency filings, and just about any other piece of printed matter you can think of. In fact, there is an entire industry of document delivery brokers who can get you a copy of any article you see referenced in an online search. (More on this in Chapter 18.)

Sometimes "retrieval" requests are anything but conventional. FIND/SVP, one of the largest information gathering firms in the world, reports that clients have asked them to locate and deliver everything from theater tickets to the front end of a 1977 Toyota. Sue's former company, The Rugge Group, was once asked to find a 1969 BMW—and a stunt driver capable of rolling it. (The client wanted to reenact an automobile accident.)

Sue and IOD also got their share of unusual requests. For example, there was once a client who wanted the floor plans to a particular Czechoslovakian hospital. This was during the Cold War, so information flow in and out of Eastern Europe was not exactly free. Surprisingly, Sue found the plans in a back issue of *Architectural Digest*. In retrospect, it wasn't that difficult an assignment, but the client was sufficiently amazed. One of the rewards of this business is that you become a miracle worker on a regular basis.

Along a similar theme, a firm in Houston was once hired by the sheik of Bahrain (one of the Arab emirates) to build a new palace. The stipulation was—and here is the kicker—that the palace had to be in the Bahrainian architectural style.

The Texas firm could have handled everything from Georgian to Bauhaus, but it had no idea what constituted Bahrainian. Sue was undaunted, however. The information had to be heavily illustrated, for obvious reasons, and there is at present no way to satisfy such a request online. Online citations specify whether or not the source article contains illustrations, but one cannot usually obtain those illustrations electronically. So Sue and her assistants concentrated on books. Books of history and architecture. Her firm's proximity to the libraries of the Berkeley campus—especially the School of Environmental Design—was thus a major advantage.

Other retrieval services are more ordinary. If you have private investigators among your clients, for example, you may find yourself searching Consumer Product Safety Commission records, newspapers, and trade literature for background information related to product liability and malpractice suits. Or you may be asked to find expert witnesses or determine what opposing experts have written and where they have testified.

At IOD, Sue used to get requests for product samples. The idea was that Company A would not want Company B to know that it was interested in samples of Company B's products and thus would use an information broker as an intermediary. One time, for instance, a load of carpet arrived at IOD's door, ordered by the firm for a client. Sue ran out to the truck and told the driver not to unload but to ship it to the client's address.

From hospital floor plans to a Bahrainian palace

And the mundane, as well . . .

At the Rugge Group in years past, Sue has also been asked to determine the worldwide manufacturing capacity for a particular chemical needed for certain drugs. This involved many, many hours of phone interviews and fax exchanges with chemical company personnel located all over the world, and long distance charges in the thousands of dollars.

Competitive intelligence, either company-specific or industry-based, is also frequently requested. Among the actual projects the large information firm Find/SVP has completed, for example, are finding the answers to questions like these:

- What ad campaigns has McCall's Magazine run for itself in the past few years?
- Is anyone actively promoting the sale of milk in glass bottles?
- What are the leading men's fashion magazines in Japan, and can you get us sample copies?
- What major articles have been written in the business press on fast-food chicken restaurants in the past five years?

"My most unusual search . . ."

Information brokers are a collegial bunch. As you will learn later, most of them hang out online in Section 0 of the Working from Home Forum run by Paul and Sarah Edwards on CompuServe. You have to be a member of the Association of Independent Information Professionals (AIIP) to gain access to Section 0.

A while back, our friend Linda Cooper, a past president of AIIP, initiated what she calls "Search Challenges." In one, she asked members to list the four or five search assignments that "demonstrate the sometimes crazy combinations of things we learn about as we do our jobs." There was only one rule: The person contributing the list must have actually done the search.

Presented in no particular order, and edited to preserve anonymity, here are some of the best ones. No one can say that information brokering isn't interesting:

- What's the market for PVC house siding in Asia in the next five years? And if there is anything left in the search budget, find out about the market for vertical blinds in Asia for the next five years as well.
- Pull all the articles published in the last three years dealing with marketing clothing to extra small and extra large women.
- Find the precise methods—diagrams, drawings, and text—for manufacturing paintball guns. Be sure to check the medical literature because the original guns were used by vets to mark animals that had mated or been vaccinated.

- What is the size of the market for fruit-based pizza toppings, primarily in hospitals, schools, and other parts of the institutional food segment?
- Are there any public or for-profit "men versus women" wrestling matches anywhere in the world? If not, why not?
- Find out about the religious cult and its members who were arrested for the ritual killing of cats in Virginia. (The client requested that the search results be faxed to him at his local 7-11 store.)
- Is there an equation for figuring out the largest number of circles that can be inscribed in a larger circle in an irregular pattern? (The client was a manufacturer of filters.)
- How can I contact Bill Murray, and what were the costs and profits from his last three films?

Market research by phone

The Rugge Group does a lot of competitive intelligence, even for large companies that have their own in-house research departments. Of course these companies hire the Rugge Group for its outstanding work. That goes without saying! But there's also the very real need for confidentiality. If you work for a company, you may be able to call out without revealing the name of your firm. But when someone calls you back, they will usually get the switchboard, and all will be revealed.

Typically, clients will want to know what their competition is doing, what the rest of the industry sees for the future. And they can get that sort of information more easily through an intermediary than if they were to assign an assistant VP, because that person would have to identify his or her affiliation.

In addition, as an information broker, you're independent and objective. Clients tell us that they've done research internally on a topic, and have come to The Rugge Group to confirm or disprove the results they found. Their people may have had even a subliminal vested interest that would inadvertently cant things a certain way.

Requests for copies of a competing firm's Securities and Exchange Commission (SEC) filings are common. As are requests for brief biographies of the company's leading executives. By law, publicly held companies must provide this kind of information to anyone who asks for it. But sometimes an information broker's client is not aware of this fact, or simply finds it more convenient to place a single phone call to an information broker, instead of sending out requests to many different companies.

Companies also like to know things on an ongoing basis, so you may get requests like "Tell me whenever Company B files for a patent," or "Give me a copy of every article mentioning the firm whenever it appears."

SDI services

Requests like these have led some information brokers to offer what in the library profession is known as an SDI service. This stands for *selective dissemination of information*, a librarian's term that simply means "current awareness." As you will see, it is possible to tell an online database to conduct a search for the information you specify each time new information is added to the database.

This makes it relatively easy to offer a current awareness service to your clients. And it is a good idea to try to do so. You probably won't make a great deal of money at it, but a monthly or weekly report from your firm helps keep the client aware of *you* as well.

Information organization

The heart and soul of the information broker's job is information retrieval. But many individuals also offer *information organization services*. These include assembling and preparing bibliographies, cataloguing book and materials collections, book indexing, library management, and consulting on library or information center design and management.

You may well wonder what doing something like cataloguing all the books in a company's library has to do with, say, preparing an in-depth competitive analysis for the same company. Where's the common thread? Are all information brokers supposed to have library management skills?

The answer once again lies in the elasticity of the information broker job description. The people who offer information organization services do so because they have had training or experience in these areas. Most hold advanced degrees in library science and thus operate as "freelance librarians" as well as search and retrieval specialists. The common thread is library science, a discipline that embraces both information organization and retrieval. Quite naturally, its masters tend to be skilled in both areas.

Go with what you know

The point every reader should take away from this, however, is that you don't have to hold a Master of Library Science (MLS) degree or have library training to be a successful information broker. These have never been requirements. Indeed, neither Sue nor Alfred hold advanced degrees.

This message seems to be getting through. In the late 1980s, for example, the vast majority of people who attended Sue's Information Broker's Seminar were female librarians, and most were not the principle breadwinner for the family. These days, librarians make up a much smaller percentage of the seminar audience, and there is an almost even split in gender. What's more, whether male or female, seminar attendees tend to have much stronger business backgrounds, and far more of them report that they intend to make information brokering their main livelihood.

The key point is that successful information brokers draw upon the training and experience they already have, whatever that may be.

For example, if you've spent the last ten years of your life as a stockbroker, you know much more than most people do about how to read a balance sheet and how to interpret financial data. You don't have to have a clue about how to prepare a bibliography or organize a library collection. Simply go with what you know.

If two years from now you've built a business offering investment research to people who prefer to deal with discount brokerage firms (which provide no research at all), your type of service could easily become "one of the things information brokers do"—simply because you're an information broker and you're doing it.

Who you know & what you know

But we're not playing fair. A stockbroker is too easy an example. Let's assume instead that you've spent the last decade as a dispatcher for a trucking company, a purchasing agent for a manufacturing firm, or a lab technician for a pharmaceutical company. Whatever it is, it's a business you know inside and out. You know how it works, you know the major problems, you know lots of people—and you know what information needs are not being met.

It is simply impossible to believe that once you have a better understanding of information, how to retrieve it, and how to package and present it that there isn't some service you could provide that the industry you know so well would pay you to offer.

This is a broad statement, to be sure. There are undoubtedly some exceptions. But knowing what we know about information and about the sorry state of information-related services in all American industries, it's a statement we make with confidence. No matter what you do for a living right now, somewhere there's an information niche in that field that is not being filled.

We would never claim that filling it will be easy. And we certainly wouldn't claim that you can make a living at it. But we *know* the niches exist. As a prospective information broker, your first job should be to find them. That will give you a base from which you can branch out to encompass industries and areas with which you may not be so familiar.

In short, the way to become a successful information broker is to first think of who you know. Then think of what you know—and find a way to combine them!

The most crucial component

We've given you just a small sampling of the kinds of things practicing information brokers do. It simply is not possible to be any more precise. Information brokers do all *kinds* of things.

You know the expression about charging "whatever the traffic will bear?" Well, when you're an information broker, you may find yourself offering "whatever the client may want." (And charging whatever the traffic will bear as well!) You may not be able to provide the service by doing the work yourself. But if you're any good at your profession, you will be able to find someone else who can. You will review the results to make sure they are up to your quality standards, add a mark-up, and present the product to the client.

In the "old days"

It takes some time to learn the mechanics of information retrieval. And you will never stop learning about all that is available. It is true that the more imagination and creativity you can bring to the job, the better off you will be. But the fundamentals of information retrieval can be learned by any intelligent, motivated person.

The real trick—whether you're an information broker, freelance writer, consultant, or some other self-employed professional—is to find out what the client really wants, what he or she is trying to accomplish. That can be the greatest information retrieval trick of all, since clients don't always know themselves what they really want or need. This is where the sheep part company from the goats, for it is the single most important skill you must develop.

There was a time, for example, when it was possible to walk into a client's office, thump a two-inch-thick computer printout of a database search on the desk, and say, "Here it is. All the information you asked for." In the early 1970s, you could be a miracle worker by handing somebody a printout created from an online database search.

Nobody knew that this kind of thing was possible. Where did all this come from? How did it get into your computer? They were amazed. Sue used to respond by explaining that the printed information was just half a loaf and then take the opportunity to explain the other services her firm could provide—like following up leads brought to light by the initial search, conducting phone interviews, obtaining actual copies of the documents referred to in the printout, and so on.

No solutions, no answers

Today, the results of an online database search are more like a third of a loaf. Today, people need—indeed, demand—more than just raw information.

This brings up an important point. As information brokers, we shouldn't consider ourselves capable of providing solutions. Let the people who call themselves "consultants" or subject "experts" do that.

What we *can* provide, and what sets a really good information broker apart from the rest, are resources. We can provide clients with the kinds of information they need—the statistics or lists or reports that make it possible for them to solve their problems.

That is probably as close as it is possible to come to defining the essence of information brokering. The mechanics of actually getting the information are, in the end, just mechanics. Performing an online search requires a good deal of knowledge and skill, for example. But any intelligent person can learn how to do it. An information broker needs something more.

3 The job of information brokering

In the previous chapter, we looked at the question, "What is an information broker?" and did our best to provide an accurate answer. Now, let's look at what it's like to *be* an information broker. Let's look at the job itself and the skills you will need to perform it successfully.

An information broker does many things. But there's one thing that all successful information brokers do and do well. *Every one of them knows how to sell.* It is in making the sale that it all begins.

It doesn't matter how good a searcher you are, how good a librarian, or how much you read or know. If you can't *sell*, you will never make a living as an information broker.

If you can't sell yourself, if you can't be credible to your prospective clients, they're not going to hire you. That's often true in other professions, but it is doubly true here. You must never forget that, to most of your clients, information is a stepchild to their own professions. It's not recognized as a legitimate profession on its own by most other professionals—chemists, biologists, management consultants, and especially engineers.

All those people think that because it's *their* subject, they're better able to gather the information they need than you are. If you're not an engineer or a chemist, how can you possibly know anything about "my" field?

Sell, sell, sell

It is a reaction you encounter in any freelance profession. After writing everything from a home economics textbook to sales brochures and speeches for Merrill Lynch executives, Alfred wrote two best-selling books on baseball with the late Charley Lau—even though he had no knowledge of the game. Then he wrote a book about computer communications. Then one called *How to Buy Software*. Osborne/McGraw-Hill published his guide to hard disk drives and sold over 50,000 copies. And Random House published his guide to Microsoft's DOS 6, as well as *Internet Slick Tricks*, a book co-authored with his wife and business partner, Emily Glossbrenner.

The point is simply this: After you've actually done it a few times and have samples to show, the questions and doubts cease. Sue has had the same experience. If someone questions whether The Rugge Group can handle a job, they have only to look at Sue's track record. Case closed.

Now this is not to say that you should expect to be equally skilled in all topics. Nor does it mean that you must be able to do all the work yourself. It is true that there are some subjects—like chemical structure searching, patents, and biotechnology—that are best left to those information professionals with training in those areas. But if you can sell a search like this, there is no reason why you can't subcontract the work to the appropriate expert searcher.

Of course we can help you

As Sue says in her Information Broker's Seminar, "If you are the person who gets that telephone to ring and you've thus convinced that potential client to come to you, then don't turn them away. Say, 'Of course we can help you. I need to consult my research staff to get you a firm quote.' Don't ever say, 'We don't do that kind of search.'"

Basically, what the client wants is a dependable source to turn to, someone who can translate his or her needs into an effective search and deliver high-quality results. The client does not care whether you yourself actually perform the search or whether you subcontract the job to a subject area expert. As we have said time and again, what you are selling and that the client is ultimately buying is your professional information expertise.

At the same time, if you know the information field and are skilled at using retrieval techniques and tools, you can obtain excellent results in many different subject areas. Naturally, that doesn't stop some people from being skeptical. Part of it no doubt has to do with clients defending their territory. Part of it is ego. It is painful, particularly for those who have spent their lives in the soft embrace of academically oriented professions, to accept the fact that an outsider—with no scholarly dissertations, no conference papers, no sabbaticals in Europe—could possibly find what they're looking for.

"But you don't know anything about the field," they say. If you try to tell them, "But I'm an information professional," they're likely to respond, "What's that? You mean you're a librarian?"

A word to the wise. You want the word *librarian* to stay as far away from this profession as possible—even if you happen to be one. It's nothing personal—some of our best friends and clients are librarians, and many successful information brokers are or once were card-carrying librarians in another life. It is strictly a matter of image.

The public image of a librarian is of someone who has all these sources at his or her disposal, all of which are mysterious. This is overlaid with the impression that somehow librarians see themselves as priests and priestesses whose responsibility it is to guard "their" information from the grubby hands of the general public.

This couldn't be further from the truth, of course. Though there are inevitably one or two bad apples, as a group, you will never find a more selfless, giving, and generous collection of people than the country's librarians. Far from jealously guarding "their" information, those whom we know are positively bursting to share the sheer joy of knowledge, particularly with young minds.

Yet the image of "Marion, Madame Librarian" presented by the 1962 movie *The Music Man* is still very much with us: a repressed female, hair in a bun, glasses, the severest of makeup—and very strict about "her" books. To say nothing of people speaking above a whisper in "her" library. It is hard to say whether the movie took its cue from the public or whether public sentiment was formed by the movie. But the fact is that this general image persists, and as an information broker you would do well to steer as clear of it and the word *librarian* as possible.

You might also want to steer clear of certain professions. You want advertising agencies, public relations firms, management consultants, and attorneys—the kinds of people who are continually bombarded with new subjects, new companies, new products, new types of cases. They are the people who have to become instant experts overnight. So not only do they need your services, they understand completely that you don't have to have a degree in a subject to be able to find information about it.

The professions to avoid are academics and engineers. Among Sue's best clients is a firm of engineering consultants who specialize in supplying needed expertise to patent attorneys. But these enlightened folks are the exception that proves the rule. In general, it has been our experience that engineers can be among the worst clients to work for. Engineers have their own networks of colleagues. They'll go down the hall. If Joe or Jane doesn't know, it probably doesn't need to be known or isn't worth finding out.

Engineers like to think that they are on the leading edge. If it has already been published in a journal, it's not worth getting because everybody already knows about it.

Chemists, in contrast, tend to be much better clients. A chemist goes to college and learns how to use *Chemical Abstracts*. We've never met an engineer who's even heard of *Engineering Index*. Yet EI started in 1898, the same time that Chem Abs started. (The online version of EI is called Compendex.)

Be confident!

Whether you're selling to chemists, attorneys, ad agencies, or even engineers, the key component is confidence. You simply must be credible. You have got to know the information field. You have got to believe in your own abilities.

To use a quick example, imagine that you're a contractor called in to bid on a particular home repair job. No two jobs are ever identical, but if you are good at your profession, you can look at the job and make a credible presentation. You may not know exactly how you will handle this specific job, but based on past experience, you know you can do it. Or you know that you can't.

Either way, your competence and the confidence it generates come through. The homeowner knows even less about what might be involved than you do. But he or she can tell in an instant whether you know what you're talking about. This is not something you can fake.

To look at things the other way, you may be a crackerjack online searcher and you may have all the confidence in the world in your ability to find anything anyone asks you to find. But if you don't get out there and sell your services, clients are not going to beat a path to your door.

Search and sell—you have to be able and enthusiastically willing to do both if you want to be a success as an information broker. Either that, or you've got to find a partner who is good at whichever activity you are not good at. Any number of successful information firms have been founded by an ace searcher and an ace salesperson, the talents of one complementing those of the other.

What does the client really want?

Now, let's assume that you have done an effective job of marketing yourself and your services using the techniques presented later in this book. You've poured your heart into marketing, and, at last, the phone rings. It's a potential client.

Now what? How do you convert that person into a satisfied, paying customer? How do you perform the job of being an information broker? Naturally enough, you start by trying to discover what the client wants.

The process begins with the initial meeting or phone interview and continues throughout the project. But it is perhaps most evident in what professional librarians and information brokers alike call the *reference interview*.

The reference interview is the conversation you have with the client to determine the goal the client is trying to achieve and the particular kind of information most likely to help him or her achieve it. Not surprisingly, it is of major importance since your ability to ask the right questions is crucial to delivering what the client needs.

It is not at all uncommon for a client to say something like "I want everything there is on solar energy." As an information broker, however, you're familiar with the information dragon. You might not know anything about solar energy yourself, but you know enough about information to be aware that literally tons of material exist on the subject.

Clearly "everything on solar energy" is not what the client really wants. It is thus your job to help the client more clearly express his or her goals. So instead of saying, "Yup, everything there is on solar energy. Got it. Anything else?", you might respond with "What are you trying to find out? What goals are you trying to achieve?"

To which the client may very well respond "Just give me everything on solar energy." As we said in a previous chapter, most people have no idea that the information dragon even exists, let alone how to tame it. So you have to be patient. You have to avoid making them feel foolish. After all, information isn't *their* profession.

Somewhere buried within the request is the goal to be achieved. And it's your job to find it. So thinking quickly, you gently suggest that there is a great deal, a *very* great deal of information on solar energy. Perhaps the client could help you out by narrowing things down a bit.

In general, you'll find that new clients either don't really have a clear idea themselves what they're after, or they don't think you can find what they want. So they make their requests as broad as possible. Through no fault of their own, their awareness of the breadth and scope of the information available on any topic and their familiarity with what can be accomplished by a skilled information broker are virtually nil.

Fortunately this is gradually changing. There is indeed a growing body of well-informed clients who recognize the need for a professional but who are also savvy enough to know what they need and what it should cost. In general, such people make very good clients because you don't have to spend your time explaining things to them. They also tend to appreciate your skills because they know what it takes to do a good job.

Give me everything!

What they don't know is that you want them to make their request as narrow as possible because that makes things infinitely easier. Among other things, narrowing things down is the whole point of using a computer. If you use the computer and get 500 citations, there's no benefit—you can whip up 500 citations in a library. But if the request is narrow enough, you can come up with perhaps *five* citations that are absolutely on target.

Narrowing it down

The biggest asset an information broker offers a client is being able to pinpoint what the person really needs to know. Or more accurately, working with the individual, asking the right questions, and offering seasoned guidance to help the client clearly define the information needed.

It is impossible to emphasize this point too strongly. If you think about it for just a moment, you'll see why. Anyone can meet with a client and blindly accept the request to provide everything there is on solar energy. And many people are familiar with the mechanics of information retrieval, particularly on such a broad topic as solar energy.

What sets the information broker apart is the ability to help a client more clearly define the goal. Without this crucial ingredient, the client will be literally inundated with information—98 percent of which is guaranteed to be useless. In fact, it's worse than useless—it is time-consuming to review, and it is expensive to provide.

As an information broker, you can save the client all that time and all that needless expense by helping the individual clarify what he or she really wants to know. After all, it takes no skill to attack a problem with an axe or a meat cleaver. Some people who call themselves information brokers actually operate that way. The true professional, on the other hand, always uses a scalpel.

The solar energy request is a perfect example. It is drawn from an actual project Sue completed for a corporate executive. As it turned out, what the person really wanted was not everything there is on solar energy. He merely wanted to build a greenhouse in his backyard to raise tomatoes. But he simply didn't think it was possible to get information specific to that problem. Then again, he had never heard of the information dragon.

Reports from the field

Discovering or uncovering what the client really wants is a key question for every self-employed professional. But it is probably even more essential in the information brokering field. It's a question we all grapple with.

Here are the assorted grapplings of information brokers who addressed the question on Paul and Sarah Edwards's Working from Home Forum on CompuServe. We have edited out names and otherwise disguised things, while preserving the essence:

- What, if any, training do you think prepares us best to zero in on what the client really wants? How significant are training, experience, and personality?

  To which another broker replied: Good question! My very humble opinion is that it takes a certain type of personality more than anything else. You've got to have an open mind, the ability to avoid jumping to conclusions, the skill to ask open-ended questions, and the patience to just shut up and listen when the client rambles on.

Experience is important, because you have to know how to elicit the information from a client. And you have to be able to think as you're talking, figuring out what questions you must get answered before you actually start a search.

_____

- A broker in Germany writes: In my opinion, we have to be more than a "gatekeeper" or "filter." We have to become an active part of the client's information resources. It is our job to help people make their business decisions more quickly. To do so, we have to look behind the client's mind and words and determine how to serve him best. And this will sometimes mean saying "no" and then suggesting a better way to do the job. Again, we have to be an *active* part of the client's resources.

_____

- I believe a good salesperson will do a good reference interview. That's because a good salesperson believes in his or her product and knows how to listen to the customer. You must listen, listen, listen! Then go back to the office and figure out how to best serve the client's needs.

  This is especially true for people who sell customized products. And boy, do we information brokers do that! We must listen to the client and we must use what we learn to customize our product to his or her needs.

_____

- When doing an information interview, I usually start with the basics and go from there. Sometimes people get a little miffed because there's usually something I think of that has not occurred to them. I can't help it—I'm an information professional and information is my life.

  But, you know, I've found that rattling off what I know about a subject tends to alienate people. Either I make them feel stupid or I look as though I'm trying to impress them. None of which is true. The key thing is to strike a balance between coming across as knowledgeable and competent and letting the client tell you what he or she really wants.

_____

- It's never good to inundate the client on the first pass with too much information. But the client should know that you do have other resources and alternatives if the information retrieved proves not to be relevant. Sometimes—more often than not?—clients can't describe exactly what they want.

At this point you should have at least a general idea of what an information broker is and does. You've been introduced to the two basic pillars of the field—retrieval and organization—and you've seen how varied the activities within each can be.

A day in the life

You've been told to go with what you know in focusing your initial efforts. And you are aware that the most important talent an information broker can have is the ability to help the client determine what he or she really wants or needs to know. We've also told you how important it is never to cease in selling your services.

We'll close with what might be called "a day in the life of an information broker." Our goal here is to give you some idea of what your workdays may be like once you enter the profession. Obviously, this is only an approximation, and it compresses into a single day the activities and tasks that may actually be done over several days. But it's the flavor we're after. As you read this day-in-the-life, ask yourself if you can see yourself doing these kinds of things on a regular basis.

Morning Get up, get coffee, scan the papers. You'll want a local paper, of course. But you should also consider subscribing to a major metropolitan daily (*New York Times*, *San Francisco Chronicle*, *Cleveland Plain Dealer*, etc.) and, if you can afford it, the *Wall Street Journal*. As an information broker, you're an information omnivore—you can never tell when something you come across in the papers will have a bearing on a current or future project.

Go to the office and boot up your computer. Sign on to CompuServe, MCI Mail, GEnie, and whatever other electronic mail services you use. Pick up and print out your mail. Answer the "hot" letters and queries immediately. Save the others for later.

Check your daily appointment book. Is anybody coming? Is there anybody you are scheduled to go see? Are there any other "to-do's" for the day?

Return to the marketing study you were writing up for Client A. Answer the phone and field inquiries. It breaks your train of thought, but any call could be a client with an assignment.

Print out the report and type up the necessary Federal Express airbill. But don't call FedEx yet. The day is still young. Between now and the 6:00 P.M. cutoff, you may have other packages to send. (Your FedEx cutoff will vary with your location.)

Take a call from a current client. He wants to know about the progress of a corporate profile you are working on. Reassure the client. After you hang up, make a note to try to get the profile done tonight.

Take another call. It's someone who has read your article in the *XYZ Magazine*. Would it be possible for you to find everything that has been published in the last five years on a certain industrial process? Explain your terms. The prospective client may offer to FedEx a check for half the fee immediately—or she may want to think about it.

Time for lunch. You eat at your desk, reading *Business Week*, *Time*, *Newsweek*, or some other magazine. After lunch, and more phone calls, you spend an hour working on the speech you will be giving next week at the local Rotary Club. It's a speech on information brokers, of course, and it is designed to both inform and, subtly, sell your services.

Tired of writing for the time being, you decide to take a break and catch up on your reading. You read two articles in *Online* magazine, scan DIALOG's *Chronolog*, and update your "bluesheets" collection (explained in Part three of this book).

At about 2:00 P.M., you start your daily round of business development phone calls. Your goal is to make appointments to get in to see people at local ad agencies, law offices, and corporations. By 3:00 you've got one lukewarm prospect who thinks he might be able to see you next month some time. You make a note to call him back to firm up a date next week.

It's 3:30 now and you're just about to pop out to pick up some office supplies when one of your very best clients calls.

"I need all you can find on artificial sweeteners, and I need it now." You calm the client down and help her more clearly define her goals. Then you agree to take a swing at it and call her back.

Forty-five minutes later, you have searched nine databases and have a pretty impressive wad of information on disk. You call the client and offer to fax it to her. She says, no, "Can you send it to me via MCI Mail?" No problem. You sign on to that system and upload the entire, unedited text file to her address. Then you make a hard-copy printout and put it into a FedEx envelope. You will bill her later, once you have checked to make sure she is satisfied.

The evening rush hour has begun. No point in going out for office supplies now. You've still got a proposal to write for a prospective client. But you decide that you've worked enough for the time being, and besides, you'll be working tonight. So you spend an hour puttering around the house or working in the garage, if you have a home office. Getting dinner started also offers a nice change of pace.

Or you make a few phone calls. Or maybe you simply take the time to think about how you will approach the next project on your list. Who will you call? What databases will you search? Do you have any contacts who could help you on this one? You make notes to yourself, of course. When you're juggling five or six projects at a time, it's the only way to remember where you were on each.

It's almost 6:00 P.M., and it is also the end of the month. Bill-paying time. Time to do the books. And next week your quarterly tax payment is due. You spend the hour with the books and the checkbook. While you're at it, you make a note to send second notices to several clients who are more than 30 days past due.

At 7:00 you break for dinner. But you are back at your machine by 9:00. You've got three online searches to do, and some online systems cut their rates dramatically after 6:00 P.M. Some databases never go down in price, but it only makes good sense to do whatever searching you can at the low, evening rate.

By midnight, you're exhausted. You think you've got all you need for two projects and have started the third. But your eyes are beginning to blur and you're no longer as sharp as you were when you started. You sign off and decide to postpone cleaning up and printing out the information you have captured until tomorrow.

Before going to sleep you either watch that television show you taped earlier in the evening or you read a novel or nonfiction book that has nothing to do with computers or the information industry. You have found that if you don't do this, if you simply climb into bed, your mind keeps replaying the last search and helpfully suggesting additional avenues of inquiry.

At the end of the day

Though hypothetical, this is very much what you can expect your days to be like as an information broker. You do spend a good portion of your day actually practicing your profession. But there are also speeches to give, articles to write, and sales calls to make. There are the mind-numbing but necessary details of paying the bills, balancing the books, and keeping the office well-supplied. There are phone calls to take—both desired and unwanted—letters to write, rush jobs to complete, and publications to read.

But there is also the freedom to come and go as you please. To make your own hours. To run an errand in the middle of the afternoon—provided a client doesn't call with an immediate need—without asking anyone's permission. To work as long and as hard as you like, or to not work at all—provided you get the check to the mortgage company on time.

No job is perfect. But some are more perfect than others. Given the fact that we must all work for a living, we must all do *something*, you could do far worse than to become an information broker. Provided that you love information.

In the next chapter we will elaborate on this theme. We will look with a cold, rational eye at the pros and cons of the information business.

4 Pros & cons of the information business

In this chapter it is our goal to scare the daylights out of you! We're not kidding. We are going to tell everything that's wrong with the information industry as a whole and the profession of information broker in particular. There is no need to exaggerate or to in any way stretch the truth. Even if we were inclined to do so. The unvarnished reality says it all. We need only present the facts.

If, after absorbing those facts, you *still* want to become an information broker, you will find that the profession has its rewards. We'll tell you about them as well. But you should be aware that there's a fundamental imbalance between the cons and the pros.

Knowing what we know, our advice is this: If there's anything else you can do for a living that meets your own personal goals, by all means do it. You will never be able to make a rational, cost-justified case for choosing this profession. The choice has to come from the heart.

We will begin by considering the information industry as a whole. Then we'll narrow the focus to a more personal level and look at the process of starting up the business, the daily work, the financial potential, and competition. We will close with some thoughts on the challenges faced by anyone seeking to set up a small business or become self-employed. In each case, we will present the negative aspects and then the positive aspects, if any, as we see them.

You're free to agree or disagree as you choose. We simply want to make you aware of the pitfalls as well as the joys of the profession. If you get into it and later decide that "this information broker stuff is not for me," you'll have only yourself to blame. No one can say you weren't warned.

Problems in the online information industry

The online industry has been good to us. We know and count as our friends lots of the people involved. They are bright, hard-working men and women wrestling with what amounts to nothing less than a force of nature. In addition, due to the relatively small numbers of online customers, these folks generally don't have large budgets to work with. But they do the best with what they have.

At the same time, however, as your guides into this realm, we have a responsibility to tell you the truth. And the truth is that if you approach online information and the companies that provide it as if this were a mature industry, you are likely to become disappointed, frustrated, and confused. If you approach it as a good consumer, your feelings may border on outrage, for the online information industry has a lot of weaknesses. Though, as one commentator we know has pointed out, the weakness never extends to prices. In good times or bad, it seems, the urge is ever upward when it comes to prices.

In short, the online information industry has more than its share of really good people. But, as Alfred says, it's still a wild and woolly place, particularly for new users. Our goal in the criticisms levelled throughout this chapter is to alert you to this fact. Keep your eyes open, and, until you feel you know what you're doing, keep your wallet close to your chest.

A product without value

We've said this so often that you're undoubtedly tired of hearing it by now, but information and the industry that has grown up to collect, catalogue, disseminate, and profit from it is the very paradigm of the word *nebulous*. None of us even knows what information actually is, let alone how to price the services required to retrieve it.

For one person, the journal articles you provide on some new antipollution process are definitely "information." But for another person, the *number* of articles that have been written on this process is the crucial point. To such a person, the actual content of the articles themselves may be totally irrelevant. As we mentioned in Chapter 1, often the simple fact that there *is* no information available on a particular topic can be valuable information in and of itself.

Information, in other words, has no clearly defined value. As such, the information industry has no clearly defined image in the minds of the people you plan to sell your services to. Many of them will know very little (if anything) about personal computers. And, while awareness is increasing, they will probably know even less about modems and online electronic databases. Worse still, those who do have some knowledge will assume that all an information broker has to do is type a few keywords into a database and—presto—the desired information appears on the screen.

"Com'on, how much time can that take? If I wasn't so busy, I'd do it myself and save your fee." This is the downside of increased information consciousness. Millions more people today are aware of the fact that information exists in electronic form online. And as is so often the case, many of these people have no humility at all about how very little they know.

Every information broker encounters clients like this. And they are among the most irritating of all. They are smart, but they're not wise. They are walking embodiments of the proverb that "a little knowledge is a dangerous thing." Remember, knowledge is proud that he knows so much, while wisdom is humble that he knows no more.

Clients of this sort are all but impossible to deal with. You're smart too, so the temptation is to plead your case and attempt some instant education. You want to say, "Listen, you stuck-up so-and-so, you think you know it all, but the truth is you don't know your elbow from first base when it comes to information."

And, guess what—your two co-authors heartily agree! Life is too short to spend very much of it dealing with, er, "potholes" like that. "Mr. Client, meet The Dragon. And good luck to you! You're so smart, you should have no trouble at all dispatching the Beast."

No one, in short, knows what you really do because they don't understand how it's done. People who willingly acknowledge the special talents and training of a doctor, lawyer, or tax accountant will thus not accord you the same respect. At least not until you knock their stockings off with a killer report or online search. That means that you start at a serious disadvantage with nearly every prospective client. You really do have to prove yourself every day.

On the plus side, once you have successfully handled an assignment or two, a satisfied client will become your biggest supporter. Often you will develop a personal relationship that probably has more in common with the doctor-patient relationship than with any standard business association. You'll become their personal miracle worker. They don't have to know what you do. All they know is that you find them the information they need.

The downside: Everybody's an expert!

Like any other industry, the information industry has its own internal technical problems. At best, these problems make your tasks more difficult. At worst, they can raise serious questions about liability.

The problem of duplicate data

Let's take a real-life example. ABC News White House reporter Brit Hume writes a computer column for the *Washington Post*. Larry Shannon and Peter Lewis each write computer columns for the *New York Times*. All three columns are excellent sources, and, as it happens, each can be found online. Let's assume that the *Washington Post* and *New York Times* are each available as a separate database. (That is indeed the case, though the *Post* is included in many multipublication databases as well.)

So far, so good. You sign on to the appropriate systems and search the appropriate databases. Perhaps you are interested in reviews of some new computer program or hardware component. You obtain the information you want—copies of each columnist's review of the product. Then you decide to broaden your search to include additional publications. You try a database that covers perhaps 50 or more newspapers, but not the *Post* or the *Times*. You get lots of hits (i.e., matches in the database for your search terms), and you begin displaying the relevant articles.

But wait a minute. You've seen the information in many of these articles before. It turns out that the columns done by Hume, Shannon, and Lewis are *syndicated*. Like press releases, their columns get picked up and printed by many newspapers, often under completely different headlines. So there you are—you've just paid perhaps $3 apiece for eleven articles, five of which are exact duplicates of what you already have from your first search.

Sue has one searcher friend who dismisses this problem, citing DIALOG's "duplicate detection" feature as the solution. But then, she's a long-time DIALOG employee and clearly doesn't get out much when it comes to other online systems. Most professional searchers like the idea of duplicate detection, but many will tell you that it doesn't always work.

What few people inside the industry will tell you is that there is a *lot* of duplication of data in online databases. And DIALOG or no, it is not always easy to detect. As we will see in Part three of this book, the databases themselves don't make it easy for you to discover exactly which publications or sources they cover. There are at least two dozen databases, for example, that cover *Business Week*. But each database starts its coverage with a different year. Some offer the full text of every issue they cover. Some are limited to abstracts. And some mix the two. Naturally, all of them have attached a different set of keywords to the same articles. And oh, by the way, the prices you'll pay to search these databases differ by several orders of magnitude.

Byzantine pricing schemes

Speaking of prices, we can think of no industry with a more Byzantine pricing structure than the online information industry. It may be that some defense contractors come close. But for sheer complexity, the online industry takes the prize. We'll go into much more detail in Part three of this book. For now, take it on faith that most of the time there is absolutely no way to compare prices across different online systems. Each has its own way of deciding how much you owe them.

When an online system is the exclusive distributor of a given database, you have no choice. But a growing number of databases are available on several systems. So as a smart businessperson, you must frequently try to figure out who is giving you the best deal. This is much more complicated than it sounds, since, among other things, some systems charge you on the basis of each article or citation you retrieve, while others charge you by the number of characters they transmit to your screen, and still others charge only on the basis of connect time.

In mature consumer products industries, one can assume that misleading pricing or other tricks are intentional. Do you really think, for example, that it's accidental when a company packs 13 ounces of gourmet coffee beans into the same size bag that for decades has always held a full pound of coffee? Of course not.

Things are different in the online industry. The industry sells a "product" whose value and price are extremely difficult to define. And in the past, the people charged with the responsibility for doing just that have not come from a marketing background. Add to this the relative immaturity of the industry and the fact that they all want to do things their own way, and the result is the incredibly complex pricing structure that exists today.

The inevitable result of this unintended confusion is that many people end up paying much more than they need to pay for the very same data. If you were a large company with lots of fat in the budget, a dollar here and a dollar there might not matter. As it is, even if you can pass 100 percent of the costs along, the shrewdness with which you use online resources can make or break you as an independent information broker.

Inaccurate data

You can avoid the pitfalls of pricing and duplicate data through trial and error and by learning as much as you can about the nuts and bolts of the online information industry. But how can you cope with inaccurate data?

Inaccurate. Incorrect. And just plain wrong! This is the industry's real Achilles heel. Most of us used to think that if something was in print it had to be true. We transferred this faith to television news programs, and then to online databases.

You need only to spend a week as an information broker to see what a fool's paradise you used to live in.

Again, we can offer a quick real-life example. In the course of writing *How to Look It Up Online*, Alfred searched the Library of Congress database for his last name. The search turned up a previously unknown publication written by a great-grandfather. (The sly old fox!) But it also turned up a book published in 1889 called *The Life of Bishop Glossbrenner*. The kicker was that the record was tagged with the named person identified as "Grossbrenner, Jacob John."

Somewhere along the line, someone made a typing mistake. But that doesn't change the fact that if you had told the database to focus on the named person field and searched on "Glossbrenner," you would *not* have found this record.

It's a small typo, of course. Merely a single letter. And the fact that Alfred located the record is proof that there are ways around errors of this sort. But the mere existence of such mistakes gives one pause. Suppose that instead of a single letter being typed incorrectly, the error occurred in a field containing numerical data. Suppose that as a result, the XYZ Company shows up with earnings either far greater or far less than it actually produced.

As an information intermediary, there is virtually no way you could detect the error. Yet it would be included in the printout or report and given to your client. If the client did not detect the error, he or she could easily make a major decision on the basis of faulty information.

Mistakes of this sort turn up *all the time*. If you're already a DIALOG user, you have only to EXPAND a few search terms to see clear evidence of what we mean. The EXPAND command on DIALOG displays a list of keywords showing you those above and below your target word in alphabetical order. For each keyword there is a number indicating how many times it occurs in the database. It is very common to find, say, 3,000 occurrences of "automobile" and one or two occurrences of "automobiel."

Again, this is a problem for at least two reasons. First, if you are searching on "automobile" you may not find the records in which that word is misspelled. And second, if mistakes can be made in text—where they can be easily detected—they can also be made in numerical data where detection is next to impossible.

Of course, the same kinds of problems occur all the time in print publications. Or, indeed, in any publication produced by human beings. No one talks about it. No one runs ads saying "Our database has fewer errors in it than the competition." But the problem clearly exists. And as a practicing information professional, you must confront it every day.

Every database is different

In this catalogue of ills, we will pass over the often poor documentation and inadequate instructions provided by online information systems. It took DIALOG and Lexis/Nexis ten years to produce what is now generally considered to be good documentation. But they are but two of over 800 online systems, and one cannot help wondering why it took these two industry leaders so long to produce good manuals.

We will pass over that other little problem—the joke about how frequently a given database is updated. It's all done with the best intentions, undoubtedly. The database producer tells an online system like DIALOG that the product will be updated on a certain schedule. The online system relays that schedule to customers in printed materials.

Sometimes the advertised update schedule is not always met. This is usually the problem of the database producer. Sometimes a vendor will get a bad tape and have to ask for a new copy. But usually vendors are told by the producers that "the update tape is in the mail."

As a customer, you have the right to expect accurate information regarding updates. But vendors tend to feel that it is also your responsibility to notice when you are not getting hits on current topics or proper names you know should be in a database that has been updated on schedule. Call the vendor to find out what is happening.

With DIALOG, you can always tell when the last update was added to a file by reading the banner that appears each time you enter a database. If you see that a given database is several months behind its published update schedule, call DIALOG customer service and find out why before you continue your search.

We will leave aside the fact that the identical database is often implemented in different ways on different online systems. That means that not all of your knowledge about a given database is necessarily directly transferable.

But we cannot pass over the fact that every online system is different. That in itself is not bad. But the fact remains that, more than a decade after the start of the online industry, there is no common command language. The commands you learn for retrieving information on DIALOG, for example, do you no good at all on NEXIS, Vu/Text, or BRS.

The concepts of searching are the same throughout the industry. But the means and commands for employing these concepts differ widely. In essence, you will have to learn an entirely different "language" for every online system you wish to search. Then, of course, each online system and each database has its own little quirks. There are things you can do on DIALOG that are not possible on BRS, and vice versa.

And those are just two of the leading online systems. As a practicing information broker, you'll have to completely master four or five systems—or hire someone with these skills—just to stay in the game. CompuServe, GEnie, and other consumer-oriented systems don't count. From an information perspective, they aren't even on the chart. Though thanks to an aggressive campaign by Information Access Company and a few other database producers, CompuServe is offering a great deal of industrial-strength information. Indeed CompuServe's progress in this area has been nothing short of remarkable.

It is very true that online searching is only part of the information broker's job. But it can be a significant part. Even if you specialize in telephone interviews, online databases offer a wealth of names, contacts, and other starting points. We thus thought it best to clue you in right from the start.

It is far better for you to learn these things now than it is to learn them later, after you have a lot of time and money in the profession. And it is this matter that we will examine next.

Start-up costs

Every new business involves start-up costs. Compared to other professions, information brokers get off rather lightly. Dentists have to buy everything from an X-ray machine to the paper bibs they snap around your neck. CPAs have to buy computers and laser printers and tax and accounting software. A prospective franchisee has to not only buy equipment and supplies, but also pay a hefty franchise fee. And so on.

As an information broker, you must basically buy the things needed to equip an office: a personal computer and laser printer, possibly a typewriter for labels and envelopes, a two-line or three-line phone system, a fax machine, stationery, a photocopier, business cards, paper clips, and all the other paraphernalia of setting up an office. You will also need a 9,600 bit per second (bps) modem, at least. Or a 14.4 or 28.8 Kbps modem, if you can afford it. And you will need software.

None of these items is unique. As you will see later in this book, there are ways to save big bucks on nearly every one of them. The start-up expenses unique to information brokers are things like subscriptions to professional journals such as *Information Today*, *Online*, *Database*, and *Searcher*. Each one will cost you $50 or more for a one-year subscription. You'll find details on crucial publications in Appendix A.

There are also subscriptions to online systems to consider. You can easily spend hundreds—even thousands—of dollars a year in subscription fees. Such fees merely entitle you to sign onto a given system. Any information you retrieve once you're on is priced separately.

Of course, if you are a member of the Association of Independent Information Professionals (AIIP), you may be eligible for discounts and special deals. So be sure to see Appendix C for more information on this essential organization.

Another expense not to be overlooked is the cost of training in using various databases and online systems. In general, you should probably budget close to $1,000 a year or more for training fees, travel, and living expenses associated with enrolling in various programs offered by databases and database vendors (online systems). You may be able to skip a year now and then, but these systems are constantly changing, so you will have to keep current.

You may spend several thousand dollars more attending trade shows and seminars. It can be vital to maintain a presence in the field, and of course, you never know when a speech you have given will lead to an assignment. Sue and Alfred both have given speeches, appeared on discussion panels, and written articles either for free or for nothing more than a token payment.

In any case, these thousands of dollars are simply the out-of-pocket expense. As a self-employed professional, you'll spend even more in "soft dollars." Writing an article or preparing a speech can take several days, for example. If you hope to make, say, $50,000 a year, with two weeks of vacation, you have to earn $200 a day working five days a week. A day here and a day there spent writing an article or preparing a speech adds up.

And we haven't even mentioned the time you will have to spend reading the professional journals and update sheets that will land on your doorstep like autumn leaves after a November rainstorm. If you were a doctor or a lawyer, you'd have to do the same thing. But it still amounts to time spent, and when you are self-employed, time is money.

It is perhaps unfair of us to refer to the day-to-day work of an information professional as "the daily grind." But after all, there's a reason why they call it "work." If you are a certain type of person, there is no experience that compares to nailing down an elusive piece of information. Sex may come close, but it's only a momentary high. If you are a skilled information professional, the high can last for days.

The daily grind

Take all the mystery movies you've ever seen, add in the nonfiction shows about dedicated scientists making important discoveries, and the designers and inventors solving "insoluble" problems, and you'll have some inkling of what it can be like to be an information broker.

You may look and dress like everyone else at the supermarket. But, as you load up your cart with the bacon and beans, the paper towels and toilet paper, you know that you're different. Through your knowledge of the information industry, your skill at manipulating its resources, and your creative imagination in deciding where to search, you have solved the mystery. You have found the patent, or located the crucial article, or otherwise performed feats mere mortals can't even dream of.

And tomorrow you're going to do it again. Another day, another miracle.

Reverie & delight

Would that it could all be reverie and delight. Would that every day could be spent confronting and besting the information dragon. Unfortunately, no self-employed information broker has this luxury. Exhilaration is definitely a part of the job. But so too is paying the bills. Literally. Hauling out the checkbook, deciding whom you can pay this month and which creditors you can let slide.

There is also the essential, never-ending work of selling. We provided a brief glimpse of a "day in the life" of an information broker earlier in this book. The portrait was essentially accurate, but designed as it was to illustrate all the various activities of being an information broker, it did not sufficiently emphasize the sales component.

It is possible—but very unlikely—that you will reach a position where you do not have to concern yourself with the sources of the next month's billing. After several years in practice, you may be able to establish a large enough client base to have your "nut" (your fundamental expenses) covered each month.

But don't count on it.

Your best client, an executive at the ABC Company, may get promoted to a distant city. (Though you shouldn't let that fact stop you from trying to maintain the relationship.) People retire all the time. People come and go. It's in the nature of things. And every time you lose a client, you face the task of starting all over again. As we have tried to emphasize repeatedly, the client-information broker relationship is a personal relationship. If Jane Smith gets promoted out, you may have to start all over again with her replacement, John Jones.

So you have got to *sell*. Always. Every day. That means "cold calls" (by telephone or personal appearances when you have not been invited). It means organizing direct mail campaigns to likely prospects—and following up with phone calls. It means soliciting speech and article assignments, preparing and issuing press releases, and making unpaid guest appearances before local community groups. Most important, it means constantly thinking about ways to (inexpensively) promote your name and the services you offer, whether it be to local or worldwide clients.

Unpleasant, stupid people

Dealing with clients is also a part of the daily grind. You may of necessity have to work at times for unpleasant people. You may have to present your skills to someone who, at best, is uninformed and, at worst, is plain stupid. You will have to smile a lot, even (especially) when you don't mean it.

You will also have to deal with smart clients who think they know how to conduct an online search. Never has a little knowledge been a more aggravating thing. They'll tell you which databases to use, ask whether you have a copy of some database thesaurus and if not, would you like to borrow theirs, and generally make a nuisance of themselves.

Smile politely. Tell them how impressed you are with their knowledge of the online world. Allow as how they have some interesting ideas and suggestions. Then go out and do precisely what you want. Under no circumstances, in our opinion, should you ever let a client sit at your shoulder when you are conducting an online search.

Follow their suggestions if you feel you have to keep them happy. But charge them for it. If you have not followed their suggestions and they ask you about it later, smile pleasantly and explain that you were searching database XYZ anyway and happened to find what they needed. Say you felt certain that under the circumstances the client would not want to incur the additional fees of searching database ABC when you already had what he or she wanted. Or words to that effect.

Compliment them on their knowledge. Talk shop with them if that's what they want to do. Don't ever let them feel ignorant or inadequate. But don't let them control your approach to a problem either. In other words, be a good politician, but stick to your principles.

Financial potential

You would think that in the Information Age, someone who was a master of retrieving information would be able to write his or her own ticket. It may eventually come to that. Knowing what we do about information and its role in the modern economy, it is entirely plausible that—someday—a company's information broker will be accorded the same respect, deference, and salary given to other leading executives considered essential to the firm. But the time is not yet.

At the very least you would think that plain common sense would cause companies to accord an information broker the same respect given to its tax accountant. That simply is not the case, thanks in large measure to the nebulousness of the information field. Everyone knows what a sharp tax accountant can do. But an information broker? You're basically a librarian, right?

It is our opinion that this situation *must* change. The potential and the value of information and the people with the unique skills needed to retrieve it are simply too great to ignore. We aren't betting the farm on seeing it change in our lifetimes, however.

As a prospective information broker, this means that you can forget about fat, easily obtained paychecks. If nothing else, your cost of making a single sale—which includes all the dead ends and false leads you had to pursue to find the one ready client—is too high. You can make a living at this profession, but you're not going to make a fortune and you will never make a killing.

That's why we have said repeatedly that you simply have to love the work. It is why we say that if you can possibly do anything else, do it. You can make $50,000 a year within two or three years—*if* you can sell and if you can produce a top-notch product.

But if making $50,000 a year is your goal, you will have an easier time selling residential real estate. At a seven percent commission, you would only have to sell three or four homes at today's prices to earn that much money each year.

And at least as a real estate agent, you won't be on the hook for hundreds of dollars in online database expenses. No matter how careful you are in negotiating advance payments, there is always the possibility that a client will not pay you for your services and expenses.

When that happens, it is one thing to write off the time you have spent and other "soft dollar" expenses. But if the project has caused you to generate $250 in DIALOG expenses, you'll have to pay that bill. If you don't, you may never be allowed on the system again, and that can be the kiss of death to an information broker. In other words, an information broker, unlike, say, a real estate salesperson, incurs certain hard financial risks. And often for a lot less financial reward.

Competition

If you were thinking of investing a million dollars in a McDonald's franchise, you would certainly be interested in whether Burger King, Wendy's, or some other competing franchise had plans to open up down the street. The competition isn't nearly as intense in the information field, but that doesn't mean it does not exist. Nor does it mean that it is somehow "bad." In fact, for the foreseeable future, the more truly good information brokers there are, the better for all of us.

That may sound surprising, but it's true. As information brokers, our major competition is not other information brokers. Indeed, you should think of other information brokers as your network of resources, not as your competition.

Our major competition is plain ignorance—client ignorance of what can be accomplished. As we have said before, your clients will not ask you to do what *they* think is impossible. But most clients have no idea of what is truly possible in the information field today. We—all of us—have got to educate them. Only then will they appreciate what an information broker can do. Only then will they unhesitatingly pick up the phone and say "I've got a problem I think you can help me with . . ."

We will say it again: Other brokers are *not* your competition. If they were, do you think we would be writing this book? Do you think Sue Rugge would be criss-crossing the country conducting The Information Broker's Seminar? In your dreams. We'd keep the good stuff to ourselves. And so would you, if you were in our position.

Anyone who is responsibly marketing information brokering services benefits every information broker. No one—no one individual, no one company—is in a position to provide everything any given client needs to know. That's why *subcontracting* is vital to any broker's ability to satisfy clients' needs. But to be able to successfully subcontract work, you've got to have good people in the field. Lots of them. With lots of individual specialities.

It is no small accomplishment to get that telephone on your desk to ring. It only happens through marketing. And if you have marketed yourself and your services thoroughly, and the phone rings, you deserve the client. If the client needs something that you personally cannot provide, don't refer him to a colleague. Subcontract the job to that colleague and keep the client for yourself.

This way everyone benefits. The colleague gets business that would not have occurred were it not for you. You are compensated for the time, expertise, and expense required for the marketing effort. And the client gets the best possible service.

Sue's rule of thumb is that even if you don't do the actual searching yourself, if you add something to the equation, you're entitled to the client. After all, there is no way of knowing what the individual will need the next time.

The bottom line is that, for very tough, practical reasons, the more skilled, responsible, information brokers there are, the better for everyone—for you, for them, and for your clients.

At this point we need to say a word or two about libraries and librarians. So let's lay it on the table: Are librarians competition for information brokers? The answer is a resounding "yes and no."

What about libraries?

There has long been some bad blood between professional librarians and professional information brokers. In general, librarians do not look kindly upon information brokers who take advantage of their "free" services and their expertise to produce a report that they then deliver to a client for a fee.

There are arguments on both sides of the issue, but there is little point in rehearsing them here. In our opinion, and in the opinion of most responsible information brokers, a library's resources should be used without using the librarian's time.

It is *our* job to ferret out the needed facts. That's what we are being paid to do. It is not fair—and it may not be ethical—to ask the librarian to do it for us. The pioneers in the information brokering field have had to work very hard to establish a positive relationship with their colleagues on the other side of the reference desk. As a new information broker, it is your responsibility not to abuse or destroy this trust.

On the other hand, while most people do not know it, many libraries have long offered research services, either for free or for a charge equivalent to database expenses. And as budgets tighten, all libraries are looking for sources of additional funds. Accordingly, some libraries have begun to charge more for research services than simple pass-through database expenses.

This could be considered a change for the better from an information broker's standpoint. For, if the library is making a profit on a search, it is difficult to see how anyone can complain if you employ these services in your own work. By entering the profit-making arena, the library and the librarians become, in effect, subcontractors.

So, in a way, libraries could be considered competitors. But the stark advantage you'll have over any library is marketing. No research librarian with a steady paycheck, benefits, and all the rest will ever have the motivation of an information broker who must make a sale to make the rent each month.

In fact, as indicated above, you can turn the entire situation to your advantage. If your library offers fee-based, profit-making research services, you may find that it is to your advantage to use them as subcontractors. (Though few public librarians have the subject expertise needed to do the type of work required of most information brokers.) That would give you more time to sell and to provide the things that librarians cannot offer. Local reference and research librarians also often make excellent freelance searchers should you ever need extra help on a particular job.

Online systems & amateurs

A more serious form of competition comes from the databases and online services themselves. Whether for reasons of profit or otherwise, many online services actively promote the idea of end-user searching. This simply means that the person who *needs the information*—the "client" in our case—does the actual searching.

Remember that these services make their money on connect time. And who do they want to be connected to their computers? Bumbling amateurs who don't know what they're doing, of course!

As time goes on, you will also face competition from people who have no business being in the information industry at all—people who have bought into the idea that all you need is a computer and a modem to make money. Folks, this is a profession! This is a specialty. It is not something that you turn on in the morning and crank out.

The problem is that the marketplace at this point doesn't know the difference between someone who has just gotten his account on CompuServe and someone who has been wending his way through DIALOG or NEXIS for years. Amateurs and quick-buck artists won't ruin the profession, but you can count on the fact that they will appear and possibly damage your business.

They will bill themselves as information brokers, just like you. And they will promise clients things they cannot possibly deliver. When they fail to deliver, or when they provide shoddy service, the entire profession will suffer. All of which makes your job as a legitimate information broker more difficult. Someone who has been badly burned by the last supposed professional is not going to greet you with open arms. You can yell "Wait a minute! I'm different!" all you want.

According to one of our information broker friends, in California it is not uncommon for a traffic cop, upon seeing some stupid accident, to record the cause of the accident as "HUA." We have it on reliable authority that this stands for "head under armpit," though, of course, you are free to make your own interpretation.

This same information broker has applied that same term to many of the online systems we all have to deal with. It is rather like the U.S. Congress—there are surely many good, dedicated people there, but the institution as a whole is strictly "HUA."

So perhaps none of us should be too concerned about so-called "house brokers." These are employees of DIALOG, NEXIS, and other systems whose job it is to conduct online searches of their respective systems for a flat fee. In the trade, they're known as "rip and ship" operations because all they do is conduct a search, print out the results, and ship the printout to their customers. There is no seasoned professional to cull, edit, analyze, or otherwise process the information. It's strictly raw data on demand. It's "information as yard goods," to use Alfred's phrase. Pull it out and cut it off!

At first glance, house broker operations like these might appear to be a threat. Certainly, they should not be ignored, and all of us should consider ways to sell against them. In fact, if you don't happen to be up-to-speed on a given system, you might consider taking advantage of these offerings yourself, marking them up as appropriate as you bill your client.

But we should not be too worried about direct competition, thanks to the "HUA" phenomenon. If the past is prologue to the future, we can rely on most house broker operations to fail. Not because of the men and women doing the searching but because of the men and women above them who are afflicted with the "HUA" syndrome.

Your co-authors have been intimately involved with the information industry for over a dozen years. We have personal friends at most online systems. Yet both they and we would agree that no information company has yet gotten its act together. In Alfred's words, they seem like battleships becalmed. You keep praying that they will rev up their engines and steam out of harbor and into the future—before some non-American company beats them to it—but they seem content to wallow in the swell.

It is tragic, but as information brokers, there is nothing we can do. We work with what's available and hope for a brighter day.

Standard self-employment concerns

Since this is not a book about how to become self-employed, we will touch only lightly on the standard concerns any self-employed person must face. Our point is that these concerns are there, and they have nothing to do with how you actually earn your daily bread.

Taxes are certainly a problem. In its wisdom the federal government has chosen to tax self-employed people rather severely for being self-employed. The tax we have in mind is even called the Self-Employment Tax, though it goes for Social Security. The bottom line is that if you are self-employed, you will pay more in Social Security tax than your friends who work for regular companies.

On the positive side, self-employed individuals have access to more legitimate deductions—starting with all that office equipment you had to buy. But the tax code is so complex that even if you have always filed the short form before, once you become self-employed, you will almost certainly have to hire a tax specialist to see to it that you are receiving every legitimate deduction.

You may also need the services of an attorney. An attorney can help you draft standard letters of agreement and contracts for your services. He or she can also advise you on issues of liability. And between the two of them, your accountant and attorney can help you structure your business in the way best suited to your own situation.

As a businessperson, you will also have to balance the books. This doesn't have to be a major undertaking, but you will definitely have to account for income and expenses. Of course, you will have to pay business-related bills in addition to the domestic ones you already pay. Even assuming that money is not a problem, one should not underestimate the time this requires each month. (Fortunately there are programs like *Managing Your Money* and *Quicken* that can largely automate this procedure.)

As "the boss," you will of course be involved in all equipment purchases. But you will also be responsible for equipment maintenance and office supplies. And, most important of all, you will have to handle dunning notices and "reminders" for clients who have not paid their bills on time.

As a small-business owner, you might as well face it—you are often the last to get paid. Your claim may be just as legitimate as that of a Fortune 500 company. In fact, you may actually have a prior claim. But your creditors know that you have little recourse. If they don't pay the big company on time, that company might cause trouble. But what are you, Joe/Jane Information Broker, going to do? Sue them? Right. Your attorney's retainer fee will probably be several times the amount in question. So politely, but persistently, dunning slow-paying clients is an unavoidable part of the job.

It is our fondest hope that this chapter will bring you up short. If it has caused you to seriously reexamine whether you really want to be an information broker, then it has done its job. Again, we must emphasize that we have told you nothing but the truth. We have not exaggerated, and we have not left anything out.

If you still want to become an information broker, then more power to you. It is an enormously rewarding profession for those who are suited to it. But it is definitely not the easy path to El Dorado. If there were any money in the information profession—any *real* money—the databases and online services wouldn't be in the state they are in, the profession wouldn't be so small, and you wouldn't need a book like this. Instead, "information broker" would be a widely understood title and accepted job description, and there would be courses in all the colleges and high schools designed to train students in this skill.

As it is, we're a small band of "happy warriors" dedicated to taking on The Dragon and, against all odds, making a living at this profession. If you're still with us, turn to the next chapter, where we will help you determine whether you've got what it takes to be happy as an information broker.

5 The crucial question: Is it for you?

With any luck, that last chapter will have scared off all the aspiring quick-buck artists!

As you are sure to have discovered by now, there are some people with a sixth sense for "the next new thing," particularly if it is something that promises to pay a lot of money for a relatively small amount of work.

For a while it was home-based water purification systems. The "900" and "976" phone services are still big. And "network marketing" (the current name for modified, and therefore completely legal, pyramid-style schemes) is an up-and-comer. Recently, we've seen it used to sell everything from residential homes to discount long-distance phone service.

Business opportunities of this sort have a number of things in common. They all tell a plausible story. They are all "new." Most emphasize their use of computers and technology to add to the intrigue and believability. Most also share the common pitch: "Look, people *want* and *need* this product or service. And with the technology we put at your disposal, it's easy to deliver. So there is no way you won't make a killing."

We'll leave it to you to deduce who's the killer and who's the kill-ee in such setups. But you can see how, on the surface at least, information brokering might appear to be ideally suited to snaring a quick buck or two. With any luck, by showing you the truth of the profession, we have convinced you that this simply isn't so.

To be sure, we have a vested interest in seeing that the profession isn't flooded with amateurs or those who think information brokering is the perfect home-based business.

But it's not what you might think. It isn't a question of there not being enough work to go around. There is plenty of work, but you've got to sell each client one at a time. Each information broker is thus a missionary.

For nine out of ten clients, you *are* the profession of information broker. You are their only exposure to the information industry. If you are not competent, if you promise things you cannot deliver—if, in short, you don't know what you're doing—you can do enormous damage to this budding profession.

Though it is not likely that information brokers will ever be licensed, at least not any time soon, work has already begun on establishing and codifying professional ethics. That, in fact, was one of the main initial goals of the Association for Independent Information Professionals (AIIP) when it started in 1987. Since that time, AIIP has participated in discussions with various online vendors regarding the establishment of "certified searcher" programs. Movements are also afoot within AIIP to tighten membership requirements so that members are more reflective of the information brokering profession as a whole.

The Carnegie syndrome

The AIIP is essential because existing information industry organizations don't always address the needs of information brokers. In fact, over the years, some people at the Special Libraries Association (SLA) and the American Library Association (ALA) have spent a tremendous amount of time and energy trying to negate the whole concept.

In the beginning, in 1972, there was an editorial by John Berry in *Library Journal* predicting that Sue Rugge would cause the downfall of the public library system. Needless to say, it came as a great surprise to Sue that she had amassed that much power.

The concept of information gathering, which is usually associated with a librarian, suffers from what we call the "Carnegie syndrome." It is the idea that somehow all information should be free.

As you may remember, Andrew Carnegie, after he created U.S. Steel, wanted to give something back to society in the early years of this century. He did a great deal of good, but he is most remembered for donating libraries. He would build and stock the facilities, on condition that local authorities provided the site and maintenance.

Over the years, this established a tradition that libraries existed to dispense information for free to everyone who wanted it. This is very much a part of the librarian ethic, and it has led to tremendous debates within the profession: Should online searching be offered as part of this charter? Should it be offered for free? Should librarians offer it at all if they have to charge for it?

In our opinion, many librarians are so caught up in this issue of whether to charge for their services or not that they are missing a lucrative opportunity: the possibility of supplementing their already tight budgets by offering the business community a higher level of service for which companies would be willing to pay a higher level of fees. The profits generated from such an approach would enable a library to offer more free services to the general public as a whole.

Please don't misunderstand. These are dedicated, often selfless, people. They will bend over backwards to satisfy a patron's request, no matter how seemingly insignificant the issue or how difficult the research task. But while many have excellent reference interview skills, many more have difficulty helping the patron define the problem. For that, you usually need an independent information broker.

You're going to think we're out to get librarians. We aren't. But it is impossible to deny that a lot of librarians went into their profession because of its job security. There was no risk-taking, at least not until everyone began to hear the whisper of the budgetary axe. It's intellectually stimulating, but if they can't find the answer, there's no financial risk for them. It is not as though they have to perform successfully each day to be assured of being able to pay the rent.

But, boy, if you're an information broker, *everything* is on the line, both personally and financially. If you're promising things you can't deliver, you're probably not going to get paid. An information broker revels in "living dangerously," as Walter Kauffman, Alfred's philosophy professor, used to say. It takes a special personality, and it is that topic we'd like to consider next.

If you've read the first several chapters, you should have at least a sense of what the information industry is all about. You know there is definitely a market for the services information brokers can provide, and you have some idea of what the job itself is like. The next logical question is "Is this profession for me? What do you have to bring to the profession to have a chance of succeeding?"

Five crucial elements

The answer can be concentrated into five elements: intelligence, personality, education, background and training, and skills—and in that order. Thus of the five, intelligence and personality are by far the most important, so we'll look at them first.

Intelligence   There are simply no two ways about it. If you're going to be a successful information broker, you've got to be smart. In virtually every other profession, there are niches for average people. Not here. There are lawyers, accountants, college professors, and even medical doctors who spend their days doing the same routine chores over and over again. They are undoubtedly of above-average intelligence—most of us would be appalled at how truly average "average intelligence" really is—but they are not above-average people. There are no such niches for information brokers.

Now, by "smart," we don't mean that you had to get straight A's in school. We mean you've got to be clever and creative. There are no instruction manuals to show you how to solve specific problems in this field. If you're familiar with the resources available, however, you can usually figure out how to manipulate them to get the job done.

You've also got to be a quick study, able to assimilate and make sense of large numbers of facts in very little time, and you've got to have an excellent memory. You never know when something you saw last week or last year will be of value in doing the current assignment.

It is also essential to be adaptable, since one day you may be dealing with nuclear power, and the next with the manufacture of low-salt peanut butter. In fact, handling only one topic each day is a luxury, and it will probably be unprofitable. Most of the time you will have to deal with them all at once. Every time the phone rings, you will probably have to shift gears as you interact with different clients or interview sources for different projects.

Personality   Your personality is equally important. When Sue was looking for employees for IOD, she always found it very hard to find people with the right combination of personality and innate ability. Like many computer programmers, people who are good at information often aren't good at relating to other people. But what's needed in the information broker is someone who is not only great with information but also great with clients.

An information broker may find information for a living, but what he or she really does—the unique service we all offer—is to serve as an interface between a client's needs and the big wide world of information. That is the essence of the profession. You must be able to make clients feel comfortable talking to you. You have to be able to draw them out and help them express what it is they are trying to accomplish.

Alfred has always said that the trick in being a freelance writer is not delivering what the client wants—it's finding out what the person wants or needs in the first place. The plain truth is that whether it is freelance writing or information, most clients have only the vaguest notion of what they really want. It is your job to help them clarify their needs by raising possibilities, suggesting alternatives, and listening very carefully to what they are saying.

You've also got to inspire confidence. You have to convince your clients, by what you say and the way you handle the situation, that you know what you are doing and that you really are going to be able to help them. Otherwise they will never invest their money in what, despite your best efforts at education, will always remain an incomprehensible never-never land.

Not everyone can do this. If client contact is not your strong point, you are certainly not barred from the profession. But you will need to team up with someone who *can* handle the client end of things. And that person will have to have far more than just a "sales personality."

Information brokers also need perseverance and adaptability. If you're blocked in one line of inquiry, you can't simply throw up your hands and quit. You should have the kind of personality that automatically begins looking for a way around the obstacle. And since you're going to be spending a good deal of time looking for things, it will be extremely helpful if you are the kind of person who enjoys the hunt.

It goes without saying that curiosity is an essential characteristic. Successful information brokers are what Sue likes to call "eclectic generalists." They are interested in *everything*. Not because they think the information they acquire by reading a wide variety of books, magazines, and newspapers (and from watching television) will necessarily be useful in some future assignment, but simply because they find it fascinating.

Finally, successful information brokers have a lot of pride. Pride in their abilities, and pride in what they produce. Sometimes that means spending far more time on a project than you should because you can't bear to put your name on something that doesn't measure up to your standards. It also means that everything coming out of your office, from business correspondence to final reports to the voice that answers the phone, should connote professionalism.

There *are* standards, ladies and gentlemen. And nothing that has happened in the past 30 years can change that. Women no longer wear white gloves to go downtown—indeed "downtown" has moved out to the mall. Men no longer have to wear ties at all public occasions. But a business letter with even a single misspelled word is and always will be unprofessional. After all, how much faith would you as a client put in the accuracy of a report by an information broker who can't even manage to produce an accurate cover letter?

Education

The third crucial quality is education, and here you are in for a surprise. Many of your competitors in the information field will hold advanced degrees, principally in library science. And many of them are not shy about waving their degrees about. Thankfully, with the possible exception of college library schools, the pernicious practice of addressing everyone who has a Ph.D. as "Doctor" has not taken root in this field. Yet.

Probably it never will, for this is the business world. Some businesspeople are impressed by degrees. But in general, businesspeople don't share the need for the constant reassurance and ego stroking many college professors require. The head of a giant corporation doesn't insist on being called Chairman Smith. It's much more likely to be "Betty" or "Bill." In the business world, you are known by your deeds, not by your doctorates.

This is certainly true in the world of the information broker. You don't need a degree—of any sort. What you need is the knowledge and some of the skills that are supposed to come with the degree but often don't. A prospective client is going to be much more interested in what you have done—the other projects you have completed, other clients served, and so forth—than in your formal education.

If you've got a degree or special training you can boast about, by all means make the most of it. But put it at the end of your capabilities brochure in a mini-resume section. The bulk of your brochure should highlight your accomplishments as an information broker and the benefits you can offer your clients. Otherwise don't give this issue a second thought.

If you are at all doubtful on this point, consider the fact that one of today's leading information brokers, someone who built the second largest information retrieval firm in the country—and then sold it for a comfortable profit—does not have a college degree. Her name is Sue Rugge.

Background & training

When someone calls The Rugge Group and says "I'm just retiring after 30 years in engineering, and now I want to be an information broker," Sue always tells them: "Capitalize on that background. You have colleagues, and those are the people who should be the beginning of your client base." It's good advice, because whatever background or training you bring to the profession offers the ideal starting point.

We cannot emphasize this point strongly enough: There isn't a profession, a craft, or a trade in existence that does not have unmet information needs. The needs may not be obvious, and certainly some businesses have more of them than others. But no matter what you're doing for a living right now, look around! Somewhere there's a need for better information retrieval, packaging, or presentation.

Most of the time you don't have to be all that clever to find it. All you need is a good, solid knowledge of your business and the ability to look at it with new eyes. Once you flip that little switch in your head that illuminates the possibility of providing information services, you will be amazed at what you see.

No one is suggesting that you can count on making a living serving the information needs of your current profession. But it is definitely a start. Many an information broker has begun with a previous employer as a first client. And as your experience grows, so too will the breadth of your subject areas and assignments.

In short, just about any background and training is grist for the mill. If you've got the brains and the personality to be an information broker, your previous work history and background can only be an asset. At worst, it will be a neutral factor. It will never be a liability.

Skills

Finally, we come to the skills component. The most important single skill you can bring to your new profession is—touch typing. Most people are under the misimpression that to be able to talk to a computer you need to be fluent in BASIC, C, Pascal, COBOL, or some other computer language. That's wrong, unless you plan to be a professional programmer. The language of computing is plain old typing.

And you don't have to be able to type 58 error-free words per minute, either. The skill level to strive for is *comfort*. You want to be able to type well enough that you can think a word and have it instantly appear on the screen, without laboring over the process of getting it there.

This is important for business correspondence and reports. But it is essential to the cost-effective use of online systems. It is true that when you are conducting an online search, most of your typing is done in very short bursts. But if you have to hunt-and-peck every word, even entering a short string of characters can be a laborious process.

The extra online time you'll spend hunting and pecking is important, of course. But the real killer is the distraction. Online searches have a rhythm and flow. You enter something. The computer responds. You quickly absorb that and enter something else. And so on. You're thinking all the time. In this situation, the last thing you want to worry about is where to find the letter *S* on the keyboard.

So learn to type. Then learn to search. Good searchers are born, not made. But you'll never know whether you were born with "the right stuff" until you try your hand at it. You have to have self-confidence, and you have to have the ability to "think on your seat" when you are online. You have to be able to instantly adapt to what you find, and change your search strategy accordingly. Of course you hear the meter running as you search, but you don't let it rattle you.

Where does this kind of confidence come from? It's probably innate. Some years ago IOD had a wonderful researcher named David who was on the staff for years. He tried online searching a couple of times. He went to all the seminars, and he read all the manuals. After three months he said, "You know, I really don't like this. I'd rather not do this anymore."

Despite David's manifest skills in other areas, he was really a lousy online searcher. And he knew it. If you like online searching, you tend to be good at it. If it scares you—if computers in general scare you—then you probably should think twice about trying to become an online searcher.

This is not to say that you can't become an information broker. As we have said repeatedly, online searching is only one part of the job, a part that you can hire out if you don't have an aptitude for it. There are many times when expert phone interviewers are essential to the success of the project. But one simply cannot escape the fact that computers in general, and online searching in particular, are essential tools of the information trade. A carpenter who can only use a hammer but has never mastered the circular saw will never be a full-fledged member of the carpenters' trade.

So, in general, learn to type. Learn to use a computer. And learn to search, both online and using conventional, library-oriented resources. And don't forget to learn to use the telephone. This is possibly an information broker's most valuable and most frequently used tool, yet few people know how to use it properly to project the friendly, interested, persona most likely to elicit information from the person on the other end of the line.

Reports from the field on information broker

The online world is definitely not the be-all and end-all of the information profession. Many's the time you will have to take the "shoe leather" approach or spend the day on the telephone tracking down the information you need. But you just can't beat the online alternative when it comes to providing an "electronic water cooler" for those of us who want to swap stories, ideas, and gossip.

This particular water cooler is located on CompuServe in the Working from Home forum (GO WORK) run by Paul and Sarah Edwards. Here's what real information brokers have to say about the profession and whether or not it is for them:

- One contributor muses: "I wonder sometimes if information professionals who go independent don't do so for what, at bottom, are serious poetic reasons." To which another replies: "If you can stretch 'poetic' to mean 'lifestyles decisions,' I would certainly agree with you."

- Another writes: "After spending a year dealing with the butterflies in the stomach and the punishing 'what-if' questions we all face, I have to ask, 'What emboldens entrepreneurs?'"
  One answer submitted by a fellow information broker consisted of four points: "Ignorance, Pioneer Spirit, Security (that is, there's another

source of income), and Problems (that is, unhappiness with the current situation)."

A second information broker weighed in with this reply: "What emboldens entrepreneurs and gets them past the 'what-ifs'? Boredom and possibly anger get you started. You threaten to start your own business. Then the teasing and encouragement of your colleagues and family get you to do it. By the way, nearly everyone I've asked tells me that this process takes about a year, from toying with the idea to actually doing something about it."

- On dealing with business problems: "Recently my mate was trying to console me over a business worry I was having. It was a tough one, and my beloved came up with the perfect comment. 'Love of my life,' she said, 'it is quite an accomplishment to have reached this level of worry.' It cracked us up, but it's true. Once you decide to own a business, you enter a completely new level of worry!"

- "When I started out, my husband said, 'Think big! He was right. If you get complacent with security and income, you do not grow. I believe you have to set an income goal so you can gauge your growth and success. The goal does not have to be high. It only has to be realistic and achievable. So, when I left my job with a large corporation, I set a goal. The goal was that after five years I would be able to take out of the business the salary I was earning at the big company (excluding inflation, raises, benefits, and the other perks). After achieving that, I set even higher goals. I'll let you know how they turn out!"

- "Why did I take the plunge? I'll be happy to tell you. I can't stand the politics of large corporations. I was sick to my soul of spending four hours a day commuting—two hours in and two hours out. To say nothing of the long days my young son had to endure being transported to distant child care. Life is too short to live it this way! It took a while, but once I made the decision to quit, the outcome was inevitable. Since making the move, I have not been sorry for even a single day that I took the steps I did."

- "About eight years ago, when I was starting in this crazy activity, some genius—I think it was Paul Edwards—pointed out that the only common denominator of a successful person was having an abundance of *unjustified* optimism. So here I am! Like the bumblebee that doesn't know the aerodynamic engineers have declared him unable to fly, he just flies anyway. There's just a chance that all of us 'bumblebees' with our unjustified optimism will indeed succeed as information brokers!"

Conclusion

It is our job here to help you decide whether you have the talents, the personality, and the desire to become an information broker. We can give you our best advice. You can, and should, read what others have to say. But the best any book or any other person can do is to help focus your attention on several key aspects. Ultimately, only you can decide whether this is likely to be an agreeable way to make a living.

If, on the basis of what you've read so far, you have decided that this is probably not the right profession for you, we are very happy indeed. We've just saved you a great deal of time, effort, expense, and disappointment.

On the other hand, if some of the aspects of this crazy profession intrigue you, if you think it's something you might enjoy, there's only one way to know for sure, and that is to actually try your hand at it. That's what we'll show you how to do when we discuss "How to Get Started" in the next chapter.

6 How to get started

As we said earlier, if you've got the brains and the personality, you can have the job. You can become an information broker.

In this chapter we're going to offer some suggestions on how to get started and how to break into the business. We will look at four major steps along the way: finding your market niche, surveying the resources, self-tests and practice, and getting your first job.

The biggest mistake most new information brokers make is assuming that their business is information-driven. They assume that the first thing they must do is learn how to retrieve information and that the second step is to go out and try to sell their information retrieval skills. In reality, things are exactly the reverse.

Finding your market niche

As an information broker, you have to be *market-driven*, not information-driven. The most important thing you can do—before you develop or further polish your information retrieval and search skills—is to find your niche in the market.

There are at least two reasons why this is so.

First, as your common sense will tell you, it is pointless to manufacture a product before you know what the market for that product might be. It is much better to try to find out what the market wants and design your product to satisfy those needs. If you are an information broker, your "product" is actually the service of locating information.

Second, so much information and so many resources are available that some kind of focus is necessary. No one can be an expert in every information resource. Nor should you try to be. But how do you decide where to direct your energies? The answer is to let the market be your guide.

Capitalize on your background. Approach people you can communicate with. Probe for their information needs (even though they may not realize that they *have* information needs). What subjects are your potential clients interested in? What would they pay you money to find? It is crucial to ask those kinds of questions first—to find your market niche—before you begin to seriously focus on specific resources, search and retrieval techniques, and the services you wish to offer.

Unfortunately, unless you are a professional librarian or have some sort of information resource background (journalism, market research, private investigations, paralegal services, etc.), this sets up something of a Catch-22 situation. You can't get a sense of the market if you don't have at least some idea of the information resources that are available, but we've just told you that you shouldn't focus on resources until you get a sense of the market and where you might fit.

Your authors are in a similar situation. On the one hand, we know how important it is for you to keep marketing and the goal of discovering your market niche uppermost in your mind. But we also know that many readers have only a glancing acquaintance with the kinds of information resources that are available. And you can't appreciate the marketing side of things without at least some familiarity with the resource side.

There is no neat solution to this problem. However, we do have a suggestion. If you are already an information professional, jump ahead to Part four, The Business Side of Information Brokering. Read Chapters 18 through 21. Then return here and continue with the book.

If you are new to the information field, finish this chapter. Then jump ahead and skim Chapters 18 through 21. Don't worry if they contain terms you don't yet understand. Return to Chapter 7, the chapter following this one, and read straight through. The *next* time you read Chapters 18 through 21, you'll have an even better appreciation for the importance of marketing and the need to find your niche and shape your services to meet its needs.

Specialization of labor

You may or may not want to follow these suggestions. But regardless of your approach, regardless of your current situation, it is vital to bear one other point in mind as you read this and the following chapters. It is a concept that will help you put everything into a personal perspective:

Figure out what you do best and then hire the rest.

It is simply not realistic, and it is extremely inefficient, to expect yourself to do *everything* required of a successful information brokerage. You will be tremendously handicapped if you try to be the researcher, marketer, and bill collector—let alone the word processor and receptionist—all by yourself. Make no mistake about it: The first year you are in business, you should expect to spend at least 70 percent of your time marketing. If you're not good at sales, find someone who is and team up with them.

One way or another, someone has got to be out there spending vast amounts of time beating the bushes and scaring up business. Establishing a client base is paramount to the success of your business. If you don't do this, you will fail. It is simply impossible to overemphasize that fact. Therefore, to be quite blunt, you've got no business spending your time doing the kinds of things—typing, filing, accounting, etc.—that you can hire temporary or part-time help to do.

Yes. We know. That means spending money. It means that even if you're a terrific typist, you should resist the temptation to do all the typing that needs to be done. Hire someone else to do it, and spend your time selling or dreaming up new ways to market your services. It's true that you may save a little money by trying to do everything yourself. But that's penny-wise and pound-foolish. It's like winning a battle but losing the war.

The concept of figuring out what you do best and then hiring the rest also applies if your talents lie not in marketing but in information retrieval. Though you are not likely to be able to hire an information services marketer through a temporary agency, you may very well be able to team up with a colleague or friend whose talents lie in that area. You could pay the person a commission on each assignment brought in. Or you could simply agree to divide the profits.

To summarize then, it is crucial to keep two points in mind. Never forget that your first job as an aspiring information broker is to find your niche in the market. And second, always remember that it is not efficient to try to do everything yourself. Realistically, you may be forced to be a jack-of-all-trades when you are just starting out. But from Day 1 onward your goal should be to free up as much of your time as possible for those things you're really good at by hiring, delegating, or otherwise off-loading everything else.

In the 1973 musical *Seesaw*, there's a boffo production number in which Tommy Tune dances up a storm while the entire company sings *It's Not Where You Start (It's Where You Finish)*.

Preliminaries

The same sentiments apply to the profession of information broker. You really *can* start from anywhere, with little more than a smile and a shine in your eyes when you think of successfully locating some obscure piece of information.

Where you start does make a difference, however, in how hard you will have to work and in how much you will have to learn to achieve professional competence. If you have not darkened the door of a library since fourth grade, you've got some big-time catching up to do.

More than likely, if you're reading this book, you are already working at some kind of a job that has an information component. You may no longer remember how to use a library's card catalogues, many of which have been replaced by computer terminals and online catalogues in recent years. But you are thoroughly familiar with how to look up prices, specifications, rules and regulations, and other job-related pieces of information.

When the boss says, "Find out how much the XYZ Company has bought from us in the last five years and how much they owe us," you're involved in information retrieval. If the boss adds, "And by the way, give me a line graph plotting their purchases by week," you're involved in information packaging and presentation. You may thus already be working as an information broker. But you're working for someone else, not for yourself.

When we say "preliminaries," we mean in part "getting the lay of the land." You are going to have to familiarize yourself with the information resources (libraries, online systems, unique sources, etc.) at your disposal. They are your tools, and you can accomplish nothing without them. Later, you will want to try to get a handle on the likely demand for your services. But focus on the tools first.

Four quick steps

1. Send for free information on DIALOG

Here are four things you should do right away. First, send for the DIALOG information kit. DIALOG is a Knight-Ridder company, and it is one of the largest online information systems in the world. At this writing, it has over 450 different databases for you to search.

If you live in the United States or in Canada, you can call (800) 334-2564 to request your free information kit. If you live elsewhere, you can call DIALOG in Palo Alto, California at (415) 858-3785, or contact your local DIALOG representative. About a week later, your information kit will arrive and you'll be on your way into the world of industrial-strength information resources.

At this writing, a DIALOG subscription requires a one-time payment of $295. This covers start-up costs, your enrollment in a DIALOG training session, and your first year's subscription to *The Chronolog*, the company's monthly magazine and updating service. This initial fee also includes $100 of free search time on the system. And, as of late September 1994, the company was still sending documentation and "bluesheets" to new subscribers free of charge. (That policy may change, so be sure to ask when you call.) After your first year, there is an annual fee of $75 to maintain the subscription and pay for *The Chronolog*.

2. Try the Knowledge Index on CompuServe

The Knowledge Index (KI) is DIALOG's low-cost, after hours service. KI contains about 125 of the databases available on the big system, and you must search it after 6:00 P.M., your local time. But the same databases that during the day cost $125 or more per hour on DIALOG cost only $24 an hour when searched on KI.

The one catch—and it is a big one—is that you cannot use KI to find information used in your information brokering business. It is expressly against DIALOG's policy for KI to be used for any commercial purpose. In addition, the search protocol is somewhat different than the "real" DIALOG system.

We're suggesting that you try KI because it offers a wonderful introduction to the world of online databases and electronic information retrieval. And at $24 an hour, you can't get into too much trouble.

Although KI used to be available as a freestanding system, the only way to gain access now is through a CompuServe subscription. (Just key in Go ki to get there.) The cost is the same $24 an hour (40 cents a minute), and it *includes* your CompuServe connect time, even if you're connected at 9,600 or 14.4.

The only real problem is that, at this writing, there is no documentation available to CompuServe subscribers who wish to use KI. We can only hope that this will change. In the meantime, you may want to look at the nearby sidebar for a quick overview of the kinds of information available on KI.

On getting a CompuServe subscription

For information on getting a CompuServe subscription, call (800) 848-8199. You will almost certainly want to subscribe, if only to gain access to the Work at Home Forum run by Paul and Sarah Edwards. As noted previously, this is the forum where most of the country's information brokers hang out.

We recommend the Standard Pricing Plan ($8.95 a month for unlimited use of a basic package of services). Time spent using non-basic services is billed at $4.80/hour for 2,400 bps access and at $9.60/hour for 9,600 and 14,400 bps access.

The best deal of all, however, is what CompuServe calls its Executive Service Option. In return for agreeing to spend a minimum of $10 on the system each month, you get all the benefits of the Standard Pricing Plan, plus discounts and access to a range of business/investment features not otherwise available. You also get to set up an automatic electronic clipping profile to monitor the newswire for items of interest to you.

Finally, the Knowledge Index is far from the only feature on CompuServe offering "industrial-strength" information. You may not be able to use the information you get via KI for professional purposes, but no such restrictions exist for many of the other databases you can tap via CompuServe.

What's on the Knowledge Index?

Although information brokers are forbidden to use information retrieved via the Knowledge Index for professional purposes, KI offers the ideal way to expose yourself to *real*, in-depth information. It is also a great way to sharpen your search skills. All for $24 an hour, after 6:00 P.M., your local time.

Here is just a partial list of the main sections of KI and the kind of information each embraces:

- *Arts.* Art Bibliographies Modern: Comprehensive coverage of all modern art, 1974 to present. Worldwide historic coverage of Western art, 1973 to present.
- *Biology, Biosciences, Biotechnology.* Worldwide coverage of research in biology, medicine, biochemistry, ecology, and microbiology, 1978 to present.
- *Books.* Books in Print: Currently published, forthcoming, and recently out-of-print books.
- *Business Information and Corporate News.* ABI/Inform, Harvard Business Review, Trade and Industry Index, Businesswire, PR Newswire, Standard & Poor's News, etc.
- *Chemistry.* Chapman and Hall Chemical Database: Physical property data on over 175,000 substances. Kirk-Othmer Online: Online encyclopedia of applied chemical science and industrial technology.
- *Computers and Electronics.* Inspec, Microcomputer Index, Computer Database, Business Software Database, and complete articles from *ComputerWorld* and *Network World.*
- *Drugs.* International Pharmaceutical Abstracts, Drug Information Fulltext, and The Merck Index Online.
- *Education.* ERIC: Research reports, articles, and projects significant to education, 1966 to present. Peterson's College Database, A-V Online, and Academic Index.
- *Government Publications.* GPO Publications Referenced file: Publications for sale by U.S. Superintendent of Documents.
- *History.* Historical Abstracts: Article summaries of the history of the world from 1450 to present.

- *Legal Information.* Legal Resource Index: Indexing of over 750 law journals and reviews, 1980 to present. BNA Daily News: Daily, comprehensive news coverage of national and international government and private sector activities.
- *Magazines.* Magazine Index: Index to articles in over 400 publications, 1959 to March 1970, and 1973 to the present. Canadian Business and Current Affairs.
- *Mathematics.* Mathsci: Research on pure and applied mathematics, 1973 to present.
- *Medicine.* MEDLINE. Cancerlit. SPORT: Coverage of sports medicine research and fitness. AIDSLINE: Complete access to the medical literature related to AIDS, 1980 to present.
- *News.* Full text of *USA Today, Washington Post, Philadelphia Inquirer, Los Angeles Times, San Jose Mercury News, Chicago Tribune, Boston Globe, San Francisco Chronicle, Newsday, New York Newsday, Akron Beacon Journal,* and scores more!

3. Look at your own area

If you are a librarian, you are already well acquainted with information resources in general, and you probably have intimate knowledge of the resources available in one or more specialty areas. If you are not an information professional, the next thing you should do is make a concerted effort to get a handle on the information resources available in your own line of work or industry. If your firm has a company library, pay it an extended visit and tell the librarian exactly the kind of overview you want to have.

If there is no company library or information center, round up all the different trade journals you can find. Every industry has trade journals and specialty magazines or newspapers. Go over them thoroughly, both to widen your vision of the field and all its various aspects and to see if there are ads or articles dealing with other industry-related information sources.

You might even consider doing a little practice phone work. For example, if some company is advertising a software package or some other custom product for your industry, you might call them up, explain that you are interested in the field, and ask if they could help you learn more. Are there any books they would suggest that you read? And, golly, how did they learn so much about the industry to be able to write a program or create a special product for it?

They will want to send you information on their product, of course. Accept the offer gratefully and have the stuff sent to your home.

This kind of exercise has many points to recommend it. First and foremost, it gives you a risk- and cost-free chance to practice your information retrieval skills and telephone personality. No one is paying you any money for this, so the worst that can happen is that the place you call will be unable to help you. You will certainly be well-motivated since you are looking for information for yourself.

In addition, this is exactly the type of query you can expect to be asked to pursue as an information professional. And in all likelihood, you would do so by asking people questions on the phone. So have at it! Plan to call several firms. Take notes, and be sure to send those people who have been helpful a short thank-you note. Who knows, you just might get lucky. One or more of these firms might eventually become your clients.

4. Support your local library

The fourth step is to pay several extended visits to your local library. Now, we know that libraries vary considerably in the extent of their facilities, so pick one that is generally considered "good" in your area, even if you have to drive a few miles to get there. The main branches of county libraries and libraries at community colleges tend to offer more than most local branches.

If you can possibly manage it, try to avoid going on a weekend or during the after-school, before-dinner period. This way there will be fewer adults and children around and the librarians can more easily answer your questions. You might even consider phoning the reference librarian first. Explain that you want to really get to know the available reference sources and ask what would be the best time to come.

However—and this is extremely important—it is against the unwritten rules of the profession for an information broker to use or otherwise rely on library staff. Many public librarians resent information brokers, particularly those who don't even know how to use a library, making demands on their time.

As an information broker, you're a professional being paid to do a job. It is unfair and even unethical for you to ask a librarian to do it for you. That doesn't mean you can't ask questions or develop a cordial relationship. It doesn't mean you can't talk to a librarian, one information professional to another. But it most emphatically means that you are not to ask the individual to do your work for you.

The pioneers of the information brokering profession have worked very hard to develop a positive relationship with their colleagues on the other side of the reference desk, most of whom are overworked and terribly underpaid. As a new information broker, it is your responsibility to honor that trust. If you don't, be aware that the information community is not all that large. People talk, and sooner or later word will get out about just what kind of information "broker" you are.

The reference section

When you get to the library, head straight for the reference section. This is the part of the library containing the big, expensive directories, books, statistical compilations, and so forth that do not circulate. Choose a corner of the room or section as your starting point and plan to work your way around until you reach the end.

Your objective is to become aware of every book in the reference section. Some you will want to pass over. Others you will thumb lightly. Still others will beckon you to plunge in. We suggest you do exactly what you feel like doing. Let your curiosity be your guide. But make every effort to cover everything, even if it takes you several visits.

By all means, take a note or two if something strikes your fancy. But there is absolutely no need to make a list of the books that are available. They're all in the card catalogue, which in most libraries these days is online and electronic. So it's usually easy to make a printout when you need one. As you will see in the next chapter, there are even reference books about reference books. So there is no need to reinvent the wheel by taking copious notes.

When you've introduced yourself to all the books, ask the librarian about non-book materials like collections of maps, photos, or prints. Make a point of learning how to use the microfilm reader and the microfiche as well, if the library uses fiche.

Then zero in on the *Readers' Guide to Periodical Literature* (RG). This is the most basic index to periodical literature, and frankly, if you've never learned how to use it, you're in for a very long learning curve on your way to becoming an information broker. It is fundamental. It is the reference work you go to when you are looking for relatively current information published in magazines. RG and its companions are available electronically on Wilsonline, but before you even think about that approach, learn to use the paper-based version.

If you're lucky, your library will have RG available as a CD-ROM. Or, if this is not the case, it will almost certainly have InfoTrak, the CD-ROM product from Ziff-Davis's Information Access Company that competes directly with RG.

Finally, return to the bookshelf and locate the multivolume *Encyclopedia of Associations*. This could be the most crucial reference work of all because it is your key to expert information on all kinds of industries and professions. Look up the associations that are relevant to the industry or field you are currently working in and photocopy the information.

Every association worthy of the name has free pamphlets and publications to distribute. Indeed, spreading the good word about their industries or professions is one of their main reasons for existing. Most have an executive director or someone with a similar title, and that is the person you should plan to call. Your goal is to learn as much as you can about the information sources that focus on what you already do for a living.

A word of warning is in order. We are sending you into the lion's den here. If you don't know "information," and even if you do, it is very easy to be overwhelmed by the reference material available in even a modest library. So take your time. Plan on making several visits.

And remember—as an information broker you do not have to *know* the information, you only have to know where and how to find it. As a practicing professional, you will frequently have assignments that introduce you to reference books that you will never use again. So rather than attempting to grasp all the details and specifics, try to feel the power.

Let yourself get caught up in the sweep and sheer breadth and depth of reference information available in the library. Introduce yourself to The Dragon. You can worry about how to twist its tail later.

Self-test & practice

The preliminaries discussed above can easily take you several weeks. But at some point you will realize that you now know a great deal about the tools at your disposal, both the industry- or profession-specific tools and the standard library reference tools. At that point, it's time to take a few practice runs.

In *Marathon Man*, a book and movie by William Goldman, the protagonist is an intense young man who is a doctoral candidate at Columbia. He's also a long-distance runner, and while he runs he asks himself the kinds of questions he expects to be asked during his final exams.

Though we hope you're not as tightly wrapped as Dustin Hoffman, the actor who played the lead in the movie, we suggest that you do the same kind of thing. Set yourself a few information-broker-style assignments and see how you do. Don't worry about preparing a report at this point. Just concentrate on developing and then executing a strategy to find the answers to the questions.

Here are a dozen general questions that you can adapt to your own particular situation. Some of them assume that you are currently employed in a particular industry or profession. If that isn't the case, simply pick an industry or profession of interest.

We suggest that you pick three of these questions and make them your assignment. We don't want you to spend any money finding these answers. The whole idea is to help you get a feel for the tools you have discovered and how to use them.

1. What is the fourth largest firm in your industry, and what were its sales last year? What is the name of its CEO, and how many children does he or she have?
2. What do industry experts (not your own personal opinion) feel are the three most significant products/services in your industry that are likely to

appear in the next five years? Which company is best positioned to exploit one or more of them?

3. Who is the leading manufacturer of baking soda in the United States, and what do Wall Street experts feel are the company's prospects for the near future? Also, what is the chemical formula for baking soda? (A cream-puff question.)

4. How are manufacturers of latex paint likely to be affected by new air pollution laws and when will the effects, if any, be felt?

5. Roughly how many plants exist to manufacture compact audio disks? Are they generally running at capacity or are more plants needed to fill the demand?

6. How do Canadians feel about orange juice? Do they drink it at breakfast like Americans? Is there evidence of an unexploited market for orange juice in Canada, and if so, should it be fresh or frozen concentrate?

7. Are T-120 VHS videotapes still the most popular format or is there a detectable trend toward longer tapes? Can you find the dollar value and/or the number of units shipped last year for each VHS tape length?

8. What ever happened with the trade agreement between the U.S. and Canada regarding cedar roofing shingles? Briefly summarize the history of the conflict and tell us the current state of affairs.

9. What are the demographic characteristics of the people who buy cake mixes especially designed for "baking" in microwave ovens? Has this product category been successful?

10. How many grocery store coupons do shoppers use in a year? And how are those coupons processed?

11. How many tons of steel did the U.S. produce last year compared to the tonnage produced by Germany and Japan? Is the fact that Germany has been reunified likely to affect steel production in the future? If so, when?

12. For many years there has been a trend toward moving out of big cities to the suburbs. Are there any indications that this trend has reversed in recent times? What kind of statistics support your findings?

Take the test

These are exactly the kinds of questions you will be asked to research as a practicing professional. We do not know the correct answers, though we are confident that you will be able to find them using a good local library. But even if we did know the answers, we would not present them, because the answers aren't the point. The point here is the *process*: What reference books will you consult? Who will you call for insight and details?

If you don't take this test, if you don't pick out three questions or create three others of similar difficulty, you will only be cheating yourself. There is much to gain. And all you have to lose is a bit of time. If you try to set up a business and your clients throw similar problems your way, you will lose a great deal more if you don't know how to solve them.

Optional assignment for extra credit

If you have answered at least three of the above questions and if you find that you enjoyed the process, then you may want to consider taking DIALOG training. DIALOG offers regular seminars and hands-on training sessions in major cities throughout the year. Indeed, you are entitled to attend one training session as part of your initial DIALOG subscription fee. Training sessions are held in most major cities on a regular basis, and there are many different courses to choose from. Your best bet is to simply call DIALOG at (800) 334-2564 and ask for the latest schedule.

Of course no seminar will make you a professional. Indeed, even experienced searchers continue to attend the seminar updates and special-focus sessions given by DIALOG and many leading database producers.

Getting your first job

The third and final major step is to go out and get your first job. As we have said repeatedly, there is no one "right path" to becoming an information broker. But it should be obvious that if you are not familiar with the reference sources available, if you haven't completed a few sample assignments, if, in short, you haven't a clue about the information industry and how it works, it is going to be very tough to convince someone to pay you to retrieve information.

So we are going to assume that at this point you have done the survey, taken the tests, and have reason to feel confident about your ability to satisfy a client. Of course you'll be nervous. Every assignment is a curve ball, even after years of experience in the business. But what the years of experience teach you is that the information is almost always there to be found. All you have to do is apply your brain, your imagination, and your accumulated skill and knowledge, and most problems will yield.

At this point, you may be saying, "Hey, wait a minute. I'm not nearly ready to begin thinking about my first job." That may be so. But don't let yourself off too easily. Your goal is to discover whether you should become an information broker. We've told you about the industry, the market, what an information broker does, and the pros and cons of the business. We've tried to guide you to the basic research sources, though we naturally hope you will use this merely as your starting point.

The one thing you don't know right now is whether you've got the knack of selling information services. Bear in mind that no one has asked you to make any commitment at this point. You've still got your day job, and your investment in exploring the profession has been long on time and short on dollars. But before taking the plunge, you've got to know the whole story. As we have emphasized time and time again, selling is a very large part of the story. If you can't sell yourself and your service, you won't make it as an information broker.

If you are already confident of your abilities, go ahead and set up a few sales calls. Do it right—send a letter requesting an appointment and follow up with a phone call. Put on your best business clothes and arrive at the prospect's office with five or ten minutes to spare. Then have at it!

Remember, at this juncture you have nothing to lose. The worst that can happen is that the prospect will cut the interview short and politely usher you out of the office. In the best case, your personal chemistry will effortlessly click with the prospect and you will have your first client. More than likely, the presentation will end inconclusively, with the prospect interested but not ready to commit.

That's fine too. Both of you will have learned something—the prospect will have learned about the kinds of things that are available, and you will have experienced some real-life client contact for the first time. Follow up the next week with a brief thank-you note. Then call the client back in a month to see if he or she has any additional thoughts on hiring you.

If the chemistry is bad—if the two of you simply are not simpatico—you should still send the thank-you. But you may want to focus future efforts on someone else. There are *lots* of fish in the sea, and there is little point in pursuing someone with whom you don't match, especially in the information broker field.

Pricing

What about pricing? For that we have a trick or two to recommend. First, most clients will understand and completely accept your statement that you want to consider the job back at the office and that you will phone them with a quote. After you've had more experience, you'll be able to offer a ballpark figure on the spot. But there is usually no need to do so if you are just starting out.

The key thing is to do such a good job presenting your case that the prospect says, "Well, that is very intriguing. What will it cost to get this information?" You, of course, don't have any idea what it will cost at this point. But you don't communicate that to the client. Instead, you say, "What level of effort did you have in mind?" The client will respond, and you will have the opportunity to get a sense of what the budget might be.

When you have a better idea of how the client sees the project and its budget, say "Let me develop a complete proposal and get back to you with the figures tomorrow, or later on today." This is a perfectly reasonable request, and under no circumstances should you let the client pressure you into committing to a specific price at this point. After all, you can do a $500 project or a $5,000 project on the same topic.

When you return to your office, sit down and map out your search strategy. Where will you look? Will any expenses be involved—long distance phone charges, photocopying, whatever? How much time do you think you will have to spend getting the answers and preparing a professional-looking report?

The goal is to come up with a price quote or "budget." You want to be able to say, "We can do this job for an amount not to exceed $X." So how do you solve for X? Basically, you have to "guesstimate" how many hours you will spend, add a third more hours as a safety margin, and multiply the total by $95 to $100 or more. (These days, information brokers charge anywhere from $95 to $200 or more per hour, depending on subject expertise and, of course, on what the market will bear.)

If you come out with an odd number, round it up. Then ask yourself how that figure compares with your sense of the interview. Would the client accept a somewhat higher figure? Or is your estimate already beyond what you think the client would pay? Pricing is an art, not a science.

Subcontracting

Now for the real stroke. Call an established information broker and ask what the cost would be to complete the identical assignment. Also, ask when the work could be completed. An experienced person should be able to come up with a quote fairly quickly. The Rugge Group is a subcontractor for many aspiring brokers and, of course, carries our highest recommendation.

Compare your quote with the professional's quote, and again view both against your impressions of how the client interview went. At the very least this gives you a frame of reference. But it also opens other possibilities. You might, for example, decide to mark up the professional's quote and convey that figure to the client. If the client accepts, you can hire the established broker to do the work and keep the markup.

Or you might decide on reflection that your own quote was too low. You might use the established broker's figure and charge even more for the job— again, assuming that the amount is acceptable to the client.

Handling the selling yourself and subcontracting the actual work is a really good way to start. Naturally, at the same time you would decide how you yourself would approach the problem. Then learn from what the established information broker does.

That's assuming you eventually want to search for yourself. If you just want to do the selling, keep in mind that there are more people out there who are skilled searchers than there are people who can sell the results. If you like the selling aspect, just go out and sell the work, and then subcontract it. There is usually room to mark up a search by at least 25 percent. Some brokers will even give you a discount because you have already secured the client, so that gives you an extra margin to work with. If you're a good salesperson, you understand what the traffic will bear; and that has a lot to do with how you quote.

There is no apprentice program in this profession, but you may be able to create one for yourself. You might, for example, establish a relationship with a practicing information broker. You could do the selling, while the information broker did all the searching. Or perhaps the person needs someone to handle some of the more basic chores, like running down documents, setting up appointments, transcribing taped phone interviews, or taking care of bread-and-butter business correspondence.

Pay close attention to how your associate operates, how problems are attacked and solved, what resources are used, and how final reports are prepared. Assuming you've picked a good broker, this will give you an excellent education in how it's done.

Such an arrangement can ultimately lead to a full-fledged partnership. Or after a time, you may decide you're ready to step out on your own. Or maybe both of you will end up doing the searching and taking on someone else to do the selling. The possibilities are endless.

There's a lot more to learn about the nitty-gritty details of the information trade. And we've tried to cover most of it in the chapters that follow. The point we want to leave you with here at the end of Part one is that there is no single, regulation path for getting into this business. It isn't like becoming a doctor, dentist, or lawyer.

To get started, you merely have to *start*. Whether you follow some of our suggestions or invent some approaches of your own, starting is exactly what we hope you will do once you finish this book.

7 At the library
Non-electronic sources & resources

Libraries are magnificent creations. Even the smallest library out in the country is a testament to human civilization and the things that really matter. Unfortunately, after listening to the required lecture in high school about how to use a library, and after pulling our share of all-nighters in college, many of us never darken a library's door again. Unless it's to drop the kids off for a little free day care.

That's a shame, of course, but it's not the topic here. We're interested in what libraries and conventional print sources have to offer practicing information brokers. The answer may surprise you: Not much. What these sources offer can be vital, and they can certainly help you round out a final report, but they are probably *not* going to supply the information and answers clients will hire you to find. At IOD and The Rugge Group, Sue always found libraries to be a tertiary source at best.

There's a very good reason for this. Libraries specialize in cataloguing and making available information that has been printed, published, or recorded in some other form. But many of the answers successful information brokers are hired to find haven't been printed, published, or recorded yet. The answers usually exist inside the brains of individual people who are experts or otherwise have special knowledge about a particular field.

This is the kind of information that, in our experience, clients are most eager to have and most willing to pay for. Clients typically want to know the state of things right *now* and, if possible, the most likely state of things in the near future. Consider a hypothetical marketing problem as an example.

A hypothetical example

Assume that the results of a study conducted at a major university have just been reported in the *New England Journal of Medicine*. The study found that when consumed in the proper quantities, a particular species of seaweed absorbs twice its weight in alcohol, chemically binding it and rendering it harmless. Five minutes after eating the stuff, people who were legally intoxicated have no trace of alcohol in their blood.

The day after the article appears (or, as often seems to happen, is leaked to the press), *The Wall Street Journal*, *New York Times*, Associated Press, and others run stories. CNN picks it up, and the following day, all three network evening news programs run special features on "The Instant Sobriety Pill." Just think of the implications.

Your client, for one, has thought of them and wants to know a number of key facts. What are all the locations where this species of seaweed grows? What is the current world supply? Can it be grown in a tank on land? Is the process for extracting the magic substance patented, and if so, by whom? Your client's goal is to get a quick handle on the feasibility of producing an actual instant sobriety pill for the consumer market. It's important to move *fast*, because you can bet the competition will do so.

Our point is that while the information you must find for this client will eventually end up in a library, it isn't there right now. The newspaper stories will be there today or tomorrow, but at least three months will pass before the first magazine stories appear, since that's the minimum lead time for most publications.

The library as an example

So do you forget the library altogether? Not exactly. As Sue says, "We don't use libraries all that much. Online searching and phone work take care of 90 percent of our research. About the only time we go to the library is to locate and copy a document that a client has requested."

Most information brokers would say the same thing. As one of them told us, "I recommend online databases as the starting point. Libraries are good for the specialized collections they have and for inexpensive access to hard-copy resources—if all you have is *time* and no money. But library research just isn't part of our normal methodology. It just takes too much time. It's too labor-intensive. And it usually does not yield the kind of up-to-the-second information our clients demand."

However, if you are a *prospective* information broker with no formal research training, your local library offers an excellent opportunity to hone your skills. Your only cost will be the time you spend.

For example, let's suppose that you've got a client interested in that seaweed-based sobriety pill. And let us further suppose that all you have to work with is a good library and the telephone. What can you do?

Well, for one thing, you can use the library as a source for the clues and directional arrows you need to locate the people who do have the information you seek. For example, who is the world's greatest authority on seaweed? We have no idea. But we're willing to bet that you can find a book on underwater plants and that at the end of that book there will be a bibliography. The bibliography will contain books by people who are experts in their fields, and one of them may have the answers you need.

No book available? Okay, look up "seaweed" in the encyclopedia. Who wrote the encyclopedia's article on the subject? Most encyclopedias will give you both the person's name and affiliation. It's also worth checking the *Readers' Guide to Periodical Literature* in the library's reference section, or the InfoTrak CD-ROM from Information Access Company. Seaweed farming could be a big topic. You never know. Or maybe you'll find some obscure little article that just happens to mention the names of several seaweed experts.

Ultimately, you'll come up with a list of names of people to phone who are likely to know the answers. Or, if they don't know the answers themselves, they'll know someone who does. And how can you find out where these folks live so you can get their phone numbers? There are lots of ways. The easiest may be to consult one of the many *Who's Who* volumes in the reference section. The volume focusing on "American Men and Women of Science" is an obvious choice.

If that fails, go back to the *Readers' Guide* or InfoTrak and look for the target individual's name as the author of an article. The byline of the article will certainly give you the name of the company or university the person works for. If there are no articles, look for books written by the individual, first in the library's card catalogue and then in *Books In Print*. If the library doesn't have the book, try calling the publisher for the person's name and address.

Be sure to check the *Encyclopedia of Associations* for the name of a professional or industry trade association to which the individual may belong. Then call the association and ask them to check the membership roster. And while you have them on the phone, ask if *they* can suggest an expert.

These are merely the first steps that come to mind. They are by no means the only ways to approach this part of the problem. Think of yourself as a ladle of red-hot mercury flowing downward through the internal cracks and crevices of a chunk of volcanic rock. There are many alternative paths leading to more and more paths. Some are dead ends, but some lead downward toward your goal.

There are so many possible paths that there is simply no doubt that you will get to the bottom of things one way or another. Your library probably won't contain the information itself, but if you know how to use its resources, they will reveal potential paths.

Our point is not to suggest that you plan to use the library as a primary information resource in your information brokering business. As we have said, most of the time, you can find the information you need online or obtain it via telephone interviews. But you simply cannot beat using the library as an inexpensive way to sharpen your skills. And don't forget: Many of today's online databases started out as print products available mainly in libraries.

The key thing, ultimately, is not so much the particular resources you use. It is developing a search mentality and imagination. A good information broker and searcher will figure out a way to use the tools at hand, regardless of what those tools may be. The fundamental search skills you learn in doing library research will serve you in good stead when you move on to electronic databases.

Survey your library resources

In Chapter 6, we suggested that as a preliminary step in getting a feel for this profession you make a point of familiarizing yourself with the reference section of your local library. Now we want you to go further.

Look in the Yellow Pages under "Libraries" or some similar heading and make a point of visiting each one in your area. Don't forget to check for community colleges as well. All of them have libraries. If you live near a state capital, check for state libraries as well since they often contain information general-public libraries don't have.

If you were going to build a manufacturing plant, you would certainly do a site survey and pay attention to the resources available in your chosen area (water, power, labor, transportation, etc.). As an information professional, you can afford to do no less for your own business. What local resources do you have to work with?

When you visit each library, give it a good going over. Ask if the library has any unique collections. Is it known to be especially strong in some area?

You will find that all libraries are not alike, even those that serve similar-sized communities within the same library system. Each has its own personality. Each has certain strengths. One local library Alfred knows of, for example, has a particularly extensive collection of books and music on tape. Another has a superior collection of magazines on file. Still another is particularly good at providing business information. Yet all three are part of the same county library system.

As you know, you have to get familiar with the mechanics. You've got to learn to use the microfilm reader, and you will want to learn how to make a photocopy of a frame of microfilm. Does the coin box attached to the machine make change, or do you have to bring nickels or dimes? Can you buy a magnetic-strip copier card to eliminate the hassle of having correct change?

What do you do if you want to look at a particular issue of a magazine? What magazines does the library have on file and how far back does the collection go? Learn, too, about *union lists* of periodicals. A union list is generally a publication produced by the libraries in a particular area telling you which library has which magazines on hand. Also, ask if the library has a pamphlet describing its various facilities and collections (many do), and get a copy.

This process is going to take some time. Don't feel you have to rush things here. Over time, as you do more and more assignments, you will get to know the libraries in your area very well. The key thing is to develop some initial sense of what reference tools and resources are readily available to you at your "site."

A second important point about libraries and the information broker is knowing enough about information to be able to *find* the tools and resources you need. This is like building the tools so you can build the tools to build a car. You couldn't have industrial robots without first having lathes to turn and shape their steel. And you couldn't have steel without blast furnaces and rolling mills. And so on.

Unfortunately, at this writing, there are few, if any, current, comprehensive directories or reference books about reference books. This situation could easily change. But right now, most of the books that address this subject are either out of print or more than two decades old!

Your best bet, in our opinion, is to start with the resources and reference works listed in Appendix A of this book (and included as a text file on the accompanying disk). In addition, you may want to order the *Information Broker's Resource Kit*, which is updated and published annually by Sue Rugge's Information Professionals Institute. (See Appendix A for information on ordering the *Resource Kit*.)

To summarize then, libraries are incredible institutions worthy of your profound respect and even awe in some cases. But as a practicing information broker, it is a mistake to assume that even the greatest library holds the answers to your clients' questions.

You may want to locate books, articles, maps, photos, readily available statistics, and other materials to round out your final report. But in general, you should go to the library to find out where *else* to go or whom to call. A

Build the tools to build the tools

Conclusion

library may be your starting point in some cases. But it is almost never your final destination.

If you have followed the advice presented earlier about going to your best local library and thoroughly examining its reference section, then your next step is to broaden your focus to include all local libraries. Get a good, solid idea of what's available to you. Then let your assignments control how well you get to know various resources at various libraries. And remember, while we would be the last to suggest that there is only one way to be an information broker, in our experience, most brokers rely primarily on online databases and telephone interviews to complete their work. Though none would deny the value of having a good library nearby.

In the next chapter, we'll introduce you to one of the greatest "libraries" of all—the mind-boggling amount of information produced by the U.S. government. Though it will not be a primary source in most situations, it is important for every prospective information broker to have at least some idea of the breadth and depth of information published or otherwise made available by Uncle Sam each year.

8 Government information sources

Professional critics, and politicians who are between jobs, often rail against government waste. But none of them ever mentions the biggest waste of all: the huge quantities of top-quality information the government produces every day that no one ever uses.

As citizens, we are paying thousands of men and women around the country to collect, analyze, and publish information on every topic imaginable (and unimaginable!). Every week a federal agency somewhere commissions a private consultant to prepare a detailed report. Every month university professors and graduate students win government grants to study some macro- or microphenomenon.

The amount of information prepared and produced each year as a result of federal government activities is simply awesome. Equally impressive are the breadth and depth of topics covered. Since government is involved in some way in virtually every aspect of our business and personal lives, there is scarcely a topic you can name that isn't covered in one way or another. There are books, booklets, maps, charts, computer programs, filmstrips, videotapes, reports, and magazines. The number of individual items is in the scores of thousands. Even the government doesn't know for sure how many items it publishes.

Small wonder that most of us have no concept of the vast amount of material that is available, let alone how to find that one crucial publication on *The*

Molluscan Record from a mid-Cretaceous Borehole in Weston County, Wyoming. (At least not when we need it.) Because of this, a great deal of government information is vastly underutilized—wasted—each year.

Government information: An endless cornucopia

As a practicing information broker, the endless cornucopia of government information is both good and bad. On the plus side, the U.S. Government Printing Office (GPO) can be thought of as a gigantic national library, a master source for almost all federally produced information. The information is usually quite good and quite reasonably priced. In fact, a lot of it is either free or downright cheap, because you've already paid for it with your taxes. You might pay $3 or $4, for example, for a government-published book that would sell commercially for ten times that amount, assuming such a title were even available.

And the information is generally considered to be top-quality. For credibility, it is still difficult to beat the phrase, "A study done by the U.S. (fill in the blank with the appropriate department, commission, bureau, panel, etc.) found that . . ." Since a great deal of government information focuses on topics of interest to businesspeople, your best clients, it can be especially useful to you as an information broker.

But of course there's a downside. Many government agencies have done the best that their budgets will allow in letting citizens know what they offer. But that isn't much, compared to what commercial magazine and book publishers typically do. And, of course, dealing with any branch of any government always involves bureaucratic red tape of one sort or another. Add to this the fact that bureaucrats typically lack the motivating incentives of the marketplace, and you can see why mastering the ins and outs of obtaining information from the government can be a challenge.

As we'll see later, for example, the *GPO Monthly Catalog* and the *GPO Sales Publications Reference File* are available for searching online. NTIS, the Commerce Department's National Technical Information Service, is another prime print and online source. The NTIS database corresponds to the biweekly publication *Government Reports Announcements & Index* and, in part, to *Abstract Newsletters*. It covers virtually all nonclassified federally funded information. Thus, locating documents that pertain to your area of inquiry can be relatively easy in many cases. (Information on contacting NTIS can be found later in this chapter.)

Obtaining copies of them quickly, however, is another matter. The government must field so many requests that it has rather stringent rules about the ordering information you must supply (publication numbers, codes, etc.). If you make a mistake or your request is incomplete, your order will almost certainly be returned to you unfilled.

In addition, while we have always found GPO people to be very friendly and helpful, they *are* government employees, and they tend to go home precisely on time. Under the circumstances, you may be best off hiring a firm that specializes in quickly obtaining and shipping the federal documents you want. You'll find some suggestions throughout this chapter.

As a professional information broker, you will probably make greater use of government data than you do of the information available in your local library. This is because government information often fits so well into a typical information broker's report and because so much of it pertains to business, finance, international trade, production figures, and so on—the very topics many of your clients are likely to be most interested in.

However, as with libraries, there is so much readily available government information that you may be beguiled into believing that it contains the answers to all of your queries. It doesn't. Depending on your needs, it may contain proportionally more usable information than a typical library. But the real information sources are still *people*. As with library information, government publications and reports are often best used as a way of identifying and locating *human experts*.

For example, several years ago Sue and Alfred had the enjoyable experience of speaking (on different topics) at the annual meeting of the Investigators Online Network (ION). This is a group of private investigators who are on the leading edge of investigative technology. The luncheon speaker was Matthew Lesko, whom you may have seen on television talk shows or starring in his own late-night commercials for *Lesko's Info-Power Sourcebook*.

Lesko is probably the world's expert on information available from the U.S. government. As the sales copy for his book notes, it gives you access to ten billion dollars worth of government research and analysis, more than two million free or low-cost publications on every subject imaginable, and over 700,000 government experts.

Speaking without notes and dressed in a black suit with pink tie and matching socks (!), Matthew Lesko regaled the assembly with the tale of how he came to found what is now Information USA, Inc., a firm specializing in locating government information for clients. The year was 1975 and Lesko's first client was someone who wanted to know about Maine potatoes.

The client represented a group of commodity investors who were concerned to know why Maine potatoes were currently selling at double their normal price. And they needed to know *yesterday*! Lesko told us with great good humor that he knew nothing about potatoes but nonetheless agreed to take the job. He agreed that if he couldn't find the desired information in one day, he would not be paid for his efforts. (This is not a policy we recommend, but

The potato man

Ten billion dollars worth!

as a rank beginner nearly 20 years ago, Lesko obviously had no choice. It is certainly not the way information brokers operate today!)

He phoned the Department of Agriculture and, on a flyer, asked to talk to the department's expert on potatoes. To his surprise, the request was handled routinely. Apparently there actually *was* a USDA expert on potatoes. As Lesko told it, he went to the man's office and found not only every reference book one could possibly imagine about potatoes, but an amiable man who had spent his entire career studying the supply and demand for the potato.

Across from the potato expert's office was another office staffed with people whose sole job it was to compile a monthly report tracking potato production and consumption in the United States. Even the number of potato chips produced each month was (and is) tallied.

Equally amazing, down the hall from the potato expert were the offices of individuals with similar expertise in beans, wheat, corn—you name it. It was an entire building of experts. As Lesko said, the only problem is that once you get one of these experts talking, you may find it difficult to end the conversation, so thrilled are they to find someone with a genuine need, seeking their expertise.

Information USA, Inc.

Matthew Lesko is an absolutely delightful speaker, and if you ever get a chance to hear him, by all means go. You will also want to get a copy of his book, *Lesko's Info-Power Sourcebook*, published by Information USA. Selling for about $35 and running to more than 1,600 pages, it is a key entry point to government information. Mr. Lesko also maintains a feature on CompuServe (key in go infousa or go lesko) that presents much of the material in his book via a series of menus. To reach Mr. Lesko or order his book, contact:

Information USA, Inc.
P.O. Box E
Kensington, MD 20895
(301) 942-0556
CompuServe: 76703,4201

The lesson for all of us here is threefold. First, regardless of the topic, the government almost certainly publishes some kind of information on it. Second, that information is frequently developed by experts who are full-time government employees. And third, many of these experts are not only willing to talk to you, they are positively eager to do so. Once again: The printed information you find can be useful to support expert statements or opinions or to otherwise round out a report, but its main value is in identifying the right person to call and interview.

The federal government publishes a host of catalogues, directories, and guides to its publications. But the two you should be most aware of are the *GPO Sales Publications Reference File* (*PRF*) and the *Monthly Catalog of United States Government Publications* (often referred to as the *GPO Monthly Catalog* or *MoCat*). You will undoubtedly be able to find both at your library. But they are also available for searching online via systems like DIALOG, Knowledge Index, BRS, and even CompuServe.

As you will learn in Part three of this book, when something is online, you can usually search it on the basis of the keywords you select. This is almost always faster than using the printed version, and it certainly saves on the eyesight, given the thin paper and fine print of most government publications. Online searching also usually lets you look for words that are not found in the print publication's index.

Now, the main difference between *PRF* and the *GPO Monthly Catalog* is this: *MoCat* covers over 375,000 items published by the federal government and indexed by the Superintendent of Documents. This does not mean *all* federally published documents, for there are many that never make it to SuDocs, as information professionals often refer to that office. *PRF*, on the other hand, covers just those items that can be ordered directly from the GPO. At around 27,000 items, that amounts to less than 10 percent of everything found in the *GPO Monthly Catalog*.

PRF is thus a subset of the *GPO Monthly Catalog*. However, here is a professional's tip: *PRF* and *MoCat* are usually out of synch. Historically, *MoCat* tends to lag behind *PRF* in its cataloguing. Thus, while many items in *PRF* eventually are included in *MoCat*, they typically appear in *PRF* first. It is therefore important to search both databases, not just the *Monthly Catalog*.

Items not available directly from the GPO (and thus not listed in *PRF*) must be obtained from the organizations that sponsored them. Or you must locate them in a federal depository library (about which, more in a moment).

Since a subscription to the print version of the *GPO Monthly Catalog* costs over $200 a year, you will probably want to save your money and look at the library's copy instead. The *GPO Monthly Catalog* lists government publications catalogued each month.

It includes citations to the publications of U.S. government agencies, including the Congress. It covers Senate and House hearings on bills and laws, as well as many studies sponsored by federal agencies. You'll find maps, fact sheets, handbooks, bibliographies, conference proceedings, computer programs, microfiche, books, pamphlets, brochures, and folders. Subjects include farming and agriculture, economics, energy, public affairs, taxes, health, law, consumer issues, and the environment.

Get to know the GPO

The GPO Monthly Catalog

The *GPO Monthly Catalog* includes items sold by the Superintendent of Documents (the GPO), items available from the issuing agencies and other bodies, items for official use, and items sent to federal depository libraries. Each issue contains between 1,500 and 3,000 items. That works out to close to 30,000 new publications a year, more than enough to keep the many GPO printing plants and thousands of printing contractors busy day in and day out.

Although a cumulative index is issued twice a year and an annual *Serials Supplement* is published, you'll still have lots of volumes to check to find the publication you need if you try to do so by hand. When you search online, on the other hand, you can search the contents of all monthly issues all at once. Indeed, you can search through years of monthly catalogues, though the further back you go, the less chance there is that an item will still be in print.

Note that at least two companies offer the *GPO Monthly Catalog* on CD-ROM: Online Computer Library Center (OCLC) and SilverPlatter Information, Inc. Subscriptions are several hundred dollars a year. You may thus wish to check at your local library to see if it offers one of these CD-ROM versions.

The GPO Publications Reference File

As noted earlier, *PRF* includes only those items found in the monthly catalog that can be ordered directly from the GPO (Superintendent of Documents). There is no printed version of *PRF*. Instead, the information is published on microfiche—which is all the more reason to search *PRF* in its online database form. When you key in go gpo on CompuServe, for example, you will be taken to a menu-driven version of *PRF*. The Knowledge Index offers the identical database but lets you reach it via a series of menus and then search it by selecting your own keywords. *PRF* is also available on DIALOG.

The coverage in *PRF* concentrates on the legislative and executive branches and includes books, pamphlets, periodicals, maps, posters, and other documents from over 60 major federal departments and agencies and from smaller federal bureaus. Between 17,000 and 27,000 titles are in stock at any one time. Most were issued in the last five years, but forthcoming and recently out-of-print publications are included as well. The file dates back to 1971, and it is updated every other week.

A free *PRF User's Manual* is available. Contact the Records Branch of the Sales Management Division of the GPO, or simply call the GPO order desk at the number given below. Though aimed at users of the microfiche product, the booklet does a good job of explaining the file and telling you whom to contact if you need more help.

NTIS: National Technical Information Service

Experts might argue about which is the more crucial, but practically everyone agrees that the *GPO Monthly Catalog* and the National Technical Information Service (NTIS) database are the two top directories of U.S. government-produced information. NTIS is a service of the U.S. Department of Commerce, and it covers all nonclassified government-sponsored research, development, and engineering reports, plus analyses prepared by federal agencies, their contractors, and their grantees.

As the DIALOG database catalogue says, "[NTIS] is the means through which unclassified, publicly available, unlimited distribution reports are made available for sale from agencies such as NASA, DOD, DOE, HUD, DOT, Department of Commerce, and some 240 other agencies. In addition, some state and local government agencies now contribute their reports to the database."

Subjects covered include: administration and management, agriculture and food, behavior and society, building, business and economics, chemistry, civil engineering, energy, health planning, library and information science, materials science, medicine and biology, military science, and transportation.

NTIS is a self-supporting agency. It is the largest single source for public access to federally produced information. Each year NTIS announces summaries of 70,000 completed and 120,000 ongoing U.S. and foreign government-sponsored research and development and engineering activities. NTIS is sustained only by its sales revenue. The costs of NTIS salaries, marketing, postage, and all other operating expenses are paid for from this revenue.

Searching for mosquitoes   For example, we just searched NTIS via the Knowledge Index on CompuServe for articles about mosquitoes. The system reported it had 1,115 entries containing the word *mosquito* or *mosquitoes*. All such entries consist of a bibliographic citation and a brief abstract of the source article or report. Here are just a few sample titles:

- Biological Control of Pests and Insects
- Downwind Drift and Deposition of Malathion on Human Targets
- Mosquitoes of Canada: Diptera, culicidae
- Third Supplement to "A Catalog of the Mosquitoes of the World"
- Aquatic Plant Management
- Research Program in Tropical Infectious Diseases
- Sensor-Triggered Suction Trap for Collecting Gravid Mosquitoes
- Japanese Encephalitis—A Plague of the Orient
- Toxicity of Methoxychlor to Fish
- Highly Efficient Dry Season Transmission of Malaria in Thailand
- Improved Laboratory Test Cage for Testing Repellents on Human Volunteers
- Parasitic Disease in the U.S. Navy
- Comparison of Artificial Membrane with Live Host Bloodfeeding

Breadth and depth   The point here, of course, is not that NTIS contains entries offering more information than you will ever care to read about mosquitoes. The point is the breadth and the depth of the coverage. And remember, these are just a few of more than 1,000 references. If NTIS contains all of this on just the mosquito, think how much it must offer on, say, the space shuttle, soy beans, or nuclear fusion.

We didn't check those topics. But we did search for information on ISDN, the acronym for the Integrated Services Digital Network that is likely to play a role in the building of the so-called Information Superhighway. We came up with 391 entries. Figure 8-1 contains just one of those records.

We've shown you the record in Fig. 8-1 for several reasons. First, we want to emphasize once again the breadth and depth of coverage you can expect from NTIS. Second, we wanted you to see what an NTIS record looks like. (Records from the *GPO Monthly Catalog* and *PRF* are quite similar.) And third, we wanted to get you thinking about the next step—obtaining copies of the reports and other items referred to in government databases.

Notice, for example, that the 67-page report cited in the Fig. 8-1 record was published in England and is available from NTIS for $272. Not all items cited in this database are available from NTIS, but virtually all records give you the information you need to order a copy from the appropriate agency or organization.

8-1

A record from the National Technical Information Service (NTIS) database.

1780480 NTIS Accession Number: ERA/93-0653R/XAB

Overview of ISDN: Integrated Services Digital Network
  Kirk, M.
ERA Technology Ltd., Leatherhead (England). Electronic Systems Div.
Corp. Source Codes: 076749010
Sep 93   67p
Languages: English
Journal Announcement: GRAI9417
NTIS Prices: PC $272.00
Country of Publication: United Kingdom
Contract No.: ERA-81-01-0697

Integrated Services Digital Network (ISDN) is the culmination of a 15-year transition period during which the Public Switched Telephone Network (PSTN) has been transformed from a wholly analog to a potentially wholly digital system.

The report studies the 2 forms of ISDN: 'Narrowband' (N-ISDN) and 'Broadband' (B-ISDN). The report begins with a brief description of existing telephone services and technologies. It then studies N-ISDN, the global wholly digital PSTN, which can interwork with existing analog telephones and is poised to offer the most economic attachment and delivery service for video, Frame Relay, point to point data and all the applications served by today's 64kbit/s circuit switched service.

Finally, the report discusses B-ISDN, the global standardization of the next generation of much higher speed telephonic communications integrated with a novel set of subscriber data services including telephone, facsimile, data and video conferencing.

Descriptors: *Communication networks; Telecommunication; Telephone systems; Facsimile communication; Teleconferencing; Telephony; Digital systems; Video communication

Identifiers: *Foreign technology; *ISDN; *Integrated Services Digital Network ; B-ISDN; N-ISDN; ATM (Asynchronous Transfer Mode); SDH (Synchronous Digital Hierarchy); PSTN (Public Switched Telephone Network); SMDS (Switched Multimegabit Data Service); NTISTFERA

Section Headings: 45C (Communication—Common Carrier and Satellite)

There are at least four ways to obtain copies of virtually any nonclassified document published by the United States Government. As we've seen in Fig. 8-1, you may be able to order a document through a specifically identified agency or organization. For other documents, you may have to turn to the Government Printing Office or one of its bookstores. A third option is to contact one of the many official U.S. Government Depository Libraries across the country to see if they have a copy you can review or use. Finally, you can often order copies through another information broker who specializes in *document delivery*.

Unfortunately, there is no single best source for obtaining all government documents. The course you follow depends ultimately on the amount of time you have and the money in the search budget. If time is short and money is reasonably plentiful, you will be best off turning to a document delivery service that specializes in government publications. If you have more time than you do money, you may want to take on the job yourself. In that case, everything depends on how the publication originated (which agency or organization created it) and who is responsible for distributing it.

As we said at the beginning of this chapter, the upside of government information is that there is so much of it that your topic of interest has almost certainly been covered, often in great detail. And the information is usually cheap, besides. The downside is that bureaucratic complexity can make it difficult to obtain what you need in a timely fashion.

It is for this reason that we suggest you strongly consider employing a document delivery service or information broker specializing in government documents. These folks know the ins and outs of government publications the way a professional lobbyist knows the ins and outs of Capitol Hill. They know who to call, where to go, and what to ask for to get a needed publication as quickly as possible.

As you know, obtaining originals or photocopies of documents and supplying them to clients is a major aspect of the information brokering business. We'll have much more to say on the topic and the "doc del" services you might consider offering later in this book. Right now it's important for you to know that, just as some brokers specialize in certain topics and fields, some document delivery services are particularly adept at obtaining certain kinds of documents.

The Document Center in Belmont, California, specializes in supplying specifications and standards documents (military, government, industrial, and foreign). Docutronics Information Services Corporation in New York City can provide you with copies of all reports filed by public companies with the Securities and Exchange Commission. Maryland-based InFocus Research Services specializes in hard-to-locate technical reports and U.S. government

How to order copies of federal government publications

Information broker document delivery

The Document Center, Docutronics, & InFocus

publications. And so on. For more information on these three firms, contact them at:

Document Center
1504 Industrial Way, Unit 9
Belmont, CA 94002
(415) 591-7600

Docutronics Information Services Corporation
130 West 42nd Street, 27th Floor
New York, NY 10036
(212) 730-7140

InFocus Research Services
P.O. Box 2172
Rockville, MD 20847
(301) 468-9310

Federal Document Retrieval

There are lots of firms specializing in obtaining government-published documents. You will find many of them in *Burwell's Directory of Information Brokers*. But Federal Document Retrieval (FDR) is typical. This Washington, D.C.-based firm has associates in major cities across the country. One FDR brochure is headlined "Name a Document. Name a City. Name a Deadline." The subhead reads "Get any publicly available document from any place in the U.S. And get it fast."

For about $25, plus about 60 cents per page for photocopying (or the actual document cost) and applicable delivery charges, FDR provides any publication from Congress, The White House, executive departments and federal agencies, the courts (decisions, briefs, pleadings from any court in the U.S.), the GPO, the National Technical Information Service, the General Accounting Office, the Consumer Product Safety Commission, the National Highway Transportation Safety Administration, and more. Photocopies of out-of-print publications are available as well.

For more information and a free brochure and current price list, contact:

Federal Document Retrieval
810 First Street, NE
Suite 700
Washington, DC 20002
(202) 789-2233

Ordering from the GPO

If you'd rather not pay a broker, the easiest way to lay your hands on a government document yourself is to simply phone the GPO order desk in Laurel, Maryland. The desk is staffed Monday through Friday, 8:00 A.M. to 4:30 P.M., Eastern time. You may use Visa or MasterCard, or you can establish a deposit account with the Superintendent of Documents. You can also order by mail and pay with a check or money order.

If you do not know a publication's stock number, you can order up to six items per phone call, including subscriptions to most government periodicals. If you know the stock numbers, you can order up to 10 items per call. (You get the stock numbers from *PRF*.) You can also enter your order online when searching *PRF* via a system like DIALOG.

Prices are very reasonable. The cost of a single issue of the *Congressional Record* is $1 domestic, $1.25 foreign. The cost of a single issue of the *Federal Register* is $1.50 domestic, $1.88 foreign. Postage is included in all GPO price quotes.

Here's how to contact the GPO:

Superintendent of Documents
U.S. Government Printing Office
Washington, DC 20402
Order Desk: Monday through Friday, 8 A.M.–4:30 P.M.
(202) 512-1800

U.S. government depository libraries

The U.S. Government Depository Library program is based on three principles. First, that with certain specified exceptions, all government publications will be made available to depository libraries. Second, that such libraries will be located in each state and congressional district to make government publications widely available. And third, that these government publications will be available for the free use of the general public.

The outline of the current program was drawn up in 1857, and documents have been accumulating ever since. By law, there are two libraries per congressional district and one for each senator, plus assorted state libraries, libraries of the land-grant colleges, and so on. The total is now close to 1,390 in the U.S. and its protectorates.

There are two categories of depository libraries. A full-blown depository library accepts everything. A selective depository library, on the other hand, is permitted to select and obtain any government publication free of charge in return for allowing the public free access to it. As one librarian we spoke with put it, "The materials are on deposit with us. We don't own them; the government does."

Due to the selectivity option, not every depository library has all government publications, though in general, the larger the library, the larger the collection. Selective depository libraries are presented with a list of government publications and are free to choose the ones they want to have.

GPO bookstores

You should also know that the GPO operates bookstores in close to two dozen locations around the country. While the bookstores carry only a small percentage of all that is available from the government, they typically stock the titles that are most in demand. And, of course, they can accept orders for any title not actually carried in the store.

The one exception is the GPO Retail Sales Outlet in Laurel, Maryland. As a part of the office's Retail Distribution Division, it has access to all titles currently in stock. This is why, if you need something quickly, it can be best to hire a document delivery service based in the area. They can go to Laurel, Maryland, pick up the item, and send it out to you for next-day delivery.

All GPO bookstores and the Laurel, Maryland, location accept MasterCard, Visa, or prepaid Superintendent of Documents deposit account charges.

This is the current list of all the GPO bookstores in the U.S. You might find it worth your while to pay one a visit. Alternatively, you can often order GPO documents by phone. (You can obtain the necessary document reference numbers by searching the GPO database online.)

Boston
O'Neill Federal Bldg.
Room 169
10 Causeway Street
Boston, MA 02222
(617) 720-4180

New York
110 Federal Bldg.
26 Federal Plaza
New York, NY 10278
(212) 264-3825

Philadelphia
Morris Bldg.
100 N. 17th St.
Philadelphia, PA 19103
(215) 636-1900

Pittsburgh
118 Federal Bldg.
1000 Liberty Avenue
Pittsburgh, PA 15222
(412) 644-2721

Atlanta
1st Union Plaza
999 Peachtree Street NE
Suite 120
Atlanta, GA 30309-3964
(404) 347-1900

Birmingham
2021 3rd Ave. North
Birmingham, AL 35203
(205) 731-1056

Jacksonville
Suite 100
100 W. Bay St.
Jacksonville, FL 32202
(904) 353-0569

Chicago
401 S. State St.
Suite 124
Chicago, IL 60605
(312) 353-5133

Cleveland
1653 Federal Bldg.
1240 East 9th Street
Cleveland, OH 44199
(216) 522-4922

Columbus
207 Federal Bldg.
200 North High Street
Columbus, OH 43215
(614) 469-6956

Detroit
160 Federal Bldg.
477 Michigan Avenue
Detroit, MI 48226
(313) 226-7816

Milwaukee
310 W. Wisconsin Ave.
Suite 150
Milwaukee, MI 53203
(414) 297-1304

Kansas City
5600 E. Bannister Rd., #120
Kansas City, MO 64137
(816) 765-2256

Dallas
1C46 Federal Bldg.
1100 Commerce Street
Dallas, TX 75242
(214) 767-0076

Houston
801 Travis St.
Houston, TX 77002
(713) 228-1187

Denver
Room 117, Federal Bldg.
1961 South Street
Denver, CO 80294
(303) 844-3964

Pueblo
201 West 8th St.
Pueblo, CO 81003
(719) 544-3142

Pueblo
P.O. Box 4007
Pueblo, CO 81001
(719) 948-2240

Los Angeles
ARCO Plaza, Level C
505 S. Flower St.
Los Angeles, CA 90071
(213) 239-9844

San Francisco
1023 Federal Bldg.
450 Golden Gate Ave.
San Francisco, CA 94102
(415) 252-5334

Portland
1305 SW 1st Ave.
Portland, OR 97201-5801
(503) 221-6217

Seattle
194 Federal Bldg.
915 2nd Ave.
Seattle, WA 98174
(206) 553-4270

Washington, DC
U.S. Government Printing Office
710 N. Capitol St., NW
Washington, DC 20401
(202) 275-2091

U.S. Government Printing Office
1510 H Street, N.W.
Washington, DC 20005
(202) 653-5075

The National Technical Information Service (NTIS) is also a major source of government documents. Indeed, as noted earlier, this agency supports itself entirely through document sales. For a copy of the free *NTIS Products and*

Documents from NTIS

Services Catalogue, call (703) 487-4650 and ask for publication PR827/HDV. For more details on the information, services, and document delivery options NTIS offers, contact:

National Technical Information Service
U.S. Department of Commerce
5285 Port Royal Road
Springfield, VA 22161
(703) 487-4929

The NTIS FedWorld BBS

Bulletin board systems (BBSs) and the Internet are covered later in this book. However, it seems appropriate at this point to alert you to a very special BBS that can be accessed directly or via the Internet.

It's called NTIS FedWorld, and it offers not only many NTIS files but also gateway service to over 100 topic-specific BBSs run by arms of the federal government. It also includes tons of information on many more government BBSs that are not part of the FedWorld gateway. The BBSs you can access are devoted to topics like:

- National Agricultural Library BBS
- Automated Library Information Exchange
- Consumer Information Center
- Superfund Data and Information
- Americans with Disabilities Act Information
- Export/Import Bank Data and Information
- Department of Labor Information and Files
- Human Nutrition Information Service
- Wastewater Treatment Information Exchange
- State and Local FEMA User Groups
- Data and Information on Fossil Fuels
- Health and AIDS Information and Reports
- Small Plane Safety Reports and Information
- Indian Health Service BBS
- Passport Information/Travel Alerts
- National Head Start BBS
- Coast Guard On-Line Magazine and News
- Public Taxpayer Statistical Information
- Radio Frequency Management Issues
- Patent and Trademark Office BBS
- Alcohol Abuse and Alcoholism Information
- National Credit Union Administration
- Department of Interior Job Announcements

This is just a small sampling of the BBSs you can gateway to by calling the FedWorld BBS. Fortunately, the system helps you get a handle on all of these BBSs by letting you first pick a broad subject category and then select a board from within that category.

You can access FedWorld directly by dialing (703) 321-8020. Set your system for 9600 bps, 8/N/1. The board has over 100 incoming phone lines. Should you experience technical problems, you may call (703) 487-4608 between the hours of 10:00 A.M. and 4:00 P.M. for assistance.

If you have Internet access, you can telnet to FEDWORLD.GOV or use the FTP (file transfer protocol) location FTP.FEDWORLD.GOV to actually download files. (If you have never used FTP on the Internet before, be sure to read the Internet chapter in this book.)

State libraries

Researching, locating, and obtaining government information is a book-length subject in and of itself. For those with computers and modems, Alfred offers more details in his book *How to Look It Up Online*. But even that book doesn't touch on the lodes of information available from local state governments.

Space does not permit a complete treatment here, either. However, you should be aware that to a greater or lesser degree, everything we have said about federal government information applies equally well to state government information. This is the place to look when you need a sharper focus than is available through the wide-angle lens of federal information. The place to start is often your state's library. But remember: A reputable information broker uses a library's sources but does not make any demands on the library staff.

Here are the numbers to call to get started looking into any state-specific topic. We found this information on Matthew Lesko's Info USA forum on CompuServe:

Alabama	(205) 261-2500
Alaska	(907) 465-2111
Arizona	(602) 542-4900
Arkansas	(501) 682-3000
California	(916) 322-9900
Colorado	(303) 866-5000
Connecticut	(203) 240-0222
Delaware	(302) 739-4000
Florida	(904) 488-1234
Georgia	(404) 656-2000
Hawaii	(808) 548-6222
Idaho	(208) 334-2411
Illinois	(217) 782-2000
Indiana	(317) 232-1000
Iowa	(515) 281-5011
Kansas	(913) 296-0111
Kentucky	(502) 564-2500

Louisiana	(504) 342-6600
Maine	(207) 289-1110
Maryland	(301) 974-2000
Massachusetts	(617) 727-2121
Michigan	(517) 373-1837
Minnesota	(612) 296-6013
Mississippi	(601) 359-1000
Missouri	(314) 751-2000
Montana	(406) 444-2511
Nebraska	(402) 471-2311
Nevada	(702) 885-5000
New Hampshire	(603) 271-1110
New Jersey	(609) 292-2121
New Mexico	(505) 827-4011
New York	(518) 474-2121
North Carolina	(919) 733-1110
North Dakota	(701) 224-2000
Ohio	(614) 466-2000
Oklahoma	(405) 521-1601
Oregon	(503) 378-3131
Pennsylvania	(717) 787-2121
Rhode Island	(401) 277-2000
South Carolina	(803) 734-1000
South Dakota	(605) 773-3011
Tennessee	(615) 741-3011
Texas	(512) 463-4630
Utah	(801) 538-3000
Vermont	(802) 828-1110
Virginia	(804) 786-0000
Washington	(206) 753-5000
Washington, D.C.	(202) 727-1000
West Virginia	(304) 348-3456
Wisconsin	(608) 266-2211
Wyoming	(307) 777-7011

Conclusion

Again, it is important to emphasize that what we have provided in this chapter is merely an introduction to the vast and deep world of federal and state government information. There is much more to learn, and, should your practice take you in this direction, you will learn it as the needs of your jobs dictate.

From an information broker's viewpoint, there are two key things to remember about government information. First, regardless of the topic, there is almost certainly some government information available that relates to it. It may not always offer you exactly what you need, but, by golly, it's *something*.

As you are executing a search assignment, you should always keep this fact in mind.

Second, as with library-based information, most of the time you should view government information as only the starting point. Use it as a means to identify the experts and professionals with special knowledge about your target subject. Then make a point of contacting *them* for their latest thinking, analysis, statistics, and additional information leads.

9 Public records searching

In the 1974 movie *Chinatown*, there's a scene in which Jack Nicholson as private eye J.J. Gittes finds himself deep within the basement of the Los Angeles County Courthouse. The year is 1941, and Nicholson is pouring over a dusty folio volume of decades-old land deeds hoping to find the key to the many mysteries that envelope him. Once he's found what he's looking for, he coughs to cover the sound he makes ripping the page out of the record book. Then he politely leaves the room and returns to the sunlight above ground.

Even if you don't remember the movie, the scene described here encapsulates the traditional view of public records. They're dusty, difficult to find, and likely to be of interest only to private investigators and other "gumshoe" types. Certainly no self-respecting librarian or other information professional would be caught dead prowling the corridors of a county courthouse.

Public records: A changing perspective

That's an unfortunate view that, fortunately, is changing. Indeed, public records searching is one of the fastest-growing areas of the information profession. The reasons are relatively straightforward. First, more and more of the country's public records are being transferred to computer databases, making them much easier to search. And what *can* be searched *will* be searched, particularly if no one has to leave home to do so.

Second, in a highly mobile society of over 250 million people, it is more important than ever to know who you're dealing with. A personnel manager can no longer say, "Oh, yes, I knew her father at Rotary Club. She comes from a good family." The person being interviewed today across the gray metal desk may come from an equally good family. But the personnel manager doesn't know that. All he knows is that this person landed in town less than a week ago from a city thousands of miles away. She could be a member of Mensa or a mass murderer, for all he knows. We just don't live in a small-town world anymore.

Third, there is the question of lawsuits. In fact, in every area of life these days, there seems always to be the question of lawsuits. A TV repair company hires a new technician without doing a pre-employment check. Six months later, the technician is on a call to fix a TV and proceeds to rape the homeowner. The company is sued because, if it had done a pre-employment check, it would have found that the individual in question had been convicted for a similar crime three years ago. Clearly the person should not have been hired. Please pay tens of millions of dollars and go out of business. Thank you very much.

Or, Company A wants to buy Company B, and it takes that firm's income statement and balance sheet at face value. After all, the two chairmen play golf together. Millions of dollars change hands. But it turns out Company B was nothing but a worthless shell. All the papers it presented were false. And now no one can find the money—or the chairman of Company B. The pension funds that own most of the stock in Company A fire its chairman and top management. But the retired people who depend on income from the pension funds's investments are out millions of dollars. If only someone had thought to check the public record!

The public record can also help you locate people who have disappeared, like "deadbeat dads" trying to avoid paying child support. It can help you uncover the assets (planes, boats, cars, real estate, and bank accounts) hidden by people who the courts say owe your client money. It can do much more as well, as we are about to see.

The essence of public records

Up to now, we've spoken in very general terms to establish the concept of public records without getting bogged down in minute detail. The general concept is simply that, to a large degree, human civilization depends on record keeping of one form or another: who owes what to whom; who owns a given piece of property; who has been convicted of what crime in a court of law.

If official records and laws and courts did not exist, the only way to protect your property would be by force of arms. The only way to collect a debt from someone who refuses to pay would be by violence. And so on. We all know the drill.

Just as we all know that the world spent centuries rolling around in that muck until it developed a better way. Laws and records, and state-sanctioned violence in the form of police powers deployed to enforce the laws, were all part of it. But so, too, was making information that concerns the public available to the public.

And just what information are we talking about? What kind of records constitute "public records"? Well, among other things, public records include bankruptcy filings; corporation records; trademarks; Uniform Commercial Code (UCC) filings; tax liens; criminal records; workers' compensation records; "vital statistics" like birth, death, marriage, and divorce records; driver history records; vehicle records (ownership, registration, title history, and license plates); hunting and fishing licenses; occupational licenses; business registration permits; even pet licenses.

That's just for openers. There are also all the various real estate transactions, each of which must be recorded and made available in the public record. And there are tons of filings required by any "public company," which is to say, any company that sells stock to the public at large. There are voter registration records, court judgments ordering one party to pay another party a set amount, and more.

If your head isn't spinning yet, it probably should be. For the field of public records is as vast as any in the information industry. And it certainly takes the prize for being the most quirky. You may be intimately familiar with all the little twists and turns of the hundreds of databases on DIALOG and NEXIS— which ones cover what publications, how far back, and so on. That's all to the good. But it won't help you at all when it comes to public records searching.

Every government keeps its own

There are a number of reasons for this. The first is that the responsibility for maintaining public records is scattered throughout every level of government. Federal, state, county, and city or township governments are each responsible for different public records.

Federal records may be generally uniform. But, to one degree or another, each state does things a little differently. Naturally, some states are more automated and computerized than others. And not every state keeps track of the same information elements in every type of record. Which is to say, some are more thorough than others.

Finally, overlaying all of this are the various federal and state laws and regulations that may restrict what public information you can obtain, how you may use it, and for what purpose.

In short, being an effective public records searcher requires a great deal of knowledge and skill. Not to mention experience. It is a bona fide specialty,

Hire a specialist

just as searching chemical formulas or searching patents and trademarks is a specialty.

As an information broker, public records searching is probably something you will want to offer to your clients. But it is the kind of work you should probably give to a subcontractor who specializes in this field. Or, if this area is of particular interest to you, you should try to apprentice yourself to an established public records searcher.

Beware of quick-buck artists!

It is particularly important to add a strong word of warning here. In recent years several franchising companies have sprung up offering to make you "an instant public records expert." All you have to do is pay them between $10,000 and $16,000!

These people know nothing about the intricacies of public records resources. There is absolutely no substitute for experience. You cannot hope to become an expert in anything, particularly not public records by taking a weekend seminar, getting a suitcase full of self-motivation books for which you plunk down your hard-earned cash. Furthermore, you may expose yourself to serious liability because you will not be equipped to handle the legalities. At this writing there are not even any really good books that can tell you how to start a public records searching business from scratch.

Indeed, we're going to assume that starting such a business is not your goal. You may very well decide to specialize in public records later. But as a current or prospective information broker, what you need right now is an introduction to the field that will alert you to the kind of information that's available and clue you in on the tools and techniques public records specialists use to obtain it.

Once you develop a sense of what's involved, you will be in a much better position to subcontract work to a public records specialist. And, equally important, you will be in a better position to offer an additional service to your clients.

Lynn Peterson, public records expert

Whenever we have a public-records-related question—or need to write a chapter on the subject—we call on Lynn Peterson of PFC Information Services. Lynn spent many years as an industrial engineer with a major California company. Then, after her children were born, she opted for the greater flexibility of self-employment. In fact, she went a step further than most and created her own employment agency.

It was that experience that alerted her to the field of public records and the growing demand for this kind of information. "We began by doing pre-employment background checks on job applicants," Lynn says. "Initially, we paid an outside firm for this, but I soon learned that there are online services providing criminal, credit, and DMV reports.

"I looked into it, signed up with a vendor or two, and the rest is history. I became absolutely 'hooked' on information." So addicted to information did Lynn become that she eventually sold the employment agency and set about learning all she could about public records.

"I started out by doing pre-employment screening and tenant screening. But I moved on to asset and missing persons searches and competitor intelligence." Today, Lynn Peterson's PFC Information Services is one of the leaders in the public records searching field.

"I've never done anything that has been as interesting, as challenging, and as much fun as this job," Lynn says. "I wish the income were greater, but public records searching is really a marvelous opportunity to keep learning and growing.

"That's where the challenge comes. The number of public records that are out there is staggering. And no single person can know it all. You can do this for your entire life and still continue to learn. That's what makes it so interesting!"

Lynn Peterson cautions, however, that public records searching is very much an art or a learned craft. Librarians can prepare for their careers by earning an MLS degree. "But there is no way to learn public records searching," says Lynn, "other than by being mentored and by just doing it. I was very fortunate to have been coached by a semi-retired private investigator who introduced me to the many records that exist at the local courthouse and in government offices. But I also learned that you can achieve the level of skill you need only through time and experience."

In addition to directly serving conventional clients, Lynn Peterson and PFC Information Services is also happy to serve as a subcontractor to other information brokers. Lynn also does professional consulting, teaching others how to search public records and thus expand the number of services they can offer their clients. For more information, contact:

Ms. Lynn Peterson
PFC Information Services
6114 LaSalle Ave. #149
Oakland, CA 94611
(510) 653-0666
(510) 653-0842 (fax)
CompuServe: 72262,2554

Four main types of searches

Like all information brokers, public records specialists are called upon to execute a wide variety of assignments. But the heart of their business centers around four types of searches:

- Pre-employment investigations
- Finding missing persons
- Asset searches
- Company profiles

The information developed by these kinds of searches frequently dovetails nicely with the information obtained by the standard "bibiliographic" research done by conventional information brokers. The newspapers, magazines, and other published information consulted in a bibliographic search typically cover only one aspect of a subject. It's helpful, of course, but it's not likely to include the kind of information on a person or company that is available through public records. And sometimes that public record information can be the very heart of the matter. So the skills of public records specialists and those of information brokers often complement each other.

For example, suppose you have been asked to do a *prior art* patent search for your client. Prior art is anything in tangible form that can be used in a patent case to support the rejection of a pending patent application. It's anything, in short, that can be used to prove that someone else had an idea first. It is not uncommon for information brokers to be asked to find such people in hopes that they can testify at a patent hearing or trial.

If all you have to go on is the name of someone your client believes may have published something years ago constituting prior art, you may not be able to locate the individual using conventional bibliographic searches. You may find that you will want to hire a public records specialist instead.

Where to find public records information

One characteristic of the public records field that may surprise you is how few records are electronically searchable. Things are definitely moving in that direction. But, at this point, only about 10 percent of all the public records that exist are available online.

So good public records specialists must not only be adept at online searches, they must also be skilled at the old "shoe-leather" approach of going to the courthouse and mining the appropriate collection of records. We should note here that, just as information brokers may use "runners" to locate and photocopy articles from distant libraries, public records specialists sometimes use trusted local researchers to do essentially the same thing at a distant county courthouse. It's often simply more convenient than travelling to the courthouse yourself.

There is really no mystery about the sources of public records. All of them are in print, someplace. Some of those printed records are available online. And some of those online databases are available on CD-ROM.

Let's start with the online sources of public records. The situation is really quite similar to what exists in the world of DIALOG, LEXIS/NEXIS, and the traditional online services information brokers know so well. In fact, just as the *Gale Directory of Databases* is the master guide to that world, *The Sourcebook of Public Records Providers* is the master guide to this world. (The *Sourcebook* is published by BRB Publications, Inc., a company whose other guides and directories we'll tell you more about later in this chapter.)

Not surprisingly, in both worlds, some systems offer highly specialized, narrowly focused information, while others offer "supermarket services." The three leading supermarket services, for example, are:

CDB Infotek
6 Hutton Centre Drive
Santa Ana, CA 92707
(800) 427-3747
(714) 708-2000
(714) 708-1000 (fax)

Information America
600 Peachtree St. NW
Atlanta, GA 30308
(800) 235-4008
(404) 892-1800
(800) 845-6319 (fax)
(404) 881-0278 (fax)

Prentice Hall Online
18200 Von Karman Avenue, Suite 1000
Irvine, CA 92715
(800) 333-8356
(714) 263-2900
(714) 263-2927 (fax)

Certainly these three services differ. But, in general, each can give you access to everything from corporate records and UCC filings to real property and court indexes.

The closer to the source, the lower the price

The fees for these services vary, as well. But here's a tip from Lynn Peterson: It's not at all uncommon in the public records field for information to be sold and resold to different online vendors. Naturally, the price is marked up at each step in this information "food chain." So, the closer you can get to the information originator, the less you are likely to have to pay for the information.

Most online vendors buy information from one another. So if you're doing, say, a real property search on some system higher up in the "food chain," you might find yourself paying twice what you would have paid had you gone to the originating vendor.

On the other hand, what you pay and where you go to get it depend a lot on what you need and in what quantity. After all, to get the best price, you may have to lay out an annual subscription fee and incur other expenses. If you don't routinely need that kind of information, you may be better off using a service that may cost more per search but does not impose subscription fees or other ongoing expenses.

Here's a good real-life example. Suppose you're doing a surname search. You're trying to locate a given individual, and in addition to surname, you can also search by state, by city, or by the entire United States. You use the Metromail Information Service's MetroNet to gain direct access to the directory assistance databases maintained by the Regional Bell Operating Companies throughout the U.S. You will pay about a dollar to retrieve up to 200 names. Yet, if you do the same search on CDB Infotek, you will be charged about $11.50 for 200 names.

The catch is that to get the one-dollar rate, you must have a MetroNet subscription, and that involves a minimum commitment of $500 a month. That's $6,000 a year! You'd have to do an awful lot of searches to make that pay off. So paying the CDB Infotek rate makes a lot of sense, even though it's substantially higher.

For more information on MetroNet and the Metromail Information Service, call (800) 793-2536 or (708) 620-2990. The firm is a division of the R.R. Donnelley & Sons Company, the huge printing concern which also happens to publish telephone books. If you are a CompuServe subscriber, you can try this service right now by keying in go phonefile. The cost on CompuServe is about 25 cents per record viewed, plus normal CompuServe connect time rates.

Keep in mind, however, that a Phonefile search on CompuServe is a scaled down version of a full MetroNet surname search since it covers only people with listed phone numbers. The full-scale MetroNet search includes address information on people with unlisted phone numbers as well.

Right to the source!   And speaking of rates, one developing trend in the public records field is the growing realization among state and local governments that "there's gold in them thar records." Increasingly, local governments are putting their public records online. Alfred, for example, lives in Bucks County, Pennsylvania, where the county government has recently arranged with the phone company to make local real estate transaction records available to anyone with a modem and $10 for the initial sign-up fee. Lynn Peterson reports that the state government of New Jersey has recently introduced a system called DAISY that gives callers access to records maintained by the New Jersey secretary of state, including corporate records throughout the state. DAISY uses the CompuServe packet-switching network. They give you the sign-on instructions, and you can dial your local CompuServe node and get right in. They take Visa and MasterCard and charge you $15 for the connection and search. Performing the same search using a commercial vendor would cost more than twice as much.

CD-ROM products

There is also a trend toward putting tons of public records information on CD-ROMs. We have no idea whether there is any real connection between the public records aspect of this trend and its manifestation in other areas, but many companies are building businesses out of offering massive quantities of information on CD.

For about $40, you can buy a CD-ROM that contains all of the telephone white pages in the country. Given the rapidity with which people move, such a product is sure to go quickly out of date. But a CD containing the full text of hundreds of classics, including the complete works of Shakespeare, Milton's *Paradise Lost*, plus *Moby Dick* and hundreds of other plays, novels, and poems will never age. And they're all on a single CD-ROM, offered at a cost of about $40!

Add to all this the computer industry's projections that a CD-ROM drive will soon become as standard a part of the typical computer package as a floppy disk drive, and you can see that the trend for CDs points in only one direction—up!

Certainly, more and more public records will become available on CD. So, for many public records specialists, it often makes sense to buy, say, the property records of a given state on CD-ROM. Yes, microfiche may still be available for that state, but, while it may be cheaper, it does not offer the convenience of being able to search an entire state all at once.

The BRB Publications directories

As we've said, things are changing. More and more records are being made available in electronic form. But it is important for everyone to remember that today, most public records are still in manila folders and large folio volumes residing in the archives of various federal, state, and local government agencies around the country.

So how does a public records specialist in California manage to retrieve a record of, say, a tax lien on a business when that record exists only on paper and only in some volume in the basement of the Chippewa County Courthouse in Montevideo, Minnesota? You could easily spend a day or more on the telephone just trying to discover the right number to call. But that, of course, would be ridiculous.

The sensible—and cost effective—thing to do is to contact BRB Publications in Tempe, Arizona, and get the appropriate directory. BRB Publications is run by Mike Sankey, former president of Rapid Info Services. And it is run aggressively. Most BRB Publications directories are priced below $30, and they have an outstanding reputation for thoroughness and accuracy. Titles include:

- *State Public Records*
- *Federal Courts—U.S. District & Bankruptcy*
- *Local Court & County Record Retrievers*
- *County Court Records*
- *Public Record Providers*
- *The MVR Book (motor vehicles registration)*
- *County Asset/Lien Records*
- *The County Locator: LOCUS*

These publications are discussed in Sue Rugge's *Information Broker's Resource Kit* and can be ordered through her. (See Appendix A for brief descriptions and ordering information.)

To contact BRB Publications directly, write or call:

BRB Publications, Inc.
4653 S. Lakeshore #3
Tempe, AZ 85282
(800) 929-3764
(800) 929-4981 (fax)

Be sure to ask about a PC software package called SNN Version 5.2. This is a brand new product that lets you enter an allegedly valid social security number. The software can then tell you whether the number is within the range of valid numbers issued up to July 31, 1994 (or possibly later, if a new version of the package has been issued as you read this). It will tell you the name of the state and the year in which the number was issued.

The idea is to make it easy and inexpensive to check the validity of a social security number. If the number in question does not pass the test, then there is no need to do a more expensive, conventional search. At this writing, the program sells for $59, plus $3 shipping and handling. Contact BRB Publications for more details.

And the answer is . . . Now then, what about that tax lien? We know it is on file in Montevideo, Minnesota, the county seat of Chippewa County. Any number of BRB Publications directories could tell us where to call, but we checked *State Public Records*. This 295-page book contains thousands of names, addresses, phone and fax numbers, office hours, modes of access, search requirements, costs, access and usage restrictions, and more.

It turns out that the place to call is the UCC division of the secretary of state's office in Columbus. The directory gives you the address, phone number, and modes of access (by mail and by visit, in this case). It also tells you that the cost is $9 per debtor name, plus $1 per photocopied page. A self-addressed, stamped envelope is requested if you make your query by mail. For expedited service, add $10 per debtor name. Prepayment is required.

At this point, you've probably begun to get a sense of what public records are, and the challenges one can face in retrieving them. By now you should also have formed the general impression that, regardless of the record in question, mechanisms exist to make it relatively easy to retrieve. The trick is in doing so at the lowest possible price. Which is one more reason to hire a public records specialist to do this kind of work for you.

Insights into public records

In short, you've got the skeleton. Now it's time to put a little meat on those bones. And here, as we have throughout this chapter, we rely on the insights, war stories, and wisdom of Lynn Peterson. As you will recall, there are four types of assignments that constitute the bread-and-butter business of most public records specialists: pre-employment investigations, missing persons, finding assets, and in-depth company profiles.

Many public records specialists rely on pre-employment checks to pay the bills. It's their bread and butter, and it's the kind of work that comes back month after month, since companies and employment agencies have a constant need for information about prospective employees. Because of this, pre-employment screening can be a solid foundation for your business, even though the fees are not spectacular.

On the pre-employment line

It's also relatively easy to learn, since it does not require a great deal of technical skill or a vast knowledge of all the public records that exist in the universe. That's why it is often a good place for a beginning information broker to start. You really don't want to dive into this kind of work doing asset searches or locating missing persons.

On the other hand, according to Lynn Peterson, the work is typically repetitive, and it can be a bit boring. It is also a field fraught with legal hazards. You *must* know the legal parameters regarding what information you may and may not pull about a prospective employee. If you don't, you can find yourself in very serious trouble, and possibly open yourself to liability.

Pre-employment screening usually involves a number of different kinds of records. Typically a specialist will start with a personal credit report. These reports provide a wealth of information about an individual—no pun intended—that extends far beyond their indebtedness.

Certainly it can be relevant whether or not a given individual pays the bills on time. But even more significant is whether the person has one or more accounts "in collection" (meaning someone is dunning them for unpaid bills). It may also include information on any tax liens that have been filed against the person, any bankruptcies or judgments against the individual, and so on. Leaving all character considerations aside, employers do not like to hear this because employees who have judgments against them may be subject to wage garnishment—a big headache for any employer.

The ins & outs of credit reports

You might argue that this information is not relevant to most jobs. But what if the person is being considered for a position that involves handling large sums of money? Employers are really in a bind here. On the one hand, if they hire someone into a position of trust without investigating the person's background and the person ends up robbing them blind, they can be held liable for negligence by stockholders. But if they do a background investigation before hiring the person, they can be sued for invasion of privacy, or for discrimination if the same level of scrutiny is not applied to all job applicants.

No one is suggesting that a given employer or job applicant would win or lose either suit. But, as we all know, anyone can sue anyone else for anything. And every lawsuit saps energy and resources, regardless of who is right or wrong or who wins in the end.

The compromise in the area of personal credit reports essentially centers around the fact that a job applicant must give written permission to allow a prospective employer to order a credit report. It's impossible to overemphasize this point.

You cannot pull a credit report on an individual for pre-employment purposes unless you have the person's written permission to do so. The job applicant must first sign a release form granting permission. And in California, as in some other states, the person is entitled to a free copy of the credit report as part of the deal.

If you are a public records specialist, you clearly must be fully aware of this. And, if you are involved in pre-employment background screening, you should have liability insurance. (You will want to comparison shop, but you should probably expect to pay premiums totaling about $1,800 a year for a million dollars of coverage, with a $5,000 deductible. Costly? Damned right. But crucial, if only for peace of mind.)

If you are an information broker looking into hiring a public records specialist for pre-employment screening or similar work, it would be a good idea to ask the person a few questions about liability, liability insurance, and the circumstances under which it is permissible to pull an individual's credit report. Pulling a report for pre-employment screening, for example, requires the person's written permission. But if an attorney has a judgment against an individual and requests a credit report for that purpose, you can pull the report without the person's permission. (Have the attorney fax you a copy of the judgment first, just to be safe.)

To a trained eye, a credit report offers far more than just a record of how much a person owes, to whom, and payment history. The credit report also includes information about former employers and former address. So it's a good way to double-check or verify the information that appears on the resume or employment application. Most job applicants select which former employers they want to include on their resume, and which they want to leave out. But a credit report can bring that information to light.

Yet, credit reports are only the first step in the pre-employment screening process. And they are the only item that requires the applicant's signature. You don't usually need permission, for example, to do a statewide check of criminal records. But state laws vary, so it's best to check. In some states a release form signed by the person must be in hand before you can do a statewide search of criminal records. In other states, the person must sign a release form to authorize you to search for workers' compensation records.

Once again, an employer can be in a bind. According to Lynn Peterson, there has been a marked increase in "negligent hiring" lawsuits in recent years. A nanny taking care of a child; someone involved in caring for the elderly; hotel employees who have access to room keys; bank tellers and security guards, of course; and hundreds of other people in "positions of trust" raise liability issues for employers.

As information brokers, we need to educate employers about these facts. We need to let them know about the kind of information—much of it public records information—that is available and accessible. Employers need to be told of their potential liability. And they need to be shown how information brokers can help reduce or limit that liability by offering pre-employment screening and related services.

Another area employers are interested in knowing about are any workers' compensation claims a prospective employee may have filed in the past. Such a report includes all "workers' comp" claims a person has filed, where they claim to have been injured on the job, the kind of injury, the date, and so on. It also includes information on whether an individual is currently being paid from a former employer's workers' compensation insurance.

Workers' compensation information

Now, before you offer this kind of information, it is crucial to review the Americans With Disabilities Act. For example, if you are an employer with 15 employees or more, you are not allowed to do a workers' compensation check unless the person has *already* been offered employment. There must be a firm offer and acceptance of employment before you can do a workers' comp check.

It's also important to check any local laws in your state. Some states do not allow access to workers' comp information under any circumstances.

Department of motor vehicles (DMV) information

Because a person's driving record can often point to substance abuse issues, employers are often very interested in having you check the state's department of motor vehicles (DMV) records. If the prospective employee has ever been arrested for drunk or reckless driving, that information will show up here.

DMV reports can also reveal certain behavioral patterns. For example, someone who has had three or four speeding tickets and several "failures to appear" or FTAs (meaning they haven't shown up in court and haven't paid their tickets) may prove to be unreliable on the job.

Social security number verification

We want to make this very, very clear: Checking or receiving information from the Social Security Administration database is illegal. That doesn't stop some criminals from doing it, but it should stop you from even thinking about joining them or doing business with them. (Do, and you could join them behind bars as well!)

However, it's perfectly legal to check a credit bureau database by social security number. Instead of entering a name, address, date of birth, and a social security number to pull the credit report, you enter just the social security number. The database will come back with whatever names and addresses are associated with the uses of that number as far as credit information is concerned.

The illegal alien problem in California, for example, has been well-reported. As noted on *60 Minutes* and in print, in the Mission District of San Francisco (and elsewhere) there are places where you can easily obtain a very authentic looking social security card. And the better cards don't just *look* authentic, they contain a number that belonged to a deceased person.

This kind of credit check will tell you when and where a prospective employee's social security number was issued. So if you have someone born in 1970 and this kind of check tells you the number was issued in 1950, you and your client know that something's fishy.

As Lynn Peterson reports, "Sometimes I've seen whole families sharing the same number. One of them will be a legal resident with a valid number, or one of them will buy a social security card. Either way, they all use the same number. Naturally, employers are *very* interested in this."

Finding missing persons

The second kind of assignment a public records searcher frequently gets is finding missing persons. To be successful, you have to have an analytical mind and enjoy puzzles. You have to have good problem-solving skills. And you have to have a very broad and deep knowledge of what public records are out there and what they contain.

That's probably why our friend Lynn Peterson likes it so much. "It's my favorite kind of work," she says. "If I could do whatever I wanted, I would do nothing else but find missing persons. I can't think of anything that I get more pleasure from. I almost don't care if I get paid—I just want to find the person. These become crusades for me."

The first step in beginning to look for a missing person is to think long and hard about what you know about the individual. Combine that with your knowledge of public records, and then consider the most economical approach. That's because, unlike the Tommy Lee Jones character in *The Fugitive*, who seemed to have endless resources to call upon in finding Harrison Ford, information brokers almost always find themselves dealing with a budget. This adds to the challenge, of course.

Where do you begin?

There is no dearth of tools to be used in finding someone. If the person has a relatively uncommon last name, you may have to look no further than MetroNet, the online database of names and addresses we talked about earlier. But most of the time, the name won't be all that unusual, and the information you want won't be online.

What tools are available?

Ultimately, your best tool is a thorough knowledge of what resides in various records in various drawers at courthouses and governmental offices across the country. In a book of this sort, it is impossible to list, let alone explain, all of the categories of information you may want to consult. But we can give you a flavor of what's available.

Vital records   Birth, marriage, divorce, and death records. Most are not available online, but some death records are on CD-ROM, and CDB Infotek offers a death search that lets you search a single state or the entire country by name, or by name and date of birth.

The Grantor-Grantee Index & UCCs   Stored at the county level, the Grantor-Grantee Index is the main guide to tax liens, power-of-attorney documents, deeds, mechanics liens, abstracts of judgments, notaries' bonds, and Uniform Commercial Code (UCC) filings.

Like an automobile "pink slip," a UCC filing establishes where the ownership of some piece of property resides. Thus, if you lease a major piece of equipment, the leasing company will almost certainly ask you to sign a UCC form attesting to the fact that, even though you have possession of the item, the company itself actually owns it.

UCCs are a good way to find people because each form contains the person's name and address—and possibly other information that can be useful in locating the individual.

Real property searches   In many states, real estate ownership records are available by the name of the individual. In that case, you can plug in just a name and get all of the properties owned by anyone with that name, anywhere in the state. Even if the person owns property but lives at another location, there is usually a mailing address on record for them.

Hunting & fishing licenses   In some states you can simply call the correct department and ask if the person you are looking for has a hunting or fishing license. If so, they will usually give you the address they have on file.

Voter registration   Often voter registration records contain a person's date of birth and, sometimes, their occupation. The occupation information can be very helpful if the person has a rather common name. (Note that in some states, "voter reg" information cannot be sold. It can only be used for political purposes.)

One of the easiest ways to check voter registration information is via the Aristotle database that is now available through CDB Infotek. This database is the only nationwide file of registered voters, and it contains information from over 3,400 counties and municipalities. (Twenty-six of the fifty states have no significant restrictions on voter registration information.)

Professional licenses   In many states this information is available online. In California, for example, there are approximately 38 licensed professions (everything from barbers to CPAs). And, again in California, you can search by name. You can plug in one name, and the database will search all 38 professions, pulling up the addresses of every name that matches your query.

Other sources & ethical considerations

This list just scratches the surface. There are also court records of many kinds, fictitious name or DBA ("doing business as") filings, bankruptcy and tax liens—there is even the National Postal Change of Address Database that keeps track of people who have filed a "change of address" card with the U.S. Postal Service.

The amount of information a skilled professional can assemble about a given individual is staggering indeed. And a little bit frightening. On the one hand, we all value our privacy. But on the other hand, there isn't a civilization you can name—ancient Greece, Rome, Persia, and China through modern Europe and the United States—that has not kept public records of things like who owns what piece of property and who owes what to whom.

There is thus nothing illegal about delving into the public record to find someone. Legally, anyone may do it. But, just as not everyone has the skills needed to perform a given operation or build an atomic bomb, few have the ability to effectively search public records. Suppose the person you're looking for doesn't want to be found? Suppose he or she has a very good reason for remaining missing? Who are we to "play God?"

For example, missing persons searches can be used to locate witnesses in court cases, an adopted son or daughter's biological parents, and deadbeat dads. Are we to be like Nemesis, the Greek god of righteous anger who never gives up and cannot be deflected in punishing all who violate the natural order of things? What if the reason your client wants you to find a given individual is so he can kill him?

It can be a genuine dilemma. If the client happens to be an individual, as opposed to a law firm or company, Lynn Peterson handles it by saying up front, "If you want me to locate this person, my condition is that if I find the person, I be allowed to notify him or her that you are trying to make contact. The person can either say yes or no. But if the answer is no, I do not give you the address. If you have any problem with that, we cannot proceed." You must let there be no doubt, however, that you expect to be paid for your efforts, regardless of outcome.

In addition, there is the purely practical matter of information availability. If we as a profession do not operate in a sensitive, ethical manner when plumbing public records, then many of those records will cease to be available. Or access will be severely restricted. There are already moves afoot in some states, for example, to seal up DMV records.

Keep public records public

Whenever we get the chance, we also need to make sure the public and clients understand the very real distinction between public records and things like a person's medical records and credit history. Unfortunately, all of these sources of information tend to get lumped together in the public's mind, to the detriment of the actual public records field.

If access to genuine public records is cut off or restricted, charlatans, swindlers, and cheats will prevail. We know of any number of cases in which a public records search helped well-meaning people avoid financial disaster.

For example, a middle-aged couple looking toward retirement was considering investing in a particular company. But the tale the company told sounded a little too good to be true. The couple ordered a background check on the principals of the firm, and discovered that the company was in Chapter 11—and the CEO had filed for personal bankruptcy. Worse still, there were multiple judgments against both the company and the various men and women involved. Talk about dodging a bullet!

Lynn Peterson reports that she had one case "in which my client, a very large hotel chain, was about to make a very significant investment. They wanted me to check out these people and the company. They sent me the letterhead of the company they were thinking of buying. And from that I learned that it apparently had offices in Boca Raton, Orange County, and Geneva, Switzerland.

"I did some background checking and found what can only be described as loads of dirt. Horrendous numbers of lawsuits all over the place. I discovered that the firm's 'worldwide headquarters' was actually a rundown apartment in Orange County. And it was the guy's home address. It also turned out that the men who ran the company had criminal records.

"All of which came as a big surprise to my client. Clearly, if it had not been for access to public records, the client would undoubtedly have made this investment and no doubt would have been fleeced!"

Asset searches

The third major activity of a public records researcher is searching for hidden assets—somebody owes your client money and refuses to pay. So your client goes to court and wins a judgment against the individual. The judgment gives your client the right to collect, but it doesn't do much more than that.

As Lynn Peterson says, "All too often clients come to me to do asset searches *after* they have won a judgment and then begin to wonder whether or not and how they can collect. Personally, I think these kinds of searches should be done *before* engaging in the litigation, because many times you'll find that the person doesn't have anything to go after anyway. So what's the point in going through the legal expense of winning a judgment?"

Still, ours is not to reason why. As long as you don't have to worry about collecting your fee from *your* client, you can take the assignment at any stage. Usually it's best to start by looking for "basic dirt." In California, this is called a *statewide public filing search*. It's a search for state, local, county, or federal tax liens, bankruptcies, judgments under $25,000, notices of default, and unlawful detainer information. It's all there in one quick and easy search.

If you find that the person has $100,000 in federal tax liens—and there are other judgments as well—your client may want to rethink whether it's worth pursuing the individual. The trouble is, you see, that your client may have to get to the back of the line when it comes to collecting. And if the client has to go behind the IRS and the other people who already have judgments against the person, there may not be anything left to collect.

Phase II

So that's the first step. Find out first who else has legal claims against the person. Then you can begin digging deeper. There are lots of places to look. We have room to summarize only a few of them here.

Real property records   In more than half the states in the U.S., you can search real property records by entering just the name of the person. The database will then "sweep" the whole state. In other states, you have to search at the county level. Which often means calling the county assessor's office.

It is also possible to search for vehicles that the person owns. You can do that by using the person's name and possibly date of birth as well.

Boats, yachts, & aircraft   If a person ever owned a boat, yacht, or aircraft, the chances are that this fact has been recorded someplace. You may be able to check state records. Or, if the yacht is over 35 feet long, it may be registered with the Coast Guard.

Divorce filings   This is a wonderful way to find out everything there is to know about a person's assets. If you can find a divorce case, you may not have to look any further. This is because divorce files contain all kinds of information about what a man and woman own, including bank account balances, cars, boats, planes, coin collections, stocks and bonds—you name it. Plus information on each spouse's personal behavior.

Corporate affiliations   It is usually very easy to locate the assets of the average person. But people who tend to have a lot of assets or "questionable" business dealings can be very adept at hiding what they own. That makes it very difficult sometimes to find their assets. Sometimes the assets are technically owned by their companies. Or they'll set up trusts to which they transfer ownership of their property. Or they will put property in the name of a relative.

A business TRW   If you know that the person is involved with a business, you can do a *business TRW* credit search. This is a great tool. The search will tell you how the business is paying its creditors. And it's good, reliable information because it comes from the company's creditors.

The business TRW will also tell you if TRW's analysts see an increasing risk factor with the particular business. And there is a section on the report dealing with public records information which can save you doing some other searches. Information like UCCs and tax liens and judgments will show up on that business TRW.

Finally, one of the main things public records searchers do for other information brokers is to create company profiles. Many of the same kinds of records examined in an asset search are consulted here as well.

Company profiles

But the search will also include corporate records to see if there are any tax problems. Is the firm in good standing with the secretary of state? Is there any litigation current or pending? What about tax liens? Are there any serious environmental violations? And so on.

Lawsuits filed by former employees are particularly helpful. Indeed, as Lynn Peterson says, "When I find a lawsuit like that, I'm often asked to locate the employee who filed it. I then find that they are only too happy to 'tell all' about a particular company."

Of course, there are the standard income statements, balance sheets, and other reports that any company whose stock is publicly traded must file with the Securities and Exchange Commission (SEC), plus the information that has been reported about the firm or its officers in *The Wall Street Journal*, *Business Week*, and many other publications.

Conclusion

Certainly the skills required to be a successful public records searcher are nearly identical to those needed to be a good information broker. But there's no denying that, like patent searching or searching for chemical formulas, public records searching is a definite specialty.

With Lynn Peterson's help, we have done our best to give you a feeling for what this area is like. But we've only scratched the surface here. Hopefully, we've given you enough information to decide whether or not you want to look into specializing in this area.

Fortunately, most information brokers don't have to decide "either/or." If your interests lie in some other area, that's great! The crucial thing is to be aware of the fact that public records exist and that there are people in our profession who have the skills and experience to search them for you. All of which adds to the range of services you can offer *your* clients.

The Public Records Seminar:

Helen Burwell is one of the pivotal figures in the information brokering profession. Not just because she's a crackerjack information broker herself, but also because she edits and publishes the annual *Burwell Directory of Information Brokers* and *The Information Broker's Newsletter*.

Helen was a law librarian for many years before she started her own very successful information brokerage. Her extensive background in legal and public records research makes her uniquely qualified to teach a seminar on public records searching. Over 500 people have taken the seminar, which offers a realistic view of the joys and pitfalls of running a public records research company. She is also a past president of the AIIP.

The seminar covers the following topics:

- Sources of information. Including courthouse records, and records from licensing boards, motor vehicles, real estate, tax, voter, UCC filings, and more.
- Information on people. Assets, background checks, financial, pre-employment, skip trace, and more.
- What's legal/illegal. The Fair Credit Reporting Act, the Privacy Act, and other laws.
- Obtaining the records. Free versus fee. Who has what? Canadian records, European records, etc.

- Database producers and vendors. Information America, LEXIS, CDB Infotek, how to choose, cost considerations, trade-offs, and more.
- Hints and shortcuts. Following the data trail. How to put the pieces together. Saving time and money.
- Uses of public record information. Business decisions, competitor intelligence, genealogy, locating people, all kinds of research, etc.

Helen's seminar will also alert you to a wide range of other resources, publications, professional associations, conferences, and "networking" possibilities. And each seminar includes a course book, sample newsletter for use in marketing, and vendor literature.

For details and the latest schedule, contact:

The Information Professionals Institute
3724 F.M. 1960 West, Suite 214
Houston, TX 77068
(713) 537-8344
(713) 537-8332 (fax)
CompuServe: 75120,50

10 The telephone
Your most powerful tool

The telephone is to the information broker what a scalpel is to a surgeon. And you should be just as comfortable holding it, manipulating it, and using it as a conveyance of your skill. But where a scalpel is an extension of a surgeon's hand, the telephone is an extension of your personality. It is you, the pleasant person on the other end of the line, to whom the expert, the recognized authority, or the Great Man or Great Woman is yielding up information, opinions, and analysis—the very gold dust that pays your bills.

Needless to say, mastery of this most powerful of tools is essential. After all, there are *lots* of people skilled at doing library research—graduate students needing extra cash, freelance or moonlighting librarians, particularly bright staff assistants and interns, and corporate information center managers come to mind immediately.

How to use the phone effectively

Relatively speaking, however, there are not that many people who can pick up the phone, call an authority or expert, and conduct a successful interview. As we have said throughout this book, it is the kind of information developed from interviews of this sort that most clients are most willing to pay for. As an important side note, mastery of the telephone is equally important in selling your services and building your business, as we will see in Chapter 20, Marketing and Sales, the Missing Ingredients.

So let's look the situation right in the eye. We can show you some techniques and give you the pointers you need to set off in the right direction. With practice, you'll develop your own style. But if you don't have an outgoing personality to begin with, if you don't enjoy talking to other people, you start at a serious disadvantage.

If you've never done anything like this before, or if you think of yourself as shy, don't be discouraged. About the worst possible thing that can happen is that the person you call will abruptly hang up on you. More than likely, protected by the anonymity of the telephone, your shyness will drop away. Your brain will take over, and you'll be so caught up in pursuing the answers you've called to find that you'll forget to be nervous. Who knows? Lurking behind that shy, retiring image you present in person could be a dynamite telephone personality. So give it a try.

A double perspective

Over the years, Sue and Alfred have both given and done countless phone interviews. We have been on either end of the conversation. We know what it's like, for example, to have the phone ring in the midst of a project and hear a voice on the other end ask for just a few moments of our time.

Though the milk of human kindness flows through our veins and though we are, of course, the most amiable, cooperative people you would ever want to meet—if someone calls who is unprepared, unprofessional, or unpleasant, a few moments is exactly what they'll get.

Well, okay, we're not exactly that tough. Like most people in this field, we're happy to answer a question or two. But, you know, if you expect your clients to pay you for your time and experience, why would you expect your co-authors or anyone else to give you their time and the benefit of their experience for free? That's why Sue charges $50 per half hour of phone consultation, Visa or MasterCard accepted. And she does a lot of it. People call, outline what they need, and schedule a mutually convenient time for a consultation.

In fact, there is even more good news. As you will see in Appendix A, Sue Rugge's highly acclaimed Information Broker's Seminar is now available on audiocassette, and the purchase price *includes* a half hour of personal consultation.

We also know what it's like to be the caller, to be under a rush deadline, and to be desperate for the information we think the expert can offer. We know the frustration of interviewing someone who really doesn't know what he or she is talking about, or the frustration of a key source being unreachable (on vacation, out of the office, in a meeting, take your pick).

And we know the satisfaction of reaching someone who is very good, very knowledgeable, and personally simpatico. After conversations like these, you hang up the phone saying to yourself, "By golly, that's what life is really all about. That's what makes this business worthwhile. Everything else just pays the bills."

As a result of this double perspective, we have some pretty definite opinions about what goes into a successful interview. Indeed, we can break it down into four major stages or steps:

1. Preparation
2. Initial contact
3. The interview
4. Assimilation of results

Step 1: Preparation

There are two reasons why we have placed such a heavy emphasis on phone work in this book. The first is to help counteract the misimpression many people have that being an information broker is simply a matter of learning to use online databases and paying an occasional visit to the local library. The second is that in our rather long experience, phone work supplies over 50 percent of the information you need to satisfy your client. The telephone thus clearly *deserves* all the emphasis we have given it.

So, while you will want and need to use information obtained from the library, from the government, or from online databases in your final report for the client, much of the work you do in these areas is really preparation for one or more telephone interviews. This preparation takes two forms. First, library and online research will reveal the names of the people you should call. Second, the information you assemble this way will give you the background you need, so that you know what questions to ask when you go to the phone.

Who you gonna call?

Selecting the right people to call when you're working on a project is something of an art. But it's an art no one has even come close to mastering. At times the person who seems like the perfect source turns out to be a real dud and a serious waste of time, while the person you dialed as a shot in the dark turns out to be a genuine gold mine. Authoritative pronouncements from your authors on this subject are thus impossible.

What we *can* do, however, is help get you thinking in the right direction. In fact, your thinking and your mindset are the key to the whole matter. If you wouldn't dream of calling up the clerk of an important Senate committee to get information on a pending bill, if it would never occur to you to phone the president of a large corporation, then seeing the names of these sources in print will do you absolutely no good.

You have got to get rid of the notion that calling people you don't know "simply isn't done." On the contrary, it's done all the time, and not just by telemarketers trying to sell you something. There are a few truths about life and about the business world that every aspiring information broker must become aware of.

Taking advantage of opportunities

The first truth to keep in mind is that anyone can call anyone. You may not always get to speak to the person you call, but a surprising percentage of the time, you will. Not everyone has a secretary, and not everyone with a secretary has that person screen incoming calls. Some people like taking their own calls. And even if you run into an initial screen, you can always ask for a callback or ask to make an appointment to call again.

Interestingly, as Sue points out, many times you may end up speaking with the people who work for the person you had hoped to reach. That can prove to be a real opportunity, since these folks don't get to tell people what they know very often and thus may be more helpful in your quest. In general, the higher you go in an organization, the more you are apt to meet with suspicion, resistance, and lack of cooperation.

As Sue says, "I always start by asking for the ultimate person. But if that person isn't available, I'll say to the assistant, 'Well, maybe I don't really need so-and-so. Perhaps you can help.' Then I explain what I need. If the assistant cannot help, at least I've given a detailed message that can be relayed to the boss, and, hopefully, I'll get an answer when I call back. It's amazing how often this works: You can accomplish your goal even if you never get to speak to the person you set out to interview.

"The same thing's true with voice mail. Since nearly everyone uses voice mail these days, it's important to develop the habit of being as specific as possible in the messages you leave. The more detailed you can be in what you need from the person when you leave a voice-mail message, the more likely you are to get a call back. And don't forget to specify the best time to call you, or to say that you would be happy to call again if the person would just get back to you with a preferred time."

The same thing goes when talking to the "ultimate person's" assistant. Tell the assistant the best time for the person to return your call. And then be there! When you start on a telephone-based research project, it is really important to be by your phone, often for two or three days, so you're there to get the callbacks. After all, not everyone you leave a message for will call you back, and those who do aren't likely to try your number more than once.

The second truth to remember is that people like to talk about their work. And who can blame them? We all like to talk about our work. We spend at least a third of our day and more than half our lives doing it. What makes you think some august authority on a subject is any different?

Third, most people are predisposed to help other people. Who among us wouldn't want to help someone else who was in trouble? We might not do it—if there was danger, if the cost to us was too high, or if the individual didn't appear to "deserve" assistance—but the instinct is there.

So a polite, pleasant-sounding person who has obviously done some homework calls you up. The person has a problem. And it turns out that not only can you help at no cost to yourself, but doing so requires you to talk about your work or area of expertise. Are you really going to say, "Go away, kid, you bother me."? Of course not. You're flattered, and you want to help. If at all possible, you're going to say, "Okay, I've got a few minutes. What can I do for you?"

Now that we're agreed that anyone can call anyone else—now that we've opened our minds to this possibility—who do we call?

<aside>**Use your imagination**</aside>

Often the answer is obvious. If a reporter has done a story on hi-tech hog farming, that reporter is a good place to start. The sources the reporter interviewed and quoted or credited in the article are equally good. And bear in mind when doing any phone interview that people know other people and experts know other experts. If the reporter or the quoted sources cannot themselves give you the information you seek, the chances are good that they know someone who can. Always ask, "Who else do you think I should contact?"

If the article appears in a magazine devoted to a particular subject like, say, *Hog Producers Daily*, consider calling the editor. You might ask if the magazine has covered the hi-tech angle in other issues. Or you might simply ask if the editor can steer you to the leading experts in hi-tech hog farming.

If the experts are professors, there's a good chance that they've written other pieces on the subject and will love to tell you all about them. Be sure to ask. More than likely they will be happy to send you copies of their works—saving you the trouble and expense of locating them on your own. Indeed, sources like these tend to send you far more than you need (or want to look at), but you accept it all graciously and gratefully.

The *Encyclopedia of Associations* is another wonderful source of people to call. And again, each person you call is a potential gateway to other people with the expertise you need. The *Encyclopedia of Associations* is available in all but the smallest of libraries, and it can be searched online, as we will see later. But it is so useful that it is the first print media tool every information broker should consider buying.

There are trade associations for every conceivable industry, profession, and subspecialty. Virtually all of them have a magazine of some sort. And every last one of them exists primarily to dispense information about their area of focus. A given association may be so small that it will have just an executive director and no staff. Or it may be large enough to have an entire library.

Some will not give statistics to nonmembers. But most are very helpful. And often they provide or suggest resources that may not have occurred to you.

Incidentally, if they have a "members only" policy, you will want to tell your client that. The client may want to call as a potential member, or actually join. It's even possible that the client may already be a member and never thought of calling.

There may be another alternative as well. More and more trade associations have begun to offer fee-based information services. So it may be possible for you to spend $50 or $60 or whatever and get a tremendous amount of information from the association. This can be good for all concerned—it means you won't have to beg for the information, and the association personnel will be motivated to help you because they know the organization is being paid for it.

The importance of the audit trail

You always want to tell the client all the people you called, their affiliations, and their phone number. Providing an audit trail of your sources is part of what the client is paying you for. It also protects your credibility when the information you have been asked to find turns out to be unavailable. In addition, your clients may want to follow up on their own, even six months or a year later.

Articles, editors, and associations don't make tremendous demands on your little grey cells of imagination. These are obvious sources to any information broker. Now let's carry things a little bit further.

Your subject is hi-tech hog farming. You've got an article on the subject that focuses on machines and devices to automate the feeding process. One of the sources quoted in the piece makes a passing reference to inoculating the animals against disease. But the article does not explore this avenue.

A light bulb goes off in your head. Inoculation wasn't something you had thought of in connection with hi-tech hog farming. But clearly it is an important part of the process. No source or other reference is given. So, assuming you have not yet reached the reporter or the editor, who can you call for information on this aspect of the topic?

There are many paths you could follow, of course. But for the sake of argument, let's assume that all print and online sources are closed to you for the time being. All you've got to work with is the phone.

You might start by calling a local hog farmer and asking how the problem of inoculation is handled. That could lead to the name of a drug manufacturer or a local veterinarian. Assume it's the drug company. You call there and ask to talk to the public information or public relations office. If it's a big company, you can count on getting bounced around to three or four people.

But eventually you will find someone who can give you information about the drugs the firm makes for swine and probably the names of the companies who make the equipment for administering them. The person will probably also be able to supply you with trade journal or other articles discussing the merits of the firm's products. Accept them gratefully.

You repeat the phoning process with the equipment manufacturers suggested by the drug firm. They too have articles and press releases for you, complete with black-and-white glossies illustrating their latest shot-giving machines.

As we said, there are many ways to attack a problem like this. But one must agree that the "phone-alone" scenario we have just presented is entirely plausible. And, as we hope we have shown, your own imagination—your own answers to the self-imposed question "Who would know?"—is the key. That and good phone work.

Getting your ducks in a row

The final stage in your preparation is deciding exactly who you want to call and what you plan to ask. We do not want to give you the impression that you can complete most projects by simply narrowing down a list of names and phone numbers, spreading them out before you, and picking up the phone. That may indeed happen. But usually you will have no idea when you make your first call how many additional people you will be speaking to before the project is finished. In fact, if you are doing your job right, there is no way you *can* know, since one source so often leads to two or three others. You may well find that you need to grow an "information tree" for each project.

In short, you'll go through the "ducks in a row" stage many times in the course of a job. At least once for each call you place.

Start by putting the person's name, address, and phone number on a separate sheet of paper. Then, on the same sheet of paper, list the major points you want to cover in the interview. Leave plenty of room between your questions since you will need the space to make notes on the answers. Do not use the back of the paper. It's too easy to overlook. Instead, start a second sheet if you need more room.

Good organization is crucial. And keeping each source on a separate sheet (or sheets) of paper makes it much easier to prepare your final report to the client. You will be able to tell the client who you called, the addresses, what you asked, how each person responded, and so on, without shuffling through a pile of disorganized notes.

It is also crucial to know what you're talking about when you call a source. Obviously you won't know the answers to your own questions. But you have got to have done your homework. Nothing turns a source off quicker than someone calling and saying, "Gee, I've got to find out about hi-tech hog farming. Can you help me out?" Remember, you are asking the source to give up time and share knowledge with you free of charge. If you yourself cannot be bothered to spend enough time to learn something about the subject, you can't expect the source to look kindly on your request for a free education.

On the other hand, if you have read enough about the subject to be able to say, "I think I have the basic concepts of the new trends in hog farming down, but there are one or two points for which I need more detail," you will get a much better reception. And if the source presses you to explain your areas of confusion, you had better be prepared to do so. Fakery and bluff are as apparent in an interviewer as they are in a source.

Is tape recording legal?

There are a number of purely mechanical details to prepare as well. First, we recommend that you consider using a telephone headset. A headset leaves your hands free to type notes at your computer or to write them by hand. And they eliminate the chronic crick in the neck that many phone users suffer from. Headsets are available from catalogues and office supply stores. But you may want to check at your local AT&T phone store.

Second, you may find it convenient to use a tape recorder. Radio Shack sells a device that makes it easy to connect a tape recorder directly to the phone line. (They cost about $25.) Please note, however, that in some states—like California, for example—taping a phone conversation is not legal unless both parties are aware that a recorder is being used.

There is an important caveat to enter here. If taping a conversation is legal in your state and you decide to turn on the recorder, the tapes you make of your interviews must be held in the strictest confidence. They are for your exclusive, personal use only. In our opinion, it is unethical to either provide them to the client or to even suggest this as a possibility—unless you have notified your source at the beginning of the conversation that a tape recorder is being used. The same logic applies to transcripts. To do otherwise is to violate the unspoken trust between you and your source.

The sole reason for using a tape recorder is that it frees you from worrying about whether you have accurately noted the source's answers. This lets you concentrate on the give-and-take of the conversation. It lets you really listen to what the person is saying and react with follow-up questions.

One should never rely on a tape recorder alone. You will find that going back and transcribing or taking notes on a taped interview takes too much time. It is much better to make notes during the conversation—typing them at your computer, if convenient—and to assume that they are your only record of the conversation. If some point gets missed or is otherwise unclear from your notes, *then* go to the recording to check what was actually said. Tape recordings are also helpful when you want to quote one or two sentences verbatim in preparing your final report.

If you are going to use a tape recorder, make sure that it's working before you place the call. Put it on RECORD. Pick up the phone and punch a number to stop the dial tone. Then say something. The needle on the recorder should react. Verify that everything is in working order by rewinding and playing the tape you have just made.

If you subscribe to the phone company's Call Waiting service, be sure to disable it before you make your call. You don't want the disruptive Call Waiting signal to interfere with your interview. Check the front pages of your phone book under Tone Block for instructions. In most areas of the country, dialing 1170 or *70 will disable Call Waiting for the duration of the call. It goes into effect again as soon as you hang up.

The nuisance of Call Waiting

Whether or not you are using a recorder, Call Waiting can be a real nuisance during an interview if you forget to turn it off before placing the call. For this reason, we strongly recommend getting a second phone without the Call Waiting feature. Use it for your interviews and let your answering machine pick up calls coming into your original line.

Now you're ready for the second phase—actually making the call. There are a number of ways this can go. In the best of all possible worlds, you would reach every person the first time you tried. The interview would give you everything you need. You could write up the final report for the client that afternoon, and we could all go home early.

Step 2: Initial contact

Sometimes that does happen. But not often. Usually you'll run into a screen of the "And what may I say this is in reference to?" variety. We're assuming here that you have the name of a specific individual you want to call. Calling a large company or government agency without a specific name, though necessary at times, is to be avoided whenever possible.

When you encounter a screen, it is important to be able to phrase your goal as succinctly as possible. You do not want to have to explain every detail to a screening secretary or executive assistant. At the same time, you want to pique the interest of the source you are trying to reach.

How to make the most of a screen

If the screen says, "Perhaps there's something I can help you with," don't disregard the offer. As we said earlier, many "lower-level" people are very eager to talk. Often they know a great deal about a topic, but no one ever asks them to discuss it.

It is even possible that the person serving as a screen actually wrote the article or the program or whatever that caused you to call, although the boss got credit for it. Everything depends on what you are after. If nothing but the insight and analysis of the particular individual you are trying to reach will do, then you will have to make every effort to speak to that person.

Tips on technique   But if all you need is more information on a particular topic, "Perhaps I can help?" can be a wonderful opportunity. You might say, "Why, yes. I'd like to know more about your firm's automated hog inoculator." Ask your questions and really listen to the answers. Don't interrupt to ask your next question until the person has run out of things to say. Sometimes silence can provide a golden opportunity because people quite naturally feel obliged to fill it. By all means let them. Don't make the person uncomfortable, but don't rush in to raise a follow-up question until the person has finished. Instead, make a note of the follow-up point and bring it up later, during the next lull in the conversation.

Use this technique regardless of who you are speaking with—screen or target source. And don't forget to be complimentary. Extol the article the person has written. If John Doe has told you that this particular person is the leading expert in the field, be sure to mention the recommendation. If someone else has said that this is the ideal person for you to talk to, mention that as well. Never forget that these people are doing you a favor. In most cases, talking to "inquiring minds who want to know" is not part of the job. So be pleasant, polite, and appreciative.

Making an ally   Of course, not all screens are information gold mines. But that does not mean you should dismiss them out of hand. Often a screen can save you some time. It may be, for example, that the source you wanted to speak with no longer covers your area of interest. The screen doesn't have to tell you that when a simple" I'm sorry, Ms. Smith is not available" will do. But if you are personable and don't treat the screen as a roadblock, you may hear something like this: "Ms. Smith no longer covers that area. The person you want to speak to is Mr. Jones. Hold on a moment, I'll ring him."

At this point, you've got an ally. The screen has become your temporary advocate within the organization. The call to Mr. Jones comes with the screen's introduction and approval. Consequently, Mr. Jones is much more inclined to be helpful than if you had called him directly.

On some occasions, you may receive a counter-request to submit your questions or query in writing. In an earlier age, submitting a written request for an interview would have been everyone's first step. But not today. Today, we advise trying the phone first. If that doesn't work, you can always fall back on sending a letter. In fact, you can fax the person a letter so it will arrive immediately.

Seizing (& keeping) the initiative   Only you can decide whether to play this game if it is imposed upon you. It all depends on how badly you need this particular individual's input. (And bear in mind that through no fault of their own, the sources you think you want to interview may not have the information you need.) If you do decide to send or fax a letter, be sure to include a phrase at the end of your missive noting that you will be calling back to follow up later on today or tomorrow. You may or may not wish to give the person a bit more time, but under no circumstances should you leave the next move up to the source.

The most likely outcome of your initial call is that the person you want to speak with will not be immediately available. Your response here is to ask the screen, or whomever else you are talking to, when would be a good time to call back. Again, keep the initiative firmly planted in your own hands.

If the screen demurs, ask if there is someone else you could speak to who may be able to help. If the screen suggests Ms. Jones, do whatever you can to contact her. The idea is first to see if Ms. Jones can give you the information you need, and if not, enlist her in your quest to talk to your original source. You want to get beyond the screen, in other words. It may be that Ms. Jones will be seeing your source in a meeting tomorrow. Perhaps she could mention that you are trying to get in touch?

When you call your source again, you may then be able to say that "Ms. Jones told me she would speak to Mr. Smith and tell him I would be calling." That will give even the most diligent of screens pause. The person will almost certainly have to check with Mr. Smith to notify him that you are on the line.

These are only a few possible scenarios. The key thing, as when conducting the interview itself, is to sense your opportunities and to improvise freely. What Sue says about searching online applies equally well to working the phone—you have got to think on your seat.

You will undoubtedly find that the first few calls are the most difficult. This is because at that early stage you probably will not have "referral information." You won't be able to say, "Dr. Perkins suggested I give you a call," or "I was referred to you by Susan Evans." Sometimes, however, you can finesse the situation by searching to see if your target source has written any articles. As you will discover in Part three of this book, conducting such a search can be relatively easy using an online database. Often if you can say, "I've just read the piece Ms. Jones did in the *Journal of Enlightened Hog Farming* and I'd like to ask her a few questions," the screen will put you right through.

Winning at telephone tag

It's entirely possible that all of your sources will be eager to talk to you, but are simply unable to do so at the time you call. In such cases, ask when would be the best time for you to call them back. If at all possible, do not leave the callback up to the source. You're the one who needs the information, after all.

Callbacks are an unavoidable part of phone work. The trouble is that when you are working on a project and calling several people, you can generate a long list of people who will be calling you back in no time at all. This presents a real dilemma for which there really is no ideal solution.

You can take it as given that if you have arranged for callbacks, you are tied to your office for the rest of the day. The trouble arises if you have a list of ten people to call and currently have five callbacks pending. What will almost certainly happen is that as you are interviewing Source Number 7, Source Number 3 will be trying to reach you.

If you have a single phone line equipped with Call Waiting, this does not present a technical problem. But it does present an interpersonal problem since in order to deal with the second call, you must put your current source on hold. Some people will be understanding, but most will resent it.

Add a second line & a "roll-over" feature

A much better solution is to eliminate Call Waiting completely. You can do this by adding a second phone line and equipping both Line 1 and Line 2 with answering machines. Better still, equip Line 1 with an answering machine and plug Line 2 into a fax machine with a built-in answering machine. (Alfred uses a Panasonic KX-F250 combination fax and answering machine for this purpose.)

Next, contact your phone company and tell them to cancel Call Waiting and replace it with a feature that causes any call coming in on Line 1 while Line 1 is busy to "roll over" to Line 2. This service doesn't cost any more than Call Waiting, and it is much nicer for all concerned.

Line 1 is the number you give out as your voice number, and Line 2 is the number you give out as your fax number.

This means that if someone calls your voice number and you don't pick up, the call will be taken by the answering machine attached to Line 1. Alternatively, if someone has called you on Line 1 and you are speaking with him as another call comes in, that call will be rolled over to Line 2. If it is a fax call, the fax machine will accept the fax. If it is a voice call, the fax machine will activate its built-in answering machine.

Whatever happens, nothing gets through the net you have raised. And no one gets irritated by Call Waiting signals.

There are two other refinements you might want to consider. First, people may be more willing to call you back if they can reach you by dialing a toll-free "800" number. Sprint, AT&T, MCI, and other carriers offer 800 numbers at reasonable rates—usually for a monthly fee of $25 or so, plus any long-distance charges. And, of course, you don't have to publish your 800 number. You can give it out only to those folks you want to encourage to call you back. You will be charged for the call, but you can pass those costs through to your client.

Second, you may want to consider adding a third phone line. You may not want to do this right away. But suppose you want to be able to do an online search using Line 3, while you are talking to someone on Line 1 and receiving a fax on Line 2. This sounds like a lot of activity, but it isn't unusual at all in either Sue's or Alfred's offices. So it is something to think about when you're paying the phone company to come out to activate a second line. Only you can be the judge, but why not go for a third line while you're at it?

Now we're ready for the main event. You've gotten through the screen, and the person on the other end of the line is indeed the source you want to interview. Like the "friendly letter" you learned how to write (or at least *should* have learned how to write) in high school, an interview has several distinct stages.

The first is the salutation. The second is the body—the real meat of the matter. And the third is the closing and gracious good-bye.

Each stage is important, but the salutation is the most important of all. "Meeting" someone on the phone is no different than meeting them in person. First impressions count. It's not impossible to counteract a bad first impression and to turn things around in the interview, but it's certainly not the best way to proceed.

The best advice we can give you about making your best first impression is simple—let your own personality shine through. If you've got a lousy personality, you probably won't be aware of it, since even those few friends you have will probably be loath to tell you. So you might as well assume that you have a wonderful personality. You're a bright, imaginative person with knowledge and interesting comments to make on a whole range of subjects. You're exactly the kind of person anyone who is also bright and imaginative would like to sit down with at a cocktail bar for a stimulating chat.

And, oh, by the way, you've got this job to do researching hi-tech hog farming. You've read up on the subject, but there are still a few points for which you need more details. Could the source possibly take just a moment to help you understand thus and so?

In other words, be yourself. Let the inner "you" shine through. Make every attempt during the salutation phase to establish rapport with the source. This should not be mechanistic. If you're the type of person who's good at phone work, it will come naturally. Be cheerful and optimistic. Leave no doubt in the source's mind that you are going to be a bright spot in his or her day.

At all times, put yourself in the shoes of the person you are calling. During the first few moments of a call, your source is wondering who the hell you are, what you want, and why you want it. The person is also likely to be thinking: Are you going to make me look stupid by asking me questions I can't answer? Are you going to be like Dan Rather or a similarly obnoxious reporter? Will you use my name and get me into trouble? And how much time is all this going to take from my day?

Step 3: The interview

Be yourself

Put the source at ease

That's why you should make every effort to put your source at ease immediately. You know the person is busy. You promise not to take much time. But your research leads you to believe that this person holds the answers to some of your unanswered questions. In other words, take the "you approach," not the "I approach." Never forget that your sources are doing you a favor. They do not *have* to talk to you.

The best way to introduce yourself is with complete honesty. Don't volunteer more information than you're asked. But don't be coy and expect your source to accept it. One technique that Sue uses is to say something like, "I'm Sue Rugge, and I'm calling from Berkeley." Often the source assumes that Sue is calling from the University of California at Berkeley. And if they don't press the issue, she doesn't explain further.

At other times, you may have to go into more detail. Often the way you introduce yourself depends on the assignment. If you're doing competitive intelligence, you will naturally be more circumspect than if you are researching some obscure subject.

You must never lie to a source. Not ever. It is not only unethical, it is also bad business, for lies will come back to haunt you. They destroy your credibility, and as an information broker, credibility is paramount.

Protecting your client's identity

But at the same time, if it is important to protect the identity of your client, you must do so. If the source presses you further, you may simply have to end the interview. Unless you have your client's permission beforehand, you can never tell anyone who you're working for.

Let's say you're working for a client interested in buying up a large number of hog farms and melding them into a lean, mean, high-tech hog producing machine. Tens of millions of dollars are involved. You call the editor of *Hog Producers Daily* to pursue a relevant story published in that estimable journal:

Sue "Hello, I'm Sue Rugge from Berkeley, and I'm doing a market research study on hi-tech hog farming."

Editor "Oh, and who are you associated with, Ms. Rugge?"

Sue "The Rugge Group. We do market research."

Editor "I see. And are you doing this work on speculation or for a client."

Sue "For a client."

Editor "And might I ask just who this client is?"

Sue "I'm afraid that's confidential. I can't reveal the client's name. But if you would be willing to speak to them directly, I will include your name in my report."

Sometimes, that stops the conversation. The source may simply refuse to be interviewed if you don't reveal the client's name. And unfortunately, there is no way to get past this fact. The source may say, "If they tell me who they are, I'll talk to them."

It's not uncommon for people to say that initially. They may say that they don't want to talk to an intermediary. But in reality, 75 to 85 percent of the time you never have to go through an interview of the sort we've shown you here. Most people will not press you like this. Most will be cooperative.

However, when you do encounter a uncooperative subject, you can simply make a note of the fact and pass it along to the client. It may very well be that the client will want to call personally.

And what do you do if this individual is the only one in the country who has the information you need? In that case, you try to keep the person on the line. Explain how much you value the information the person could impart. You're sorry you can't reveal the client's name, but it's a company highly respected in the industry and you would really appreciate just a few moments of time to discuss a couple of issues . . .

Does No mean NO?

Sometimes sources will try a gambit. They may say they only talk to principals, not intermediaries, just to see what *you* will say. We're not advising "Don't take 'No!' for an answer." We merely want to point out that once a source has refused you, you have very little to lose by persisting. Nicely, of course. But it doesn't hurt to keep them talking. People's opinions change from moment to moment like the colors of a 1970s-era "mood ring." So even a "No!" doesn't always mean "No! No! A thousand times, No!" Sometimes it means "Let me think about it." By keeping a source talking, you allow time for that to happen.

Another thing to remember is that all the people you talk to are potential clients. A lot of times sources are very interested in what you're doing. It occurs to them that maybe you could do the same kind of thing for them, and you end up sending out your literature to those people. This is all the more reason to represent yourself as legitimately as possible.

Go with the flow

Let's assume that you've overcome any objections and that the source has said, "Okay, what is it you want to know?" You follow with the first of your prepared questions. But the source warms to the subject and continues talking, even after you have gotten the information you need.

Here you must remember the cardinal rule of conducting an interview. We've discussed it in general terms earlier, and now here it is in all its stark glory: Never cut off a source. You might have your own agenda, your own list of questions that you want to ask. But let the source go on as long as he or she wants. You have no way of knowing what pieces of information or additional lines of inquiry the source may offer this way. Many, many times in such situations a source will mention someone or something you haven't thought of or considered.

When that happens, you must be ready to follow up. Don't slavishly return to Question Number 2 on your list. Listen to what the source is actually saying and engage with the person as if you were holding a real conversation, not a Barbara Walters-style interview. It is one of the sad but typical ironies of our age that Barbara Walters is considered one of the greatest interviewers. She gets the name celebrities, yes. But as any viewer can tell, she is so focused on asking her next prepared question that she never listens to what her subjects are *saying*.

An interview should be a real conversation, with each person reacting to and building upon what the other has just said. As a skilled interviewer, you will naturally want to bring the conversation back to the questions you need to have answered. But you should also go with the flow. If you're really good, your sources won't be aware that you have a list of "must answer" questions. Instead, they will feel that they've had an enjoyable conversation about their area of expertise.

The closing   Just as the friendly letter has a natural winding down and ending—the traditional technique used by Alfred's nephews is "Well, gotta go now"—so too, with interviews. When you reach the natural end of the conversation, you might consider saying, "Gee, that covers it all. Is there anything I forgot to ask?" This gives the source one last chance to interject points that may have been passed over. And it sometimes brings to light other people or lines of inquiry you should pursue. Indeed, if no additional names or contacts surface, it doesn't hurt to press the point: "And can you direct me to any other sources on this subject?"

As the interview draws to a close, put on your most gracious self. Thank the source for cooperating. Indicate that you have really enjoyed the conversation. Summarize any promises the source may have made to send you additional information. Suggest that the information be faxed to you, or give the person your Federal Express number to emphasize the immediacy of your need. Then say "good-bye."

We have said it before, but it bears repeating. As information brokers we must never forget that an interview is an imposition. Yes, the source may willingly grant it. Yes, it may be—indeed, we hope that it will be—an enjoyable experience. But it is still a favor and good manners demand that you acknowledge that fact.

This last stage may be the most important of all. You've hung up the phone and put the recorder on rewind. Your impulse is to either get up from your chair and do something else or, in the frenzy of the hunt, pick up the phone and make another call.

Take our advice: Neither impulse is good for you.

Upon finishing a phone interview, the absolute best thing you can do is to review, annotate, and expand your notes. Your source's comments will never be fresher in your mind than they are at this very moment. Make yourself take the time to review them and, if possible, write them up. The idea is to capture the relevant points of the conversation you just had as completely as possible. This is especially important if you are not legally permitted to use a tape recorder. But even if a recorder is permissible, you will find that thoughts, questions, additional avenues to pursue, and many other ideas popped into your head during the conversation but were never verbalized and thus never recorded.

Much of the time it is very difficult to make yourself do this right away. Your body's tired. Your brain is full. You need a break. But you will thank yourself a week from now when you must return to your notes to prepare your client's report. At this very moment, you know exactly what information the source had to convey to you. A week from now, the ashes will be cold. You'll have to spend time bringing yourself back up to speed as you try to recall the conversation. It is so much easier in the long run to bite the bullet and summarize the interview now, even if your summary is nothing more than a long note to yourself about what was asked and what was said.

Finally, you may want to consider sending your source a thank-you note. Written thank-you's are so rare anymore that anything you send is bound to make a positive impression. Only two or three lines are necessary. Just a small token symbolizing your appreciation for the time the source gave you. If appropriate, on the basis of the conversation, you may want to include literature about your information/research service.

No surgeon reaches for the scalpel without a good deal of advance preparation. No information broker should reach for the phone without being equally well prepared. But while successful preparation is a function of the mind, a successful interview is largely a matter of personality. Your brain has to be working all the time, but it is not your brain that the human being on the other end of the line is talking to—it's you, the person.

So just be yourself. But be yourself at your best. Try not to do an interview when you're tired or feeling glum. If need be, take a moment before you call to meditate on everything that is good about your life. Push the bad thoughts away and focus on how much you enjoy the hunt and on how this source is going to supply a key piece of the puzzle.

Step 4: Assimilation of results

Conclusion

Always assume that the source does indeed have the information you seek and that obtaining it will not be a problem. You'd be surprised how often that proves to be the case. If your preparation and preliminary research have been thorough, there is an excellent chance that you will indeed be calling the right person. Even if you have your doubts, conveying a feeling of optimism that the source can help often stimulates the individual to go the extra mile for you.

And as we said earlier in the chapter, don't forget to be genuinely complimentary. If the source is an authority in the field, make it clear right up front that you are aware of that fact and grateful for the opportunity to speak with him or her. If you can say that, on the basis of your research, the source is clearly the one person who can best answer your questions, by all means say it.

People will see through blatant flattery. But by the same token, if you are aware of these kinds of facts about a source, there is no reason to leave them unspoken. By acknowledging them, you are not merely being complimentary. You are also demonstrating that you have done your homework and thus automatically raised your credibility in your source's eyes.

Always take great care to listen—really listen—to what the person is saying. Nuance, inflection, hesitancy, tone, nervous laughter, and all the vocal devices people use to convey nonverbal information become crucial when you're on the phone. With no body language or other nonverbal cues to support them, they are all you have to work with. It is entirely possible for someone to convey a meaning that is completely the opposite of the words he or she speaks, merely by the way the words are spoken.

Above all, have fun with it. Normally we hate it when people say that about a task or a job. But in our experience, phone work really is fun. On many levels. It's an intellectual challenge; it's a test of your interpersonal skills; and it is almost always rewarding to encounter another human being.

In the next chapter, we will look at phone work of an entirely different sort. We'll introduce you to the many marvelous things you can do with a computer, a modem, and a telephone as we introduce you to the "electronic universe" of databases and online communications.

11 Welcome to the electronic universe!

In this chapter we'll introduce you to the electronic universe of personal computer communications. You will see that this vast realm divides naturally into five parts: information, communication, Special Interest Groups (SIGs), services, and interactive games.

We'll help you get acquainted with each of these areas and what they can do for you as an information broker. We think you'll enjoy the tour.

Don't worry about the technology just yet. In the next chapter we'll show you exactly what you need and what to do to go online. And in the chapters after that we'll go into much more detail about how to use the power that exists at your fingertips. Here we'd like you to concentrate on getting the lay of the land. We want you to start developing a feel for the kinds of things that are available and how this universe is structured.

Sue Rugge founded her first professional research business in 1971, and for the first year or so the business was literally based in a shoebox. Not until 1974 did she buy a terminal to begin accessing the six databases the newly formed DIALOG system began offering in 1972. As you'll learn in the next chapter, a terminal is not a personal computer. The first personal computer didn't appear until 1976.

Alfred began writing professionally in 1973, using the same Royal Ultronic that had seen him through college. Some years later he bought a Smith-

Why the electronic universe is essential

Corona, the one with the cartridge ribbons that load from the side and pop in and out. Alfred wrote five books on that machine and in 1980 wanted nothing more in the world than a correcting IBM Selectric.

Things have changed considerably since then. It is hard to believe, but for a number of years, there was a good deal of doubt about whether one needed a personal computer at all. It was a nice option, apparently, but no one really understood what it could do or what it could mean. In some circles, much more effort was spent debating whether a dot-matrix printer produced output of acceptable quality for business correspondence than on how a PC could boost productivity.

Alfred vividly remembers his first encounter with a dedicated word processor, a personal computer that is optimized for text production. Though a business associate swore by it, Alfred thought it was a toy. A correcting IBM Selectric—now there was a machine to conjure with.

It took an hour of "playing" at the word processor's keyboard one afternoon. After that, Alfred was hooked. Within six months, he had a CPT word processor of his own, complete with a half-screen black-on-white display and a single eight-inch disk drive. It was simply self-evident that no writer, at least no writer who makes a living at his trade, could possibly do without the power such machines made available.

The same is true in the information business. An information broker needs a personal computer for all the normal business chores—correspondence, accounting, keeping track of inventory or clients, and so forth. But that's not what makes it *essential*. What makes a personal computer essential these days for writers and information brokers alike is the electronic doorways it opens via the telephone.

A simple process

The basic process is easy to explain. When you hook your computer to the phone line using a device called a *modem*, you can connect your machine to a distant computer. That's called "going online." Once the connection is made, each time you hit your *A* key, the code for that letter goes out over the wire, ending up inside the distant computer and being displayed on its screen. When someone sitting at that computer hits his *B* key, the process operates in the other direction, and a *B* ends up on your screen.

Now, remove that other person and substitute a computer program designed to respond to the commands you send it from your keyboard. You want to know what the *Wall Street Journal* has written about the XYZ Company? The distant computer will check its files and transmit the full text of those articles to your screen, just as if they were being typed by some incredibly fast secretary.

All you have to do is tell your own computer to capture the incoming text and save it on your disk drive. You can then say good-bye to the distant computer and break the connection. Once you're offline, you can review the text you have captured with your word processing program, print it out, incorporate key paragraphs (properly credited, of course) in your report, and so on. We'll go into more detail later, but basically that's all there is to it.

The electronic universe

Obviously, the value of a service like this hinges on the remote computer and the information it has access to. If all that remote system could offer was a database of recipes or people interested in yoga, or national potato production figures, it would be of limited value.

But suppose it's a system like DIALOG, that offers over 500 separate databases, including files like "America: History and Life," files containing every report published by the Associated Press since 1984, the Arab Information Bank, Biography Master Index, databases of every federal or state registered trademark, a database listing every book in the Library of Congress, and a database of world patents.

All of a sudden, that system becomes very interesting indeed. For not only does it give you access to concentrations of information you aren't likely to find in any library, it also gives you the power to search through that information in the twinkling of an eye.

Imagine standing in front of your library's card catalogue—with its thousands and thousands of three-by-five cards neatly arranged in row upon row of little drawers. Imagine being able to stand there, snap your fingers and say, "Give me all the cards for books on home energy conservation published after 1983 but before 1994," and have them appear instantly in your hand. *That's* the kind of power these systems place at your disposal. Indeed, that's why more and more libraries are getting rid of their card catalogues in favor of terminals that you can use in exactly this way.

Hundreds of systems, thousands of databases

Database vendors like DIALOG, however, are only part of the story. There are many smaller systems, some of them offering only one database, like the one operated by Bloodstock Research that gives you access to the pedigrees, breeding records, and race records of all thoroughbreds in North America since 1922. The database is called Horse, of course.

There are also consumer-oriented "online utility" systems like CompuServe, America Online, Delphi, GEnie, and Prodigy. And there are 60,000 or more bulletin board systems (BBSs), most of which consist of a single PC sitting in someone's bedroom or basement. In years past, online utilities and the bulletin boards have not offered what we would call "industrial-strength" information. But that is no longer the case. CompuServe, in particular, has begun to assemble a very impressive array of major-league databases, and many bulletin boards exist for the sole purpose of covering some subject in great depth.

And we haven't even mentioned the Internet, that vast "network of networks" that links more than three million sites around the globe. As we will see later in this book, the Internet is filled with traps and treasures. When it's good, it's very, very good, and when it's bad, it's awful! But it cannot be ignored.

Nor have we mentioned the communications-oriented systems. A system like MCI Mail, for example, lets you instantly send letters, reports, memos, and other text files to fellow subscribers. If your correspondent is not a subscriber, you can order MCI Mail to print out a copy of your document at a location near your correspondent's home or office and put it in the U.S. Mail. With MCI Mail, you can also exchange messages with any telex or TWX machine anywhere in the world, and you can transmit text files to any fax machine (a great feature if you don't happen to have a fax machine yourself). Some of these features are also available from systems like CompuServe, GEnie, or Delphi.

The features, the services, the information—the sheer power that a communications-equipped computer places at your disposal—are so vast that they constitute nothing less than an entire universe. An *electronic universe*. The phrase is as accurate now as it was when Alfred coined it in 1983, particularly since, like the physical universe of stars and planets, this one has continued to expand since then.

Guidebooks for the tour

There are books you can refer to for more detailed information. Recent Glossbrenner books include *The Little Online Book* from Peachpit Press, *Internet 101: A College Student's Guide* from McGraw-Hill, *Internet Slick Tricks* from Random House, and the forthcoming revision of *How to Look It Up Online* from John Wiley & Sons. But these aren't the only books on the subject. Check Appendix A for other recommended Internet books.

While you're at it, check the reference section for the *Gale Directory of Databases*, edited by Kathleen Young Marcaccio. This is a two-volume set that is published twice a year. It is truly the authoritative guide to the industry. Volume 1 covers online databases (over 5,300 of them) and database producers (over 2,220 of them). Volume 2 covers CD-ROM, diskette, magnetic tape, handheld, and batch-access database products.

Gale Research and the many editors and advisors involved in the project have done a wonderful job. For more information, contact:

Gale Directory of Databases
Gale Research, Inc.
835 Penobscot Building
Detroit, MI 48226
(800) 347-4253
(313) 961-2242

As we suggested at the beginning of the chapter, the best way to get a handle on all of the various options at your disposal is to realize that everything in the online world falls into one of five categories:

1. Information
2. Communication
3. Special Interest Groups (SIGs)
4. Services
5. Interactive games

A handle on the universe

Of these, information and communication are the two major categories. Services and special interest groups are really just combinations of the other two, as we'll see later. And so, to some extent, are interactive games. For now, however, if you keep this five-part matrix in mind, you'll have a much easier time figuring out where everything fits.

The online information industry has two main types of players. There are the *database producers*, also called *information providers* or IPs (pronounced "eye-pea"). And there are the online systems or *vendors* like DIALOG, Dow Jones News/Retrieval, Newsnet, and others.

Information

The relationship between IP and database vendor is often very much that of wholesaler and department store. The IP supplies the database and the vendor makes it available to the public. Often this works well for all three parties—IP, vendor, and customer. The IP is free to concentrate on database development. The vendor handles software development, updates, billing, and advertising. And the customer can take advantage of one-stop shopping, using the same set of commands to search many databases on the same system and paying one itemized monthly bill.

A database can contain absolutely anything. It might consist of every article in *Time* or *Newsweek* magazine, or the most important economic and demographic reports and tables from the Census Bureau, or a catalogue listing and describing almost every piece of software for Macintosh computers. It could be the Yellow Pages or the White Pages of the nation's phone books, or the full text of a major reference book like *The Encyclopedia of Associations*. Basically, if there's a market for the information (and sometimes, even if there isn't), a database will be created to provide it.

What's in a database?

It is crucial to understand the wide open nature of the field. There are no standards. Thus one company can choose to create a database that contains, say, only the cover stories published by *Time* magazine, plus "other selected articles." It may choose to begin its coverage with, say, 1962. A different company might also choose to offer *Time* magazine in its database, but include every article. Its coverage, however, might begin with 1979. Still another database could decide to include only article *citations*—not the full text of the articles themselves—from *Time*. All three could say in their promotional literature that they cover *Time* magazine, but as you can see, their coverage is quite different.

We confected the above example to make a point. In reality, competitive pressures virtually rule out the existence of differences in coverage as significant as those in our example. The actual differences are more subtle. But they're there, and if you're going to hire or become a professional searcher, you have to be aware of them.

What format does the information take?

Because the information in databases can vary so and be so eclectic, it's impossible to classify them by content other than to refer to their coverage: "This one covers every U.S. doctoral dissertation written since 1861, and that one covers over 300 English-and French-language Canadian periodicals."

In terms of information format, however, things are a bit more uniform. There are three major formats you can expect to encounter online: statistical, full text, and bibliographic. Not every database falls into one of these three categories—some databases offer directory listings, for example—but as a new denizen of the electronic universe, you can't go far wrong if you keep these three categories in mind.

Most of us are familiar with statistical tables, though you may want to look at Fig. 11-1 for a classic example of online statistics.

Full text, of course, is full text—the complete text of a magazine, newspaper, or other article. All that's missing are any photos, graphs, or other illustrations. That can be an important omission, since photos, graphs, and illustrations may be vital to your quest. Undoubtedly illustrations of this sort will become available online one of these days. Until this happens, however, you may find that you must still track down the actual article.

Bibcites & abstracts

Bibliographic citations or *bibcites* are another matter. The closest most of us have ever gotten to a bibcite is having to prepare a list of them for a high school or college term paper. (Bibcites are the items that appear in your bibliography when preparing such papers.) Since most electronic information exists in bibcite form, it is worth taking a moment to understand what you can expect to find online—and how to find it.

By the way, you'll find that most information professionals truncate the term *bibliographic citation* even further than *bibcite* and simply refer to them as *cites*. We will use *bibcite* here to prevent confusion, but you may encounter the shorter term in practice.

Online databases, like those you might create yourself with Paradox, Microsoft Works, or some other personal computer database management package, are called *files*. Each complete item in the file is called a *record*. Each piece of information in the record is called a *field*.

Shown here is one of the many tables you will find in CENDATA, a database prepared by the U.S. Census Bureau. This database is available in a command-driven format on DIALOG as File 580. An easy-to-use menu-driven version is also available on DIALOG and on CompuServe (key in go cendata).

Some statistical databases contain only tabular matter, in which case you must search on the basis of the title of the table. CENDATA contains both statistics and paragraphs of text summarizing the data. For reasons of space we have not included the portion of the table that presented the data in 1987 dollars, and we have presented only a few paragraphs from the textual summary.

11-1

CENDATA (U.S. Census) online.

11.5.2 - November 1, 1991
TABLE 1. VALUE OF NEW CONSTRUCTION PUT IN PLACE IN THE UNITED STATES, SEASONALLY ADJUSTED ANNUAL RATE (BILLIONS OF DOLLARS)

Type of construction	Sep(p) 1991	Aug(r) 1991	Jul(r) 1991	Jun 1991	May 1991	Sep 1990
	Current dollars					
Total new construction	406.5	402.1	400.6	398.2	399.0	437.2
Private construction(1)	295.9	293.2	289.6	290.9	291.0	330.3
Residential buildings(2)	167.7	162.9	157.8	158.3	154.6	175.4
New housing units	119.0	114.6	109.7	106.7	103.2	121.6
1 unit	104.2	101.0	96.1	91.9	87.9	102.9
2 units or more	14.8	13.6	13.6	14.8	15.3	18.7
Nonresidential buildings	90.1	91.9	93.9	94.2	99.0	117.6
Industrial	20.0	20.4	20.9	20.9	20.7	22.5
Office	21.3	21.6	22.2	22.6	23.2	28.6
Hotels, motels	5.2	5.3	5.3	5.4	7.3	9.7
Other commercial	23.2	24.6	24.7	24.9	27.0	34.0
Religious	3.4	3.3	3.6	3.4	3.3	4.0
Educational	3.8	3.6	3.8	3.8	4.2	4.5
Hospital and institutional	9.0	8.7	9.0	9.1	9.2	9.9
Miscellaneous buildings	4.2	4.3	4.3	4.1	4.1	4.3
Telecommunications	(NA)	9.2	8.9	9.4	8.6	9.9
All other private	3.9	3.9	3.8	3.8	3.7	3.3
Public construction	110.6	108.9	111.0	107.3	108.0	106.8
Housing and redevelopment	3.8	3.4	3.5	3.6	3.7	3.7
Industrial	4.0	1.5	1.4	2.2	1.8	2.1
Educational	22.7	23.1	24.3	22.4	23.6	21.1
Hospital	2.7	2.6	2.7	2.5	2.6	2.5
Other public buildings	17.5	18.6	17.6	16.2	17.2	17.8
Highways and streets	28.2	30.0	28.7	28.8	29.2	29.8
Military facilities	2.2	1.8	1.8	1.9	1.9	2.5
Conservation and development	4.4	5.0	8.2	5.8	5.1	3.4
Sewer systems	10.8	9.8	8.9	9.9	10.1	10.2
Water supply facilities	4.6	4.9	5.1	5.2	4.8	5.3
Miscellaneous public	9.7	8.2	8.8	8.9	7.8	8.4

(NA) Not available. (p) Preliminary. (r) Revised.

11-1 *Continued.*   (1) Includes the following categories of private construction not shown separately: residential improvements, railroads, electric light and power, gas, petroleum pipelines, and farm nonresidential.

(2) Includes improvements.

Textual summary:

SEPTEMBER 1991 CONSTRUCTION AT $406.5 BILLION ANNUAL RATE

New construction put in place during September 1991 was estimated at a seasonally adjusted annual rate of $406.5 billion compared to the revised August estimate of $402.1 billion, according to the U.S. Commerce Department's Bureau of the Census.

During the first 9 months of this year, $301.1 billion of new construction was put in place, 11 percent below the $337.3 billion for the same period in 1990.

(etc.)

The easiest way to keep these terms straight is the classic example of a collection of canceled personal checks. All the checks together constitute the file. Each individual check is a record. Each piece of information on a check (the date, the payee, the numerical amount, etc.) is a field.

In Fig. 11-2, for example, all of the downloaded text constitutes a single record in the ABI/INFORM database file. The fields include each discrete piece of information in the record: the article title, the author, the name of the journal, the publication date, the ISSN (International Standard Serial Number) of the publication, and so on. The summary paragraph or abstract, the full text, and the collection of keywords at the end of the record are fields as well.

All records in a bibliographic database contain at least two components: the bibcite and a list of keywords or *descriptors*. The bibcite includes the article title, author's name, and all relevant facts about the source publication. Often the author information will include professional affiliation, which can be helpful if you need to reach the person for more information. Ultimately, the purpose of a bibliography is to make it easy to locate the books, articles, and other publications it contains.

In Fig. 11-2, the bibcite occupies the first several lines of the downloaded text. As you can see, it includes everything you need to know to quickly locate the original article in a library. But it doesn't include any real information.

Nor does it contain enough information to make it practical to search for this record. Remember, computers are nothing if not literal-minded. If a word does not exist in a record, there is no way the machine can find it, and the bibcite alone doesn't give you much to work with. For this reason, the creators of bibliographic databases almost always add a field of *keywords*. These words may also be called *indexing terms* or *descriptors*.

Here is a full-text record from the ABI/Inform database on DIALOG. (We've truncated it to save space.) The article title, publication, publication date, and other individual pieces of information constitute the fields. This record can be searched for and retrieved based on the contents of any of its fields, including the contents of the summary paragraph or abstract or the full text of the article itself.

11-2
*File, record, and field—
Bibcite and Abstract.*

DIALOG(R)File 15:ABI/INFORM(R)
(c) 1994 UMI. All rts. reserv.

00903394   95-52786

Core competence
Gillin, Paul
Computerworld v28n34 PP: 34 Aug 22, 1994
CODEN: CMPWAB
ISSN: 0010-4841
JRNL CODE: COW
DOC TYPE: Journal article
LANGUAGE: English
LENGTH: 1 Pages
AVAILABILITY: Fulltext online. Photocopy available from ABI/INFORM
WORD COUNT: 452

ABSTRACT: An editorial discusses Apple. The company is going in a lot of different directions at the same time, and unless it gets focused, it may spin out of control.

TEXT: Apple is enjoying relatively good financial health right now and has just completed a difficult hardware transition, but I sense that the hard part is just beginning for The Other PC Company.

Apple is arguably the most consistently innovative company in the business. But it is going in a lot of different directions at the same time, and unless it gets focused, it may spin out of control. Depending on whom you talk to at Apple today, you'll hear that the company is committed to the corporate market, small business, the home, education, personal digital assistants, electronic services and set-top boxes. No one has been able to establish a beachhead in all those markets. And Apple won't either because it's got other worries right now.
.
.
.
Apple can try to be all things to all users and settle for 10% corporate market share. Or it can focus on doing one or two things really well. Right now, it seems to have selected option A. I'm not sure that's such a great choice.

THIS IS THE FULL-TEXT. Copyright CW Publishing Inc 1994

COMPANY NAMES:Apple Computer Inc (DUNS:06-070-4780 TICKER:AAPL)

GEOGRAPHIC NAMES: US

DESCRIPTORS: Computer industry; Software industry; Competition; Market strategy
CLASSIFICATION CODES: 9190 (CN=United States); 8651 (CN=Computer industry); 8302 (CN=Software and computer services); 7000 (CN=Marketing)

The people who add these keywords work for the database producer and are called indexer/abstracters. They are professionally trained to read each source article and decide which keywords best describe its contents (the issues, topics, or concepts it covers) and where it fits in the overall scheme of things. The keywords the indexer/abstracter decides on may or may not appear in the source article.

Controlled vocabularies

How does the indexer/abstracter know which words to choose? The answer is that indexing terms are almost always drawn from a predefined list of words called a *controlled vocabulary*. The complete controlled vocabulary used to index a database is called a *thesaurus*.

For example, John Wiley & Sons, the producer of the Harvard Business Review Online (HBRO) database, has established a list of 3,500 authorized index terms that includes everything from *ordnance* to *x-ray apparatus*. The words *ammunition* and *x-ray machine*, in contrast, are not on the list and are thus not used as keyword descriptors. The only way to determine this fact is to look up *ammunition* in the HBRO thesaurus, where you will be told, "See ordnance." Needless to say, if you plan to do much searching of a database that uses a controlled vocabulary, it's essential to either have a copy of its thesaurus or learn how to take advantage of the online version that's sometimes incorporated in the database itself. Wiley, incidentally, sells the 400-page HBRO thesaurus for about $50. (Of course, many databases also use additional identifiers and descriptors which are not "controlled.")

Including abstracts—the other bibliographic option

A record consisting of a straight bibliographic citation and a list of key index words can be quite serviceable. Indeed when the information industry was starting and computer storage costs were high, most of the time it wasn't economical to offer anything but bibcites and keywords. Of course there were exceptions. The National Technical Information Service (NTIS), for one, has had searchable abstracts from the beginning.

There is also the fact that communications speeds were four to six times slower than they are now, making it impractical to transmit significant quantities of text. There were few complaints from end users, however, since most were librarians with easy access to the source material and since online databases represented such a leap forward.

Some commercial databases, like Information Access Company's (IAC) Magazine Index, still offer nothing but bibcites and keywords. (IAC's companion product, Magazine ASAP, offers the full text of many of the articles referenced in Magazine Index.) But it is much more typical these days for the producer to include short summaries or abstracts of the source article as well. They are usually prepared by the same professionals responsible for indexing a database.

The abstract of the article in Fig. 11-2 is quite short, and the full text of the referenced article follows. But often a good abstract will not only give you a better idea of whether it would be worthwhile to obtain a copy of the source article, it may well contain exactly the fact, figure, or statistic you're looking for. In such cases, the abstract can eliminate the need to obtain the source article. As noted, the abstract itself is considered a field in the record, and it is almost always searchable on most vendors' systems.

As a new online searcher, you may be tempted to believe that because it is more complete, a full-text database is *ipso facto* better than one offering bibcites and abstracts. But that is definitely not the case. In fact, much of the time exactly the opposite is true.

A database of abstracts is usually much easier to search, particularly if you are a new user. Unless you are looking for a very specific and unique combination of words, searching a full-text database can be treacherous. With so many words, the potential for unexpected (and thus irrelevant) combinations and occurrences of your search terms is enormous. You can easily end up retrieving and paying for articles that have nothing to do with your subject of interest.

Abstracts can also save you both time and money. For example, if you wanted information on the bacteriocide market in Japan, would you rather read a complete 1,000-word article or a short, fact-packed abstract of the article? You might pay as much as $2 for the full text or about $1.50 for the bibcite and abstract. Not a great difference, but if you are looking at a lot of articles, it can mount up.

When searching for bibcites and abstracts of interest, the fields of each record are obviously crucial. Records are what you are after when you search a database, and fields are the only way you can hit them. In fact, each time a system finds a record containing one of your keywords, it's called a *hit*.

Finding information is thus a lot like the carnival game in which the object is to dump the pretty girl, good-looking guy, or perhaps a clown into the water by hitting a target with a baseball. You know someone's there. You can see your victim through the protective cage. But you'll never knock the person into the pool unless you hit the target.

In the carnival game there is only one target. In a database record there are many. That's important because the more fields a record contains, the more precisely you can focus your search. Needless to say, the number of fields a record contains is up to the database producer and the database vendor or online system on which the database resides. We'll have much more to say about online databases and how to search them later in this book.

How to find the information you want

Communication

The second main part of the electronic universe is communication "from any machine—to any machine—any place in the world." If industries had mottos, that would be the stated goal of the various telex, fax, personal computer, and electronic mail providers and equipment makers that constitute the world's data communications industry.

Computer communications is an entire sub-universe all by itself, so we cannot cover it in depth here. As an information professional, however, it is important for you to be aware of what *can* be done if the need arises. If you happen to hook up with a particularly computer-savvy client, for example, you may want to be able to offer to deliver your search results and/or reports by electronic mail.

If you have international clients, you may want to be able to communicate via the worldwide telex system—without buying or leasing a telex machine yourself. Though, these days, it is more likely that both you and your client will be able to use Internet e-mail. And, of course, everyone these days knows the value of fax machines. What most people don't know, however, is how easily faxes can be sent from a personal computer. It's easy to receive faxes as well, if you have a little inexpensive equipment.

What follows, then, is a whirlwind tour of the main communications options available in the electronic universe. These include electronic mail (e-mail), computer-generated paper mail, file exchanges, telex/TWX connections, and facsimile messages. We'll give you names and addresses to contact when appropriate, but for a more complete treatment, see Alfred's *The Little Online Book*.

Electronic mail

All electronic mail is rooted in a single concept: the ability of computers to store messages just as they store information. It is very simple. When you want to send a letter, you go online with another computer—usually a commercial system with e-mail capabilities—and transmit the message you have prepared. The distant computer stores that message on its disks or tapes or whatever. At that point your job is over and you can sign off.

The complementary phase occurs when the person you have sent the letter to goes online with the same host computer and, with hope in his heart, keys in a command saying in effect, "Is there any mail for me?"

The computer responds with the equivalent of a bespectacled postman leaning over an oak countertop and saying, "Why yes, Mr. Jones. I believe I did see something in your box. Would you like me to get it for you now?"

That's it.

The only hardware components, other than the telephone system, are your personal computer and modem, the main computer, and your correspondent's machine. Everything in the field of electronic mail involves those three components and the options and possibilities available through each of them.

The many advantages of e-mail Electronic mail offers many advantages. For one thing, it gives the sender complete control over when a message is sent, and it gives the correspondent complete control over when it is received. This is something a voice telephone call cannot deliver since the recipient has to be ready to receive when the "sender" (caller) is ready to send. When you are separated by 3,000 miles of real estate and three hours of time difference, as Sue and Alfred are, the "on-demand" sending and "on-demand" receiving advantages of e-mail are particularly apparent.

In addition, electronic mail is the ideal way to quickly transmit information that would be far too detailed to convey in a voice conversation. Can you imagine what it would be like to have to verbally communicate the contents of the CENDATA table shown in Fig. 11-1, for example? With e-mail, you simply transmit the entire file to the other person's mailbox.

Though you don't read much about it, one of the main contributions the Internet has made is providing connectivity among electronic mail systems. For years the industry wrestled with something called the X.400 standard, a set of formatting rules promoted by the communications arm of the United Nations that was intended to make it easy for various e-mail systems to exchange messages.

Cross-system connections via the Internet

Unfortunately, the world's e-mail systems never really supported the idea. Thus, prior to commercial availability of the Internet, among the leading online systems only CompuServe and MCI Mail set up X.400 gateways. Certainly there were some exceptions, but basically, all the other systems dragged their feet.

The availability and popularity of the Internet changed everything. Customers demanded Internet e-mail access, and once every e-mail system was connected to the Internet, transmitting e-mail messages among them was a done deal, with or without X.400. This means that you can send mail from CompuServe via the Internet to an associate on America Online, and vice versa. And someone on GEnie or Delphi can send mail, via the Internet, to you.

Policies regarding charges for Internet e-mail vary, so be sure to ask your online system vendor. At this writing, for example, CompuServe charges a minimum of 15 cents for receiving any message sent to you via the Internet, but it does not charge you for sending a message.

It is also possible to exchange files over the phone with other computer users. Graphics or paint files (graphics files created by drawing programs like MacPaint or PC Paintbrush) are exchanged among Macintosh and IBM-

File exchange via e-mail

compatible users all the time, for instance. Program files are exchanged as well, though only among users of compatible computers. Indeed, finding and downloading files—whether on the Internet, on a BBS, or on systems like America Online and CompuServe—is probably the most popular activity in the electronic universe.

Files can be exchanged directly, from one personal computer to another. All that's required is that communications software at the receiving end be set for "host" mode. The sender can then call that system just as if he or she were going to log onto CompuServe.

Most of the time, however, it is much easier to simply send a file using the electronic mail feature of one of the commercial online systems. The only complication is that you have to be aware of whether the file you want to send is *plain text* or *binary*. If the file is plain text, you can simply transmit it to the mail system as if it were a message you had prepared before signing on. A good example would be a letter or report you prepared in WordPerfect and then saved to disk as a plain ASCII (pronounced "as-key") text file. ASCII is explained in the next chapter.

A binary file, in contrast, contains characters that are not meant to be displayed, so you can't send them like a text message. A good example would be a program file like SORT.EXE or a graphic file like PIECHART.GIF. Files of this sort have to be *uploaded* (sent) and *downloaded* (received) using an *error correcting protocol*. The leading protocols in the microworld have names like XMODEM, ZMODEM, Kermit, and CompuServe Quick B. It's not important to know how they work. All that matters is that both parties use the same protocol.

Electronically transmitted paper mail

MCI Mail, brought to you by the phone company of the same name, is the premier electronic mail system. It offers no information or databases but concentrates instead on superb person-to-person or person-to-group electronic communications. Other online systems have some of the same features, but no one does it better than MCI, so we'll use it as our example.

One of MCI Mail's most fascinating features is the option of generating paper-based mail. The company has printing facilities at various locations around the country and around the world. If you choose the paper mail option, your text will be transmitted to the location nearest your recipient. A copy will be printed and stuffed into a distinctive MCI Mail envelope and taken to the post office to go out with the first-class mail. Letters can be delivered by regular mail to any location in the world.

Domestic and international   The cost for domestic paper mail delivery is $2 for three pages and $1 for each additional three pages. For international paper mail, the cost is $5.50 for three pages and $1 for each additional three pages. For purposes of comparison, if you were to send three pages to Europe via air mail, your cost would be about $3.67. Domestic and international overnight delivery is available as well.

Among other things, MCI Mail will let you put your letterhead and your signature on file with its main computer. You can then tell MCI Mail to use either or both when it is preparing a given paper mail letter. Since the company uses laser printers at all of its locations, it is easy to generate a cover letter bearing your letterhead (black ink only) and a facsimile of your signature.

Fax options   If your computer does not have a *fax modem* (a modem capable of talking to remote fax machines), you can tell MCI Mail to take care of things for you. You can, for instance, send the same letter to one person's MCI Mail mailbox, another person's CompuServe mailbox, and a third person's fax machine, regardless of where that third person is in the world.

In fact, the MCI Mail fax option can be particularly handy, even if you have your own fax machine. If a client does not have a modem, for example, you can transmit your search results to MCI Mail and tell it to send the file to the client's fax machine. This is often much more convenient than running the same pages through your own fax machine and, for technical reasons, it produces a higher quality printout on the client's machine.

MCI Mail is a system well worth checking out. It offers even more options than we have space to describe here. You can contact the company at:

MCI Mail
Box 1001, 1900 M Street NW
Washington, DC 20036
(800) 444-6245
(202) 833-8484 (in Washington, D.C.)
Mon–Fri, 9 A.M.–8 P.M., Eastern

Telex & TWX

It may very well be that you will never have to send or receive a telex message as an information broker. But, while it is rapidly being supplanted by fax, telex is still a major factor internationally. The word *telex* is short for "teleprinter exchange." The machines are also called teletypewriters (TTYs) or teletypes. Developed in the 1920s and 1930s, the telex machine overcame the most severe restriction imposed by the telegraph networks—namely, the fact that you had to know Morse code to be able to send and receive messages.

The telex machine is an electric typewriter-like device plugged into the telegraph network. A TWX ("twix") machine operates on the same principle. It sends and receives somewhat faster and is used only in North America. Like fax machines, telex and TWX machines provide "forced delivery," meaning that a hard copy is produced as the message is sent. With e-mail, in contrast, you've got to wait until the recipient actually signs on to a system or otherwise takes steps to check an electronic mailbox.

The only other thing you need to know is that you can use systems like CompuServe, MCI Mail, AT&T EasyLink, and other providers of e-mail services to send and receive telex and TWX messages. It's as easy as e-mail. The only twist is figuring out the address you will need to give your correspondents so they can send to you. Your best bet is to call customer service at your chosen e-mail system and ask.

Facsimile options

It's not impossible to do business these days without the ability to send or receive fax messages, but it is becoming increasingly difficult to do so. We would be hard-pressed to tell you which piece of equipment to buy first: a personal computer, a fax machine, or a photocopier.

It is a virtual certainty that sooner, rather than later, you are going to need to be able to send and receive facsimiles. It is quite natural to assume that this simply means buying a standard fax machine. And, indeed, for most people, this is what we would recommend.

But you should at least be aware that there *are* other options. If you want to send faxes, you can easily do so via MCI Mail, GEnie, CompuServe, and many other online systems. The process is identical to sending an electronic mail letter, except that instead of specifying a person's e-mail box, you specify a fax number.

This approach essentially eliminates the need to deal with busy signals, since the e-mail system will automatically make many attempts to get the fax through. There are two main drawbacks, however. First, you can usually send only standard ASCII text files (the same sort of file you would upload to someone's e-mail address). Second, you can send, but you cannot receive faxes via most e-mail systems.

Data/fax modems & laser printers

Another option is to buy a data/fax modem. Fax machines and online systems use different signalling techniques and thus require the use of different modem hardware. When they first appeared, fax modems were sold as free-standing products. But these days, it is much more common to find a single modem that offers both data and fax capabilities.

Most come with a data communications software package and a fax communications package. Though, of course, you are free to use any other software you like. Fax software varies in its capabilities but is essentially designed to fool your word processing program into thinking it is a printer.

The word processing program thus "prints" to the fax modem. That means that all the special fonts and graphical elements in your text are preserved. Your correspondent will receive a fax that looks like one you might have sent had you first printed your message and then used a conventional fax machine.

Getting set to receive   As for receiving faxes yourself, all you have to do is make sure your data/fax modem is on and that you have loaded the appropriate fax software. Whether you use Windows, DOS, or a Macintosh, the fax software is designed to sit "in the background" watching the modem. When a call comes in, the software will be activated and start to receive the incoming fax. The fax will be stored on your disk as a graphics file, which you can look at, print out, or send to someone else via fax or e-mail.

The data/fax modem solution is cheaper than a regular fax machine. If you have a laser printer, it has all the output advantages of an expensive "plain paper" fax machine. And, depending on your software, it can give you access to all kinds of computer-powered features like scheduling transmission to take advantage of the cheapest phone rates or broadcasting the same fax to many different people automatically.

But you'll need a scanner   The main drawback of the data/fax modem approach is that there is no provision for sending something that is not already in your computer. The only way to fax someone a newspaper clipping or magazine article with this setup is to add a scanner.

The scanner acts like a photocopier. The difference is that it pumps its output to your computer's hard disk instead of making a paper copy. Once the scanned image is on your disk as a file, you can fax it or e-mail it anywhere. It's neat. But expensive. The $600 or so you are likely to spend on a flatbed scanner is likely to be better spent buying a good fax machine.

The one time when a data/fax modem is clearly essential is when you are travelling with your notebook or laptop computer. In fact, such a modem can even eliminate the need to lug a portable printer with you. When you want a hard copy of something, you can simply fax it to the fax machine at the hotel where you're staying.

And the winner is a real fax machine!

Back at your office, however, you will probably find that you really need a conventional fax machine. There is simply no other sensible way to fax marked up pages, clippings, and other documents. As a bonus, you may discover that your fax machine can be used as a "convenience photocopier" as well. And many units now come with built-in answering machines. All for around $400.

Since you will almost certainly want a modem as well, however, you might as well make it a data/fax modem. These days it seems modem manufacturers throw in fax capability for free, since there is virtually no difference in price between comparable data/fax and data-only units. There are sure to be times when you find it convenient to send a fax directly from your word processing program. And, if you've got a fax machine, a data/fax modem, and two phone lines, you can use the fax machine as a convenience scanner. Just have it send a fax to your data/fax modem!

Special Interest Groups (SIGs)

The third major section of the electronic universe is comprised of the online Special Interest Groups or SIGs. These features go by different names on different systems. On CompuServe they are officially called Forums. On GEnie they are called RoundTables or RTs. Prodigy calls them Bulletin Boards and America Online calls them Clubs. Only Delphi actually calls its Special Interest Groups *SIGs*. Regardless of what you call them, the underlying concept is the same.

There are literally thousands of SIGs. The interests they are devoted to range from law to health and fitness to fine wine to sports, investments, or political issues. There is at least one SIG devoted to each brand of computer and one devoted to each leading software product. There is almost certainly a SIG devoted to any hobby you'd care to name.

Since a lot of information brokers are trained in traditional library science, many have little or no concept of how valuable this nontraditional source can be. Get acquainted with the SIGs on various online systems, and you just may be able to steal a march on your competitors. Or not. It all depends on the subject you have set out to investigate.

But one thing's for sure: SIGs have become too important for any information broker to ignore. Like online databases, they represent rich concentrations of specialized information. Better yet, they are interactive in that you can raise a question and be pretty sure of getting a response.

The three parts of every SIG

All online Special Interest Groups have three main areas or features:

- The Message Board
- The Conference Area
- The File Libraries

The message board is very much like a cork-and-thumbtack bulletin board. One SIG member will post a query or a comment. Other members read it, and some of them respond with answers, suggestions, or comments of their own. The discussion takes place over time. The result is a *message thread* that's the rough equivalent of a transcript of a meeting.

The conference area allows SIG members to "chat" among themselves by typing at the keyboard. CompuServe refers to this feature in general as a *CB Simulator*, harking back to the days when citizens band radio was all the rage. It is an excellent image, since the comments of each person are always preceded by a "handle," and multiple conversations take place at once, all jumbled up.

Online chat is an acquired taste. But sometimes the conference rooms are used to present guest speakers, and that's a different matter. Pick a field of interest and pick an expert. There is at least a chance that the expert has done a guest appearance in a SIG somewhere.

Among others, Steve Wozniak and John Sculley have appeared as guests in Apple-related SIGs, *Entertainment Tonight's* Leonard Maltin has appeared in a SIG devoted to show business, best-selling thriller author Tom Clancy has appeared several times in a writers' SIG, and so on.

The moderator will have introduced the person and made a few comments. Then SIG members will be allowed to ask questions of the guest. Some SIG member will have been given the role of recording secretary to make sure that a complete transcript of the interview is preserved.

That transcript will be stored as a file in the SIG library section, where you can find it, even years after the event took place. The transcript may be wonderful, or it may be useless, but the chances are it exists no place else. There are lots of other files in most SIG libraries as well. Computer programs, graphic images, press releases, price lists, files of the phone numbers of BBSs devoted to the SIG's main topic, and more.

Of course, not every SIG is worthwhile, or even terribly active. And you really do take pot luck when using a SIG's message board or file libraries. Certainly we cannot recommend relying on SIGs as a primary source of information. You may want to use them to simply post a message like, "Can anybody recommend an expert in Roman coins minted before 75 A.D.?" Post that in a SIG devoted to coin collecting, check back in a day or two, and you're sure to have one or more answers.

The "Information Broker's SIG"   If you are an information broker today or if you aspire to become one in the future, you cannot afford to be without a subscription to CompuServe. Brokers from all over the country meet to exchange tips in the Working from Home Forum operated by Paul and Sarah Edwards. (Key in go work once you have logged onto the CompuServe system.) This CompuServe forum is also the online home of the Association of Independent Information Professionals (AIIP). Once you become an AIIP member, you will be granted access to the infamous "Section 0" of the forum. (Okay, so it's not exactly "infamous," but it *is* invisible until you are granted access.)

We're going to touch only lightly on the fourth and fifth aspects of the electronic universe—services and interactive games. You need to know about them to have a well-rounded picture, but more than likely, they won't have a bearing on your professional activities.

Services & interactive games

Most services-style features are offered through general interest online utility systems like CompuServe, America Online, GEnie, Delphi, and Prodigy. Many systems, for example, give you access to Shoppers Advantage (formerly Comp-u-store Online), a shopping service offering discounts on over a quarter of a million brand name products. You can use the power of the remote system to search for the product or model offering exactly the features you specify. You can read a description, and if you like it and the price, you can tap a few keys and order it.

Electronic malls & banking

A number of systems have also created "electronic malls." These consist of a variety of "shops" sponsored by various merchants, including McGraw-Hill, Waldenbooks, Long Distance Roses, Gimmee Jimmy's Cookies, Sears, and many others. All such "shops" offer only a limited selection of merchandise, but ordering any item is as easy as hitting a few keys.

It is also possible to buy and sell stocks and securities online through companies like Charles Schwab or Fidelity Online Express and E*Trade. There are ways to pay your bills online. And on Prodigy, you can even do your banking—checking your balance, moving funds from one account to another, and so on.

At this writing, the services component of the electronic universe is thus centered around online shopping, stock trading, and to a very minor extent, online banking.

Carnage on the Information Superhighway

Now, to complete the picture, a word about games. From the very beginning, users of every kind of computer have found ways to play games with their machines. Indeed, games were among the first features to be offered by the consumer-oriented online systems. But, whether it was hangman, blackjack, or the classic text-based game, Adventure, your opponent was always the computer. This was a novelty more than a decade ago, but it's a real snoozer today.

Then someone figured out how to play a game like StarTrek with several people participating. Games of this sort show you a sector of the universe as a grid of X's, O's, dashes, and other text characters. You make a move by keying in a command, and the computer sends you a new screen of text characters reflecting your move and those of your various opponents. It's about as exciting as watching ice melt.

The next iteration was much closer to Sega and Nintendo. The game Air Warrior appeared on GEnie, and over time it came to support not only its original full-color graphics and joystick or mouse controls, but also multimedia-style, Soundblaster-compatible sound. Imagine being able to engage in a real-time dogfight with multiple players located all over the country. Your engines roar. Your guns rata-tat-tat. You hear a "ping" when your fuselage is hit. And your screen looks like Microsoft's Flight Simulator.

It may not sound like much to most readers. But Rupert Murdoch has recently bought Kesmai, the company that created Air Warrior, and the game is now up on Murdoch's Delphi system, as well as on GEnie. Dare we suggest that interactive games are likely to be the real motivating force behind the drive to build the Information Superhighway? (What happened to the "information"?)

Conclusion

No one knows what will happen. And anyone who claims to is just guessing. But as we hope this brief tour has shown, the electronic universe and Information Superhighway are destined to play an ever greater part in our personal and professional lives. As we have said repeatedly, however, the online information offerings—impressive as they are—will not be able to supply the answers to all your questions.

Regardless of whether you use any or all of the electronic universe features, it is essential that you at least have some idea of all that is available. That's what we've shown you here. In succeeding chapters, we will concentrate exclusively on the information side of things as we look at how to search an online database and how to make the most of a SIG library. But first, we've got to get you online. That's the subject we will turn to next.

12 How to go online

In this chapter we'll tell you everything you need to know to equip yourself to go online. Then we will walk you through the process step-by-step. With just a smidgen of practice, in no time at all, you'll be ready to stride into the electronic universe with confidence. Hundreds of thousands of people have done it, many, we are happy to say, with the help of Alfred's books on the subject.

However, so there won't be any misunderstanding, we should note right up front that "going online" and doing an "online search" are two very different activities. Some people may think that they mean the same thing. They don't. Going online simply means making a successful connection with a remote computer, a connection in which you type something and the distant computer responds.

Doing an online search means actually tapping into a database and looking for some of the information your client has hired you to find. Online searching is a complex, brain-intensive activity that requires an intimate familiarity with databases, online systems, and search commands. We'll give you a preview of what it's like in the next chapter. But you should know right now that years of study and experience, and a certain amount of inborn talent, are required to become a really good online searcher.

Still, everyone has to start somewhere, and we can say without fear of contradiction that all would-be online searchers have to start by learning how to get online in the first place. That's what we'll cover here.

What you need to go online

You don't have to be a computer expert to go online. But you do need to know a bit more about your system than how to turn it on. Either that, or you need the support of a competent computer dealer, if that phrase is not an oxymoron in your town. In truth, communications capabilities are so basic that even an incompetent dealer would have difficulty screwing it up. We are not talking about brain surgery here.

Any computer, regardless of make, model, or size can be equipped to go online. The equipment is ridiculously cheap—you can get out for slightly more than $100. You need at most five basic things: a serial port, a modem, a cable to connect the two, communications software, and a telephone line. We will start with a bit of background material and then explain each of these items in enough detail to help you see what's going on.

Note that Sue and Alfred have a little disagreement about how much "technical" information most information brokers need. Alfred feels that it is important for every online communicator to have a basic understanding of what's going on. Otherwise how can you hope to solve problems when they occur?

Sue feels that most information brokers would be better off spending their time drumming up business. As one of her friends says, "Who cares? The computer is a tool, like a pen. I don't want to know how they made the ink!"

Both points of view have merit. Fortunately, in a book, both can be satisfied. Thus, if you want to, feel free to skip ahead to the heading labelled "Telephone." If you are interested in more detail, some of it a bit technical, simply continue reading.

Bits, bytes, & ASCII

Computers operate with voltage pulses called *bits*, a term that is short for "binary digits." These are the famous 1's and 0's you have undoubtedly heard about. A single voltage pulse by itself doesn't amount to much. But when you put eight of them together, then you really have something. What you have, in fact, is called a *byte*. And what makes a byte useful is the large number of patterns of 1s and 0s it lets you create. When you've got eight bits to work with, a total of 256 patterns are possible, ranging from 00000000 to 11111111.

In a computer, each pattern has a different meaning. When operating in what we can call *text mode*, for example, the first 128 patterns represent the letters of the alphabet. There is a separate pattern or byte for each letter in uppercase and each letter in lowercase. There is a pattern for each of the Arabic numbers from 0 through 9, and one for each major punctuation mark.

About 31 patterns symbolize control functions, like "stop transmitting" or "move the cursor to the left margin," and so on.

All computers agree on what each of the first 128 patterns mean. This is what makes it possible for different kinds of machines, whether they are PCs and Macintoshes or mainframes, minis, and micros, to exchange information. None of this happened by accident, of course. The first 128 patterns make up what is known as the American Standard Code for Information Interchange or ASCII ("as-key") code set. The term ASCII thus means "text."

For easy reference, each pattern is referred to by its number. So each capital letter has a number—a capital *R*, for example, is an ASCII 82. Ditto for each lowercase letter—a lowercase *r* is an ASCII 114. The eight-bit patterns of 1s and 0s, you see, really *are* numbers. But they are numbers expressed in the binary or *base 2* system that is the foundation of machine language. Human beings use the decimal or *base 10* system, and it is as decimal numbers that most people refer to each ASCII code.

If you have a PC and would like to demonstrate the ASCII code for yourself, get to the DOS prompt. Then hold down the Alt key and punch in 82 on your numeric keypad. When you release the Alt key, a capital *R* will appear on your screen.

PC users can generate any ASCII code by holding down the Alt key and punching in the desired ASCII decimal number on the keypad. If you have a Macintosh, use your Keycaps Desk Accessory to do the same thing. Or you may be able to use your Options key.

Now, if you want to communicate with a remote computer, you must somehow find a way to get the patterns you are generating with your machine into the distant machine over the phone lines. That is what online communications is all about.

Serial or RS-232-C ports & cards

Your first problem is the phone line. Most wall jacks offer four wires, but only two of them are used for a telephone connection. (The other two are not used at all.) Your computer, however, uses 8-bit bytes. Inside the machine everything is connected by 8- or 16- or 32-line cables or printed circuits, and bits travel eight-abreast in parallel formation.

To follow the same procedure with the phone line, you would need at least eight wires going out and eight wires coming in (to carry the responses of the distant computer). Somehow you've got to convert the parallel formation of eight bits travelling together into a serial formation in which the bits in a byte travel single-file. That is the job of the *serial card* or other circuitry lying behind your machine's serial port.

A serial port, also called an *RS-232-C interface*, is one of your computer's doors to the outside world. You will see it as a spot at the back of your machine to plug in a cable connecting the machine to some other piece of equipment. On a Macintosh, the port is round and marked with a telephone icon. On a PC, the port is shaped like an elongated capital *D* containing 25 pins. Parallel printer ports look the same, except they have sockets instead of pins.

Today, most machines of every make and model come with at least one serial port and one parallel port as standard equipment. So you probably won't need to even think about this. In addition, if you choose an internal modem—one that is designed to be plugged into your computer's main circuit board—the modem board will handle the conversion from parallel to serial and back. Internal modems present you with a standard phone jack, not a round or D-shaped plug.

Modem

Why do you need a modem? Why can't you just plug the phone line into the serial port on your computer? The simple answer is that phone lines were designed to carry sound signals generated by the microphone in the telephone handset, not computer voltage pulses. If you want to send computer bits out over the phone, the voltage pulses must be transformed into sound. And if you want to receive computer information, the incoming sound signals must be converted back into voltage pulses.

The modem performs these transformations by *modulating* and *demodulating* the signals. The word *modem* is a combination of these two words.

There are two main types of modems: external and internal. To install an internal modem, you must open the computer's case and insert the modem into an empty slot on your computer's main circuit board. You then plug it into the phone line just as if it were a telephone.

External modems are free-standing "boxes" requiring three connections: They need to be plugged into an electrical outlet, connected to your computer's serial port with a cable, and plugged into the phone line.

Cables & comm programs

The computer industry seems to thrive on complexity. How else can one explain the fact that there are at least three different types of plugs that can be used to cable a modem to a computer? This is only an issue if you opt for an external modem. The way to deal with the problem is to be sure to ask your salesperson if the modem you're buying comes with the cables you will need to connect it to your particular computer. If it doesn't, have the person sell you the correct cables. The cost is usually no more than about $10.

A communications or "comm" program is needed to tie all the hardware components together and to get them functioning as they should. It is the comm program that opens the serial port and lets you talk to the modem. And it is the comm program that, on your command, records incoming information as a file on disk. Comm programs are also responsible for negotiating the connection between you and the remote system.

Communications programs are among the most widely available of all commercial and public domain or shareware programs. They all do the same basic things, and undoubtedly because of this, they tend to compete on who can offer the most exotic add-on features. Like feature-laden microwave ovens and VCRs, however, you will find that most of these extras go unused. Many modems come with comm programs. The software is usually quite basic, but it may be all you need.

Any telephone connection can be used to exchange data between two computers. It is even possible to go online with a portable or laptop computer and a car phone, though if you will be moving at the time, you will need a special cellular phone modem.

Telephone

If you are just starting out, you may be tempted to get by with one phone line to handle everything: voice, data, and fax. That may indeed work for a while, but we don't recommend it. If you're serious about being in business, you'll need at least two phone lines—one for voice and one for your modem and fax machine to share. More than likely, though, you will want at least three phone lines, and one of them should be a "business line."

As Sue says, "A lot of people try to save money by using residential lines instead of business lines. But I think that's a mistake. As an information broker, you need to have a business listing, both in the Yellow Pages and in the White Pages of the phone book. The only way to get that is to tell the phone company that you want one of your lines to be considered a business line. It costs a little more, but it's worth it.

"I leave my business line open for incoming calls. If at all possible, someone calling your business line should always get an answer, either from you or from your answering machine. That's why you don't want to tie up that line making your outgoing calls.

"I make my outgoing calls on a second line, and I do save money by designating it 'residential.' And I have a third residential line for my fax and modem. I'm a strong believer in having a dedicated fax line. The thing that drives me crazy when I'm trying to send a fax to someone is running into one of those systems that is either supposed to detect whether a human being or a fax machine is calling or that tells you to hit the pound key if you want to send a fax or the star key if you want to leave a message. Or whatever.

"Half the time the automatic detection system doesn't work. And if you do an automatic dial on your fax machine, you won't hear the recorded voice telling you which key to hit. So you have to pick up the fax machine's receiver and do the whole thing manually.

"I don't want to put my clients and potential clients through that. So I really recommend dedicating a phone line to nothing but your fax machine. You can always use that line to dial out, should you need the use of a third line."

Three lines will probably do it: A business line that you keep free for incoming calls; a residential line dedicated to your fax machine; and a residential line for making outgoing calls. As for your modem, you can connect it to either the fax line or your outgoing call line, whichever better suits your business.

For maximum flexibility, you may want to get a manual two-way switch that will let you connect your modem (or any other piece of phone equipment) to either of two phone lines at the turn of a dial. The cost is about $40 from Hello Direct, a mail-order firm that specializes in all manner of handy phone-related gear. For a free catalogue, call (800) 444-3556.

Finally, remember what we said in Chapter 10 about the need to disable Call Waiting before making a modem call. Depending on your preference, you may want to consider eliminating Call Waiting in favor of the phone company feature that will cause incoming calls to roll over to one of your other lines if the initial line is busy.

What kind of modem should you buy?

The answer to this question is easy. First, check to make sure that your computer doesn't already have an internal modem. That's not as stupid a suggestion as it sounds. Many brand-new machines these days come equipped with modems as a matter of course, and we know many new computer users who haven't the slightest idea of what their computers contain.

If you look behind your machine and do not see a regular phone jack or two, then you will have to buy a modem. How does $180 sound? At this writing, that's what you would pay for a 28.8 data/fax modem made by Zoom Telephonics and sold by the award-winning mail order firm, PC Connection/MacConnection. You can reach this company at (800) 800-0004 at any time of day or night, except between 5:00 P.M. Sunday and 8:00 A.M. Monday, Eastern time.

With a plug like that, it's important to emphasize that neither Sue nor Alfred have any "secret relationship" with Zoom or PC Connection. There are many other excellent modem makers and many other top-quality mail-order firms. But you're not going to get a significantly better price, and no one will treat you as well as these two companies. Zoom modems are made in the United States and they come with a seven-year warranty. The company has been in business since 1977, so it must be doing something right.

Why so fast?

Modem speeds are measured in bits per second (bps), and we have just told you to get a unit that can operate at a top speed of 28,800 bps or 28.8 kbps (kilobits per second). All modems are downward compatible. Which is to say, a modem with a top speed of 28.8 kbps can communicate with any slower modem as well.

At this writing, none of the online systems information brokers typically use supports 28.8 connections. (The "kbps" is often left out, since, presumably everyone knows that it is implied.) Only a few, like CompuServe, support the next level down, 14.4, and even then, only in a limited number of cities. The top speed most online systems widely support is 9600 bps.

So why not recommend a 9600 bps modem? Three reasons. First, you probably won't be able to find a 9600 bps unit for sale anywhere as you read this. The 14.4's and 28.8's have pushed them out of the market. Second, the price difference between a 14.4 and a 28.8 modem, at this writing, is only about $30. Third, if you ever plan to get what's called a *SLIP or PPP connection* to the Internet, you will definitely want to be able to use it at 28.8. As for the fax capability, it adds virtually nothing to the modem's price. And it can be nice to have.

Make sure it says "V.34"   It probably won't come up. But if someone offers you a 28.8 modem at an unbelievably low price, beware! The reason is that the official international standard for 28.8 modems wasn't approved until June 1994. It's called V.34 and pronounced "vee dot thirty-four."

Prior to this, modem companies made modems based on their best guesses as to what the V.34 standard would look like. They labelled these units *V.Fast*. Do *not* buy a V.Fast modem, should any still be around as you read this. You simply cannot be sure that one maker's V.Fast modem will work at 28.8 with any other maker's model or with models implementing the full, official V.34 standard.

Internal or external or PCMCIA?

As we said earlier, modems usually come with the basic software you need to use their features, whether it is data communications, fax, or even voice mail. Such software usually isn't the most powerful available. But it is almost always serviceable.

Thus, the only other thing you need to consider when buying a modem is what the industry calls its *profile*. There are essentially three modem profiles:

- Internal
- External
- PCMCIA

As we said earlier, internal modems are just circuit boards that you plug into a vacant slot on your *motherboard* (the computer's main circuit board). Once installed, you can plug an internal modem into the phone jack just as if it were a telephone.

External modems are free-standing boxes that require three connections: to the computer, to the phone line, and to an electrical outlet.

PCMCIA modems consist of shirtpocket-sized circuit boards that are protected by a plastic case and equipped to be temporarily plugged into a PCMCIA socket. The letters stand for Personal Computer Memory Card International Association, and while any kind of computer can have a PCMCIA socket, they are most often found on notebook computers.

Externals: pros & cons An external modem offers two main advantages. It can be used with *any* computer. As long as that computer has a serial port, you can plug in your external modem. Just mind your cable connections and plugs, as discussed earlier.

Second, external modems have little lights to let you know what's going on. The SD (send data) light flashes when you hit a key and the RD (receive data) light flashes as the remote system sends you information.

On the negative side, external units tend to be a bit more expensive than comparable internal models. And they are bulky to carry around. Ideal for a desktop system. Lousy for a portable.

Internals: pros & cons The two main advantages of an internal modem are, first, that it saves space on your desktop and causes less clutter. Internal modems draw their power from your computer, while externals need to be plugged into an electrical outlet. More cords, more cables.

Second, if you have an older PC, you won't have to worry about replacing your old serial card to be able to use a modem that operates faster than 9600 bps. It's techno-gobbledy-gook, but unavoidable. If you got your computer sometime prior to about 1992, you may not be able to use a 14.4 or 28.8 *external* modem with your current serial card because such cards have a top speed of 9600 bps.

The key question is: Does the computer have a 16650A UART? The UART is the Universal Asynchronous Receiver/Transmitter chip that is the heart of your serial communications port. If you're in doubt about what you've got, ask your favorite computer guru. Or run the program UARTID.EXE, available on the Glossbrenner's Choice disk Utilities 9, System Configuration Tools. The program will check your serial communications ports and tell you what it finds.

If it finds a 16650A UART chip, then you can indeed operate at 14.4 or 28.8 with the appropriate external modem. If it doesn't, then you will have to either replace the serial port connection or go with an internal modem.

PCMCIA: pros & cons Most notebook and other portable computers come with a serial port, so you can plug in a conventional external modem if you want to. Some external modems are no bigger than a pack of cigarettes. Alternatively, you might be able to equip your notebook with an internal modem. No muss, no fuss, just plug in the phone line whenever you want to communicate. It's neat, but then you are always carrying your modem with you as part of your computer.

The PCMCIA modem-on-a-card solution addresses both problems. It's very light, self-contained, and detachable. You don't have to take the modem with you unless you want to. And if you do want to, it can be carried someplace else. All of that is to the good.

The downside is the expense: PCMCIA modems tend to cost more than comparable external or internal models. And there's the convenience factor. An internal modem may add a bit of weight to your system, but it eliminates the need to think ahead. Who knows where you'll be before day's end or how many times you will want to be able to go online? If you've got an internal modem, you may not even have to worry about bringing along a phone cord, since you can simply unplug a telephone and plug in your computer at many locations.

Two other considerations: First, you may have to pay a bit more for a notebook equipped with a PCMCIA socket. Second, battery life. Internal modems and PCMCIA modems alike draw the power they need from your computer. If the computer is plugged into an electrical outlet, no problem. Otherwise, they will both drain your battery unless you remember to shut them off.

Buying or obtaining comm software

Selecting a communications program today isn't nearly as tricky as it was only a few years ago. Today almost all comm programs offer the same set of basic features and differ only in the "whistles and bells" department.

As we said earlier, most modems these days come with a communications program of some sort. If the modem can handle both data and fax, the software supplied with the unit will be able to do so as well. These programs, however, tend to be watered down versions of some commercial program. That's why you will almost certainly want to get something else.

At this writing, Procomm Plus from Datastorm Technologies and Qmodem from Mustang Software are among the leading comm programs in the PC world. Both products are available in DOS and Windows versions. In the Macintosh world, MicroPhone Pro from Software Ventures Corporation is among the most popular programs. White Knight 12 from The FreeSoft Company may also be worth considering.

The shareware alternative   Commercial comm programs like these are available from mail-order houses for between $90 and $140. But you should also be aware of the shareware option. As you may know, shareware is "software on the honor system." You get a fully functional program, with a ready-to-print manual on the disk. If you like the product, you are honor-bound to "register" it by sending the programmer the requested fee. Registration fees typically range from $25 to $40 for a major package, and registration often gets you a printed manual and telephone support.

Shareware packages can be downloaded from bulletin boards and online systems like CompuServe and America Online, but they can also be ordered through the mail for about $5 a disk. That's what Glossbrenner's Choice is all about. As you will see when you turn to that section of this book, Qmodem is the recommended shareware program for DOS users, and CommWin by Gerard E. Bernor is the one to get for Windows.

If you're a Macintosh user, call Educorp, one of the leading distributors of Mac shareware, and order Disk #4910. This disk contains Zterm, an excellent Mac comm program, plus StuffIt, the widely-used Macintosh file archiver and compression program. The cost is $6.99, plus $4 per order for shipping and handling. The phone number is (800) 843-9497.

Specialized comm programs

You should also be aware that some online systems offer communications software that has been optimized for their systems. In most cases, this special software is not required to access a given system. Any comm program will do. But in some cases, the special programs can make things easier and more automatic.

In the consumer world, for example, CompuServe offers the CompuServe Information Manager (CIM) and CompuServe Navigator. In fact, *PC Magazine* recently reported that there are some 20 "front-end" programs available for CompuServe, including the shareware favorite, TAPCIS. GEnie offers Aladdin. Many Delphi users swear by a shareware offering called D-Lite. Among the leading consumer systems, only America Online and Prodigy require you to use their own software, which is supplied free of charge as part of your subscription.

All such consumer-system programs are designed to save you money by making it easy for you to read, prepare, and respond to e-mail and SIG messages while you are offline. A typical session thus consists of three phases: the front-end program signs on to a system, picks up your mail and SIG messages, and signs off; you read and respond to same; then you direct the program to sign on again and transmit your replies and any new letters you want to send. Connect time, which is often billed by the minute, is thus kept to a minimum.

Information systems like DIALOG, NEXIS, Dow Jones News/Retrieval, and others also offer special programs designed to automate your sessions, keep track of the money you spend on the session (a great feature for information brokers), or process and analyze financial data once you are offline. You will want to check into offerings like these, of course. But remember that life will be simpler if you can use one communications program for all your online chores. No one should have to learn how to use a different software package for each individual online system.

We urge you to read the manuals for your comm software, your modem, and the online system you plan to use. Indeed, although many comm programs these days have excellent pop-up, context-sensitive help features, there's really no way to escape at least looking at the printed manual.

Fortunately, we can help by telling you what to look for. First, in all likelihood, you will not have to do anything with your modem. It will probably work just fine as it comes from the factory. Load your communications software and get into its "terminal mode." Key in AT. If you get an "OK" or "Okay" on the screen, the modem is almost certainly doing everything it should.

If you don't get the "OK" response, check to make sure that you used capital letters for *AT*. If you are using an external modem, make sure that it is turned on and the cable connecting the modem to the computer is firmly seated. If you still don't get "OK," check your modem manual and your software manual to see if they say anything about special requirements. Or call a computer guru friend for help.

Second, communications programs are capable of a variety of settings but only two combinations are widely used: 8 data bits, no parity, and 1 stop bit (abbreviated as 8/N/1); and 7 data bits, even parity, and 1 stop bit (abbreviated as 7/E/1). The setting of 7/E/1 is the lowest common denominator in the online world, and certainly the one you should use in the absence of any specific instructions to the contrary.

Third, you should also set your system for *full duplex*. The only exception is GEnie, which requires you to be set for *half duplex*. And finally, set your "baud rate" or speed to the highest speed your modem can deliver. Your modem will negotiate the speed of the connection with each system you call, attempting, of course, to connect at the highest possible speed.

At the risk of confusing you, two speeds are involved. There is the speed between your modem and the database or other online system you call, and there is the speed between the modem and your computer. Thus, if you set your comm program for a speed of 28.8, that is the speed that data will flow from the modem to your computer, even if the system you're calling communicates at a top speed of 9,600 bps. The reasons why this is a good idea have to do with on-the-fly data compression/decompression, a topic which is far beyond the scope of this book. So, as your Mom or Dad used to say, "Just do it. Don't worry about why."

Packet-switching networks

You also need to know about packet-switching networks. These are special telephone circuits designed to carry only computer data. Packet-switching networks are what make it affordable for you to call DIALOG's computers in Palo Alto, California, from your home office in Bangor, Maine. Most online systems can be reached via one or both of the leading packet-switching networks, SprintNet (formerly Telenet) or BT Tymnet. But many systems, like DIALOG, GEnie, and CompuServe, operate their own networks as well.

If you're going to call a bulletin board system, you will probably use regular phone lines and dial direct. But if you are going to call a commercial online system, you will almost certainly use a packet switcher of some sort. The key thing is to find a packet-switcher access number (to connect you with a "node" on the network) that is as close to your location as possible. That way, the connection will be a local call.

Commercial online systems have a vested interest in making it as easy as possible for you to access their computers. So many supply detailed instructions on how to connect. If they don't, or if you have any questions, you can always call their customer service number and ask for help.

The process itself

Now let's walk through the process of going online and capturing incoming information. We can do it using the free facilities of SprintNet, the packet-switching network that used to be known as Telenet. There is no need for you to have a subscription, account number, or password. The procedure is illustrated in Fig. 12-1. Here are the steps to follow:

1. Load your comm program and get into "terminal mode." Then open your capture buffer so that everything that follows will be recorded in a file on your hard disk.
2. Once you're in terminal mode, key in ATDT 1-800-546-1000. You will hear your modem go "off hook" and dial the number. The phone will ring. When your modem connects, the noise will go away, and you probably will see "Connect" or "2400/ARQ" or some other screen response from your modem.
3. After "Connect" or something similar appears, key in @. You should then see "Telenet" on the screen. You will be prompted for "Terminal=."
4. Respond to the "Terminal=" prompt by keying in D1. That's the terminal type for all personal computers, as far as SprintNet is concerned.
5. You will next see a prompt like this: YOUR AREA CODE AND LOCAL EXCHANGE (AAA,LLL)=.
   Your area code is obvious. Your local exchange number consists of the first three digits of your telephone number. So if your area code is 212 and your phone number is 555-1234, key in 212,555.
6. When the SprintNet "at" sign (@) network prompt appears, key in MAIL.
7. When you are prompted for a user name, key in PHONES. Key in PHONES again when prompted for your password. (The password PHONES will not show up on your screen.)

8. You will then be welcomed to the system. Some bulletins will appear. And, finally, you will see a menu—which we will leave you to explore on your own.

Here is a complete sign-on session to guide you and to show you what to expect. Just follow along, matching what you see here with the seven steps presented in the text.

12-1
Free online information from SprintNet!

```
AT
OK
ATDT 1-800-546-1000
CONNECT 2400/ARQ

TELENET
800 12.60

TERMINAL=d1

YOUR AREA CODE AND LOCAL EXCHANGE (AAA,LLL)= 212,555

@mail

User name? phones
Password?

Welcome to Sprint's online directory of SprintNet local access
telephone numbers.

For customer service, call toll-free 1-800/877-5045 (option #5).
From overseas locations with non-WATS access, call 404-859-7700.

                    US SPRINT'S ONLINE
        LOCAL ACCESS TELEPHONE NUMBERS DIRECTORY

            1. Domestic Asynchronous Dial Service
            2. International Asynchronous Dial Service
            3. Domestic X.25 Dial Service
            4. New Access Centers and Recent Changes
            5. Product and Service Information
            6. Exit the Phones Directory
```

When you are finished testing the SprintNet system, tell your communications program to close its capture buffer and the capture file. Then tell the program to have the modem hang up the phone.

Checking your results

Now for the moment of truth. Did you successfully capture incoming information to disk while you were online? To find out, get out of your comm program, load your word processor, and tell it to bring in the file your comm program used to capture text. With many comm programs, you can switch to your word processor or text editor and look at a file without actually leaving the communications software.

The entire session you have just conducted should be there as a plain text file. You can edit, reformat, and print the information you have captured, just as you would with the contents of any text file. After all, that's exactly what a "capture file" is.

If you are not successful in looking at the file with your word processor, check to make sure that you are using the correct filename. It's easy to forget the name you told your program to use as its capture file. And even if you do not forget, you may have mistyped it.

If you are certain that no capture file is on the disk, load your comm program again and immediately open your capture buffer. Then key in AT several times. Your Hayes-compatible modem will obligingly supply an "OK" each time, and these will be captured. Close your capture buffer, leave your comm program, and see if the file can be looked at with your word processor. If you are successful, sign on to SprintNet again and repeat the exercise.

Two final points on capturing

First, remembering to close a capture file before leaving your comm program can be as important as remembering to open it in the first place. If you don't close the file and tell the comm program to stop capturing, you could lose the last few lines of text, or even the entire session, depending on how your comm program handles things.

Second, plan to capture *everything*. Open your buffer either before you dial or as soon as you get connected and leave it open until just after you sign off. When you are doing an online search, particularly if you are an inexperienced user, you have a great deal to think about. And the connect time meter is always ticking. The last thing you should have to worry about is deciding what you want to save to disk as it comes in on your screen.

Once you are offline, with your capture file safely stowed on disk, you can easily edit it or otherwise clean it up with your word processing software.

Conclusion

That's the basic process for going online and getting information. Clearly, there is nothing to be afraid of. It is true that there are a number of little pieces you have to bring together—access phone number, account number, password, commands for controlling the remote system, and commands for controlling your own comm program. But after you've done it a few times, it will become second nature. Besides, many comm programs offer a "script" capability that lets them automatically dial the phone and sign you on to a specific system.

These are very simple scripts, and they are not hard to create. Our point here is that as an information broker, you should focus on how to use the online system you're calling and avoid getting caught up in the technicalities of hardware and software. In Alfred's opinion, you need enough information about how things work to be able to solve the common problems most people encounter. But we've tried to avoid telling you more than you really need to be able to go online with confidence.

Now that you've got the basics, you're ready to learn about the kinds of systems information brokers access nearly every day. In the next chapter, we're going to show you what you can expect once you connect with an online database. We're going to introduce you to the high art of online searching.

13 Databases & how to search them

This chapter is designed to do two things. It will give you a series of quick snapshots of some of the leading database vendors, and it will introduce you to the art of online searching. As you would expect, there is far more to know about the systems discussed here than a mere snapshot can reveal.

But the point we must emphasize in the strongest possible terms is that the discussion of online search techniques presented here is intended to serve as merely a brief *introduction* to the topic. A complete treatment is far beyond the scope of this book. Indeed, trying to learn online searching from any book or manual alone is like trying to learn open heart surgery by mail. It can't be done. Hands-on practice, supplemented by instruction from a seasoned professional if at all possible, is essential.

Our goal here is to give you a sense of what online searching is all about. We want you to see some of the tools you'll have to work with, and we want you to "try on" the special mindset you must adopt when you're in search mode. If you are an experienced searcher, you know these things already. So please feel free to skim lightly over this chapter.

If you've never done an online search before, you will want to continue reading. We'll show you the doors into this part of the electronic universe and try to guide you in the right direction. But only you can turn yourself into a professional searcher.

A consummate search artist

As it happens, we have a wonderful real-life example of the level of skill you can aspire to. Several years ago Sue and Alfred spoke at a conference organized by a fellow who was very high on "online." (The adjective *online* is rapidly becoming a noun and is used by many people to refer to the entire electronic universe.) Wouldn't it be great, he thought, if a professional searcher could be available at the back of the hall? During the meetings and the speeches, the searcher could use his or her skills to locate the answers to any questions people might pose. About anything.

As a promotional gesture, DIALOG agreed to provide a no-charge guest account number and password for the duration of the conference. All that was needed was someone to actually do the searching. Could Sue make any suggestions?

The conference organizer had great ideas, but he didn't really know what he was asking. It is one thing to sit down with a client, conduct a reference interview, and then return to your office where you can scream, tear your hair out, or pound your head against the desk trying to figure out where to start looking. It is quite another to sit at a PC at the back of a hotel meeting room and calmly accept any information request—*any request*—conference goers cared to throw at you.

The very model of a modern online searcher

There are perhaps only a handful of people in the world with the knowledge and skills to take on such an assignment. And it is our great good fortune to count one of them among our very best friends. Her name is Reva Basch, and for two days she sat at her machine accepting any and all questions from conference attendees. To watch her work was like watching a harpist magically stroke DIALOG's strings to produce the most elegant melodies.

Reva, as we have told her many times, is a consummate search artist. (She's also an award-winning writer, gourmet cook, and many other things, but that's another story.) If you ask her a question, she knows immediately which three or four databases are likely to produce the best results. And not just DIALOG databases. She is equally at home using NEXIS, Dow Jones, or any of the other major systems. She knows the approach to use and the commands to enter to get the most out of these databases at the lowest possible cost.

None of this is accidental. There is no button you can push that will automatically imbue you with this kind of knowledge. You've got to be clever, and smart, and you've got to know how to imaginatively apply what you've learned. But you've got to learn it in the first place. And the only way to do that is to study and practice and study some more. Reva Basch has been searching *every day* for nearly 20 years, and, as she says, she continues to learn and hone her skills.

Much of her knowledge, as well as that of many other top-notch information brokers, has been distilled in *Secrets of the Super Searchers* by Reva Basch. Published by Online, Inc., this book is available in bookstores and from Sue's Information Professionals Institute. (Use the order form in Appendix A or call (510) 649-9743 to order by phone. The cost is $39.95 plus shipping.)

Available training

When you contact DIALOG, NEXIS, and other systems for subscription information, be sure to ask about the training and seminars that are available. Most of the major systems offer training of some sort. Though, of course, the emphasis is always on the commands and procedures used on one particular system.

That's all to the good. But systems like DIALOG are actually "supermarkets" offering hundreds of individual databases, each of them different. Thus, you may also want to look into training programs offered by the producers of those databases. Companies like Information Access Company, Dun & Bradstreet, and UMI/Data Courier, for example, hold regularly scheduled training sessions designed to show you how to best use and search their products. Again, be sure to ask!

Snapshots of the leaders

At this writing, the online world is in a greater state of flux than at any time in its history. Mergers, consolidations, and closings are taking place everywhere. As you read this, the Data Star and Vu/Text systems have been absorbed by Knight-Ridder's DIALOG. The Mead Corporation has sold Mead Data Central and its LEXIS/NEXIS system to Reed Elsevier in a move to concentrate on its core business of paper products. The fates of BRS and ORBIT are uncertain, at best. And CompuServe is coming up fast as a source of major-league databases and information. (If you need any evidence of this fact, take a look at Glenn and Ruth Orenstein's *CompuServe Companion: Finding Newspapers and Magazines Online*, published by BiblioData and available from the Information Professionals Institute. See Appendix A for ordering information.)

Fortunately for you, magazines like *Database*, *Online*, *Searcher*, and others make a point of tracking what's going on. Better still, you can almost always find out the latest by checking into the Working from Home Forum on CompuServe, the place, as we've said before, where most information brokers hang out.

But you've got to start somewhere. That's why we recommend you contact DIALOG, NEXIS, Dow Jones News/Retrieval, and NewsNet. Explain that you're an information broker and would like as much information as they can send you about their systems (database catalogue, price list, list of available publications, etc.), including anything they offer in the way of training. When the information arrives, read it carefully.

Wait before you subscribe

But don't subscribe just yet. For one thing, subscriptions cost money. For another, you may be able to get a discount on your subscription. The Association of Independent Information Professionals (AIIP), the professional association for information brokers, has negotiated a number of attractive special subscription arrangements with many of these systems. (Sue Rugge is a past president of AIIP.) If you're going to be an information broker, you will want to join AIIP and thus, you might as well take advantage of these deals.

DIALOG

Far and away the industry leader, some of DIALOG's hundreds of individual databases are DIALOG exclusives. Some can be found on other systems as well. Most offer bibliographic citations and abstracts, though many full-text databases have been added in recent years. DIALOG also carries many directory, statistical, and chemical structure databases. The trademark database offered by DIALOG even includes graphics files for various "marks." This allows you to see what various registered trademarks look like. Costs vary from $35 an hour to nearly $300 an hour, and there are additional charges tied to how much and what kind of information you opt to display.

Contact:

DIALOG Information Services, Inc.
A Knight-Ridder Company
3460 Hillview Avenue
Palo Alto, CA 94394
(800) 334-2564
(415) 858-3785

NEXIS from Reed Elsevier

The system long known as Mead Data Central's LEXIS/NEXIS has recently been sold by the Mead Corporation to Reed Elsevier.

This system has always specialized in full-text databases offering the complete article or transcript. The LEXIS part of the system contains so much full-text legal information that it can virtually eliminate the need for an extensive law library. Since legal searching is a highly specialized field, we have not discussed LEXIS in this book. (Nor have we discussed WestLaw, LEXIS's main competitor.)

The NEXIS system offers the full text of hundreds of magazines, worldwide newspapers, wire services, and industry newsletters. The only bibliographic citations and abstracts on the system are those found in The Information Bank section, a collection of databases acquired by Mead Data Central from the now-defunct New York Times Information Service. The full text archive of the *New York Times* is available only on NEXIS, though Dow Jones News/Retrieval now offers the full text of the current issue.

Contact:

LEXIS/NEXIS
Reed Elsevier, Inc.
P.O. Box 933
Dayton, OH 45401
(800) 227-4908
(513) 865-6800

The Dow Jones News/Retrieval Service (DJN/R) offers scores of separate databases or services. None of them is bibliographic in the classic sense of the word, and many are produced in-house by Dow Jones and follow their own special formats. They include a variety of stock quotes, news, and the full text of the *Wall Street Journal*, a DJN/R exclusive.

DJN/R also offers access to the complete DataTimes database of local newspapers, and much more. There is even a special feature called DowQuest that uses artificial intelligence techniques to make it possible for the average person to enter a search request in plain English.

Contact:

Dow Jones News/Retrieval
Dow Jones & Company, Inc.
P.O. Box 300
Princeton, NJ 08543-0300
(609) 520-4000

Dow Jones News/Retrieval Service

NewsNet offers full-text access to nearly hundreds of trade, industry, and investment newsletters, and over 20 separate newswires. The newsletters you'll find on NewsNet are the sorts of publications that typically charge $250 or more a year for subscriptions to their printed versions. Some 20 percent of NewsNet newsletters have no printed counterpart and are available only on the system. NewsNet offers many other features as well, including access to both TRW and Dun & Bradstreet business credit reports.

NewsNet

Contact:

NewsNet, Inc.
945 Haverford Road
Bryn Mawr, PA 19010
(800) 345-1301
(215) 527-8030

Now let's look at the various fees you will have to pay when you set up and use an account on a database vendor's system.Unfortunately, there is no standardization. Subscription policies vary widely. As do the various ways you will be charged for using an online system.

Costs & account-related matters

In general, all the online systems or "database vendors" mentioned earlier operate in essentially the same way. Their suppliers, the database producers, provide the information in return for a royalty or percentage of the income derived from selling that information online.

The vendors incur certain costs in making this information available. They have to pay for their computer or "host system." And there are disk farms (rooms packed with mainframe disk drives); software; maintenance; computer center and customer support personnel; not to mention all the traditional business expenses of rent, advertising, and taxes. They have to count the cost of paying royalties to the database producers, and, of course, they have to make a profit.

Given these facts, one would think that deciding how much to charge would be fairly straightforward. In reality, exactly the opposite is true. You don't have to spend much time perusing the rate cards of the various vendors to realize that the information industry has no one consistent way of pricing its products.

As an information broker, you must be very aware of costs since they can rapidly eat into your profit margin. Among the various ways online systems levy charges are these:

Connect-hour charges

Most vendors charge you for each minute you are connected to their system. You don't have to be doing anything to incur a charge. As long as the connection is open, you are at the very least using packet-switcher resources and occupying a port on the host system.

The actual connect-time cost varies with each database. This is due to differing royalty arrangements between the vendor and the information providers (IPs) who create the databases. A database created by the U.S. government might cost $45 an hour (including telecommunications costs), while one created by a private company might cost anywhere from $55 to nearly $300 an hour.

It is also worth noting that some vendors quote a single connect-hour rate that includes everything. Others quote a basic system connect rate, a database royalty rate, and telecommunications (packet network) costs. To get the actual cost you must add all of these components together.

High-speed surcharge

In the days when there were just two speeds—300 and 1200 bits per second—it was common for a system to charge double the 300 bps rate if you connected at 1200 bps. The idea was that although you are paying double, you are obtaining your information four times as fast and will thus spend far less time connected to the system.

In more recent years, as 2400 bps has been supplanted by 9600 bps, policies have changed. On one system you may be charged a different connect-time rate based on the speed of the connection. On another, the charges may be based on the number of characters, including blank spaces, you receive, not on the speed with which you receive them.

"Type" or display charge

The word *type* is a throwback to the days of "dumb terminals" with printing capability. These machines had no video display and were basically electric typewriters hooked up to the telephone.

Though many vendors still use *type*—it is still alive and well on DIALOG, for example—the term is thankfully being replaced by the more accurate word *display*. Both terms refer to displaying on your screen information retrieved from a database. (You may also hear the terms *hit charge* or *citation charge* used by some vendors to refer to the same thing.) Since display charges are assessed on top of connect-hour charges, when they were introduced they were generally viewed as a way to raise prices without being obvious about it.

As discussed next, display charges come in several varieties and often depend upon how much of a given record you elect to view.

"Print" or offline print charge

Databases that have display charges usually give you the option of having a record or parts thereof printed offline at the vendor's computer facility instead of being displayed on your screen. The hard-copy printout is then mailed to you by the vendor.

When terminals were dumb and communications speeds were limited to 300 bits per second, offline printing was more relevant than it is today. If you have done the search on DIALOG, you also have the option of telling the system to send the offline "prints" you have requested to your DialMail electronic mailbox. The cost is the same as a paper "print," but you will have to pay DialMail's connect-time charge (20 cents per minute) to pick up your "prints." On the other hand, when you use DialMail, you will have the information within 24 hours. You won't have to wait for it to arrive by mail. Better still, if your are a regular member of the AIIP, you can use DialMail free of charge!

Per-search charges

NEXIS is the only major database vendor to use this method. At this writing, you are, in effect, charged a minimum of $6 or more each time you hit the Enter key to transmit a new search command. This is in addition to a basic connect rate of about $40 per hour, including telecommunications charges. You will want to review the documentation and price list carefully. But in general, you can expect to pay at least $30 to $60 per search, depending on your skill and on the specific database you are searching. Mead also charges two and a half cents per line when you request certain online or offline output formats.

Pay for display

Variable display charges are almost always associated with bibliographic and directory databases, though display charges also apply to many full-text databases. A bibliographic or directory record is by its very nature divisible into discrete fields. It is thus relatively simple to impose a charge for each field a customer asks to have displayed.

It works like this: You enter a search command and the system goes away and locates the records containing your hits. Then, like a casino dealer holding the cards close to his vest, the system says in effect, "I've got all the fields for the records you asked for right here. But it's gonna cost'cha. Now, which cards would you like to see: Just the title and author? Just the title and abstract? The title, author, abstract, and indexing keywords? The full text of the article?"

Under this system, the more you ask to have displayed, the more you will pay.

The bottom line on database and online system charges is to make sure you are aware of all the charges that will be assessed when you search a given database on a given system. Do not take anything for granted. Do not assume that anything is included. On some systems, for example, you may be charged a different rate depending on which packet-switching service you use to access the system.

A quick-start introduction to online searching

As we have tried to emphasize, no single book can even begin to tell you everything you need to know about online searching. And even a book completely devoted to the subject is no substitute for actual online searching and practice.

In addition, every vendor's system is different. Every database on a vendor's system has its own little eccentricities. However, we can give you our best advice for getting a sense of what it's all about. It is a five-step process:

Step 1: Get a subscription to CompuServe

Since many modem makers include subscription offers to online systems in their packages, you may already have a CompuServe coupon of some sort good for an hour or two of free time. Policies can change, but in the past CompuServe has not charged a sign-up fee. Under the Standard Pricing Plan, the monthly subscription fee is $8.95 for unlimited access to a basic package of services. Call CompuServe at (800) 848-8199 for the latest details, and be sure to ask about the Executive Service Option, the subscription plan we think makes the most sense for most people.

Unfortunately, neither the Working from Home Forum nor the Knowledge Index is among CompuServe's basic services. So you will be charged $4.80 an hour for using that forum at 1200 or 2400 bps, and $9.60 per hour for accessing it at a speed of 9600 or 14.4.

Using the Knowledge Index (KI), on the other hand, costs $24 an hour, regardless of speed. And access to KI is available only after 6:00 P.M., your local time, on weekdays and all day during the weekend.

It is important for us to emphasize yet again that KI and the information you obtain by searching its databases is to be used only for your own personal needs. You are not permitted to use KI to fill information broker requests. You must use DIALOG instead.

When you key in go ki on CompuServe, you will be taken to a menu of information items, including items offering an overview, instructions, pricing, hours of availability, and so on. When you select the last item on the menu, CompuServe will actually connect you to the Knowledge Index system. (Assuming, of course that the local time is after 6:00 P.M. or that you are doing this on a weekend.)

Step 2: Use KI's menu system

The next menu that appears will give you a choice of using KI in *command mode* or in *menu mode*. Pick menu mode. Set a kitchen timer for 30 minutes and put it by your computer. Then settle back and explore. You may want to open your capture buffer to log everything to disk. A half hour will cost you $12, and at 9600 bps, you will be amazed at how much information you can collect.

At this writing, no printed manual for KI is offered. All the instructions you need are available online, but don't worry about that now. We suggest you plunge right in.

Some other time, you will want to sign on, key go ki, open your capture buffer, opt for instructions, and get everything you see on the resulting submenus, including "advanced techniques."

The searching information in this chapter will give you general concepts and techniques, all of which will make more sense after you've spent a half hour on KI.

Step 3: Read this chapter

Try finding a list of every book by your favorite author, for example. What can you discover about lead solder and domestic drinking water? What articles have been published in medical journals about some disease or condition? What substance is currently being used in place of Red Dye Number 4? And so on. The databases on KI hold the answers to all these questions—or they can tell you whom to call.

Step 4: Test yourself using KI

Since it is very easy to lose all track of time when you are searching for something online, you may want to set your kitchen timer once again. Give yourself 10 minutes from the time you actually enter the Knowledge Index system. If you haven't found what you're looking for when the timer beeps, sign off KI and CompuServe and review the results you have achieved.

Should you be looking in some other KI database? Is your search term or phrase too broad? Is it too narrow? In other words, *think* about each of the steps you have taken so far and the results they yielded. Then ask yourself what other steps you can take.

Step 5: Practice, practice, practice

Don't be too hard on yourself. Searching is anything but easy. And there is always the possibility that the information you seek does not exist in the 125 or so databases KI offers. Also, not everyone is cut out to be an online searcher. If you don't enjoy this kind of thing, don't do it.

As we have pointed out time and again in this book, there are two very distinct parts to a successful information brokerage business—sales/marketing and searching/information retrieval. You may enjoy doing telephone research and making sales calls a lot more than online searching.

If you do enjoy searching, however, it is not a bad idea to take advantage of the Knowledge Index to develop and sharpen your skills.

Eventually, you will probably want to learn to use KI's command mode, for example. And of course there is always more to know about any given database. The answer is practice, practice, and more practice.

Learning to use the Knowledge Index is clearly the best way to introduce yourself to the field of online searching. The experience will certainly help you decide whether searching is something you want to do, and it will prepare you to get the maximum benefit from the seminars offered by DIALOG, NEXIS, Dow Jones, and others.

How to search a database

Now let's turn our attention to the actual search process. We can only give you a preview of what it is like. But even so, you will find that there are two essential elements to successful online searching. The first is your mental approach to the problem at hand. The second is your familiarity with the tools available to get the job done.

The mental element is the more important of the two. Indeed it may be the most important factor of all. Certainly it's the most difficult to explain.

Here we will rush in where most others have feared to tread and attempt to offer some of our insights about online searching. We'll start with a discussion of how to develop the proper mental approach. Then we'll discuss many of the major tools and techniques you will use to start searching. We will use the Knowledge Index as our main example. But you should know that the concepts and approaches apply to all databases, even those which, like NewsNet, NEXIS, and most of Dow Jones, are not based on bibliographic citations and abstracts.

The best way to find the answers to questions about using a system is to spend some time with the database vendor's manual. Strive to get a handle on what the database contains and how it presents its information. Do your best to bring yourself up to speed.

Then call customer service. The information industry, unlike the computer hardware and software industries, has always put a heavy emphasis on telephone support. They've got the toll-free lines, the trained staff, and the years of experience to do the job right. Top-quality customer service is part of what you're paying for when you use an online system.

Often a customer service representative will not only tell you what commands to enter, but will also enter them at a nearby terminal to test them for you and make suggestions on how to improve on the results. You can then hang up, sign on to the system, and enter the same commands in "cookbook" fashion.

But don't stop there. Learn from the experience. After you are finished, log off and *think* about how and why the search strategy worked. You can't rely on "cookbook commands" forever, after all.

The database vendor's hotline is only your first option. There is an entire second level of customer support provided by the database producers. In the industry, these companies are known as *information providers* (IPs). Many IPs publish and sell their own reference manuals. The manuals and other materials explain how the database is set up, what it includes, and how to use any special codes or controlled vocabulary terms for precision searching.

Many IPs also maintain their own customer support hotlines, many of them toll-free. In fact, though it will stunt the growth of your information retrieval skills, you can often phone an IP with nothing more than a question like "How can I find information on Company X?" and receive a complete, blow-by-blow set of instructions on what commands and search terms to enter on a given system.

It really is crucial to have the right mindset when you are embarking on an online search. If you don't, you will simply burn up time and money and have nothing to show for it.

A mindset is a difficult thing to define. But we have done our best by offering what we call "The Five Rules of Search Success." And here they are:

Rule 1: Respect your opponent.
Rule 2: Define your target.
Rule 3: Consider the source: Who would know?
Rule 4: Don't go online unless you have to.
Rule 5: Know your databases.

Call customer service

IP support

The five rules of search success

Rule 1: Respect your opponent

It is vital to begin by developing a healthy respect for your opponent—the vast quantity of information that's out there. With so much information now online, it is exceptionally easy to simply dive in and drown.

Consider all the various forms the information you seek could take. If we assume, for example, that you have a client who wants to know about the market for decaffeinated tea, you could expect to find information on this topic in any or all of the following: general interest, trade, and technical newspapers and magazines; specialized newsletters; doctoral dissertations; government studies; and possibly even films, filmstrips, and videotapes. Multiply all of these by the number of countries in the world, and you can begin to appreciate the scope of what's available on this topic alone.

Rule 2: Define your target

One of the biggest mistakes new searchers make is to go online without a clearly defined idea of what they're after. If you do this, your information opponent will swallow you alive. For example, suppose your client is interested in industrial robots of the sort that weld cars together on a modern assembly line. We searched the ABI/INFORM database and discovered that there were over 70,000 articles containing the word *industrial*, nearly 5,000 containing the word *robot* or *robots*, and 396 containing the phrase *industrial robot(s)*.

Then we narrowed things to just the magazine *Business Week*, one of the more than 800 magazines that ABI/INFORM covers. It turned out that from 1971 through September of 1994, *Business Week* had published eight articles containing the phrase *industrial robot* or *industrial robots*. The most recent was a June 1993 article focusing on IBM's robotized tape-library data server machine.

Rule 3: Consider the source: Who would know?

One way to begin any search is to start with a methodical inventory of the resources at your disposal. The library card catalogue (paper or online) over here, the library's magazine and newspaper racks over there, several hundred books from A to Basque in the stacks across the room, right next to several hundred more from Cable TV to Czar.

That can be a useful approach. But it may be more productive to ask yourself, "Who would *publish* this kind of information? And how would each type of publication treat the topic?" In other words, instead of allowing your actions to be limited and channeled by what happens to be close at hand, whether it's a collection of databases or a collection of books, take control of the situation. This forces you to focus on the source material, and that has a number of benefits.

First, it emphasizes the fact that the information in an online database, whether it corresponds to a printed publication or not, has to come from somewhere. It isn't enough for an IP to say, as many do, "We've got a business database! Come search! Come search!" If information is to have any value, you've got to know where it came from. Is it from a reasonably impartial government study, a guaranteed-to-be-partial trade group, a reputable magazine, a newspaper with a particular viewpoint to sell, or what?

Focusing on source material is also one of the most important steps you can take toward ensuring successful online searches. For example, *Business Week*, *Scientific American*, *Beverage World*, and the *New York Times* could all be expected to publish information on decaffeinated tea. And you know, almost without thinking about it, that each one is going to take a different angle on the story.

Business Week could be expected to profile one or more leading firms and CEOs. *Scientific American* would report on the clinical evidence regarding the effects of regular and decaffeinated tea. Or it might go into great detail about the process of removing caffeine from tea leaves.

Beverage World, good trade magazine that it is, would zero in on market trends: who's doing what and what their plans are for the future. The *New York Times* might cover decaffeinated tea as a trend in a "Life Style" report or as a science report (if some new process were involved) or possibly as a business story (if some new company's shares were rocketing upward). But however it covered the story, the *Times* would not go into great scientific or business detail.

If you think about the kind of coverage you want, and if you think about the kinds of publications most likely to provide it, you can begin to zero in on the *databases* you should search by looking at the publications each database covers.

Databases don't always offer the easiest solution to your information problem. It is crucial to be aware that an electronic database is only one of *many* options. It's part of a continuum of information tools that includes all of a library's standard reference, index, and directory volumes (some of which are online); encyclopedias and handbooks; the card catalogue; interlibrary loan programs; and every other library resource. This continuum also includes the telephone and the U.S. Mail.

Rule 4: Don't go online unless you have to

There are lots of times when you will have to go online, of course. But when you've got a question, you might also ask yourself: "Who would know about this kind of thing?" One of your friends, contacts, or business associates? Maybe they know somebody who knows somebody you could call.

No luck? Okay, let's go online. But instead of trying to find the actual information you need, consider a different approach. Instead of looking for the answers to your client's questions, use the online tools to find an expert who can tell you what you want to know.

Let the reporters do the legwork   When you're looking for an expert, you'll frequently discover that the nation's magazine and newspaper reporters have done much of the work for you. If you search for even general stories on a topic, you'll find that most will quote one or more experts and cite their credentials and affiliations. The stories will also give you important background information and alert you to issues you may not have considered. When you use a database in this way, it doesn't much matter whether the abstract or referenced article contains the exact facts and figures you're after. If it contains the name of an expert or recognized authority, you've got the entry point you need.

Sign off the system, pick up the phone, and call directory assistance to get the telephone number of the university, corporation, consulting firm, or other organization with whom the individual is associated. You may have to make several calls. The expert may or may not be able to help you. But the chances are that he or she knows someone who can, and probably has that individual's phone number in the Rolodex.

When you do make contact with the right person, you'll be able to ask questions and explore topics in a way that you will never be able to do with a computer. And, thanks to your online search, you will be able to sound more intelligent and better informed since you will have picked up the basic vocabulary, learned the issues, and discovered the current trends.

Elementary, my dear database   When searching for information it generally makes good sense to turn first to those publications and sources you know best. But no one can be familiar with every information source. The real challenge, and much of the satisfaction, comes when you apply your Holmesian powers of deductive reasoning.

For example, if you're aware that almost every industry has a trade journal of some sort, you can deduce that one exists for the industry you are interested in without ever having seen or heard of it. Similarly, you can assume that most industries have at least one trade association. Even if it is a small industry, you can assume that some investment banking concern has prepared a detailed report on it, or on one or more of its leading companies. You can also assume that it falls under the jurisdiction of a governmental body somewhere that has probably prepared a report on it.

What are the names of the leading companies? Who are the executives of those firms? Is it possible that one or more of them has been quoted in a national magazine? In a local or regional newspaper? Have any of them written books on their experiences? You can obtain all of this information and much more from online databases.

On becoming an information detective   Information retrieval, in short, is anything but a passive activity. It is a skill that requires imagination, brainstorming, curiosity, and an ability to combine and extrapolate what you know into areas you have never explored.

Consider the problem of getting financial information on privately held companies. Because they do not sell securities to the public, privately held companies are not required by law to publicly reveal their balance sheets, income statements, and other financial data.

At first blush, you might think, "Well, that's that. No way to get the information." But you shouldn't give up so easily. Instead, ask yourself: Are there any circumstances under which a private company might voluntarily report its financials to someone? How about when it is applying for a loan? Come to think of it, don't most companies at one time or another have to fill out a credit report before their suppliers will do business with them? Who would have that kind of information?

If you're a businessperson, you can probably make a pretty good guess at the answer: Dun & Bradstreet (D&B), the country's largest credit reporting organization. Certainly it is worth a phone call to D&B to see if the information you want is available and to find out what D&B is likely to charge you to deliver it. Knowing what you now know about electronic information, it is also worth checking one or more database catalogs to see if the information is online.

Either way, you would almost certainly discover a file called D&B-Dun's Financial Records. Available on DIALOG, this file contains financial information, sans credit and payment history, on nearly one million firms, 98 percent of which are privately held. It is important for you to know, however, that while D&B information can be helpful, it may or may not be accurate. Through no fault of Dun & Bradstreet, reports contain only the information the subject company chooses to report. And there is usually no way to verify the accuracy of the information.

If you need credit and payment history information as well, you can get that through the NewsNet, DIALOG or other gateways to D&B or TRW, D&B's main competitor. You can expect to spend $50 or more for a business information report or a report providing you with payment history information. Contact D&B and TRW for the latest information and options. But note that these reports apply only to companies, not to individuals. And special restrictions may apply regarding what you as an information broker can do with them.

Of course things rarely work out as neatly as in this example. And no one is suggesting that you should have been able to arrive at the same solution on your own. The point is the *process*. The most successful searchers are those who adopt the creative, imaginative approach of an information detective.

Rule 5: Know your databases

How do you know which databases to search? How do you know which ones cover, say *Beverage World*, *Business Week*, and similar publications? It would be wonderful if there were a master database of databases that could give you an instant list of every database that covers a specific topic or every database that includes a particular publication. You could then simply search for every database that covered, say, *Time* or *Forbes*. Someday such an all-encompassing product may exist, but there is no such thing today.

Today, we have what amounts to a patchwork of database information sources. To begin with, there are the print or online versions of the leading database directories—like *The Gale Directory of Databases* cited earlier in this book. But, once you plug in, you will undoubtedly hear of other database reference works, both in print and online.

Ultimately, the only way to become an effective searcher is to become familiar with the databases and online systems that focus on your fields of interest. And that takes a considerable effort.

Just remember, each database is a separate product. You can't expect to bring yourself up to speed on all of them overnight. As with computer software, you will probably begin by using two or three databases fairly frequently and thus get to know them well. Gradually you'll branch out, and as your familiarity grows you'll add more databases to your repertoire.

Tools & techniques

Once you've got the right mindset, the next area of concern is the collection of tools and techniques databases offer to execute your search strategy. Here is where the pedal really meets your mettle as an online searcher, for there are so many tricks, twists, and turns to online systems and the search commands they offer that you could spend a lifetime studying them.

That certainly is not our purpose here. In this book we merely want to introduce you to the process of online searching so you can get some sense of what it is like. We have made no attempt at being comprehensive and we have not included all of the various refinements a professional searcher would weave in as a matter of course.

The importance of fields

As you will recall, databases like those on DIALOG, NEXIS, and the like typically consist of files, records, and fields. Most other databases use similar divisions, though they may not call them by those names or permit you to search them in the same way. Records are what you are after when you search a database, and fields can be one of the best ways to hit them.

For example, imagine a database created from your address book or Rolodex cards. If there is a field in each record for "Phone Number," you could tell the database software to retrieve every record containing the phone number "800-555-1234." That's not terribly useful. After all, how often do you know someone's phone number but not their name?

Suppose we break up the phone number into more precise fields. Suppose we restructure the records so that there is a field for "Area Code" and one for "Phone Number." If you were planning a trip to Los Angeles and wanted to be sure to call all of your friends when you're there, you could easily produce a comprehensive list. Simply tell your database software to retrieve every record in the file in which "Area Code=213" or "Area Code=818" or "Area Code=310," since these are the main codes for Los Angeles. (If you wanted to broaden your coverage to include surrounding suburbs to the north and the south, you might include "Area Code=714" and "Area Code=805.")

Now, look at the abstract in Fig. 13-1. We searched the ABI/INFORM database via CompuServe's Knowledge Index on the word *decaffeinated*. Then we narrowed the focus to *decaffeinated and tea*. We came up with 25 records, the first of which is shown in the figure.

As you can see, the first record summarizes an article that appeared in *Beverage World*, May 31, 1994. Each line that appears above the abstract paragraph contains one or more searchable fields: title, author, journal name, etc.

Thus, using KI's search commands (explained in the KI online help files), if you wanted to limit the search to just articles that appeared in the "journal" *Business Week*, you would include the following line in your search statement: JN=BUSINESS WEEK. If you wanted to limit things further by publication year, you would include: PY=1994 or PY=1992:1994. These two statements specify a "publication year" of 1994 and the range of years from 1992 to 1994.

In addition, the entire abstract is also a searchable field. So if you searched on *snapple* and *fruit drinks*, you would retrieve this record, since both terms can be found in the abstract. Now look at the end of the record. Company names, geographic names, descriptors (keywords), and classification codes are also searchable fields. (We'll have more to say about them in a moment.)

Our point is simply this: The fields in a database record let you fine-tune a search. If databases were not organized into fields, you would not be able to zero in on specific publications, date ranges, or anything else. Just imagine, for example, if you could *not* say to Knowledge Index, "Okay, I want you to look for '1994' in the date field."

Without this power, if you included *1994* in your search statement, you would retrieve everything in the database that contained *1994* somewhere in the record. If an abstract of an article published in 1984 contained the phrase ". . . may take until 1994 before things are straightened out," that record would be retrieved.

Full text as a field We should note that the full text of an article may also be treated as a field. This is the case in the example shown in Fig. 13-1. Notice that at the very beginning of the record there is a line reading "**USE FORMAT F FOR FULL TEXT**." As you will see in a moment, this record was retrieved by searching on *decaffeinated and tea*. Neither word appears in the abstract, but both can be found when you use "Format F" to view the full text of the article.

In this particular case, then, the entire ABI/INFORM record consists of all the fields we've discussed, including the abstract, and the full text of the article. Together, they form a single discrete unit of information. By displaying only the abstract in Fig. 13-1, we are, in effect, displaying only part of the "complete" record.

13-1

A complete ABI/INFORM search on Knowledge Index.

?BEGIN BUSI1

Now in BUSINESS INFORMATION (BUSI) Section (BUSI1) Database ABI/INFORM(R)_1971-1994/Sep W3 (c) 1994 UMI

?EXPAND DECAFFEINATED

Ref	Items	Index-term
E1	1	DECAFF
E2	4	DECAFFEINATE
E3	88	DECAFFEINATED
E4	1	DECAFFEINATING
E5	5	DECAFFEINATION
E6	2	DECAFFINATED
E7	3	DECAFS
E8	1	DECAGON
E9	2	DECAGW
E10	1	DECAHES
E11	3	DECAHYDRATE
E12	1	DECAID

?FIND E3 AND TEA

```
                88  DECAFFEINATED
              1979  TEA
S1              25  "DECAFFEINATED" AND TEA
```

?TYPE S1

00871776   95-21168

USE FORMAT F FOR FULL TEXT

Keeping up with the Snapples

Prince, Greg W.

Beverage World v113n1567 (Periscope Edition) PP: 18 May 31, 1994 ISSN:
        0098-2318 JRNL CODE: BEV

DOC TYPE: Journal article LANGUAGE: English LENGTH: 1 Pages

AVAILABILITY: Fulltext online. Photocopy available from
        ABI/INFORM 80095.00

WORD COUNT: 440

ABSTRACT: When Snapple Beverage Co. went public in December 1992, it boasted 52 varieties. Since then, 15 more varieties have been added to great corporate fanfare, including several hitting the market now. One change in the Snapple lineup is in the balance of presence between fruit juices and fruit drinks. In early 1993, there were 11 juices and 7 drinks. Now, there are 14 drinks but only 7 juices. In addition, all 4 diet sodas have been taken off the market, replaced by 3 diet fruit drinks.

COMPANY NAMES: Snapple Beverages Corp (DUNS:06-385-3998)

GEOGRAPHIC NAMES: US

DESCRIPTORS: Beverage industry; Market strategy; Product development; Changes

CLASSIFICATION CODES: 8610 (CN=Food processing industry); 7500 (CN=Product planning & development); 9190 (CN=United States); 9000 (CN=Short Article)

Do you have to specify fields?

We know what you're thinking. Suppose you just sign on to a system, enter a database, and type in the word or phrase you are looking for. Suppose you do not tell the database to look at specific fields. What then?

Well, the answer is simple. Like most online database vendors, DIALOG and the Knowledge Index are preprogrammed to search certain fields in each database. For example, if you simply key in a search term or phrase on KI, the system automatically searches the title, the abstract, the full text (if available), and the descriptors. On DIALOG, this preprogrammed selection of fields is called the *Basic Index*, and it varies with each database. The fields included in the Basic Index for each database are listed in the corresponding DIALOG "bluesheet."

You can tell a system to forget about its Basic Index and zero in on a particular field or series of fields if you like. Or you can tell it to search the Basic Index for a database as well as the other fields you specify. Although the specific commands differ, other online systems follow a similar practice.

Special fields

Most of the fields we've discussed so far require no further explanation. We all know what to expect in a date or author or journal name field. Even company names or geographic names (see Fig. 13-1) are relatively easy to figure out. But what are we to make of fields for *descriptors* and *classification codes*?

The answer is rooted in the information provider's desire to help you retrieve records with a high degree of precision. After all, finding and displaying records is what this business is all about. So not only is it the "right thing to do," it is also in the best interests of an IP to make it as easy as possible for you to locate the records you want in its database.

As an example, look at the descriptors at the end of the record shown in Fig. 13-1. None of the words found there (*beverage industry*, *market strategy*, *product development*, etc.) appears in the abstract. Nor, in fact, do they appear in the text of the complete article. (We checked.)

Yet someone who was interested in trends and niche marketing in the beverage industry would almost certainly want to see this record. Since none of those words is used in the abstract or the full-text article, if these descriptors were not attached to the record, that person might not find it. Descriptors are added to a record by an indexer/abstracter to give you a helping hand. The terms themselves are usually drawn from a special word list or *controlled vocabulary*, as explained earlier in this book.

Sometimes, in addition to indexing terms selected from a controlled vocabulary, a database producer will use subject or topic code *numbers*. These may simply be the U.S. government's SIC (Standard Industrial Classification) codes you may have heard of. Or they may be some elaborate and very precise system created by the IP. ABI/INFORM and the various Predicasts databases, among others, make extensive use of code numbers. There are codes for companies, major topics, subtopics, "events" like the announcement of a new product, codes for specific types of products, and so on.

The code numbers can be used exactly as you would use controlled vocabulary terms. You look up the topic you want on an IP-supplied list, note the corresponding code, and enter the number in your search statement.

Supplementary documentation

Every information provider does things its own way. You can thus expect each database to have its own unique array of fields. The Marquis Who's Who database on DIALOG and KI, for example, has at least five fields dealing with a person's education (degree, name of school, school location, years of attendance, and certification).

The Merck Index Online on DIALOG, a database of chemicals and drugs, has over 40 fields—everything from chemical names to boiling point to refractive index. The database Magill's Survey of Cinema has fields not only for film title, actor/actress, and screenplay author but for running time, videocassette availablility, cinematographer, releasing studio, and more.

The fields a database includes will always be mentioned in the "bluesheets," if it is a DIALOG database, or in equivalent publications on other systems. Keep in mind, however, that "bluesheets" and their equivalents are merely capsule summaries intended for quick reference. For a full explanation of how to use, say, ABI/INFORM's classification codes, you will need more documentation.

In almost every case, you will find complete explanations of the type of information you can expect to find in each field in the appropriate DIALOG documentation for "chapter" of the database. Database chapters are sold separately at a cost of about $6 each. All such chapters begin with a general explanation of the file and the fields included in its Basic Index (the preprogrammed collection of fields that will be searched unless you specify otherwise). They then explain each searchable field in turn. The chapters always conclude with several search examples and a list of additional documentation or search aid material that may be available.

We highly recommend buying the DIALOG database chapter for any database you think you may be searching on a regular basis, regardless of whether you will be searching the database on DIALOG or some other system. It is true that the commands used on different systems will be different. But translation usually isn't a problem, and the information a DIALOG chapter provides about a database can be equally useful.

But don't stop with the DIALOG database chapters. Contact the company that *created* the database to inquire about additional manuals, controlled vocabulary thesauri, code lists, booklets, training materials, and anything else that may be of use.

As we said earlier, the online information industry operates on two tracks when it comes to providing customer service and database documentation. The vendor offers things like "bluesheets" or their equivalent and possibly database "chapters." But to get something like a controlled vocabulary thesaurus, you must go to the information provider—the company responsible for creating and maintaining the database.

Of course, you'll have to pay for this supplementary documentation. Indeed, since sales volumes are low, the prices tend to be relatively high. A price of $50 or more for an IP thesaurus or special manual is not uncommon. Steep, perhaps. But when you consider that the information such supplementary documentation contains can easily save you that much in one or two search sessions, and when you realize that it will help you serve your clients better, the high price is easier to accept. Ultimately, buying supplementary documentation is simply one of the costs of doing business if you are an information broker.

Boolean logic & proximity operators

There are two final points we need to make in this whirlwind tour of online search tools and techniques. The first concerns the matter of "AND . . . OR . . . NOT" or *Boolean logic*. The manuals for nearly every database vendor system go into much greater detail, but basically, Boolean operators are used to tell the online system what you want. (George Boole, the man for whom this term is named, was an English mathematician who died in 1864.)

Picture yourself standing at a counter talking to a clerk. You want the clerk to get you recent articles mentioning certain American presidents and energy policy. You might say, "Get me everything you have that mentions Presidents Bush AND Clinton—but NOT Carter OR Ford—AND the word *energy* within one word of *policy*."

To qualify for retrieval, an article would have to mention *both* Bush and Clinton. But if it mentioned Bush, Clinton, and Carter, the article would not meet your specification and would not be retrieved. Similarly, if the record's only reference to *energy* and *policy* was in a sentence like "The President attacked the policy of imposing import duties with great energy," the record would not be retrieved.

This leads to our second point—*proximity operators*. As you can see from this little example, specifying *energy and policy* can produce articles that have nothing to do with the subject of energy policy. As long as both words are in the record somewhere, the record qualifies for retrieval.

That's why most online systems include proximity operators and/or phrase-searching capabilities. If you wanted to specify a particular phrase, you might have to put it in quotation marks ("energy policy"), for example. Or you might be able to enter a command telling the system to find only records in which *tax or taxes* occurred within five words of *increase*.

The tools at your command

There is much, much more to learn about the tools and techniques used in online searching. But already the outline of the process is becoming clear. You can key in a word or a phrase to have the system search its preprogrammed set of fields. You can use additional fields to focus a search on one or more specific aspects (publication date, controlled vocabulary descriptor, special subject or concept code). And you can use operators (AND/OR/NOT, etc.) to control which of these various focal points are considered and in what way.

Online searching really is like standing at a counter and telling a clerk what you want. The difference is that you may or may not know precisely what you want, and you almost certainly don't know every item that the clerk has in the back of the store. So searching becomes an interactive process and a process of successive approximations.

You stroll in and say, "Okay, I'm looking for something in energy policy. Not too old, but with lots of facts, figures and statistics. I'd like it to mention Presidents Clinton and Bush, but not Carter or Ford. Show me what you've got."

In a twinkling, the clerk tells you that the store has, say 1,200 items that meet your specifications. "Well, that's more than I had in mind," you say. "Could you take those 1,200 items and tell me which ones mention shale oil and the recycling of automobile tires?"

The clerk might say, "Sorry. There aren't any items in that 1,200-unit set that mention both of those topics." You think for a moment and then say, "Gee, that's too bad. I really was looking for an item like that. Well, how about everything I said before, but this time include President Carter."

The process—the "dialog"—between you and the clerk continues as you use the tools at your disposal to turn the dials and fine-tune your inquiry. That's what online searching is like. There is no guarantee of success. But it stands to reason that the more you know about the tools and how to use them, the more likely you are to walk out of the store with the merchandise you want at a fairly reasonable price.

Now let's put it all together and look at a real online search. The search was conducted on the Knowledge Index since this is the system we suggest you use for your own practice sessions. Once again, you are not permitted to use KI for business purposes. It is strictly for personal use and practice.

The five rules in action

We have used KI's command-line option since it is closer to what you will face on DIALOG and other major-league systems. As noted earlier, KI also offers an easy-to-use but less powerful menu option. The concepts demonstrated here apply equally well to virtually any command-driven system. The process starts with the Five Rules of Search Success we discussed earlier:

Rule 1: Respect your opponent.
Rule 2: Define your target.
Rule 3: Consider the source: Who would know?
Rule 4: Don't go online unless you have to.
Rule 5: Know your databases.

No problem with Number 1. If you don't have a pretty good idea of what you're up against by now, there's nothing we can do to help you. Now let's invent an imaginary client, say, someone who has developed a new process for removing the caffeine from tea. She's a scientific type with little exposure to marketing, but she wants you to prepare a report of the market for decaffeinated tea. That subject will be your target.

Who would know about such a thing? Well, there might be an industry association of beverage makers. Perhaps they have a study they can send you. Since the main outlet for coffee, tea, and the like is grocery stores, you might check to see if there is a trade group or association of American grocers you could call. What the heck, there's probably even some kind of group responsible for promoting tea consumption, funded by the tea industry, of course. The American Tea Council? It might be worth looking into.

Though we have not checked ourselves, our experience tells us that somewhere in this country there is almost certainly an organization that can send you some information about tea consumption in the United States. It might be a private industry group, or it might be some arm of the U.S. government. (Remember our earlier discussion of the potato expert Matthew Lesko found at the USDA? Why not tea?)

Naturally there's no way to tell what the information such groups may provide will consist of. There might be press releases and photocopies of articles published in various trade magazines. It may be nothing but a corporate annual report. But more than likely there will be something you can use: the names of the companies who make or are considering making decaffeinated tea, the names of key people at Lipton or Twinings or whichever companies own those brands. Your next step might be to contact one or more decaffeinated tea manufacturers.

Should you go online? Sure you should. The materials you receive from the firms and/or organizations you've contacted can help you refine your search. But you want to know a lot more about the topic, and a database search is ideal for that kind of application. But which database should you choose?

Before making up your mind, stop for a moment and ask yourself about the kind of information you want. Do you want a *Scientific American*-type treatment or the kind of article you'd expect *Business Week* to do? Whatever you decide, by asking yourself these questions you have automatically made the database selection process ten times easier. If you are new to the field, there's no way for you to know which databases cover which publications. But there are people you can ask and, as noted previously, there are directories you can consult.

Here's a professional tip: In general, if you are interested in a business topic, you should almost certainly begin by consulting PTS PROMT, ABI/INFORM, or Trade & Industry Index, or all three. These databases offer superb coverage of business magazines and trade and industry journals. Indeed, they are so good that no one else even comes close.

Twelve steps to online information retrieval

Yes, it's beginning to sound like a crazy New Age self-help guru has gotten loose on these pages. But lists can be wonderful things, and frankly we know of no better way to cut through the fog that surrounds information retrieval. Let's assume that you have decided to conduct an online search as part of your assignment to investigate the market for decaffeinated tea.

Step 1: Select your database   We've covered this pretty thoroughly. All that remains to be said is that you may eventually want to search *several* databases. Be aware, however, that at some point you're going to encounter diminishing returns. Overlapping coverage is fine since one IP's abstracts can complement another's. But if you search more than a few databases, you can very quickly end up with more information than you can successfully digest, and you will have lost much of the benefit of using electronic information retrieval.

Step 2: Check the vendor & the database documentation   Please, please, please do not omit this step. Discipline yourself to do it every time until you know the database so well you don't have to think about it. Which fields are searchable? Can you search by phrases or must you use words and proximity operators? What kinds of information does each field contain: words, code numbers, dates, controlled vocabulary terms?

Step 3: Meditate   Seriously. You may not be a ninja warrior preparing for battle, but it's not a bad analogy. If you ride in like a cowboy with six-guns blazing, firing off search terms as they come into your head, you'll stir up a lot of dust, expend a lot of ammunition, and be presented with a hefty bill—but very little relevant information—when you're done.

Think about the topic beforehand. Let your mind run free and flow into the subject. What do you know and what can you extrapolate about decaffeinated tea? What are the names of the companies known for selling tea? Have you read anything recently about the popularity of herbal teas? Could there be a connection? Who buys or is likely to buy decaffeinated products? Is there a health angle? And so on.

Try to develop a list of search words that come close to defining what you want. Some searchers try to think in terms of synonyms and word variants. The database thesaurus—if one exists for your target database—can help you there. We prefer an approach that's closer to free-association. Ultimately you'll develop a technique that works best for you.

Think about the source material and types of magazines or whatever you are searching. Then pick the words that you feel could logically be expected to appear in the kind of document you're looking for. The process is similar to writing up a bid specification. The document you want will have this, this, and this. It will be published between these dates. It will deal with such-and-such a topic, and so on.

Step 4: Select your fields   We can't tell you what fields to search since they vary so with the database. The author (AU) field may be virtually useless in a database of general interest magazines, but crucial in a database of book titles. The database documentation is your best guide to selecting the fields most likely to retrieve what you want.

Step 5: Write out your first search statement in full   Don't try to keep all of your search terms and search logic in your head. Free yourself of them by putting them on paper. When you are actually online, you'll have many other things to think about, and unless you're awfully quick, you don't want to be thinking about all the various words and commands you could use while the meter's running.

Keep a pad of paper and a pen within easy reach, as well. You will need them. And remember this professional's trick: Use the macro key function of your comm program or use a macroing utility program to record your first-pass search strategy *before* you go online. That way, you can enter a database and blast your first search statement into it at the touch of only one or two keys.

Step 6: Check the display options & verify how you sign off   The ultimate point of going online is to display the records that your search statements have selected. Make sure you know what formats are available and what pieces of information are included in each format as it applies to the database you're going to search. Again, this is not the kind of thing you want to look up while you are connected and paying for online time. The same thing goes for making sure you know how to sign off. What is the correct command?

Step 7: Set your computer to capture incoming information   This is so important that it's worth the emphasis of making it a separate step. During your search you may want to dump a screen to the printer for easy reference. So leave the printer on and enabled, but don't toggle on the "printer echo" from within your communications program.

Instead, open your capture buffer or set your communications program to record to disk or do whatever else is necessary to save incoming text to a disk file. You can always go back into the file and edit out the portions you don't want with a word processor. In addition, a record of a complete online session can be a wonderful self-teaching tool since you can review it to see where you went wrong, the number of hits on a term that you did not follow up on, etc.

Step 8: Sign on & check the inverted file   Systems like DIALOG, Knowledge Index, and others maintain files of every searchable word in every database. In the trade, these are called *inverted indexes*, and it is really these files that you are searching when you are online. Each keyword in an inverted index is tagged with an invisible pointer identifying the records in which it appears.

It can be extremely worthwhile to look at this list of keywords before you begin displaying records. In fact, most professional searchers would say it is essential. The command to do so on both DIALOG and Knowledge Index is EXPAND followed by the keyword—or first part of a keyword. As an example, take a look at Fig. 13-1. At the top you will see the command BEGIN BUSI1. This tells KI you want to start searching ABI/INFORM. (As a new user, you will be better off taking KI's menu approach to do the same thing. But we wanted to show you what "command-line" activity is like.)

Note the command that reads EXPAND DECAFFEINATED. By entering this command, we told the system to look for *decaffeinated* in the inverted file for the fields in its Basic Index.

Step 9: Enter your first search statement & note the results   Our first and, as it happens, only search statement told the system to look for *E3* ("expand" term 3 or *decaffeinated*) and *tea*. We could have entered FIND

DECAFFEINATED AND TEA with the same effect. It's a small point, but once you "expand" a term on KI or DIALOG, you can avoid typing it by following the procedure shown here.

In checking the results of this command, we see that the word *decaffeinated* appears 88 times in the database; *tea* appears 1,979 times; and both *decaffeinated* and *tea* appear in 25 records.

Step 10: Add qualifiers to narrow the search   Some searchers like to put all of the qualifiers they can think of in their initial search statements. Many of the commands that clutter the vendor system manuals are designed to make this possible. For our money, this makes things needlessly complex.

We prefer to think of searching as a process similar to repairing a household appliance at a well-equipped workbench. There are certain tools (search terms and search logic) you know you're going to need to open the case or remove the housing. But from then on there are no definitive steps to follow. At this point we've got the case off and are peering into the machine's innards to try to get an idea of the situation.

If the initial search command had located, say, 50 or 100 records containing the words *decaffeinated* and *tea*, we would have had to reach for another tool. Through experience, we know that 50 to 100 hits indicates that the search needs to be more sharply focused. It's a good start, but perhaps records should be winnowed further by setting some kind of date limit. Say, just the last two years. If that were the case, one could zero in on this first "set" of records with a command like FIND S1 AND PY=1991:1992. As the KI documentation explains, *PY* stands for publication year.

Generally speaking, it is not a bad idea to try to narrow a search down until you are left with about 20 records. Though we hasten to add that this is merely a rough rule of thumb. Naturally, everything depends on the subject you are looking into and the database you are using. There are too many other variables in online searching for this to apply across the board. As it happens, in our sample search, we have found eight records, which is fine for our purposes here.

Step 11: Display results   This is the easy part. There's nothing like conducting a search that appears to be on the beam and yields a manageable number of results. Here we merely keyed in TYPE S1 to display all the records in "Set 1." That showed us the first and most recent article containing the words *decaffeinated* and *tea*.

Of course there are variations. Nearly every online system offers commands to control how much of each record you display. As discussed earlier, DIALOG and most other information systems charge you a different rate for nearly every display format, under the general principle of "the more you display, the more you pay."

KI is different. All that matters on KI is the amount of time you are connected to the system. So, because a full-text record or a "long format" record takes more time to display, viewing it costs a little bit more. "Short" and "medium" formats are also available on KI.

Step 12: Log off & write your capture buffer to disk   Now log off to stop the connect-time clock. On both DIALOG and KI, the official command is LOGOFF, though QUIT, BYE, and OFF also work. Close your capture buffer and write it to disk. Because of the way most personal computers do things, if you neglect this step, you may lose all or part of the material you have downloaded, and the information that has already been written to disk may be rendered inaccessible because the file was not properly closed.

Conclusion

Although we have reproduced only one of the 25 records retrieved for our search on *decaffeinated and tea*, all were typical of what one could expect from a search of this type. The abstract shown in Fig. 13-1, and the full text of the article to which it refers, do not provide the ultimate answer regarding the current state of the decaffeinated tea market. But they, and the other 24 articles we found, offer good leads to additional information.

Certainly there is a lot more searching to be done. And, budget permitting, a lot more phoning, interviewing, and possibly library research. But as you work through the process, it is important to remember that the definitive article you envision may not exist. With all the information that's out there, it may seem like a paradox that no one has written the one article that can fill all of your needs. But very often that will be the case. As we have said from the beginning of this book, the best way to view online is not as the source of all answers but as the source of many starting points.

14 Special Interest Groups (SIGs) & forums

DIALOG, Dow Jones, NEXIS, NewsNet, and the other industrial-strength databases form the core of online information retrieval for any information broker. Of the *consumer-oriented* online services—services like America Online, CompuServe, Delphi, GEnie, and Prodigy—only CompuServe offers much in the way of "real" information.

But the consumer-oriented services, including CompuServe, have one thing the industrial-strength information systems lack: online Special Interest Groups (SIGs). As mentioned earlier in this book, these features go by different names on different systems. But they all follow essentially the same format, and they all offer unique information retrieval possibilities.

This is crucial to understand, because most search professionals come from a library school background and can operate DIALOG or NEXIS blindfolded. But most have never heard of the "SIG" concept and have no idea what a really good SIG can offer in the way of information and expertise.

It is important to remember once again that often what you're really after when you go online is a contact—a person you can call on the phone for more information. And, since SIGs are about nothing if not about people, they are often an excellent place to look. Of course, you'll find interesting and useful text files and programs to download as well.

In this chapter, we'll help you get familiar with the basic SIG structure. We'll tell you where to find SIGs, and we'll give you some general instructions on how to use them. Every consumer system—and many bulletin board systems—have SIGs of some sort. Not all are equally good, of course. But some can offer spectacular results. In any case, regardless of your background, SIGs are something that cannot be ignored.

The basic SIG floor plan

All consumer-oriented systems have multiple SIGs, and it is often convenient to think of them as fraternity or sorority houses on college campuses. All SIGs on any one system have an identical floor plan and, in general, this floor plan varies little from one system to another. Once you know how to use one SIG on one system, you automatically know how to use all the other SIGs on that system. And, although the actual commands differ, you will have little difficulty translating your skills so that you can easily use a SIG on some different system.

You will undoubtedly find that mental images of your "physical location" are very helpful while you are online. Never is this more appropriate than when contemplating a SIG. That's why the image of a frat house or a community building is so useful. You can see yourself physically opening the front door and entering the building as you enter a SIG.

After you join a SIG, every time you enter you will be greeted by name and notified of any major developments that have taken place since your last visit. The system will display bulletins and announcements prepared by the *sysop* (pronounced "sis-op," short for "system operator"). Then you're on your own.

Let's imagine that you've just walked through the "door" of a SIG. On your right is the club message board. It's a very big board, with lots of messages organized into lots of categories and topics within those categories. You might pause for a moment and read any new messages in any or all categories that have been posted since your last visit.

You might want to post a question or an announcement here yourself. Or you may have the answer to someone else's question and scribble them a quick note. You might even disagree with something someone else has said and feel moved to comment at length.

When you're finished there, you might stroll into the lounge ("conference" area) to have a real-time chat with anyone or any group of members there at the time. Most SIGs have regularly scheduled get-togethers during the week, and many invite guest speakers. Individuals as diverse as Steve Wozniak, Tom Clancy, and Barry Manilow have been guests in various SIGs in the past. Indeed, you can never predict when a "name" in a particular field will appear.

If conferencing doesn't appeal, you can go upstairs to the library. There you will find a series of alcoves, each devoted to a particular topic and each containing all manner of useful information, including transcripts of notable online conferences and guest appearances of the past. In most cases, you'll find tons of free, public domain software as well—all of it yours for the downloading. And you can upload any of your own programs or files, usually free of charge.

In almost every case, SIG usage is billed at standard connect-time rates or is included with your monthly membership fee. On CompuServe, for example, the connect-time rate of $9.60 an hour applies to most forums, regardless of time of day, if you sign on at 9600 bps or 14.4 kbps. Commercial online systems are, by their nature, designed to make a profit. So, while policies vary on what's included in your monthly subscription fee, in general, you can expect the really good stuff to be billed separately.

All this at no extra cost

After you've spent some time in a really good SIG you can't help but become aware of all the hard work that's gone into making it what it is. That may naturally lead you to wonder about the sysops and their assistants, and how they are paid for their labors. The answer is that while many of the sysops undoubtedly put in many long, undercompensated hours working on their SIGs, the SIGs themselves are designed to be small enterprises. Many sysops receive from 2 to 15 percent of the connect-time revenue generated by the forum or SIG they operate.

All of this is invisible to the user. You pay the same connect-time rate regardless of the online system's compensation policies. But, as with anything else, there are sharp, well-run SIGs and there are SIGs that are not so well run. Generally, the policy of compensating sysops works to the benefit of everyone. Sysops who operate their forums in a way that makes subscribers want to come back and spend time there are rewarded financially for their efforts, while subscribers have a wealth of unique places to go and things to do at no extra charge.

Why are SIGs important information sources?

Think back to our description of one entering the clubhouse, looking at the message board, peeping into the conference room, and going upstairs to the library. Now multiply that activity by several thousand people—sometimes, even several tens of thousands of people—for each SIG. Imagine thousands of people each evening doing exactly what you're doing.

At this writing, CompuServe claims some 2.3 million subscribers. America Online (AOL) claims over a million. And some people estimate that the Internet connects over 20 million people. All the other online systems have their membership figures as well. But specifics are not the point here.

The point is that, leaving aside the traditional information systems, your computer can quickly and easily link you to literally millions and millions of people around the world. So posting a query on a SIG message board (or on an Internet newsgroup) can be like buying space on a billboard at a prime location on the Santa Monica freeway—or any other major highway you'd care to name. You're bound to get replies from people you would never have met—ever—in a million years any other way.

A wide variety of expertise

Naturally, you will find lots and lots of SIGs devoted to computer and software topics. But there are countless SIGs devoted to noncomputer subjects as well. For example, on GEnie you will find groups devoted to topics like genealogy, home offices, legal issues, medical issues, photography, scuba, science fiction and fantasy, space exploration, travel, television, show business, and freelance writing.

On CompuServe you will find forums focusing on topics like fish, astronomy, aviation, cancer, wine, coin and stamp collecting, diabetes, education, foreign languages, organic gardening, ham radio, journalism, religion, rock music, and sports.

In each of these noncomputer SIGs you will find current topics of interest being discussed on the message boards. You will find topic-relevant software to download. And you will find files, like the one on the GEnie Scuba RoundTable detailing the best places to dive for shells on the East Coast or the one on the CompuServe HAMNET forum offering reviews of the latest ham radio equipment from people who have really bought and used the products.

Magnets for experts

Most important, you will find people you can reach, either by phone or by electronic mail, who can either answer your questions or put you in touch with experts and authorities in the field. Online SIGs, in short, act as magnets for people who have a particular interest, curiosity, or expertise. They won't provide everything you need as an information broker. Not by a long shot. But they are clearly too powerful and unique a source to be ignored.

Looking at libraries

A SIG's *message base*, as the comments, messages, and postings on its message board are sometimes called, is but one source of valuable information. If you use the system's search function to locate messages likely to be relevant to your search assignment and come up empty, don't automatically leave the SIG. Go check the SIG library as well.

Again, since self-employment is a subject most of us can relate to, let's look at the libraries available in the Working from Home Forum on CompuServe. As you can see from Fig. 14-1, this particular forum offers some 22 different libraries. A *library*, we should point out, is simply a way of making a first cut at classifying files. When you enter, say, Library 9—which is Accounting & Tax in the Working from Home Forum—you are telling the system to concentrate on those files that pertain to that library topic.

Working From Home Forum+ Libraries Menu

```
 1 General Information
 2 Business Info
 3 Member Showcase
 4 Info Professionals
 5 Specific Businesses
 6 Forum Help Files
 7 Getting Business
 8 Med Trans & Claims
 9 Accounting & Tax
10 Independent Writers
11 Jobs/Teleworking
12 Legal Matters
13 Word Processing
14 Office Hdwr & Sftwr
15 Virtual Corporation
16 Policies & Legislat
17 Home Business Assns
18 Mgmt. Consulting
19 Auditing Businesses
20 International Biz
21 Training & HR
22 DTV & MultiM Biz
```

Enter choice !9

Working From Home Forum+ Library 9

Accounting & Tax

```
 1 BROWSE Files
 2 DIRECTORY of Files

 3 UPLOAD a File (FREE)
 4 DOWNLOAD a file to your Computer

 5 LIBRARIES
```

Enter choice !1

Enter keywords (e.g. modem)
or <CR> for all: TAX

Oldest files in days
or <CR> for all:

[72144,1233]
OBBK30.EXE/Bin Bytes: 227694, Count: 12, 26-Sep-94

Title   : OWL Basic Bookkeeping 3.0
Keywords: ACCOUNTING BOOKKEEPING TAX FINANCE SMALL BUSINESS IBM OWL

OWL Basic Bookkeeping 3.0: PC WORLD's BEST OF BUSINESS SHAREWARE (Feb. 94).
Very easy to use bookkeeping system for small businesses and individuals. NO
ACCOUNTING EXPERIENCE IS NEEDED. Tracks income and expenses using single entry
method recommended by the IRS. Produces easy to understand income, expense, profit
and general ledger reports. Supports fiscal or calendar year accounting. Intuitive mousable
menus, on-line help & user's guide - VERY EASY TO USE. REQ: PC/MS DOS, 640K &
Hard Disk. Shareware: $39.00

Press <CR> for next or type CHOICES !

Why are SIGs important information sources?

You can search a library on the basis of keyword, date, and the e-mail address of the uploader. But on CompuServe, the search will be limited to just the files in the library you have selected. On GEnie, in contrast, you can specify that you want to "search all libraries" at once.

How to use a SIG

For years there has been talk (and little else) in the online industry of introducing a "common command language." The idea is that users would learn one set of commands and be able to apply them on DIALOG, NEXIS, and any other industrial-strength online information system. There has been no such talk in the consumer-oriented online utility field.

Every online utility is different, requiring you to learn a separate set of commands for each system whose SIGs you plan to access. As noted, however, the concepts are the same across SIGs, so this does not present a terrible difficulty. It is true that there are little differences in features and capabilities across systems, but there is enough *de facto* standardization that we can tell you in general how to make the most of any SIG.

Step 1: Get a list of all SIGs on the system

The first step is to get a list of all the SIGs available on the system. Check your system manual for instructions on accessing or searching the index feature. When you do access that feature, search on the appropriate keyword. If you are looking for scuba SIGs, search on *scuba*. But if you want a complete list of SIGs, search on the name the system uses for these features. Search on *forum* on CompuServe, for example, and *RoundTable* or *RT* on GEnie.

Note that the list may or may not be 100 percent complete. Updating files is a persistent problem affecting all areas of the online world. It is always possible that a SIG has been added to the system but its name has not yet been added to the list.

Step 2: Select a SIG of interest

Step 2 is to select the SIG of interest and enter the command needed to get there. The first time you access any SIG you will be considered a visitor. On GEnie this status causes the system to display "Hi, sailor. Welcome aboard!"-type bulletins and announcements. These will not appear the next time you enter.

On CompuServe you will get similar treatment and then be offered a menu, one selection of which is "Join." By all means do so. There is no cost for joining a forum, and if you don't join, you will not be able to download any files.

Step 3: Zero in on the library

Step three is to learn how the SIG library works. This is an experience that can make you wistful for the controlled vocabularies of major league information systems. The problem is that any SIG member can upload a file. Since part of the uploading process is a prompt for keywords, and since most uploaders are not information professionals, you can imagine the variety of keywords they use for their files.

One user might use the keyword *IRS*, while another might use *I.R.S.* But as you know by now, computers are the very definition of literal-minded. So if you search on *IRS*, you will not find the file tagged with *I.R.S.* Alfred once wrote an article for *Database* magazine titled "SIGs: On the Frontier of Civilized Searching" (October 1989). Discrepancies like the one just described—plus the inevitable misspellings of keywords on the part of the uploaders—add new meaning to the term *uncivilized*.

The best way around this problem is to download (capture to disk) the complete list of keywords used for all files in a given library. Then sign off and print it out. Circle the keywords of interest and sign back on again to do your search.

The way to do this on CompuServe is to select a library and open your capture buffer. Then, at the library menu prompt, instead of selecting "Browse" or some other menu item, type in the command key. This will give you a list of every keyword used in the library and the number of times it appears. Close your capture buffer when the scrolling has finished and key in off to leave the system.

Similar commands exist on other consumer-oriented online systems. For hands-on, step-by-step instructions, see the "Online Cookbook" section of Alfred's *The Little Online Book*, published by Peachpit Press.

Step four is to actually download a file. Again, you will want to consult your system manual or online help function for the appropriate commands to do this. You will have to know either the name or the "accession number" of the file, and you will have to know which error-checking protocols your comm program supports.

Step 4: Download a file

The best protocol to use in any situation is Zmodem. But if this is not available, the lowest common denominator is Xmodem. If you are on CompuServe, opt for CompuServe Quick B, assuming your comm program supports it.

Finally, step five is to master the message board. Check your system manual or online help for instructions on searching message topics to find just those that are likely to be relevant to your quest. On most systems, you can choose to read just those messages that are "new" to you (that is, that you have not read before). Or you can select individual messages or ranges of messages.

Step 5: Master the message board

Conclusion

As a prospective information broker, consumer online systems have the advantage of being very cheap by information industry standards. However, they are also very unconventional.

The heart of the online information field will always reside in systems like DIALOG, The Knowledge Index, NEXIS and their relations. But, these days, it would be foolish to ignore the burgeoning area of special interest groups or SIGs (and their newsgroup equivalents on the Internet). These resources can often help connect you with the expert or group of experts who can help you solve your problem. That's why we strongly recommend that you take the time to learn how to use the SIGs one of the leading consumer-oriented online systems.

15 How to tap the Internet

You can't pick up a newspaper or magazine these days without encountering at least one story about the Internet. Either some company is announcing that it will now be doing business on the Internet, or someone else is concerned about the copyrights being violated by Net users, or the FBI is worried about unbreakable data encryption programs being distributed via the Net. Or some new user is gushing on about the wonders of electronic mail and public domain software and searchable information, as if these things were something new.

What's new, of course, is that at long last the public as a whole has begun to discover the electronic universe that many of us have been living, working, and playing in for over a decade. The Internet has become the latest fad.

So much so that, while cocktail party conversation used to center around the number of miles you ran or bicycled each day or the finer points of tennis or racketball, it is now just as likely to focus on FTP, Telnet, Gopher, and WAIS. "Yeah, I FTPed that file from Marvel-dot-com. Then I used the University of Michigan Gopher to telnet to Wiretap. You should see the files they've got there. Outrageous!"

Clearly, the Internet is here to stay, and a smart information broker will learn to take advantage of it. Doing so, however, requires two things: the mastery of certain skills and a lot of hands-on experience. Regrettably, this book can provide neither. What we *can* provide here, however, is an overview and

What you need to know

explanation that will make the Internet make sense, as well as some recommendations on what to do next.

This chapter will thus answer the following questions:

- What is the Internet?
- How can you get connected?
- What are the Internet's major features?
- How can these features be used by an information broker?
- What are the most essential tools to have?

What is the Internet?

The best quick definition of the Internet is to say that it is "the network of networks." Think of all the state colleges and universities in the U.S. Imagine a mainframe computer system at each of them, and visualize all the terminals and computer modem connections scattered across campus. Every person who has access to one of these connections can communicate with every other person who has access via e-mail.

Every person can also tap the central mainframe computer for files, whether it is the reading list for next semester's course on French Impressionism, or a copy of the U.S. Constitution that some good soul has typed in and stored on the system, or even the university library catalog.

Now imagine that all of the mainframe computers on all of the campuses of every state college or university were connected via continually operational telephone links. Imagine that all of these individual campus-wide networks were linked together to form a *gigantic* network.

That would mean that students in Texas could tap into the mainframe computer system that's the heart of a campus network in Maine or Nebraska or California as easily as they tap into the local Texas system. It would mean that students in all of these states could easily exchange e-mail and files.

Now expand the concept even further. Add in not only every college or university in the U.S., but in the entire world! Add in corporate mainframes and small-business local area networks (LANs). Add in the computers operated by agencies of the U.S. government.

At this point, the awesome scope of the Net should start to become apparent. In some respects, you can say that the Internet links everything to everything else. It really isn't important to understand how all of this is accomplished. The only thing that really matters in that respect is that the links that connect various parts of the Net operate at dramatically different speeds. And the speed of your connection has a direct influence on whether or not you will be able to get all the wonderful graphics and photos that are featured in most magazine stories about the Internet.

The Internet has often been cited as at least one instance where the federal government "did it right." Specifically, the government provided the funding and then got out of the way. That made it possible for the Net to develop organically. The people who created it were the people who used it, and so the Net did a very good job of meeting the needs of those for whom it was intended.

Originally, those people were all working in one way or another for the U.S. Department of Defense (DOD). They were defense contractors, university researchers and professors, and, of course, the Pentagon. DOD created the network in 1969 and called it the ARPAnet. (ARPA stands for Advanced Research Projects Agency.) The idea was to link companies, universities, and the military electronically and to do so with a network that no single nuclear warhead could destroy.

At the time, there were no personal computers. The model of centralized mainframe computers and terminals ruled the computing world. Under this model, the big mainframe sat at the center of a starfish-like system with a dumb terminal (a CRT and a keyboard) at the tip of each tentacle. The concept of *networking*, in which many machines are connected so they can share resources—but nothing is centralized—was quite new. Innovations in both hardware and software were required to bring it off, which made it perfect for the Advanced Research Projects Agency.

The origins of the Internet are important to today's users for at least three reasons. First, some 20 years elapsed between the inception of the Net and its opening to the general public. In that time, a very distinct "Net culture" developed. Thus, one way or another, you will encounter some aspect of the "This is the way we do things here" mentality. Which is fine. People who don't know DIALOG or CompuServe or any other online system other than the Internet will encounter the same phenomenon.

After all, it's "free!"   Second, anyone can use the Internet for "free." Or almost "free," thanks to the subsidies provided by the government, the universities, and the companies the Net connects. The end of the Cold War has opened the Internet up to everyone.

This has led to a very interesting situation. Namely, the spectacle of those same people who wail and moan about how difficult it is to use CompuServe, GEnie, or Delphi without a graphical user interface to shield them from the horrors of the command line eagerly plunging into the Net—even though it means dealing with complexities far greater and interfaces far uglier than those of any commercial online system.

Why? Because it's "free!", of course. This has led to what Alfred has elsewhere called "the crowding of the Net." Don't forget that no university, government, or corporate computer system is likely to grant access to an *unlimited* number of people coming in from the outside via the Net. After all, these computer systems were not bought and installed for the purpose of serving every person in the world with access to the Internet.

If they grant access to outside users at all, they limit the number to 30, 50, or maybe even 100 at a time. That's very generous. But when you consider that there may be as many as 20 million or more Internet users, even 100 "slots" for outside users is insignificant. The "net net" (no pun intended) is that you cannot count on being able to connect to any given Internet site whenever you want. You may find that you have to keep trying until an opening occurs.

The eclectic nature of Internet information   The third reason why the origins of the Net are important is the eclectic nature of the information it offers. Until late 1993, no significant number of people or organizations even considered using the Net to offer real, commercial-quality information retrieval resources. People have always "done their own thing" on the Net. As a result, while there are tons of information available via the Internet, the collections are spotty at best.

If someone at a company or university, for example, decided to transcribe every stand-up comedy routine done by, say, Bob Newhart or Shelley Berman, and store the results as a file on some system connected to the Internet, then that file will be an Internet resource.

Finding the file or even discovering that it exists is another matter. When you're looking for information on the Net, you cannot simply open a DIALOG database catalog and select a database. Nor can you call the database producer to get more details on the type and extent of information the database includes. You are very much on your own.

There are ways to search for Net resources, but they are crude and time-consuming, at best. And, for an extra, added sense of adventure, there is always the very real possibility that the file you have learned about may no longer exist on the system you were told to check. In the course of writing the Random House book *Internet Slick Tricks* and the McGraw-Hill book *Internet 101: A College Student's Guide*, Alfred and his wife and co-author Emily encountered this problem any number of times.

The reasons why a file might disappear are many. The person who created it may have changed jobs or moved. He or she may have been contacted by attorneys who expressed a deep concern about copyright matters. The system administrator at the site may have decided that the disk space occupied by the file was needed for other purposes. Or the file may have been inadvertently erased.

At least when a database is removed or ceases to be updated on DIALOG, NEXIS, or some other online system, there is an announcement to that effect. And said announcement appears in various trade publications read by information brokers. On the Internet, files come and go all the time. And there are no official announcements of the fact.

It is our hope that what we have said here has begun to ring warning bells in your head. Access to the Internet may be free or so cheap that it makes no difference. But the main thing you have to sell as an information broker is your time. And you can waste an awful lot of it trying to track down information on the Internet. There is simply no question but that in some instances you will be better off doing a quick search on a commercial system at commercial rates than spending hours wending your way through the Internet in hopes of coming up with the same information for "free."

How can you get connected? Let us count the ways. Better still, let us make it real simple. At this writing, the fastest, easiest, and possibly cheapest way to get full Internet access is to subscribe to Rupert Murdoch's Delphi system. At this writing, America Online (AOL) has the prettiest, most graphical interface to the Net—but does not yet offer access to every feature. CompuServe, too, is moving toward offering more Internet features, but isn't quite there yet.

How can you get connected?

It's important to emphasize that all of this can—and undoubtedly will—change. Delphi has announced plans to implement a graphical interface. America Online has promised to add all Internet features in the near future (though whether this "family service" will ever offer the X-rated newsgroups is an open question). And CompuServe is sure to keep pace. At this writing, Prodigy seems confused and GEnie is clearly dead in the water. But that too can change.

So it comes down to Delphi. Which you can reach by voice line at (800) 695-4005. Or send Internet e-mail to INFO@delphi.com. Delphi will give you five hours of weekend and evening access to try out the system and its Internet offerings for free when you sign up. Your monthly cost will be $13 for four hours of non-prime-time access to Delphi and the Internet. After that, it's $4 an hour.

You are sure to read about other types of connections to the Internet. Namely, SLIP (Serial Line Internet Protocol) and PPP (Point-to-Point Protocol) connections that will cost you anywhere from $20 to $200 a month. The only advantage these connections offer, in most cases, is the opportunity to use whatever Internet software you like. When you use Delphi or some other online system, in contrast, you are limited to whatever that system offers.

At this writing, for example, Delphi does not offer the famous Mosaic program—the one that can display pictures and graphics in real-time. But that's okay, because, if you have a SLIP or PPP connection and are running Mosaic, you will find that photos and graphics take forever to transmit, even if you are connected to your Internet service provider at 14.4 Kbps! Thus, after about the first day or so of using Mosaic, many users simply toggle off the "graphics" function and return to plain text. Which is just what Delphi offers.

Please, please remember that all the wonderful things you see in magazines and newspapers with graphical screens and photos and drawings are only practical if you have a high-speed Internet connection. Which, for the sake of simplicity, means a connection that does *not* involve a modem. Even at 28.8 Kbps, photo/graphical functions are barely usable. And 28.8 is the top speed of any modem you will find!

Bottom line: Plan to at least start with Delphi. Or with America Online, CompuServe, or some other system, as long as it offers full Internet access. You can always cancel your subscription and replace it with a subscription to NetCom or Pipeline or some other Internet service provider. But your Delphi/America Online/CompuServe experience will give you the background you need to fully understand and appreciate the offerings of the various service providers.

What are the Net's major features?

There are all *kinds* of things you can do on the Net. You can play text-based interactive games modeled on Adventure or Dungeons and Dragons. You can carry on real-time conversations as if you were typing into a CB radio. You can explore resources using a hypertext system that lets you click on highlighted words to get more information.

This is great fun. Unfortunately, none of it is relevant to the profession of information brokering. Forget about everything else you've read or heard and listen to your authors. In the end, the Internet boils down to four crucial functions:

1. Getting files with the File Transfer Protocol (FTP).
2. Exploring distant computers as if you were onsite (Telnet).
3. Sending and receiving mail (e-mail).
4. Reading and participating in discussions of any topic you can imagine (newsgroups and mailing lists).

The four features: FTP, Telnet, e-mail, & newsgroups/mailing lists

Let's start with FTP, the Internet *File Transfer Protocol*. The key to understanding FTP is realizing that many systems on the Net have set aside special areas containing files for you to download. When you FTP to one of these sites, you are locked into one area. You can't go anywhere else on the host system. You can't upload files to the system. All you can do is move around the directory structure of the FTP area, getting the files you want. Which is fine, since there are lots and lots of files to choose from.

Now let's consider *Telnet*. This feature is also called *remote login*. Telnetting to a site is a lot like signing onto CompuServe, GEnie, Delphi, or a local bulletin board. You log in and are usually presented with a menu system. Though still limited, your access to the host machine is much broader than is the case with FTP. You can use the menus you find to move all around, running programs, downloading files, and searching for information. Good examples of Telnet sites are interactive library catalogs and campus-wide information systems.

E-mail is the third main feature. And, ironically, it may be the most important. That's because the popularity of the Internet has forced almost every commercial system everywhere to offer Internet e-mail at the very least. The result is that anyone on any commercial system can send an e-mail message to anyone else on any other commercial system. Naturally, there are exceptions, but as the Internet juggernaut rolls on, they are fewer and fewer.

The fourth feature consists of *newsgroups* and *mailing lists*. If you've ever used a bulletin board system (BBS) like those systems discussed in the next chapter or an online special interest group (SIG) like those discussed in Chapter 14, then you already have a very good idea of what Internet newsgroups and mailing lists are all about.

Newsgroups are ongoing discussions devoted to a particular topic. People transmit comments, questions, answers, and opinions to a group. When one comment leads to another, a "message thread" develops. Reading a message thread is like reading a conversation that has taken place over time.

At this writing there are close to 10,000 newsgroups, though individual groups come and go all the time. To make this mass of groups more manageable, each group bears a name that indicates its subject. The longer the group's name, the more specific the subject. At the first level are the major classifications like ALT (alternative), COMP (computer), BIZ (business), SCI (science), NEWS (Internet issues and news), etc. Every newsgroup will begin with a major category like that.

Then things become more specific. For example: rec.gardens, rec.outdoors.fishing.fly, alt.comedy.firesgn-thtre, alt.comedy.british.blackadder, and so on. Not every Internet site gives you access to all of the existing newsgroups. The newsgroups that are available and the length of time any given message in a group will remain posted are decisions made by the system administrator.

Mailing lists are simply a variation on this theme of one-to-many communication. They exist because the software that runs one of the major networks hooked into the Internet—a network called Bitnet—cannot handle newsgroups. Every comment or question or whatever that gets transmitted to a mailing list goes to everyone on that list, whether they want it or not.

Information-finding functions: Archie, Gopher, and Veronica

Three other terms you are sure to hear about are *Archie*, *Gopher*, and *Veronica*. All three can be thought of as subsidiary functions designed to help you *use* the four main Internet functions. Here's a quick summary:

Archie   The name *Archie* comes from *archive*. Archie is basically a database of filenames and their locations. It is as if you signed onto every major FTP site and keyed in dir to get a listing of the filenames in each directory, saved the results to a text file, and created a special program to search that huge text file for a given filename or partial filename.

The result is a huge file that lists the locations of lots of FTP sites and the file directories of each. This file, as it were, exists and is regularly updated at a handful of Archie sites around the world. These sites are called *Archie servers*.

Thus, to do an Archie search you log onto a server at an Archie site. Then you are asked for a filename or part of a filename. The Archie software will search its database of such names. Whenever it finds a match for the filename or partial filename you request, it gives you relevant filenames and FTP site locations in its database. You can then use the FTP feature to go to the designated system and download the file.

Gopher   The name of this feature comes from *go fer*, as in "go fer coffee, my lad, will you." (There is also a lame connection to the Golden Gophers, the football team of the University of Minnesota, site of the very first Internet Gopher.) An Internet *Gopher* is a menu system designed by some good soul to help you identify and actually obtain information from the Net.

Imagine creating a menu system on your disk that embraced all of your word processing files. Each item on the menu describes a file. Select any item and the menu software automatically issues the command needed to run your word processor and load the desired file. When you finish with the file, you are returned to the menu system from which you can make a different selection.

That's essentially what a Gopher does, except it uses many levels of menus. There are two things to remember about Gophers. First, a Gopher can give you access to just about *every* aspect of the Net (FTP, Telnet, Archie, newsgroups, etc.) Second, while there are many more Gopher sites than Archie sites, every Gopher is unique. No single Gopher covers the entire Internet. Instead, each tends to be strong in one or two individual areas.

That's because Gopher menus are created by a site's system administrators and their staffs. So if a particular college has a strong collection of environmental literature and files, the Gopher menu that the system administrators at that college create will be very strong in that subject area. After all, many gopher menus are created mainly to make it easier for the students of some college or university to access the file collections on the campus computer. Though, of course, many gopher menus go well beyond one campus. It all depends on the "Net knowledge" of the system administrator or staff.

Veronica   The name *Veronica* comes from Archie's girlfriend in the old comic strip. The Archie and Veronica concepts are essentially the same. The difference is that Archie offers a searchable database of the file directory listings of many *FTP* sites, while Veronica offers a searchable database of the menu items on hundreds of *Gopher* sites.

Since the Veronica database is made up of menu item entries, you've got a *lot* more to work with than obscure filenames. You can search on the basis of topic or concept. Veronica also permits much more powerful searches. You can use ANDs and ORs, for example, to link terms.

This is a wonderful concept. And when Veronica works, it is great! Unfortunately, Veronica doesn't always work the way it is supposed to. But it is certainly worth trying. Veronica is available as on option on most Gopher menus. But don't accept without question all the results it produces.

How can these features be used by an information broker?

It's tempting to say in answer, "Good question," and let it go at that. In reality, however, the Internet and your access to it can be useful in a number of ways. Remember that the main features are file transfer via FTP; remote access via Telnet; e-mail; and newsgroups and mailing lists. Let's look at each from an information broker's perspective.

FTP file transfer

As an information broker, there is never any way to predict what your clients will want. It's entirely possible that they will want the full text of *Moby Dick* or *Love's Labour's Lost* or the full text of some U.S. Supreme Court decision. All of these things are available on the Net.

But, in our experience, it is rather rare for a client to want a copy of full-text files like that. Usually the client is more interested in an executive summary prepared by you or an associate that may be based on the full text of a number of files. This is simply the nature of the business.

Thus, from an information broker's viewpoint, finding files with Archie and obtaining them with FTP may be of less interest than other features.

Remote access via Telnet

The Internet Telnet function essentially says, "Key in this particular Telnet address, and see what happens." What happens depends entirely on the software running at that Telnet address. The software could be designed to give you access to the Library of Congress catalog. Or it could have been created to prompt you for two subway stops in some world city, in which case it will provide you with a complete list of station stops and transfers along the way.

The information broker business being what it is, it is entirely likely that you will have a client someday who will request something that can be supplied only through the Internet Telnet function. But in most cases you will probably find that Telnet has little to offer.

Making the most of e-mail

It may well be that you will find that Internet e-mail is the single most important function of all. That's because it eliminates the need for you to get a subscription on the same systems your clients use. Thanks to the Internet, almost all online systems can freely exchange messages.

And these days, nearly everybody has an account on an online system of some sort, whether it's a consumer system or a corporate e-mail system. So you and your client can probably communicate via e-mail, using the Internet as your transport mechanism and intermediary. There must be some exceptions, but nearly every commercial and corporate online system these days can send and receive e-mail via the Internet.

So you can ask questions of your client, receive answers, and deliver your results (if appropriate) directly from your computer. No need to go to the expense of Federal Express or take the time to send a fax.

Not that we necessarily recommend it, but with Internet e-mail, you can deliver the results of a search to a client an hour before it's due! If that turns out to be what is needed.

Sending e-mail to & from other systems

If you subscribe to one of the commercial online systems and someone asks you, "Are you also on the Internet?", the answer is "Yes." The trick is to know how to convert your e-mail address into one that is recognized by the Internet. Similarly, if you are on one commercial online system and have a client or business associate on another, you can use the Internet to communicate with each other—as long as you each know what address to use. Here's a quick overview:

- **America Online (AOL)**

To convert an AOL address to an Internet address, add @aol.com to get an address like jsmith@aol.com.

To send mail from AOL to an Internet address, just put the person's Internet address in the "To:" field before composing your message. Thus, bjones@company.org.

- **CompuServe**

Although you may soon see English language "aliases" introduced as CompuServe addresses (EMILYG, for example), CompuServe users have traditionally had numerical addresses in the form 71234,567.

To convert a CompuServe address to an Internet address, change the comma to a period and add @compuserve.com. That gives you an address like 71234.567@compuserve.com. (CompuServe users are charged a minimum of 15 cents for each message received from the Internet.)

To send mail from CompuServe to an Internet address, use an address in the form >INTERNET:bjones@company.org. Both the greater-than sign (>) and the colon (:) are required.

▪ Delphi Internet Services

To convert a Delphi address to an Internet address, add @delphi.com to get an address like jsmith@delphi.com.

To send mail from Delphi to an Internet address, the form is internet"jsmith@company.org". (The quotation marks are required.)

▪ GEnie

To convert a GE Mail address to an Internet address add @genie.geis.com to the end of the GEnie user name. For example: jsmith@genie.geis.com.

To send mail from the GEnie Mail system to an Internet address, use the person's Internet address plus the constant INET#. The address will look like this: jsmith@company.org@INET#.

▪ MCI Mail

To convert an MCI Mail address to an Internet address, add @mcimail.com to the end of your name or numerical address. For example: 555-1234@mcimail.com or jsmith@mcimail.com. You're better off using your numerical address if you have a relatively common name, since there can be no doubt about the John Smith at 555-1234, but considerable doubt about JSMITH.

To send mail from MCI Mail to an Internet address, at the "To:" prompt, key in the person's name and (EMS). At the resulting "EMS:" prompt, key in internet. At the resulting "MBX:" prompt, key in the recipient's Internet address.

▪ Prodigy

To convert a Prodigy address to an Internet address, add @prodigy.com to the Prodigy user ID. For example: jsmith@prodigy.com. As with CompuServe, Prodigy users must pay extra for Internet e-mail.

To send mail from Prodigy to an Internet address, you'll need Prodigy's Mail Manager software, which is available for download from the system.

After composing your message offline using Mail Manager, send it to the person's normal Internet address, like jsmith@company.org. No special punctuation is required.

Newsgroups and mailing lists

In our opinion, while the various file collections that exist on the Net can be useful, the most important Internet information resource consists of the newsgroups and mailing lists. That's because, like special interest groups and forums, newsgroups and mailing lists are magnets for people interested in very specific topics.

A word of explanation is in order at this point. Each individual newsgroup is in effect a "piano roll" of messages related to a specific topic. And, at this writing, there are some 10,000 individual topics and subtopics on the Net. Newsgroup messages are presented to you by "newsgroup reader" software running on the online system you're using, or on your own computer if you have a SLIP or PPP connection.

Anyone, anywhere in the world, with an Internet connection can contribute a message, comment, or whatever to any newsgroup. And, of course, the same person can read any contributions made by anyone else. This makes it very easy for arguments and discussions to develop, whirl, eddy, and flow over time. And, often, the men and women who are contributing their thoughts are world-class experts in their chosen fields.

All of which means that you cannot only grasp the essence of their thinking on some topic, you can also communicate with them directly, since every posted message includes the creator's e-mail address on the Net. What's more, you can pose questions to the group as a whole, if it seems appropriate.

Don't barge right in!   You will want to tread cautiously, though. A group that has been formed to exchange information among colleagues is not likely to take kindly to someone barging in and saying, "I have a client who would really like to know . . . can any of you help me?" Do not forget that, while many of them may not be paying for their Internet connections, they certainly are not being paid by you or anyone else to yield their knowledge.

Read several dozen exchanges in the group first. Make friends with the people. Then ask politely what you want to know. Most people on the Net are happy to share what they know. Like the online world as a whole, it is a very giving culture. But no one likes to be taken advantage of. So do unto others as you would have them do unto you.

The mailing list difference   As we said earlier, mailing lists exist because Bitnet, one of the major cooperative networks linked by the Internet, is built on software that cannot handle newsgroups. Here's the difference.

With a newsgroup, everyone "drives by a building" and tacks up messages. Other people drive by and read the messages and tack up responses. Or they tack up new messages of their own. In short, you, the user, decide what messages you will read in the newsgroup, and when or if you will read them. It is entirely up to you whether and when you "drive by the building."

With a mailing list, in contrast, everyone on the list gets every message every other member of the list decides to post. The messages arrive in your e-mail mailbox, whether you happen to be interested in them or not. There are variations on this, of course. Some mailing lists are *moderated*, which means all postings go to a single individual who then decides what will go out to the list as a whole.

To add even more interest to the affair, there are some Internet newsgroups that have been created to "mirror" Bitnet mailing lists. The group is thus a "subscriber" to the mailing list, which means you the user can treat the output of that mailing list as if it were postings to an Internet newsgroup. You can read the postings or not read them as you please. Nothing ends up in your mailbox.

The documentation produced by commercial online systems like DIALOG, CompuServe, and Dow Jones News/Retrieval may very in quantity and quality. But at least it exists. At least there's an instruction manual, and often a customer support number, to guide you in using the system.

What are the essential Internet tools?

No such materials exist for using the Internet. Or, more correctly, there are no *official* instruction manuals. How could there be? The Net isn't a discrete online system owned by some company. Indeed, many of the computer systems linked by the Internet operate in different ways and may require different commands to accomplish the same thing.

Thus, on the one hand, you have unprecedented public interest in the Internet, and on the other, you have the fact that there is no Internet "manual" to tell people how to use it. The result has been an explosion of books on the subject. And, just where do the authors of such books get their information? From what can only be described as "unofficial guides" to Net resources.

Over the years, various individuals have taken it upon themselves to create and maintain information files about the Net. The files are often called *FAQs*, short for "frequently asked questions." Or they may consist of lists of other files that are particularly noteworthy. Such lists may or may not offer an elaborate description of each file, but they always include the information you need to obtain a copy yourself.

Internet 1— Internet Must-Have Files

These FAQs and resource directories are the files you should start with. Many of them are famous on the Net and are available from numerous FTP sites. But, as you will see in Appendix F of this book, they are also available from Glossbrenner's Choice on high-density 3.5-inch disks. The files are plain ASCII text, which means that you can read and use them even if your computer is an Apple Macintosh. In all, there are seven disks—Internet 1 through Internet 7—in what Alfred and Emily Glossbrenner call their "Internet Toolkit."

The latest versions of the six key text files every Internet user should have:

- *The Internet Services FAQ* by Kevin Savetz
- *Special Internet Connections* by Scott Yanoff
- Kevin Savetz's *Unofficial Internet Book List*
- The List of Subject-Oriented Internet Resource Guides
- John December's *Internet-CMC List*
- John December's *Internet Tools Summary*

The Internet Services FAQ   Kevin Savetz is not only one of the most knowledgeable Internauts you are ever likely to find, he is also one of the best writers you are likely to encounter on the Net or in real life. His Frequently Asked Questions (FAQ) file on Internet basics is must reading for everyone. It includes sections like "I'm new to the Internet—Where do I start?", "What kind of information is on the Internet?", and "Are there any magazines about the Internet?"

Mr. Savetz has written a book based on his file. Look for *Your Internet Consultant: The FAQs of Life Online* by Kevin Savetz. Or call Sams Publishing (800) 428-5331 for more information.

Special Internet Connections   This is the famous "Yanoff List." It tells you about what Scott Yanoff feels are the best resources available on the Net for specific topics. Those topics range from Agriculture to Weather, Atmospheric, and Oceanic information. The Yanoff List calls on you to use all your fundamental Internet skills to get the information or goodies you want. So you will have to learn how to FTP a file.

If you want to get the list online and need to know where to look, use the Internet Finger utility. Finger yanoff@csd4.csd.uwm.edu and you will get a list of locations where you will find the current version.

The Unofficial Internet Book List   This is another super list prepared and maintained by Kevin Savetz. The reviews are only two or three sentences long, and Mr. Savetz makes no claim at comprehensiveness. (That's probably what the "Unofficial" is all about.) But in our opinion, he is right on target.

Emily and Alfred were especially pleased to get a letter from Mr. Savetz after he read their *Internet Slick Tricks*. "I just wanted to let you know that I think it's great. I mean really great. I haven't seen a book this honest, readable, and fun since, well, mine :-) or *Internet Starter Kit for the Mac.* Congratulations on a fine job!"

The List of Subject-Oriented Internet Resource Guides   Prepared by the Clearinghouse for Subject-Oriented Internet Resource Guides at the University of Michigan, this file is probably the single most important file for an information broker to have.

The file itself is a directory—a list of *other* files and where to get them. These other files have been prepared by professors and students at the University of Michigan, and each one pulls together and presents in one neat package information on the main resources available via the Internet on a particular subject.

At this writing, the subjects for which there are corresponding resource files (some 130 in all) include everything from anthropology, animals, and astronomy; to Buddhism, dance, and environmentalism; to theater, film and television; to women's studies and feminism. In each case the subject file shows you the newsgroup names, Telnet and Gopher locations, mailing lists and list servers, electronic newsletters and journals, key e-mail addresses, and FTP sites that are relevant to that subject.

John December's *Internet-CMC List*   The full title of this incredible resource is *Information Sources: The Internet and Computer-Mediated Communication* by John December. This list is essentially a wonderfully detailed table. It organizes and categorizes resources by topic and gives you the Internet feature to use (FTP, Gopher, etc.), the address to target, and the path to follow once you get there.

There are so many wonderful things to say about Mr. December's continually updated publication that, instead of saying anything, we will say the one thing that matters: Get the list! It will not mean a great deal to you until you have learned to FTP files and Telnet into sites. But, once you have that knowledge, the December CMC list will prove to be a gold mine.

John December's *Internet Tools Summary*   Ditto for this John December file as well. The topics covered by this 21-page document, at this writing, include Network Information Retrieval Tools, Computer-Mediated Communications Forums, Protocols/Standards, and References.

Consider the first category as an example. Among the Internet Information Retrieval Tools this file discusses are Finger, Netfind, Nslookup, Ping, WHOIS, X.500, Archie, FTP, Jughead, Knowbot, Maltshop, Trickle, and Veronica.

In each case, Mr. December gives you a quick handle on the tool and then tells you where to get more information on how to use it, tips, demos, and so on. Once again, you must have some idea of what Telnet and FTP mean and how to use these features to be able to understand this document.

Internet 2—FTP Essentials

Internet expert Perry Rovers has written an excellent FAQ on how to use the Net's FTP file transfer function. He also maintains a list of FTP sites that's about as comprehensive as one can imagine. Both documents are supplied on this disk. Updated monthly, Mr. Rovers's FTP list gives you:

- The site address, country, time zone (number of hours plus or minus Greenwich Mean Time), and date of last modification for the site.
- Source of the most recent information for the entry, aliases, administrative address, organization, e-mail server address, and hardware/operating system.
- Any general comments or restrictions, types of files, archives, or mirrors available.

Internet 3—Telnet Essentials

For DOS and Windows users only, this disk contains Peter Scott's remarkable Hytelnet package. This package contains a gigantic database of Telnet locations that includes at least one screen per location describing what you'll find there. It is, in effect, a gigantic, computerized directory of Telnet sites.

For ease of use, the entire thing is organized as a hypertext-style menu system. Also on this disk is Bruce Clouette's optional Subject Guide for the main Hytelnet menu, as well as a Windows front-end (WINHytelnet) program.

Internet 4—Newsgroup Essentials

Here you'll find two lists of Internet newsgroups, organized by newsgroup category (alternative, computer, recreation, science, etc.). The best way to use these files is to put them on your disk and then bring them into your word processing program, where you can use a "search" feature to locate keywords on the lists. The lists include:

- The List of Active Newsgroups (Parts 1 and 2)—This list includes newsgroups for all categories except ALT (alternative), which has its own list.
- The List of Alternative Newsgroups (Parts 1 and 2)—This list includes *only* newsgroups in the ALT category. Alternative groups can be focused on absolutely anything. The most popular, however are those in the ALT.SEX hierarchy.

Internet 5—Mailing List Essentials

This disk contains two gigantic lists of Internet and Bitnet mailing lists, plus the LISTSERV REFCARD command summary to help you communicate with robotized, mailing list "servers." Nearly every existing mailing list gets a meaty paragraph-long write-up, usually prepared by the list's creator. These write-ups offer lots of keywords for you to find when you bring one of the following files into your word processing program and apply its "search" function:

- The SRI List of Lists—Covers both Internet and Bitnet lists.
- Publicly Accessible Mailing Lists—Mainly Internet lists, with about a dozen or so Bitnet lists.

This disk is for DOS and Windows users only. It contains all of the programs you will need to uncompress or unarchive the various files you will find at FTP sites around the Net. File compression and archiving (bundling several files into a single file for easier downloading) have long been popular in the world of commercial online systems and bulletin boards. And fortunately, only a few main techniques and formats are used, principally ZIP and ARC in the DOS/Windows worlds and StuffIt in the Mac world.

Unfortunately, this kind of simplicity does not rule on the Net. Over the years Net users have developed any number of ways to compress and/or archive files. If you want to be able to uncompress and unarchive those files, you've got to have the correct utility program. That's what this disk provides. Among many others, it gives you the programs you need to deal with files that end in .ARC, .ARJ, .BTOA, .CPIO, .GZ or .Z, .HQX, .SIT, .TAR, .UUE, .Z, and more.

Internet 6— Compression Tools

On this disk you will find two things. First, there is the gigantic 100-plus page FAQ Index listing all of the FAQ files currently available on the Internet. The FAQ Index includes precise filenames to help you locate the files via Archie. Second, there are what we feel are some of the key FAQ files you may want to have on hand (in addition to the ones already described). Here's just a sampling:

Internet 7—Just the FAQs

- Addresses FAQ—How to find e-mail addresses and locate people on the Internet.
- Compression FAQ—All about compression programs. Where to find them, how to use them, troubleshooting, and more.
- Gopher FAQ—Questions and answers about using Internet Gophers.
- Pictures FAQ—Information on graphics images on the Internet, newsgroups devoted to graphics, decoding and encoding images, image formats, and so forth.
- Veronica FAQ—Answers to frequently asked questions about using the Veronica search utility on the Internet.

The Internet has become a fact of life for all of us. But no single chapter can tell you everything you need to know to use it. What we have tried to do here instead is to give you a solid introduction to the Net that is free from all the hype and misinformation found in the laymen's press. We have tried to put the Net into perspective, alerting you to both its positive and its negative characteristics.

Conclusion

From an information broker's standpoint, however, the most salient feature of the Internet is *chaos*. There's an old saying that if you put 100 monkeys in a room and gave each of them a typewriter, they would eventually produce all the plays of Shakespeare—by accident. Certainly those who have built the Net and generously prepared and contributed files for all of us to download are bright, giving people. But to someone accustomed to the order and clarity of a DIALOG or a NEXIS, the results can seem just as random as if the monkeys had been in charge.

There are gems to be found, to be sure. And it won't cost you much to get them, once you discover where they are. The problem is that, as an information broker, your time is essentially all you have to sell. As you will see later, we definitely do not recommend that you bill your clients on the basis of hours spent. We recommend that you quote and bill on a project basis.

But, internally, you've still got to keep track of your time. Thus, you have got to ask yourself whether it is likely to be worth the time required to check the Internet to see if one of its sites contains the information you need.

Suppose, for example, that someone said to you, "You can spend 15 minutes searching a DIALOG database and be certain of finding the needed information—but you'll have to pay for it. Or you can spend at least an hour locating and searching Internet resources for the same information. The difference being that there is no assurance that the information you want exists on the Net, but, if it does, obtaining it will cost you next to nothing."

This is not an either/or situation. Everything depends on how much you know about the information resources available commercially and the resources available via the Net. Ultimately, the Internet represents a promising new resource for all information brokers. But it is only one of many, many resources. And, just as with any information system, you will have to plan on spending a lot of time learning its ins and outs and how to use it effectively.

16 Bulletin board systems (BBSs)

Bulletin boards! What on earth are you talking about? I'm a trained information professional. I know DIALOG, DataTimes, and Dow Jones like the back of my hand. But bulletin boards? What's in it for me?

Possibly nothing. It may very well be that you will never have an assignment for which bulletin boards would be helpful. But then again, depending on the question at hand, a bulletin board may hold the only answer to one of your client's requests. It is difficult to tell—bulletin boards cover so many subjects, attract such a wide variety of people, and change so rapidly.

We would be the last to suggest that the 60,000-odd bulletin board systems (BBSs) in the country today are likely to be a prime source of information or leads to information. At the same time, however, it is impossible to deny that BBSs attract articulate, experienced experts in various fields. Unorthodox as they may seem to trained information professionals, BBSs are not only a legitimate information source, in some instances they are the *only* easily accessible information source for a particular subject area.

What is a bulletin board?

Now, before we go any further, we must define terms. It is true that the term *bulletin board* is often applied to systems like CompuServe, America Online, and GEnie by the lay press. But, as you know by now, CompuServe, GEnie and their competitors are far more than message-exchange systems. Well, real bulletin boards are anything but the products of large corporations. They are very much a private, individual effort.

A real computer bulletin board system consists of the same components everyone uses to go online: a computer, a modem, and a telephone connection. The difference is in the software. Bulletin board software can be thought of as a specialized form of communications program. Instead of allowing the computer owner to *dial out*, BBS programs are designed to allow other users to *dial in*. They can thus turn any personal computer into a "host" system. Like the people who run SIGs on commercial systems, the person who owns, sets up, and runs a bulletin board is called its system operator or *sysop* (pronounced "sis-op").

The board's personality

The sysop is also responsible for the board's personality. Indeed, most sysops view their boards as their own unique creations, and they are forever tinkering with them the way some people tinker with souped-up stock cars. Thus, even if you are an experienced user, you never know what you'll find when you sign on. For example, at your option, some boards are capable of putting on quite a show, complete with pseudo-animated graphics, music, and other surprises.

Other boards are more sedate, channeling their originality into the selection of files they offer for download or the lively discussions and message exchanges they host. The sysop can focus a board on any topic he or she finds interesting. Most give their boards a name and publicize its existence throughout the BBS community. Once the word gets out, they have merely to sit back and wait for people with the same interests to call. The makes and models of the host system and the callers' computers are irrelevant since any communicating machine can talk to any other.

No one really knows how many BBSs are in operation today. Our statistic of 60,000 or more comes from Jack Rickard, publisher and editor of *Boardwatch*, the leading magazine in the field. (For subscription information call (800) 933-6038. At this writing, a year's subscription is $36 domestic and $99 overseas.) And that's just in the United States. There are BBSs, or "mailboxes" as they are sometimes called abroad, in many other countries as well. The number and variety of topics covered is breathtaking. For example, here are the names and primary focus of just a few of the boards in operation today:

Family Keeper—Genealogy and sports.

Civil Net: The Civil Engineer Network—Dedicated to the civil-engineering professional. Let's create a national community of CEs!

The T.E.R.N. BBS—Police/fire/EMS/REACT. Member FidoNet, JerseyNET, Policenet, SafNet, & Adult Links.

Vault BBS—For NASCAR fans. Internet online, VGA Planets offline game hub, adult areas.

The Financial Experience—Dedicated to financial-and accounting-system applications.

Gray's Anatomy—Research and serious discussion on topics of UFOs, paranormal, and newsworthy events.

H.E.M.P. BBS—Dedicated to the legalization-of-marijuana movement. Internet/VNet, drug-related E-mail/newsgroups.

Eye Contact—Available through CompuServe network. Technical forums, focus on gay men's issues.

Maryland Catholic (Washington Node)—Catholic Access Net, Catholic Infonet, K12Net message areas. All are welcome. Religious and educational files.

UNitek Research BBS—Home of WORLDTLK conference, United Nations news, education, and distance learning.

Most sysops operate their boards as a hobby, but even so, running an active board can be a lot of work. There are questions to answer, messages to respond to, programs to test for viruses, and old files to remove. Consequently, some sysops offer download-only systems with virtually no messaging capabilities. These systems can serve as "publishers" of news, information, and selected topic-specific articles, but most act as distribution points for public domain (PD) and shareware software.

The number of megabytes of PD software a system has to offer is a mark of distinction in the BBS community, with some boards boasting four or five gigabytes or more, plus access to a wide selection of CD-ROM disks. Although some BBSs offer software for PCs *and* Macintoshes, it is more common for a board's file collection to be aimed at one or the other.

From an information standpoint, BBSs offer all of the advantages of a SIG on a big online system. But they have a number of disadvantages as well. The main problem with "boards" is the width of the pipeline. You can dial up CompuServe or Prodigy at any hour of the day or night and be virtually certain of making a connection. After all, these systems are set up to handle scores of thousands of users at the same time. The vast majority of bulletin boards, on the other hand, are connected to a single phone line.

A narrow pipeline

There is a thriving entrepreneurial trend in the field, however, with some boards offering a dozen or more lines. Such BBSs typically offer three-month or one-year subscriptions. At this writing, Wisconsin-based Exec-PC is the largest BBS in the world, with 280 modem lines, 30 direct Internet connections, 98 CD-ROMs online, and 75 gigabytes of files for every brand of computer. The board handles 6,000 calls a day.

Exec-PC is run by Bob and Tracey Mahoney, the same husband-and-wife team that started the system—with a single phone line—in November 1983. Subscriptions are $25 for three months or $75 for a full year. For more information, call the Exec-PC voice line at (414) 789-4200.

How to plug in: Getting lists of good numbers

This is only a brief sketch of the kinds of things you'll find once you enter the BBS world. More than likely, making your initial sojourn will cost you little or nothing. As noted, some bulletin boards charge subscription fees and issue passwords like a commercial system, but the vast majority are free to all callers. Your only expense will be any long-distance charges for the call.

The key thing is to find a list of *good* BBS numbers, by which we mean numbers that are still connected to operational boards. The attrition rate among new sysops is high. Many novices publish their board numbers only to find that they really don't want to make the required commitment.

A high attrition rate

As we said earlier, operating a good board can take a lot of time and energy. In addition to routine computer housekeeping, a conscientious sysop will review all uploaded files for viruses and to make sure that no one has put a copyrighted program on the board. Most also review each day's messages for stolen credit card numbers and other dicey information.

Of course there is also the time spent tuning, tweaking, and tinkering with the hardware and software. Add to this the fact that every sysop is a target of opportunity for all the addlepated computer punks who get their jollies by trying to wreck every board they call, and it's no wonder BBSs come and go with such frequency.

The ephemeral nature of bulletin boards is a fact of online life, however, and it simply means that you must pay particular attention to the freshness of the BBS phone lists you use. Because of this, books and magazines are not usually very good sources. The lead time between the submission of the last bit of copy and the publication date can be three months to a year, and inevitably many of the numbers will be out of service by the time the book or magazine hits the stands. However, there is at least one exception—the *Computer Shopper* list.

The Computer Shopper list

Computer Shopper is a tabloid-sized magazine that regularly runs to 800 pages or more. It makes a valiant attempt at providing editorial content and articles, but people really buy it for the ads.

The reason we mention *Computer Shopper* here, however, is that it publishes what is generally considered to be one of the best, most accurate lists of BBSs available. Boards are listed by state and area code and each listing includes a sentence or two giving the name of the sysop and the special focus—if any—

of the board. Only BBSs operating 24 hours a day, 7 days a week (except for maintenance) qualify to be included.

To enter a board on the list, its sysop must call a BBS operated by the BBS Press Service in Topeka, Kansas, and fill out a questionnaire. To remain on the *Computer Shopper* list, the sysop must call that board and review the listing at least every three months. Otherwise, the board is dropped from the list.

Though not perfect, the *Computer Shopper* approach does indeed come close to making sure that every number on its list is connected to a real bulletin board system. There are just two other points to make. First, the complete list of BBSs has grown so large that *Computer Shopper* publishes only one half of the list in each issue. So, to get the complete list, you must consult two consecutive issues. Second, *Computer Shopper* is among the full-text publications offered on the Ziff-Davis *Computer Select* CD-ROM that is available at many libraries. And it is available for search and retrieval on Ziff-Davis's Computer Database Plus, which can be accessed through CompuServe, the Knowledge Index, DIALOG/Data-Star, and the CARL Systems Network.

Lists online: The electronic alternative

The main point in favor of a conscientiously prepared printed BBS list is the amount of information it provides. The main disadvantage of all printed lists, aside from the problem of currency, is simply that they are printed: the numbers are on the page instead of in your computer where they belong.

Since you have a modem, however, there's an easy solution. One of the best places to look for bulletin board numbers is on other bulletin boards. Virtually every board will have at least one list of numbers in its file or library area. Better still, *Boardwatch* magazine publishes a "List of List Keepers" in every issue. These are the names and BBS phone numbers of people who "compile and maintain lists of bulletin boards, either by topical category, or by some geographic area or definition—often by area code."

Equally rich and varied phone number collections can be found in the SIG libraries of the online utility systems. Look for a SIG devoted to telecommunications, bulletin boards, a particular communications software program, or simply to your brand of computer. Use the system to search a SIG data library for lists by specifying the keyword *bbs* or *list*. (Please see Fig. 16-1 for a sample search on CompuServe.)

You could also select CompuServe's "Browse" option from the data library menu and simply specify *bbs* or *list* as your keyword when prompted to do so. You will probably want to search separately on both words to be sure of finding all relevant files.

The lists in Fig. 16-1 make for fascinating reading. There are lists of non-U.S. boards. And there are some local area lists—in this case for New Hampshire

The following file descriptions are from CompuServe's IBMBBS forum library, which is devoted exclusively to BBS lists. To obtain a similar printout yourself, sign on to CompuServe and key in go ibmbbs. Then key in dl7 to get to Data Library 7, the one that contains BBS lists. Finally, open your comm program's capture buffer and key in s/des/key:list .

[71565,1532]
MED101.ZIP/Bin Bytes: 12253, Count: 9, 03-Oct-94

Title   : Latest Black Bag Medical BBS list - 10/10/94
Keywords: MEDICAL FIRE EMS RECOVERY SCIENCE ALCOHOL AIDS DISABILITY BBS
              LIST

Latest Black Bag Medical BBS list current of 10/1/94. The list contains over 400 systems with interests in medicine, science, Fire/EMS, Psychology/Mental Health, Self Help, Recovery, AIDS and Disabilities. ENUMERABLE interesting systems. All numbers have been verified within the last 21 days. Now in its eighth year of publication. A worthwhile download. Please distribute.

UPL/AUT Edward DelGrosso M.D.
Black Bag BBS (1:2614/706)   610-454-7396 4 nodes - V32b
CIS: 71565,1532
Internet : ed@blackbag.com

[70322,2063]
NHBB10.ZIP/Bin Bytes: 12277, Count: 3, 02-Oct-94

Title   : New Hampshire BBS List for OCTOBER 1994
Keywords: MAGGI BBS NH LIST MARIOS

New Hampshire BBS List for October 1994 ....

[100274,1040]
IS0994.ZIP/Bin Bytes: 6519, Count: 6, 19-Sep-94

Title   : The ISRAEL National List
Keywords: ISRAEL BBS LIST

The sep-94 list of BBSs in ISRAEL. Contain system name, phone,
sysop name and short description.

[76320,204]
EN0994.ZIP/Bin Bytes: 43856, Count: 57, 12-Sep-94

Title   : The Engineering BBS List: September 1994 edition
Keywords: ENGINEERING BBS LIST ENGINEER ENGRXXXX COMPUTER PLUMBER

Engineering BBS List; 9-94; 177 listings September 1994 version of The Engineering BBS List; 177 listings with complete information and descriptions. Since May 1990, the source for Engineering related BBS's. Current version always available on The Computer Plumber BBS @ 319-337-6723.

[100332,1726]
RUSBBS.ZIP/Bin Bytes: 33874, Count: 27, 07-Sep-94

Title   : A major list of Russian Bulletin Board Systems
Keywords: BBS LIST RUSSIA RUSSIAN

List of Russian Bulletin Board Systems - sorted by locations. For private use only! Any commercial distribution strictly prohibited!

[73240,2046]
BBSEUR.ZIP/Bin Bytes: 481428, Count: 56, 26-Aug-94

Title   : BBS lists and listholders in Europe
Keywords: BBS LIST LISTHOLDERS EUROPE SYSOPS TWO BBSCON SWITZERLAND
             GERMANY RUSSIA

BBSing in Europe - many BBS lists from all over Europe including Switzerland, France,
Hungary, Belgium, Benelux, Bulgaria, Croatia, Denmark, Spain, Finland, U.K., Germany,
Ireland, London, Milano, Russia, Soviet Union, Sweden, Yugoslavia, Norway, East Germany,
and others

[100101,1270]
RLUK94.ZIP/Bin Bytes: 87758, Count: 87, 13-Aug-94

Title   : ROBLIST UK verified BBS Listing for AUGUST 1994
Keywords: UK BBS LIST

ROBLIST is the only *verified* UK BBS listing available in the UK. Not only is it growing into
the most comprehensive listing available, but it also contains editorial and advertising
directed at the BBS community. With powerful search and sort functions it has to be the most
unique list on the planet. Download it TODAY!

[72240,2230]
USB123.ZIP/Bin Bytes: 123072, Count: 670, 31-Jul-94

Title   : USBBS National BBS list for August 1994
Keywords: BBS LIST USBBS

USBBS National BBS list for August 1994

[70007,4634]
SUP407.ZIP/Bin Bytes: 20098, Count: 552, 08-Jul-94

Title   : Technical Support BBS List for July 1994
Keywords: TECH TECHNICAL SUPPORT VENDOR SHAREWARE HARDWARE BBS LIST

Technical Support BBS List for July 1994 - Lists over 500 BBS's ran by Commercial and
Shareware Hardware/Software Manufacturers for the support of their products. Also
includes a list of Faxback numbers that offer product support and product information.

[70007,4634]
EVV407.ZIP/Bin Bytes: 5173, Count: 20, 08-Jul-94

Title   : Evansville Indiana Area BBS List for July 1994
Keywords: EVANSVILLE INDIANA EVV IN EVVIN BBS LIST

Evansville, Indiana BBS List for July 1994

and Evansville, Indiana. But notice the special interest lists—medical boards,
boards devoted to engineering, product and technical support, and so on. And
pay particular attention to the file USB123.ZIP. This file contains the best,
most current list of boards running IBM-compatible software. As its filename
indicates, it has been continuously issued every month for 123 months
to date.

The best way to "work the boards" is to take advantage of your
communications software's dialing directory or phone list. Most comm
programs these days let you create lists of numbers to call. Enter the phone
numbers once, and you can tell the program to dial them by simply picking
an item off a dialing directory menu.

How to implement "attack dialing"

If you're a novice user, start by keying in five or six numbers that are geographically close to you. You will find them on the *Computer Shopper* list and on others. Take extra care to get the numbers right or you'll end up with an irate voice on the other end of your line instead of the familiar modem tone.

Many comm programs will let you specify a list of dialing directory entries for them to dial in turn. If the first number is busy, they automatically dial the second one, and so on until they get a connection. This technique is sometimes called "attack dialing," and it offers the best way to deal with constant busy signals.

If you really get into bulletin boards, you will want to search boards and online utility libraries for any public domain programs capable of *automatically* converting a file of BBS numbers into a dialing directory for your comm program. There is no guarantee that such a program exists for your communications software, but some user may very well have written exactly the program you need. If you're lucky enough to find one, you may never have to key in another BBS number by hand.

The Communicator's Toolchest disk available from Glossbrenner's Choice, for example, includes CVTT, a Windows program to convert among Procomm, Procomm Plus 1.0, Telix, and text dialing directories. Plus DIRCOPY to convert among Telix, Qmodem, Procomm, Procomm Plus, Bitcom, and text formats. The disk also includes the programs needed to add ZMODEM and CompuServe B+ support to almost any comm program.

Conclusion

Bulletin board systems, like the electronic universe as a whole, offer you information, adventure, and a sense of community. Dialing up a board is an ideal and virtually cost-free way to enter that universe. And it's easy, particularly if you follow our advice and put several board numbers in a dialing queue so your comm program can cycle through them seeking a connection.

Once you've plugged in, you'll discover store-and-forward mail systems like FidoNet that can pass your locally uploaded message across the country or even around the world at little or no cost to you. You will discover Internet connections. You'll encounter oceans of public domain and shareware software.

And you'll find that the BBS community is so diverse that it can answer virtually any question on any topic—or at least help you turn up some expert or contact who can. It's simply a matter of locating a board frequented by the kind of experts you seek.

As a current or prospective information broker, the main question in your mind is the one we put forward at the beginning of this chapter: What's in it for me? It's a question that we simply cannot answer. However, there can be little doubt that BBSs are a legitimate information source. And it can be well worth your while to look into this new medium.

17 CD-ROM possibilities

This chapter discusses what many feel is the most exciting technology to hit the information industry in over a decade—CD-ROM. It's a technology that lets you put an entire database—or an entire encyclopedia—in your pocket. With a database on a CD-ROM disk, you can search to your heart's content without being subject to the various charges levied by online database vendor systems.

The one caveat is that as an information broker it is especially important to check the terms and conditions for use attached to each CD-ROM database. You may find that there are copyright restrictions on how you may use the data. You may even find that there are CD-ROM producers who refuse to sell their products to information brokers, insisting instead that they do their searches online. Policies vary and vary widely.

When you are not restricted in any way, there's no question but that purchasing the CD-ROM version of a database you search frequently can be a very cost-effective solution. For the same reason, a CD-ROM also offers new searchers the opportunity for unlimited practice at a fixed price. The commands required to search a given CD-ROM database may differ from those used by an online system. But the search concepts and approaches will be the same.

If you like, you can skip the other details presented here and jump to the end of the chapter where you will find a sampling of CD-ROM titles and the names of two of the leading directories of the products that are available. On the other hand, if you'd like to know a little more about the pluses and minuses and the technology that makes it possible to pack all that information on a little disk, read on.

Too important to ignore

The term *CD-ROM* stands for "compact disk, read-only memory." The disks themselves are identical in appearance to the CD audio disks that have all but replaced vinyl records in music stores across the land. They are of interest here because of their incredible information-holding capacities— entire encyclopedias, the text of literally hundreds of books, tens of thousands of images, all packed onto thin plastic disks measuring a mere 4.7 inches in diameter.

These days, if you're interested in information, you have to be interested in CD-ROM, since more and more information is being made available in this format. Fortunately, more and more computer models these days include a built-in CD-ROM drive as a matter of course. And the cost of adding such a drive to an existing system has fallen to as low as $140.

As for the cost of databases on CD, it all depends on the database. Some go for as little as $45, while others sell for several thousand dollars.

As Sue points out, "If you follow our advice and find your own special market niche, you may indeed find that using CD-ROMs can save you a lot of money. But CD-ROM prices have come down, while database search costs have gone up. Today, I'd say that if you specialize in any of the technical or medical areas in particular, it can be well worth your while to look into buying appropriate CD-ROM databases. But do not neglect to pay attention to any copyright restrictions and to the terms and conditions under which you may use each product. Assuming you're okay there, you will find that CD-ROMs really are a realistic and cost-effective alternative to online searching in many cases."

There's nothing like a real-life example to clarify a point, and Alfred's got the genuine article for you. We'll let him tell it in his own words in the section that follows.

Alfred's most excellent CD-ROM adventure

As many of you know, over the past decade or so I've made a profession of writing books about telecommunications, databases, software, and computers. In support of this effort, I have subscribed to a *lot* of topic-relevant magazines. In fact, I've still got the premier issue of *PC Magazine*, a thin little saddle-stitched affair that bears no resemblance to the perfect-bound monster that now appears in my mailbox twice each month.

Actually, I should say "appeared," since I no longer subscribe to *PC Magazine*. In the computer business that's rank heresy. If you're going to be a computer pundit and author, at the very least you must subscribe to *PC Magazine*,

InfoWorld, and *PC Week*. You should probably add *PC World* as well, and possibly *PC Computing*. And that's if you're concentrating on the DOS and Windows world. If you are concentrating on the Apple Macintosh, at a minimum you need *MacUser* and *MacWEEK*, in addition to *InfoWorld*.

Unfortunately, there are a number of drawbacks to subscribing to all of these magazines. First and foremost is the expense. A one-year subscription to *PC Magazine* costs $50. A subscription to *PC Week* is $195 a year. *InfoWorld* is $130. And so on. Yes, this is simply a cost of doing business, and as with all magazines, special discounts are available. Still, magazine subscription costs do mount up.

There is also the problem of storage and retrieval. I used to keep every issue of every computer magazine in row-upon-row of boxes in a room on the third floor of our house. When a box filled up, I would move it out to the barn for long-term storage and put an empty box in its place. Eventually the long-term storage space began to fill up and so, with great reluctance, I got rid of several years' worth of publications, resolving to keep only the last two years' worth from then on.

I don't know why I was so reluctant. Trying to find, photocopy, and file the articles relevant to whatever topic I happened to be working on at the time was always a royal pain. I won't say that the magazine collections were useless. But they were certainly difficult to use. I used to spend hours sitting on a battered old stool on the third floor pouring over magazine tables of contents by the light of a single bare bulb.

So why not do my searching online? Two reasons. First, the online database to use for this is Ziff-Davis's Computer ASAP. But it did not offer all of the publications I needed in full-text format.

Computer Database Plus on CompuServe

Second, I wasn't keen on paying $108 an hour in connect time and nearly a dollar for every record I asked to have displayed and $2 for each full-text article I wanted to see. (Those were DIALOG's rates at the time. The current rate is $60 an hour and $2.70 for each full-text article viewed.)

As it happened, at about this time Ziff-Davis began to offer a product called Computer Database Plus on CompuServe at a cost of $24 an hour, plus $1.50 to $2.50 for each full-text article retrieved. (The display charges are the same, but the connect-time cost has been reduced to $15 an hour, plus your normal CompuServe connect-time rate.)

The price was right. And since I was on CompuServe every day anyway, I decided to give it a try. It was great! No more scuttling up to the third floor to spend half an hour trying to find an article on some topic. I would use the database to simply (and cheaply) locate citations. Then, armed with the article title, page number, and publication date, I could go straight to the target magazine.

To make a long story short, I spent over $300 using Computer Database Plus on CompuServe in this way in the course of writing my *Complete Hard Disk Handbook* for Osborne/McGraw-Hill. That sounds like a lot, but the time I saved was well worth it. To say nothing of the richer vein of information I was able to incorporate into my book.

The Computer Select CD-ROM

When I heard that Ziff-Davis was introducing the same database on CD-ROM as a product called Computer Select, I was extremely interested. Fortunately, I'd acquired a Hitachi CD-ROM drive in the course of doing another project. I'm not sure I would have been so interested in Computer Select if I'd had to add the cost of a CD drive ($500 at the time) to the product's $800 subscription price.

I decided to give it a try, and can say without hesitation that it forever changed the way I work. The boxes of magazines are now gone from my third floor and from the long-term storage area in the barn. They have been replaced by a single CD-ROM disk for each year.

Each month, a new disk arrives containing 12 months' worth of magazines—the full-text of some 62 magazines and newsletters and citations and abstracts for 65 more.

The disk also offers a directory containing the addresses, company officers, phone and fax numbers, and financial data for 11,000 computer and software companies. And there is address information on nearly 70,000 hardware and software firms. Plus Alan Freedman's *Computer Glossary* and Harry Newton's *Telecom Dictionary*. And you can search everything with all the power available on a system like DIALOG.

At prices like these . . .

This is an enormously impressive product. But then, it had better be: A subscription now costs nearly $1,200 a year. No question, that's a lot of money. It clearly would not pay you to invest in this product unless, like me, you have a continual and constant need for the information it offers. The same applies to other CD-ROM titles, almost all of which are much less expensive.

But if you *do* have that kind of need, consider the fact that a Computer Select subscription costs the equivalent of $100 a month. That's less than a single hour of connect time on some databases. And it is only slightly more than the $75 that DIALOG has for years claimed is the cost of one typical search on its system.

Or consider the fact that if you were to subscribe to all of the 62 magazines and newsletters Computer Select offers in full text, special deals notwithstanding, you would pay much more than that. (Divide $1,200 by 50 and you get $24 per publication, far less than even the most aggressive magazine can afford to charge for a yearly subscription.) And you would have all those issues to store in your attic.

There are drawbacks, however. At this writing, like most online and CD-ROM products, Computer Select does not include graphics and illustrations. Fortunately, for my purposes, photographs and graphics aren't all that important.

**Overload!
Overload!
Mass critical!**

There is also the "information overload" factor. This is something I've never seen anyone talk about when discussing CD-ROM. The fact is, however, that in the course of researching this chapter for your indefatigable writing team, I found 5,269 articles containing the keyword *CD-ROM* on the most recent Computer Select disk—1,228 of them with *CD-ROM* tagged as their principle topic.

Had I opted to print them, the result would have been a stack of hundreds of pages. Had I opted to read them, I would probably still be doing so, and this book would never get written. Of course, CD-ROM is a very broad topic, and I had in effect said to the database, "Give me everything you have on CD-ROM." I didn't have to do that. The search software provided with this and many other CD-ROM products is easily capable of executing a much more refined and sharply focused search.

A time sink of a different sort

But, since it didn't cost anything, I decided to go for the whole enchilada. Yes, I ended up producing far *more* information than I would have come up with had I been limited to the boxes of magazines in my attic. But I also ended up producing far more information than I need or could possibly absorb.

There's nothing wrong with this, of course. But I know from previous experience that, freed from the discipline of cost, I have indulged myself far too often and too long reading articles that I've pulled up from my Computer Select CD-ROM. To an innately curious person, it's "kid in a candy store" time. Besides, reading is a lot easier than writing. It's a great way to procrastinate, and easy to justify if the reading is work-related.

A word about CD-ROM technology

Don't worry. We're not going to make you sit through a chapter-and-verse explanation of how CD-ROMs are created and how they work. Still, it is important to have a very general idea of what CD-ROMs are all about and how it is that they can store such massive quantities of data, if only so you can sound reasonably intelligent when someone asks you how all that information can fit on such a little disk.

The answer is the *laser*. Laser beams can be focused with incredible fineness, and they can be turned on and off very quickly. These two facts are at the heart of CD-ROM technology. When an inscribing laser beam is focused on a spinning CD and turned on, it makes a very, very tiny pit in the CD's surface. When it is turned off, there is no pit.

Ones and zeros—again! Thus, as a reading laser beam traverses the CD's surface, at any given second it is over a pit or a solid place on the disk. If it is over a pit, the laser light reflected back from the disk looks one way. If it is over a solid area, the reflected light looks another way. But these are the only two ways the light can appear: either a "pit" or "not a pit;" either an "on" or an "off;" either a "1" or a "0."

Laser disks or CD-ROMs, in other words, are a *binary* medium, just like a hard or floppy disk drive. The reading laser is either over a pit or over a "nonpit." There is no in between. Just like your disk drives, CD-ROMs can record the numbers needed to represent ASCII characters or any other kind of computer data.

What sets a CD-ROM apart is the terrifically fine precision of that laser. The pits and nonpits are much, much smaller than the magnetized or nonmagnetized areas used to represent 1's and 0's on a floppy or hard disk. Indeed, it has been estimated that if you were to stretch out the spiral data track of a 4.7-inch CD-ROM, the track would extend to three miles or more.

How many megabytes? That's about all you need to know about CD-ROM technology. It will certainly satisfy any nontechnical person who asks. Accordingly, please feel free to skip ahead to the next section, if you like. The paragraphs that follow are for those who are interested in learning a bit more.

The image of a three-mile long track of data is certainly striking. But let's put it into more conventional terms. Because of the fineness of lasers, a single side of a single CD-ROM can hold 650 to 700 *megabytes* of data. That is the equivalent of more than 1,850 5.25-inch 360K floppy disks. A disk of 650 megabytes is also equivalent to 325,000 double-spaced typewritten pages or 650 reams of paper. Or a stack of pages 135 feet high. If you were to transmit all the data on a CD-ROM using a 2400 bps modem, working round the clock, the process would take you 23 days.

Great economics It is also worth noting that the media cost of a single compact disk is now around 75 cents, probably less than the cost of the packaging. In contrast, producing the printed version of an encyclopedia might cost a publisher $10 a book—or $200 for an entire 20-volume set. And, of course, 20 printed volumes take up far more space and cost much more to warehouse than single CD-ROM disks.

So, given a choice, which would you rather sell if you were the publisher: The printed version at a discounted price of $500 or the CD-ROM version at $400?

Your gross profit on the printed version will be $300. But on the CD-ROM version, your profit will be nearly $400. Plus, the CD-ROM version will involve far fewer intermediary costs. Just think what it costs to ship a 20-volume encyclopedia—compared to the 98 cents or so you would spend to ship a single CD-ROM in its jewel case.

The economics of CD-ROM publishing are *very* attractive. Particularly if you are primarily in the business of producing a printed product anyway. For a very low entry fee, you can offer a CD-ROM version of your print product that holds the potential of making you nearly 100 percent profit.

As the prices for the equipment needed to create CD-ROMs drops, even corporations are looking to the technology as a money-saver. For example, the cost of the machine needed to make a master CD-ROM is now about $6,000, and the cost of the media used to hold that master ranges from $20 to $40 a disk. The machine can be hooked up to any recent-model computer. Dataware, a Cambridge, Massachusetts-based publisher of CD-ROM mastering and search software tools, estimates that the cost of storing one megabyte of data on paper is about $4, on floppy disk about $1, and on CD-ROM, less than one-quarter of a cent!

At this point, there are three things you need to know: What to look for when considering a CD-ROM drive, how to add such a drive to your current system, and where to get information on what CD-ROM titles are available.

How to buy a CD-ROM drive

If you are buying a new computer, and if the manufacturer offers a built-in CD-ROM drive or multimedia package as an option, give it strong consideration. But make sure the drive offers the characteristics listed below. If it does not, then you should consider adding a drive, sound board, and speakers on your own at a later date instead.

- Double speed. The very first CD-ROM drives were essentially audio CD units that had been adapted for data. The rotation speed of the drive was thus the same as that used for an audio CD. Fine for music, but too slow for data and computer graphics. Most of today's units, in contrast, can operate at two speeds—one for music and audio and a faster speed for data. There are even "triple speed" drives, but it is not clear that they are worth the extra money you will have to pay.
- Average access time of 320 milliseconds or less. This is the so-called "seek time" of the drive—the average amount of time it takes to locate and move to the track containing the requested data. Hard disk drives, in contrast, have average access times of between nine and 15 milliseconds these days.
- Data transfer rate of 300 kilobytes (300K) per second or more. Transfer rate is the same as "throughput." A transfer rate of 300K per second is typical in a double-speed drive. More expensive drives transfer data at 470K per second or more, which is close to the rate of most hard disk drives.

- Buffer size of 64 kilobytes (64K) or more. In both hard disks and CD-ROM drives, built-in RAM chips are used to speed up and smooth out the flow of data. In simplified terms, the notion is that if you have commanded the drive to go to a certain track and read the data occupying half that track, there's a good chance that the next bit of data you want will be located on the remainder of that track. So why not read the data while you're there? There's just one problem: where do you put the data after you've read it? The answer is in the drive's buffer of RAM chips. A 64K RAM buffer or "cache" is typical of today's drives, though more expensive models boast caches of 256K or more.
- Multisession photo CD-compatible. This is often referred to as "multisession Kodak Photo CD ready." It means that the drive is able to read images on a given disk, even if those images were recorded at different times, in multiple sessions.

Upgrading an existing system

If the maker of the computer you are interested in buying offers a drive that meets or exceeds these specifications, you should probably add it to the options you want. If not, or if you want to add a CD-ROM drive to your current machine, you will be pleased to learn that it's no more difficult than adding a standard floppy drive. Though, if you are at all trepidatious, you can have a friend do the job or pay a technician at your local computer store to do so. If you're a Macintosh user, adding a drive is merely a matter of plugging it into one of the ports at the back of your system unit.

Your main consideration is whether you want to add a sound board and speakers at the same time. These two items, plus a CD-ROM drive, will equip your computer to run all multimedia titles. Since multimedia kits that give you everything you need, *including* several CD-ROMs, sell for around $270, if you can possibly afford it, we strongly suggest you take the plunge. Get some advice from your local computer guru. Check the "buying guide" articles you will find on the Computer Database Plus feature on CompuServe. But basically, for that kind of money, you can't go too far wrong.

Directories of CD-ROM titles

If you need a comprehensive list of what's available, see *CD-ROMs in Print* from Meckler Publishing at (203) 226-6967. This book is published each year at a cost of $100.

You should also look for Volume 2 of the *Gale Directory of Databases*. This volume covers databases available on CD-ROM, disks, magnetic tape, and other media. Both Volume 1 (Online Databases) and Volume 2 are published every six months. The cost is $315 for both, $210 for just Volume 1, and $130 for just Volume 2. Purchasers receive the current issue, plus the next issue. Call Gale Research at (800) 347-4253 for more information.

You might also consider *The CD-ROM Directory* from TFPL Publishing. Updated semiannually, this directory covers titles for all kinds of computers. The cost is $165 for the book, $220 for the CD-ROM version, or $320 if you want both book and disk. For more information, call TFPL Publishing at (202) 296-6009.

18 Services to sell

It is a cardinal rule of success in any business to know what business you're really in. It is thus appropriate to begin Part four of this book with a brief discussion of the kinds of services you can expect to offer as an information broker.

We have spent most of our time up to now discussing *information gathering*. That will always be your bread and butter, and we will assume that you have at least a preliminary understanding of what that service is. There are two other services, however, that many information brokers offer as well—*alert services* (sometimes referred to as "electronic clipping" or "current awareness" services) and *document delivery services*.

Of course, these services involve information gathering. But it is information gathering of a type that is different from what is likely to be your main line of business. These services may or may not be profitable for you. As Sue says, "You should be able to make money on an alert service, but document delivery can be a real sinkhole. It can cost you far more time to locate an article or other document for a client than you can ever charge for the service, if you try to do it yourself." However, as we'll show you in a moment, there are alternatives. So read on.

Whether you make or lose money, however, there are good reasons to consider offering these services. For one thing, they are part of the full-service concept many brokers want to project. For another, they offer a natural way to keep your name in front of a client's eyes. And that, of course, can lead to more assignments.

Document delivery, yellowsheets, & DIALOG

Document delivery—or *doc del* as it is called in the profession—is basically the service of providing clients with photocopies of documents referred to in an online search. The document can be anything from a magazine article to a corporate report to an out-of-print book. The term originated in the days when online systems offered only bibliographical listings of source material pertaining to a particular topic. But, of course, the practice of interlibrary loan that preceded doc del has been in existence since the invention of libraries.

At the time, there were no full-text databases. If you saw a reference to an article in, say, a scientific journal that looked like it might be relevant, you could order a copy using a document delivery service. DIALOG, for example, has arrangements with over 100 doc del services. (Their capabilities and areas of specialty are listed on DIALOG "yellowsheets.") So if you are on DIALOG and you see a bibliographical citation of interest, it is an easy matter to key in a command telling the doc del service of your choice to send you a copy of the article.

A matter of choice

Choosing the right document delivery service is one of the skills you will develop as a practicing information broker. In virtually every case, you will have to make a decision regarding the doc del house you wish to use. If you have found a citation in a database that provides its *own* document delivery service, then it is often most cost-effective and expedient to take advantage of that fact and order your documents from them.

Some of the many database producers who provide doc del services include ISI (Sci Search and Social Science Search), Chemical Abstracts, Predicasts, and ABI/INFORM. As you would expect, one of the features that makes using an IP's own doc del service attractive is speed. The information provider almost always has the actual documents (magazine articles, reports, etc.) on file. It does not have to go looking for them. For this reason, in-house doc del services can usually offer those services at a relatively low price.

Full-service document delivery firms

On the other hand, if you need something that is not referenced online, or if the item is from a database that does not operate its own in-house doc del service, then you should order from a full-service document delivery company. We've dealt with several such firms over the years, including Information Express, Infocus, Instant Information, and Infotrieve. See your DIALOG "yellowsheets" for details on contacting many of these firms.

A full-service doc del firm will usually be able to obtain anything from anywhere, even if you can't provide them with the complete citation. They typically take longer to deliver the goods than a databases's in-house doc del service because, for the most part, they do not maintain their own document collections. Instead, they rely on their networks of runners stationed at or near major libraries.

The service will consult its records to determine which library has the originals of the documents you need. It will then issue an electronic work order to the runner who covers that library. The runner will locate and photocopy the document and send it to the doc del service's home office or directly to you, depending on how you and the company have arranged things. Either way, there are all kinds of options, ranging from first-class mail to fax to using an overnight delivery service like Federal Express.

Our point here is that mechanisms and organizations already exist within the information industry to locate, copy, and deliver virtually any document you may want. Some documents are easier to get than others. But just about everything cited, whether online or in print, is available as a photocopy of the original. Markups are added and fees are charged, of course.

At IOD, Sue had her own network of library runners to provide document delivery services to clients. It was profitable. Generally there was a gross margin of around 60 percent on document delivery, compared to a gross margin of about 25 percent on research. However, you need considerable volume (15,000 requests per month or more) to make that kind of profit margin. There is always the chance that one especially difficult doc del assignment can significantly eat into the profit made on the easy ones. You may find yourself spending far more time on one of these tasks than you can possibly bill for.

Competition from the IPs

It takes a lot of time to build an organization like the one Sue established at IOD, and it certainly isn't something a new information broker should attempt to do today. The market has changed, and, as noted, there is significant competition from the database producers themselves.

For example, ABI/INFORM, as well as Predicasts and Trade and Industry Index (both of which are owned by Information Access Company), offer customers document delivery through Information Express. The rates are very competitive since, in keeping with the current trends, Information Express actually owns the collection of the relevant print materials, so most orders can be filled on-site.

There is also competition from small one- and two-person operations, many of which do not pay copyright clearance fees. We strongly advise you to avoid firms like this. After all, one of the benefits that a good doc del house provides, in addition to speed and cost-effectiveness, is freeing you from the liability and overhead associated with copyright issues.

If you are new to the field, you may not be aware of the fact that anyone who provides articles, book chapters, or any other copyrighted material may be required to pay a royalty fee. A doc del firm that does not pay royalties as required can be sued for damages and costs. And if you are a customer of that firm, you may be dragged into the suit as well.

But forget about the penalties. Paying a copyright fee is the right thing to do. As Sue says, "I'm often asked by people, 'How do I get around copyright?' I want to make it very clear that I feel that it is our obligation as professionals to adhere to the copyright requirements.

"We should really welcome the fact that we can pay the publishers a fee that will help them stay in business. Because, after all, as information gatherers, if we end up with very few publications to gather information from—because the publishers have had to go out of business—everyone loses. Remember, a publisher is just as entitled to reap the rewards of his or her work as we are to be paid for our expertise.

"Copyright requirements are not something to be gotten around. The fees they generate for the publishers and authors are the water that helps nourish new growth. If you play by the rules and insist that your colleagues do so as well, the entire profession benefits."

The Copyright Clearance Center

To facilitate the granting of permissions and payment offees, in 1977, in accordance with the expressed desire of Congress, an organization called the Copyright Clearance Center(CCC) was established. Corporations pay site-licensing fees to the CCC to cover photocopies made and distributed internally. Document delivery services are required to pay a fee to the CCC for each document they photocopy. The CCC then passes the fee along to the appropriate publisher.

Thousands of publishers participate in the CCC, but every now and then a doc del company will receive a request for a document whose publisher is not a CCC member. In those cases, the doc del firm will usually contact the publisher and negotiate a permissions agreement. The phone calls and letters involved make this a labor-intensive process.

They'll give you the hard stuff

When Sue was running IOD in the 1980s, the competition in the document delivery end of the business wasn't nearly as intense. But as more and more database producers began to offer documents from their own collections at cut-rate prices, it became increasingly difficult to make any money offering doc del services.

"We began to get all the tough requests," Sue says. "The ones requiring us to contact the British Library Lending Division or some library in Russia. The clients would use the document delivery services provided by Predicasts and ABI to handle the easy stuff and turn to us for the real toughies.

"The problem was that our rates were established on the assumption that we would get *all* of a client's doc del business. The money we made on the easy ones would offset the money we lost on the really hard ones."

Today, in Sue's opinion, it is very difficult to make money offering document delivery unless you happen to own a "captive collection." Some information specialty firms are in this position, and, of course, many databases are. But for the aspiring information broker, document delivery is not a viable option.

Bruce Antelman, founder of Information Express, (415) 494-8787, has come up with an imaginative solution. Bruce combines an in-house collection with a worldwide network of runners. This combination enables Information Express to provide quick service (24 to 48 hours via the core "captive" collection), and to respond to esoteric and unique requests for information available in only one or two libraries in the world.

Information Express, a great example

The Rugge Group uses Information Express for almost all of its document delivery needs. We know the company and thus feel confident in using it as an example of what a superb doc del house should offer:

- Document requests are processed the same day they are received.
- Regular orders go out via first-class-mail or UPS ground. (Other delivery options are available at the client's request.)
- The base rate includes up to 10 pages. There is a charge of 25 to 60 cents per page after that, depending on where the document came from.
- Expenses like telephone, purchase, verification, and shipping are charged over and above the base rate.
- Documents are provided in compliance with the Copyright Act of 1976. Copyright fees are charged back to the client and are paid directly to the Copyright Clearance Center.
- The base rate runs from $8.50 to $20.00 per document, depending on your monthly volume of orders and on where the document comes from.
- There is a charge of $12 for rush service.

Information Express is an example of a document delivery service that has done it right. They are a pleasure to deal with. And, one final point, whether you use Information Express or a different company to fulfill your client's document delivery request, do not neglect to add an appropriate markup to the delivery service's fee. After all, you had to spend your time and use your expertise to contact the service and order the document.

We should make clear that, while years ago at IOD document delivery was a money-maker, these days, Sue doesn't view it as as a profit center. "It's a convenience we offer clients, not something we push. Whether they take advantage of it or not usually depends on the client's access to collections of printed material or the client's familiarity with document delivery services."

A convenience, not a money-maker

If you are working for a corporate information center staffed by a full-time librarian, the chances are that he or she will know about the most economical document delivery services. If the client is not "information wise" and does not have easy access to the doc del mechanisms of the industry, you might consider offering the service at a 50 to 100 percent markup.

The Rugge Group might charge $15 for a document delivered by Information Express at a cost of about $7. If the price of the document is higher, the markup percentage might be smaller. A markup of $8 to $10 is hardly unreasonable considering the time, effort, and handling that go into obtaining a document, even from a document delivery service. Remember, you are offering the client the convenience of one-stop shopping. Most clients don't want to deal with the details. They just want "the facts."

If the client balks at the price you charge, fine. Let them get the document elsewhere or do without. Document delivery, in most cases, will not be your primary business.

Electronic clipping or alert services

The information industry is as bad as any other when it comes to jargon. For years, long before President Reagan proposed the Strategic Defense Initiative, the information industry has offered SDI or *selective dissemination of information*. But the term *SDI* is rapidly being replaced in the information industry with the much more descriptive *electronic clipping service* or *alert service*.

Call it what you will, the concept is not difficult to understand. Suppose you conduct a search on a DIALOG database to find information on, say, the most effective colors to use in packaging a snack food. You do the search today, capture all the information it produces, and prepare a final report. But two weeks from now the database is updated to incorporate citations of articles published in the last 14 days.

For a small fee, you can store your search strategy on DIALOG. Then, when the database is updated in two weeks, DIALOG's computers will *automatically* run that search strategy against the new information. Any hits will be automatically transmitted to your DIALOG electronic mailbox. So when you sign on two weeks from now, you will have a "letter" containing the latest hits generated by your search strategy in your mailbox. DIALOG will also let you store a search strategy and run it yourself at a time of your choosing.

You capture this new information, clean it up as need be with your word processor, and send it to the client along with a bill. That is what an alert (or *current awareness*) service is all about. It's easy to do, as long as you are certain that your search strategy is the right one to use.

Every online system does things a bit differently, but all major online systems offer some version of an alert service. DIALOG calls its version DIALOG Alert. Fees vary with the database, but they typically range from about $2 to $10 per update and include all charges for the first 20 records. Additional hits are printed at the normal per-record display price.

To calculate your monthly alert service expense, multiply the per-update charge by the number of times the database is updated during a month (daily, weekly, monthly, etc.). Updating schedules and alert fees for each database are given in the DIALOG price list.

An alert service depends on computer technology and thus has a "sexy" feeling to it. You can make much of this in selling a current awareness service to a client. Figure your costs beforehand and add a comfortable markup. If you have to pay DIALOG $12 a month, plan on charging your client at least $75 a month for the first 25 records, plus your cost on any records above 25.

Add a comfortable markup

Remember, you'll have to pay connect-time charges for using DIALOG's electronic mail system to download the hits. (Although, as noted elsewhere in this book, if you are an AIIP member, DialMail connect time is free.) You'll have to spend time word processing out all the elements in a record likely to confuse a nonsearcher (accession number, keyword descriptors, etc.). Then you'll have to print it out, package it up, and mail it to the client. It's not all gravy, in other words. A lot of processing and handling are involved.

Like document delivery, an alert service is not something to build your business on. But it's an easy add-on service, and that's how we suggest you sell it. Wait until you have done a search your client is happy with—that way you'll know your search strategy is producing the desired results—and then suggest a current awareness service using the same strategy. At the Rugge Group, the cover letter that accompanies most reports to clients notes that "the search strategy has been saved. If you feel updated information would be useful to you on a regular basis, we can provide it for x a month or y a quarter. Just let us know."

You probably won't get rich on alert service income. But offering this kind of service has the extra advantage of helping to keep your name before the client's eyes. Someone who is getting a report from your office every week or every month is much more likely to remember your firm when the next search question comes up.

There are all *kinds* of things an information broker can offer a client. The field is so wide open that we would hesitate to set any limits. But the three conventional services most information brokers offer are information gathering, document delivery, and current awareness or alert services. Regardless of where your future takes you, this is an excellent triumvirate to start with.

Conclusion

In the next chapter, we will show you how to create the basic materials you need to project a suitable image so you can sell this triumvirate of services. Then we'll look at how to sell and how to market your services (two different activities entirely!).

19 Projecting an image of credibility

In Chapter 20 we're going to focus on the things you can and should do to market yourself and sell your services. But before we can get to that point, you've got to prepare your business materials. You've got to have stationery, business cards, and a brochure designed to sell your services. These components are not to be taken lightly or treated casually, for they are your basic marketing tools.

Like it or not, everyone who hopes to sell his or her personal skills to someone else is *ipso facto* in the image-making business. The image happens to be one of yourself and your business, and every piece of paper a client or a prospect receives from you reinforces it. The image you want to project as an information broker is, above all, one of *credibility*. When you hand your business card to someone, you don't want the person to look at it and silently say, "Hmm, cheap. I wonder if this is really my sort of person?"

Nor do you want your card to communicate flashiness. Flashy people cannot be relied upon to be discrete. And discretion and confidentiality are *crucial* in your relationship with a client.

Your business card should therefore be cleanly designed and of the best quality. If the traditional white card with black lettering is too boring for you, consider a different colored stock and/or a different ink color. But keep it "quiet" and avoid the temptation to get cute.

Business cards

Stationery

The same thing goes for your stationery. It should be 24 pound, 25 percent cotton bond. This is the kind of paper that carries a water mark (visible when you hold it up to the light).

Paper "poundage," incidentally, refers to the number of pounds registered by a stack of 500 sheets of the 17-×-22-inch master stock from which letter sheets are cut. The conventional range is 9 to 28 pounds. Photocopy paper, by comparison, is usually 16 or 20 pound paper, really too flimsy for your professional letterhead.

Good paper costs more, to be sure. But nothing else communicates the same look and feel of quality. It says you care about how clients and prospects perceive you and that you take pride in anything that bears your name.

You will have to decide what information to provide on a business card and letterhead in addition to your name, address, and voice phone number. It is a good idea to use the nine-digit ZIP code for your address since it really will speed up your mail delivery. Call your local post office for details.

A fax number, if you have a facsimile machine, is good to include. In fact, in today's fax-happy world, a fax number is a virtual necessity. You may also want to include your electronic mail addresses—MCI Mail, CompuServe, DialMail, and, of course, your Internet address. It is worth noting here that the Internet connects virtually all commercial systems. So, if you are on MCI Mail, America Online, and Delphi, for example, you can receive Internet mail on all of them. For our purposes here, however, it is best to include only e-mail addresses on those systems that you check regularly. One of them can become your "Internet mailbox" as well.

Describing your business

You should also include a line on your business card and letterhead describing your business. There are no hard and fast rules here. When Alfred was more heavily involved in freelance corporate communications and copywriting, he used the simple term *Wordsmithing*. This was a deliberate—and effective—attempt to avoid being pigeonholed as someone who specializes in a particular kind of writing.

On her stationery, Sue includes the line "The Rugge Group" followed by the line "Information Specialists and Consultants." Given the breadth of services you may perform, there is no reason to be more specific than that in most cases. In our opinion, the one term you should not use is *information broker*. Yes, that's what we all call ourselves. But your prospects won't know what it means, and you risk embarrassment trying to explain it. "I see," your prospect will say, "but what exactly do you *broker*?"

Hiring a professional designer

One thing you may want to strongly consider when producing your letterhead and business card is hiring a professional designer. This doesn't have to be expensive, particularly if you are not asking for a special logo or other custom device. And, as tempting as it may be to try to do it yourself with a desktop publishing package, the results you produce are not likely to be comparable to those of a professional.

Tell the designer that you want your letterhead and business cards to match (same color paper, same color ink, same typestyle, etc.). This presents a uniform, professional image. You will also want to consider carrying the same design elements through to your brochure. Indeed, we suggest you use the design on *everything*.

One thing to be aware of, however, is the "faxability" of your letterhead. If the design does not provide enough contrast between, say, the color of the paper and the color of the letters, it will not look good when you use it to send a fax message. One solution is to have the designer give you a "stat" or other image in black and white. You can then photocopy this to produce "faxable" letterhead sheets.

As for quantity, if you are just starting out, go with the print shop's minimum. That's likely to be 500 sheets (one ream), although the extra cost of getting a total of 1,000 sheets is likely to be so small that you may want to consider it. You may want to get 1,000 matching Number 10 business envelopes as well. (You will find yourself using your envelopes for everything.) Of course there's a tradeoff here. The larger the quantity, the lower the price. Sue uses about 1,000 letterhead sheets and about 2,500 envelopes a year. But then, she is well established in the business.

In any case, whether you buy your own paper and take it to the print shop or use the stock it offers, don't forget to get a ream of matching blank paper to use as second sheets. Many printers offer package deals that give you letterhead, envelopes, and business cards at a reduced price. So be sure to ask.

Other printed pieces

There is absolutely nothing wrong with using your letterhead as your invoice form. Simply key in the date and the client's address, just as if you were sending a letter. Then draw a solid line several lines below the inside address. Allow a few more blank lines, and type in your billing information (item descriptions, amounts, total due, etc.) just as you would on an invoice form.

Paper for client reports

There are a number of additional printed pieces to consider, though none of them are crucial. You might consider ordering a ream or two of good grade copier paper printed with a discrete header or footer that displays your address and phone on a single line. Use a colored ink, but don't make the type too large. If you use this special paper for your client reports, you will subtly remind the client on each page that you and your firm are the ones who tracked down and delivered the information.

Of course, there is nothing wrong with using plain copier paper for client reports. If money is tight, you may wish to do so. As an inexpensive compromise, see if your word processing program can supply appropriate headers or footers for each page in a smaller type size than your regular text.

Note and memo paper

Note or memo pages bearing your letterhead design are also a possibility. The printer will create these by cutting an 8.5-x-11-inch page in half to make 5.5-x-8.5-inch sheets. These are ideal for brief notes to clients while you are working on a project. Whether typewritten or handwritten, a little three-sentence note looks much better on a note or memo sheet than swimming around on a piece of full-sized letterhead.

Report envelopes & labels

Large, letter-size envelopes are another possibility. The standard size is 9×12 inches, though we strongly recommend you consider a size of 10×13 inches to give yourself a bit more room. Whenever possible, you should avoid folding a client report, so you will be sending reports in 10-x-13-inch envelopes. The slightly larger size will accommodate more pages, in case you have a really big report. And it is essential if you use any kind of report binder or cover.

You may be tempted to have these letter-size envelopes imprinted with your letterhead design as well. That's a nice look, but there's a better alternative. Consider using good looking pressure-sensitive address labels instead. This will give you the flexibility you need. You can use such labels to address boxes, book mailers, report envelopes, and anything else you send through the mail, except a conventional business letter.

Most print and copy shops offer three or four standard label designs, often in color. The problem is that everyone uses them. To rise above the ordinary, you might consider ordering special labels that use the same design and ink you selected for your stationery. It costs a little more, but you may feel it's worth it.

Do-it-yourself mailing labels

That's probably the ideal solution, and it certainly makes a wonderful presentation. On the other hand, there may be a way to get similar results without the expense. After all, a client can be expected to file your cover letters. But the mailing label and the envelope to which it is attached are almost always thrown away.

Often a simple typewritten label will do. But, thanks to the Avery Dennison Corporation, an excellent compromise is available. Avery offers a low-cost program that makes it incredibly simple to produce professional-looking labels—LabelPro for DOS and Windows systems and MacLabelPro for the Macintosh. The program comes with a nice selection of business-related clip art that you may want to incorporate in your label design.

The program will also accept graphics files created by programs like PC Paintbrush and MacPaint. This means that you can scan your letterhead design into the computer and use the resulting file as the basis for your label design. In fact, since copy and print shops have become so computerized in recent years, your printer may even be able to supply the letterhead design as a computer file and save you the trouble of running the image through an optical scanner. It certainly doesn't hurt to ask.

The list price is $100 for the DOS and Macintosh versions, $130 for the Windows version. For more information, contact Avery Dennison Corporation at (800) 252-8379.

The laser printer alternative

Just as a modem will turn your personal computer into an information machine, a laser printer will turn it into a typesetter. The output is so good and the machines are so versatile (and quiet!) that they are almost as essential as fax machines in today's business world.

Prices start at around $650, at this writing. But that's for a four-page per minute machine rated for "personal use." More than likely a "business" machine will cost you around $900. That's likely to include two megabytes of printer memory, 40 or more built-in fonts, and a top resolution of 600 dots per inch (dpi). It will also have a paper tray that holds 250 sheets or more and will operate at about four pages per minute.

A few pointers on laser printers This is not the place to discuss laser printers in detail. But you should know two things. First, when it comes to laser printers, you will never be unhappy if you go with Hewlett-Packard. It is simply the best laser printer company in the world. Everyone else is trying to play catch-up.

Second, in recent years printer makers have decided that speed isn't nearly as important as price. Accordingly, lots of powerful, feature-filled printers these days have speeds in the "slow" range of 4 to 6 pages a minute. Only the top-of-the-line units operate at "high" speeds like 6, 7, or even 11 pages per minute.

In our opinion, unless the FedEx truck is waiting at your door, the speed of a laser printer is not that important. Much more crucial is how quickly you can use your computer again after you have told it to print a document. Let the printing take 5, 10, 15 minutes or more—as long as the process doesn't tie up the computer in the meantime.

The solution is *memory*. Unless you routinely print lots of complex graphic images, two megabytes of printer memory should be fine. But if you're a DOS or Windows user, you will want to have four to eight megabytes of memory in your computer itself. This memory can be used by programs like PrintCache from LaserTools [(800) 767-8004; street price, around $40] to temporarily hold the data you want to have printed. PrintCache and other *print spooling* programs fool your software into thinking that a print job has been completed. Your software returns control of the computer to you instantly, and PrintCache feeds the data to the printer in the background. (Similar programs are available for the Macintosh.)

Do-it-yourself letterhead   A laser printer makes it possible for you to produce your own letterhead and pressure-sensitive address labels on an as-needed basis. We still feel that everyone can benefit from the services of a professional designer. After all, what do we know about typefaces and design elements? But, as noted, that doesn't mean that you can't take the designer's work and put it into your computer as a graphical image. Once you do that, you can scale it, flip it, color it, alter or add to it, or do anything else you want. Such is the magic of digital images.

To perform this magic, however, and to produce your own letterhead, notepaper, and labels on demand, you will need a desktop publishing program or a paint program. PageMaker, Quark Express, MacPaint, Corel Draw, PC Paintbrush, and others are all well-suited to the job. Our advice is to ask your computer-using friends for their recommendations.

Use this approach if you have to keep costs to the bare minimum. But be aware of the hidden costs. No truly powerful desktop publishing (DTP) program is easy to use. So, unless you are an experienced DTP user, you may spend a lot of time preparing your letterhead. And, regardless of how skilled you are, in all likelihood, you will be limited to using black as your ink color.

Producing your own letterhead as you need it can be a real convenience. But, as we have said several times, let the pros handle your design.

Designing your brochure

Finally, you will need a "capabilities" brochure. A few large information specialty firms produce saddle-stitched booklets on glossy paper with photos. You don't have to do anything nearly as elaborate. Some people use a legal-size sheet of card stock printed on both sides and folded into thirds, so it fits neatly in a Number 10 business envelope. That gives you six narrow "pages" to work with. This is a standard offering at most print and copy shops.

Actually, even that may be more than you need, particularly when you are just starting out. Alfred, for example, uses his letterhead second sheets to list books, articles, and all the other stuff he's written. The pages are laser-printer-typeset, and they are simply stapled in the upper left corner.

On the other hand, if you attend trade shows or even sometimes take a booth at a show, it is worth thinking about a commercially produced brochure that will really stand out.

So many people waste their money doing brochures that are black ink on grey or beige stock. They look good all by themselves, but they fade into the background when placed next to a variety of snazzier offerings. Once again, this is the kind of thing a professional designer can help you with. Just bear in mind that the cost of adding a bit of color is relatively small compared to the results it may bring by getting your brochure noticed, opened, and read.

Sue uses letter-sized pages typeset with a laser printer to have a professional look and feel. But she varies the pages depending on the client or the prospect. If you are sending material to someone you have already spoken with, this is really the ideal way to do things.

The easy way to customize your brochure

On the other hand, a brochure designed for direct mail—unsolicited by the client—will look quite different. We should note that we definitely do not recommend the direct-mail approach. It is far better to establish yourself with a client by phone and then send a more meaty package. That way the prospective client is ready to receive your information and will pay much more attention to it.

If the client knows virtually nothing about information resources and information brokers, you can include in the brochure sample pages of database output to help bring the person up to speed. For more knowledgeable clients, there is no need to include those pages.

The same thing applies to the pages you include listing your past clients and accomplishments. If you feel that the prospect you are trying to sell is likely to have a special interest in, say, competitive business intelligence, you can include pages that describe your previous work in that area. If you feel the person is more likely to be interested in scientific topics, you can substitute pages detailing your work in science-related areas instead.

No hard & fast rules

Clearly, there are no hard and fast rules about the contents of a brochure, though we offer some strong suggestions below. If you are just starting out, you won't have any previous work to highlight or any past clients to call on for favorable recommendations. But you can produce a list of typical projects. You might say, for example, "Here are examples of the kinds of projects we can execute for you:" and follow with a bulleted list of the kinds of questions you might expect to be asked to explore.

Even if you lack past experience, there may be other achievements you can cite: articles published, awards earned, areas of special expertise, and so forth. You might include reprints of magazine articles about the crucial role of information and/or information brokering. And, if you happen to have written articles yourself, by all means include reprints of them.

Use your imagination. There really are no rules. However, we strongly suggest that you avoid presenting yourself as a one-person operation. You want your clients to think of you as a *business*, not as a single individual. Therefore, *do not* include a *resume*! If your current resume contains important pieces of information, find a way to work them into the brochure. But do not present the information as a conventional resume.

Above all, remember that your brochure is a *sales* document. That fact should be your guiding principle. This means you must put yourself in your prospect's shoes and try to create a brochure that will convince the person that you are the one to call to discuss any and all information needs. You're smart. You're professional. You have the knowledge and skills to do the job. You are . . . *credible*.

The cover letter

For both Alfred and Sue, as for you, a cover letter on letterhead bond is an essential part of the brochure package. The cover letter should never be more than a single page. And since much of it is likely to be *boilerplate* (material that will appear in every letter) it can be produced rather quickly. Create a master copy and just make a duplicate of it under a different filename each time you need to prepare a letter. Customize the duplicate as necessary for the particular prospect.

You should start by saying "Enclosed is the material you requested," or words to that effect. This serves as a subtle reminder to the recipient that the material is not unsolicited junk mail but information that you were asked to send. Make that point right up front so the recipient does not inadvertently assume that this is yet another mailing destined for the "circular file" of the wastebasket.

Then move on to some sales copy about your firm and what you can do for a client. You might want to close with the friendly statement that you will call the client in a week to answer any questions or to further explore how you might be of assistance. For an example of the cover letter prepared by Sue for The Rugge Group, please see Fig. 19-1. You'll also find a copy on the disk accompanying this book.

Later, when you have had time to develop a track record, you may wish to use a folder of the sort that opens to reveal two pockets. Your capabilities brochure could go in one pocket. The other pocket could contain reprints of magazine articles you have written for trade journals (more on this later) or even a sample client report or two. (You must have each client's permission for this.) Be sure to paper clip your business card to one of the interior pockets and add a cover letter.

Production values

As with your stationery and business cards, production values are important. You want everything you send out to add to your credibility. But as long as your brochure is cleanly designed and produced, it does not have to be elaborate.

Once those conditions are met, the most important thing is what you choose to say in the brochure. Don't tell your audience what you do. Don't say "We search this and that database, and we have document delivery from these 10 libraries."

Your prospects don't care. What they want to know is how you're going to save them time and money.

Shown below is a copy of the kind of cover letter you may wish to create to accompany your sales and capabilities brochure. The text shown here is adapted from a letter used by The Rugge Group. This is the firm's basic letter. When contacting attorneys, private investigators, or other potential clients in special areas, a more focused letter is used. (The types of samples and lists of satisfied clients also vary with the type of letter and potential client.)

Please remember that as with brochures, there are no hard and fast rules regarding cover letters. You can assume, however, that even if prospects don't read all of the materials in your brochure, they will almost certainly read your cover letter. So make the most of this opportunity.

19-1

A sample cover letter.

[The Rugge Group
letterhead logo, address,
and phone number.]

(Date)

Dear ——:

Thank you for your inquiry about the services of The Rugge Group. We are a coalition of highly experienced, internationally based, information-gathering specialists. We offer a wide range of research expertise from competitive analysis, market research, and company profiles to legal, medical, and scientific literature searching. Enclosed you will find our brochure and a short description of the capabilities of some of our researchers.

Our clients range from small businesses to law firms (Pillsbury Madison Sutro, Fliesler Dubb Meyer and Lovejoy, Graham and James) to Fortune 500 companies (Arthur Andersen, Westinghouse, Varian, Sun Microsystems, Citicorp, Weyerhaeuser) to many local biotech firms (Metra Biosystmes, Keravision, Berlex, Cygnus). We save them time and money by providing the information they need to make informed decisions.

The cost of an "average" online search ranges from $350-850. Our report to you will include the full text of the pertinent articles or a reference to where they were published and an abstract of their contents.

While online searching is a powerful tool, many market research and other types of investigative projects need manual work which can include in-depth interviews. We formulate the approach for your approval and then interview the pertinent competitors, experts, trade associations, trade journal editors, or government agencies. Budgets for these projects vary widely, but we always work within a pre-arranged amount.

Please feel free to call if you have questions on our capabilities or would like a quote on an upcoming project. We look forward to working with you.

Sincerely,

Jim Hydock
Managing Director

Follow the tried and true principle of selling the *benefits*, not the features. Mention the features, but take the next step for the reader and explain what the features mean to them. Explain the benefits.

Benefits, not features

Here's a familiar example of a feature: This car gets 35 miles to the gallon on the highway.

And here are some of the benefits: That means you'll save money, particularly on long trips. In fact, on a 100-mile trip, you'll save $x compared to what you'd spend driving your current car. And you'll be able to go longer between fill-ups. Think how much time that will save you.

Examples are the key

One way to make the benefits of what you offer instantly clear is with examples. Examples are crucial. You can explain until doomsday what you do, and then if you say "I did this for so-and-so . . .," something clicks in your prospect's mind. All of a sudden, *the prospect* begins coming up with the benefits that hiring you could provide.

We should add that you should always get permission before using a client's name. It is usually okay to provide prospective clients with a list of clients you have served. But under no circumstances should you publicize a list of "satisfied clients" without the permission of each and every one of them. And never, ever link a client with a particular subject without getting permission. That's part of the confidentiality you offer. Information is a sensitive issue, and some clients would just as soon others not know what they are interested in knowing.

Be careful!

The Rugge Group uses client testimonials about the quality and timeliness of its service, without mentioning the actual topic. But large companies usually have policies against endorsing a specific firm. You might find that a large company will let you say "We did thus and so for a major adhesives company in Minneapolis," but not let you say "We did this for 3M."

The bigger the company, the less likely they are to allow you to use the company's name. In doing her brochure, Sue will call the people she knows well at a particular company and say, "We're putting a brochure together. Would you be willing to contribute any of the comments you've made to me over the years . . ." Sometimes the response will be "Sure, tell me what you want me to say." On other occasions, the person will not be willing (or able) to give permission.

We cannot emphasize this enough. Information and information retrieval are *sensitive*. Sometimes, to a client's competitors, even the fact that the company has hired you can be of interest, whether or not it's clear exactly what you did for the firm. That's why it is imperative that you ask before using any client's name in any way in your brochure or sales literature.

Creating a track record

As a brand-new information broker, you won't have a track record to cite. So what do you do? Use your imagination. That sounds like a cop-out on our part, but we're serious. Think about the industries and professions you plan to focus your sales effort on. What kinds of questions would they ask? If you don't know the industry very well at first, consult its trade journals and associations.

Use your information retrieval skills to find out about your target industries/professions. What are the hot issues? What's everyone talking about? What kinds of questions might you be able to help them with? Create a few good questions, and then research them as if each were an assignment from a client. Keep track of your time and expenses. Then figure out what you would have charged each imaginary client.

Now you have a track record. You cannot say you have worked for numerous Fortune 500 companies. But you can say, "In the past we have completed the following research projects," and then list them and the price you "charged." Or you can say, "These are the types of questions we can help you with."

One word of warning: Don't try to fake it by not actually doing the research. If a prospective client asks you to name the company you did a certain project for, you must decline in any case since all such names are confidential. But if the client says, "You know, your project on current market trends in the super-premium ice cream market—the one you did for $500—sounds interesting. We have a similar problem here. How did you approach that one?", you had better be prepared to give a credible answer. The only way to do that is to have actually done the search.

Making it real

You might also consider assembling a few testimonials. Again, you can't fake this, but you can fudge it a bit. You would be amazed, for example, at how many of the blurbs you read on book jackets just happen to come from authors whose books are distributed by the same publisher. You might offer to do a project for a friend, for example, and then ask for a testimonial. Prospective clients won't know that it came from a friend. Testimonials always have more impact if they can be attributed to specific people at specific firms. But if you cannot get permission to do this, you can say "a leading law firm," "a top advertising agency," or whatever other description is accurate and appropriate.

To get ideas for your brochure's layout and contents, you might consider contacting established information brokers and requesting their literature. The source to use for names and addresses is *Burwell's Directory of Information Brokers*. (See Appendix A for more information on this publication.)

How to get sample brochures

As a professional courtesy, you should be up-front with your fellow practitioners. Explain that you are in the trade as well—and use the opportunity to identify additional resources to call on when you are overloaded or when you do not feel qualified to handle a particular subject. Ask them to send you their literature.

Use the information you receive as a guide in preparing your own brochure. Then file it carefully. You can never know when you may need to subcontract work to one of these people. It is a collegial profession, and not only will your paths cross in the future, the people you meet this way can be an excellent source of friendship and advice.

The question of rates

Should you quote your rates in a brochure? No, you shouldn't. An hourly rate means nothing to a prospect—since the person has no idea of what you can accomplish in an hour.

Instead, present a list of research project examples and the prices you charged. This will give your prospective client a much better idea of what to expect.

A client, once he or she is interested, immediately wants to know what a job is going to cost. But as we all know, every job is different. The only way to come up with an accurate quote is to meet or speak with the client to define the job.

Sue strongly recommends trying to quote by project, not by the hour. Yet, it's important to have some concept of pricing in your brochure because—surprising as it may be—most prospects think your services are more expensive than they really are. That's why a list of sample questions or research projects with an approximate dollar figure next to each one can be so effective.

Examples from The Rugge Group brochure include:

- Determining whether a Hong Kong-based company has any U.S. corporate affiliations—$600
- Locating the current address of a specific German physician—$75
- Identifying an expert witness on pit bull attacks—$700
- Researching the technology of electronic color printing—$425

Notice that there is no mention of who the client was or exactly what was delivered. Simply list the project succinctly and tag it with the approximate price for the information you found. This won't answer all of a prospect's questions about price. But it will certainly give a sense of what your services cost.

At the end of the list, be sure to include a line noting that prices will vary, depending on the scope of your project. Then, as Sue suggests, say something to the effect that "We always work within a not-to-exceed budget." After all, it is possible to do a quick survey of the floor-covering industry for $500 to $600, but it is equally possible to spend $5,000 doing an in-depth study of the same field.

Everything depends on how far the client wants you to go. Because of this, it is also a good idea to include a line suggesting that the client give you a call to discuss any particular needs. Then note that you will be happy to give a free quote after the initial reference interview.

Follow-up phone calls

Finally, always make it as easy as possible for a prospect to communicate with you. Include your address, phone, fax, and electronic mail addresses in the brochure and make sure they are easy to find. Sue's brochures are not intended to be sent as part of a direct-mail solicitation. They have always been designed as "tell-me-more" pieces, to be sent after the prospect has been contacted and expressed an interest in the company's services.

The brochure is something the prospect can file away for future reference. And, of course, it can serve as a talking point when you follow up with a phone call. Use your cover letter to tell the prospect that you will call shortly. Generally, that call should be made within about 10 days of mailing the brochure. Don't let the fire of interest you've kindled grow cold. Fan the flames.

Conclusion

One way or another, you've got to have some kind of brochure. It is true that much of your business will come via word of mouth. But whether someone calls you or you make the contact on your own, you must have some literature to send out. You should not be making sales calls or doing any kind of promotion if you don't have something to respond with.

It doesn't have to be fancy: Sample clients and projects, if you've got them; testimonials, if you've got them; and why it's more cost-effective to hire someone like yourself than to do it any other way. Emphasize that you have the expertise to provide thoroughness, and the cost-effectiveness and ability to respond immediately, with *complete confidentiality*.

In the next chapter we'll show you how to use your business materials to both market and sell your services. As you will see, there are all kinds of possibilities. Some of them are plain common sense, and some are limited only by your own creativity and imagination.

20 Marketing & sales
The missing ingredients

Nothing happens in any industry without sales and marketing. It is important to make this point because many prospective information brokers come from an academic or library background where *sales* is a dirty word. These institutions often vigorously engage in marketing and sales activities, but academics call it "development," "client education," or some other euphemism.

Of course, it doesn't matter what you call it. The fact is that if you don't actively seek out people who are likely to buy your services, you will starve. The world will not automatically beat a path to your door, regardless of how skilled you are at the art of information retrieval.

There are hundreds of professional librarians out there with all the right degrees and outstanding search skills (both online and conventional), and many of them have told us they simply don't understand why more people don't request their services. These are good, caring, service-oriented men and women, card-carrying members of a helping profession, who happen to have the most important skills in the Information Age.

Why don't they call?

Yet many of them, at least those who serve in public libraries, spend their days answering the same questions over and over again. "Here, let me show you how to use the *Readers' Guide* . . . Have you checked *Standard & Poor's*? The card catalogue? I'll be happy to show you how it works." It's like forcing Michelangelo to spend his life painting wide-eyed children on cheap black velvet!

The missing ingredients are marketing and sales. "Sell, sell, sell," says Sue, who never leaves home—even to go to the grocery store—without a supply of business cards. "You never know when you will meet someone who could become a client."

You never know, so be prepared

Now, no one is suggesting that you buttonhole every fifth shopper and thrust your business card into the person's hand. Nothing of the sort. The point is that as an independent information broker, you and only you are responsible for bringing in the business. And information is such a broad area that you *never* know when you will encounter someone who needs your services: in the checkout line, seated next to you on an airplane, train, or in a bus terminal; at a cocktail party; while you are attending a conference; wherever you happen to be.

If you are an outgoing person who enjoys conversation with others, things will happen naturally. You don't want to press or ever force the issue. But it is always a good idea to ask people what they do for a living so you can get an idea of what they're interested in. That way, when they ask you what you do, you will know how to phrase your answer in a way they will find interesting.

If someone does indeed ask what you do for a living and seems genuinely interested, it just makes good sense to be able to produce a business card and suggest using your services the next time a question comes up. Better yet, ask the person for his or her business card so you can send your brochure. Sue's rule is: Don't ever give out your business card without getting one in return. And always write on the back of the business card what you talked about. You think you will remember, but you won't. So write it down as soon as you get home.

So few information professionals actively pursue marketing that it is no wonder so many of them fail when they try to go out on their own. Remember: You're not holding a gun to anybody's head and forcing them to buy shoddy, over-priced merchandise. You're in the business of helping people solve their information problems using skills and resources you have worked long and hard to acquire. Like any doctor, lawyer, or CPA, you deserve a fair price for what you offer.

If you have told people what you do and what you can do for *them* and they don't want to buy, that's fine. But they'll have no way of knowing what you can do unless *you* tell them. That is the essence of marketing and sales.

There *is* a distinction between marketing and selling. Marketing generally includes all the things you do to make people aware of your business and the services you offer: market research, the packaging and design of the product, and sales. The coverage is broad. Sales activities—just one of the elements in marketing—are more sharply focused.

Whenever you are contacting a specific person to personally explain what you can do for him or her, you are selling. In this chapter we will look at both activities. In the following chapter, we'll show you how to play some interesting variations on the sales and marketing theme.

Basic marketing activities

Before you do anything, stop and think for a moment about your overall goals. The purpose of all marketing activities is to make potential clients aware of your existence and of the kinds of benefits you can offer. The purpose of all sales activities is to persuade a single individual to agree to pay you money for providing them. As we said, marketing is broad, sales is specific.

We're going to assume that you've got your materials ready—your business cards, stationery, and brochure. These tools are essential. It is foolish to spend time and effort doing any marketing until you have them in place. Do you remember what we said about your materials projecting an image of credibility? Well, marketing covers the techniques you use to stimulate interest and make people ready to receive your image.

That's your goal—to stimulate interest, which you can then convert into a sales opportunity. So let's look at how you can accomplish it. Let's start with standard, conventional techniques.

Personal contacts

The first and most obvious place to start any marketing effort is with personal contacts. A personal contact is usually someone who already knows you, someone who knows the kind of person you are, the kind of work you do, and so on. Often a personal contact is also a personal friend, though that does not have to be the case.

Since every information broker comes to the profession from someplace else, it's a good bet that you have contacts in some other field, profession, or industry. Don't overlook this possibility. Make yourself sit down with a pad and pen and think about the people you've worked with, the people you know, or the people you know how to reach from your "previous life."

Or as Sue says in her seminars, "Think about who you know and about what you know, and then think about how you can bring those two together. How can you make them interact? What do the people you know need in the way of information or information retrieval that you can provide?"

As we have been at pains to tell you throughout this book, one of the wonderful things about being an information consultant is that everyone in every line of work will eventually need your services. They may find a way to do without them, probably because they aren't even aware that people like you exist. But the need will definitely arise.

So. Start by contacting your contacts. Tell them what you're doing. Tell them you're going to send them your brochure and several business cards. And ask them if they know of anyone—in the office, at the plant, in the industry—who might be interested in what you are now in a position to offer.

Then think about the industry or industries you are most interested in serving. This may not become apparent until you've been in business a while. But watch for it. Then find a way to join the trade associations that focus on these industries. Go to their meetings. Get to know the people and get them to know you. Would it be appropriate for you to offer your services as a speaker? As a contributor to the newspaper or magazine the association puts out? It might even be a good idea to pay for and staff an exhibit booth at some convention or conference.

This is an important technique. The term *networking* (of the nonelectronic kind) has come into vogue in recent years. It is based on the certainty that everyone you know also knows people you don't know. But networks don't always drive themselves. Often you have to give things a gentle push. So ask: "Gee, Tony, that's great. I know you may not need me right now, but is there anyone else I might call? . . . Judy Johnson? Great idea. I don't think we've ever met. Mind if I use your name?"

What about direct mail?

The next step you might be tempted to consider, after personal contacts, is a massive direct-mail campaign. In our experience, this kind of approach *does not work* for information services. But we would love to be proven wrong, and we believe you should leave no stone unturned. If you think you might have a workable approach, here are some of the things you should know.

There are a number of crucial elements to any direct-mail campaign. First, you have got to develop a list of people to whom you can send your direct-mail piece. The key thing about the list is that the people on it be likely prospects for the product or service you plan to offer.

Any number of companies have made a business out of assembling tightly focused lists. For example, if you manufacture life preservers, you would naturally be interested in everyone who had bought a boat in the last three months. That's the kind of information "list brokers" or "mailing list houses" collect and sell.

A costly numbers game

It sounds intriguing. Wouldn't it be great, for example, to be able to put your sales message on the desk of the managing partners at every law firm in your state? Just think of the business that would generate!

Well, think again. The problem with direct mail in general is the response rate. In most cases, a one to two percent response from a mailing is considered a big success. That's just responses of the "tell me more" variety, and it assumes you are selling a tangible, easily understood product or service (which you're not). So to even have the hope of generating enough business to make the campaign worthwhile, a company must send out thousands of letters, probably at a cost of at least $1 apiece.

The short answer is that you can spend a lot of money marketing your information brokering firm through direct mail and have nothing—not one single inquiry—to show for it. In our opinion, information services simply cannot be sold in this way.

So forget about buying mailing lists. Concentrate instead on developing a highly focused, *personalized* campaign. Your goal should be to stimulate enough interest on the part of businesses and professionals in your local area to generate a few initial interviews. A small portion of those interviews will lead to assignments. Some will produce results later, as people return to their files and notice your brochure. And many will be like seeds sewn on fallow ground.

One good approach that Sue recommends is to start by sending out 10 or 15 letters a week. Make sure that you follow up on each one of them with phone calls. Just see if people will take your call. If they don't know who you are and won't talk to you, then, obviously, you've got to revamp your letter. On the other hand, if they say, "Yes, I got your mailing and it was intriguing. I'd really like to talk to you further," then maybe you're doing something right! Still, the most you can hope for from any such letter is that it will act as a knock on the door. There is no way you can expect a letter and brochure to actually sell your service.

When we say personalized and highly focused, we mean exactly that. Identify specific individuals and prepare a cover letter aimed at each one. That may mean doing some research. What are the biggest law firms in town? The largest ad agencies? What kinds of information needs do each of these professions have? How might your skills be of value? How can you save them time and money or make their efforts more cost-effective? Who is the right person to contact at each firm on your list—the managing partner? The agency president or creative director?

Personalized & highly focused

Find the right individual—the person you feel is most likely to be in a position to hire you. Contact the person by phone. Then send a letter with your brochure. Customize your letter to match the requirements of the kind of firm you will be contacting. You would not want to send the same letter to an ad agency that you send to a law firm, for example. This is yet another example of why Sue advises all brokers to find a particular market niche. It is simply not efficient to try to market to several different industries at the same time.

Who should it go to?

Notice that we are not suggesting that you create a different letter for every specific firm. We are suggesting that you create a different letter customized to each different *profession* or business. Again, that's part of "personalization." It may be tempting to create a single, general sales letter. But a piece like that will never be as effective as one that speaks to the prospect in the language of a particular industry or profession.

Get an appointment

Send the letter and brochure. Then follow up with a phone call a week later and try to get an appointment. Getting the appointment is your real goal. The letter and brochure are simply a means of achieving it. Or, as we said a moment ago, a knock on the door.

We are emphasizing the goal of getting a personal appointment here because we believe it is important for all new information brokers to experience the face-to-face contact this involves. On a day-to-day basis, however, you will probably do most of your selling over the phone. Often, in-person sales calls simply cost too much time and money—relative to the amount of money the prospect is likely to spend with you—to make them economical. Notable exceptions include the opportunity to speak to the sales team, the monthly law partnership meeting, the advertising agency creative group, or any other "group" of potential clients.

First-class mail

People *open* first-class mail. That's why so many firms strive so hard to make their third-class "junk mail" look like first-class letters. They know that simply getting someone to open the envelope is half the battle. If the letter inside piques a prospect's interest after a quick scan, the person will return to the top of the page and read it with care.

So how do you pique someone's interest? You talk about something of interest to that particular person. You give the person something to chew on—not vague unsupported statements like "We can save you money." Make that statement, then follow up with several examples. Don't just state the feature. Help the person *see* the benefit!

If someone wrote to you proposing to save you money, the first question to enter your mind would be: How? If the letter does not answer that question, if it doesn't put some substance behind this assertion, you will be disappointed. The letter writer will have raised your expectations only to let you down.

Let's look at a hypothetical example in Fig. 20-1.

Analyzing the letter

The letter in Fig. 20-1 is merely an example of the kind of thing you might consider. Your own letter may be longer or shorter, though you should try not to exceed a single page. Notice that the first sentence gets right to the heart of the matter. It instantly answers the prospect's question: "What is this package all about?" It's about how the firm Questor, Inc., can save you money. Notice too the use of the first-person-plural possessive pronoun. Call it "our firm" even if you are the only employee.

"Okay," the prospect says, "I'm always interested in cutting costs. And I see the person knows about LEXIS and WestLaw, so she must have had some experience with attorney information needs. I think I'll read on. How can this company save me money?"

February 28, 1995

Ms. Anne Howe, Esq.
Dewey, Cheethem, and Howe
1234 Via Dargent, Suite 567
Monmouth Courthouse, NJ 08540

Dear Ms. Howe:

I'm contacting you today because I believe our firm, Questor, Inc., can save you money.

For example, while I'm sure you and your staff are quite skilled at using LEXIS or WestLaw, those skills may not extend to other online systems. As a result, you may be paying far more than necessary for the information you get from DIALOG, BRS, DataStar, and similar systems.

I believe that we may be able to cut those costs substantially, and possibly improve on both the quality and timeliness of the results as well. At Questor, we specialize in efficient, cost-effective searches of *all* the leading online information systems.

However, while it may be that an online database search will produce the most pertinent results, this is not always the case. It is essential to know when to go online and when to pick up the phone. And when you do pick up the phone, it is crucial to be able to conduct a skillful telephone interview. Otherwise, your call and your time are wasted.

That's why at Questor we stress our ability to consult *all* appropriate resources, whether online, by phone, or in print.

You'll find more details in the enclosed brochure, but the bottom line is this: We can probably save you thousands of dollars a year in online charges and other information gathering activities, while freeing your staff to spend their time doing what they do best.

Of course, there's no way to know for sure whether we we can save you money, and if so, how much, until we compare notes. With that in mind, I'll plan to phone your office next week to see about setting up an appointment.

Thank you for your time and consideration. Please don't hesitate to call if you have any questions or if you have immediate needs.

    Sincerely,

    Joan R. Questor

20-1
A personalized direct-mail cover letter.

The letter continues, anticipating the reader's questions every step of the way. It makes the point that Questor offers specialized skills that enable it to provide the same information the attorney is currently getting at a potentially lower cost. Notice that—without promising anything definite—the benefits are made real by the phrase "thousands of dollars." The term *costs* is so vapid and indefinite. But everyone can identify with the image of "thousands of dollars."

The phrase "freeing your staff to spend their time doing what they do best" is a guess born of putting yourself into the prospect's shoes. That's part of personalizing your approach. You may have no definite information that law office paralegals at this firm do online searching. The firm might not even have any paralegals. But it's a valid assumption, since employing paralegals

A bit of guesswork

and having them conduct online searches (among many other things) is the kind of thing law offices do.

If this law firm matches that profile, you will have scored a bull's eye. What you're saying, in effect, is that paralegals and other law office staff don't have the training, experience, and skill to do the most cost-effective nonlegal online searches. You do, however. So it simply makes sense for the firm to hire you to do what you do best and free the paralegals to do what they do best.

If the firm does not have a staff of paralegals who do online searching, there is no harm in guessing that it does. The reader of the letter in Fig. 20-1 will take it as a sign that you know a thing or two about how a law office works, and that's all to the good.

Let the brochure do it Notice, too, that the letter directs the reader's attention to the enclosed brochure for more information. Opinions vary on how much detail you should include in your cover letter. The answer probably depends on exactly what you are selling. But if you put yourself into your prospect's shoes, you will see that he or she would prefer a brief letter. Unless you've got some absolutely irresistible offer—like how to get free money—don't do your explaining in the cover letter. Concentrate on benefits, make your points cleanly, and get out.

As you are leaving, tell the prospect that you will plan to call the following week. Don't ask for permission. Simply say that you're going to do it. Then make good on your promise.

Remember that the whole purpose of this marketing exercise is to stimulate interest that you can convert into a sales opportunity. Your goal in preparing your letter and sending your brochure is to get into that office and have the opportunity to sell your services face-to-face or, failing that, over the phone. So the follow-up call to arrange an appointment is crucial.

Ideally, there should be a specific purpose to your call. In the sample case, the purpose is to set up an appointment that will let you compare notes on what the attorney is currently paying for non-LEXIS/WestLaw searches with what you can offer. You are offering the prospect a way to determine whether she is indeed paying too much for those searches, and you are doing so at no cost to her or her firm.

What's in it for me? This is much stronger than saying you will call to see if the prospect has any questions. Or that you will call to arrange an appointment to discuss the prospect's information needs. Ugh! Put yourself in the prospect's shoes once again. Would you be enthusiastic about giving up half an hour or more of your day to let some salesperson come in and give you a sales pitch?

"What's in it for *me*?," you'd say. "Why should I give this person my time? Simply so she can make a sales call? Forget it! I've got better things to do."

In our opinion, a weak or vague closing like that is simple laziness. Take the time and make the effort to think of something you can offer. You have got to at least hold out the hope that meeting with you will lead to tangible benefits. The reason you come up with may very well be a smokescreen—for both of you. If you get an appointment, you may find that you spend no more than the first three minutes of a half-hour meeting on your ostensible reason for being there.

The prospect may have other, related concerns. There may be a hidden agenda. But you're there. Face-to-face, person-to-person. You're able to listen—really listen—to the prospect's desires and needs, and you are able to respond in a way that no brochure can ever respond. You are able to *sell* your services and—most importantly—*yourself*!

And what about the dynamics of that follow-up phone call? It's a little scary, isn't it? Well, don't worry. You're not being pushy. If the individual does not want to talk to you, a secretary or receptionist will screen the call. You will be told the person is in a meeting or not in the office today or has read your materials and they are not of interest at the present time, thank you very much.

The follow-up phone call

No harm done. No embarrassing confrontations. No reason, in most cases, not to call back again in a month or so. Sales and marketing are a normal part of business life. Everyone in every business or profession does it in one way or another. Attorneys can't afford to sit and wait for the business to walk in the door anymore than you can. So your letters and follow-up phone calls are expected.

You can be personable, pleasant—and persistent—at the same time. Again, you're not selling second-rate merchandise at exorbitant prices. You've got something special to offer. Something that can be a major benefit to the prospect. If this isn't a good time, fine. Sorry we couldn't get together this time—perhaps sometime in the future.

This leads to what is undoubtedly the most important aspect of sales and marketing: confidence. There are books and seminars galore about effective sales and selling techniques. But the fundamental component in all of them is building up the confidence of the salesperson. That's not always an easy job. To be a confident salesperson, you've got to believe that the product or service you are selling is the best on the market.

Confidence is the key

As consumers, we all know that much of the time there's not a dime's worth of difference between many products. Understandably, perhaps, many of these "motivational" courses and books are really about the art of self-delusion. The hidden message is that it does not matter whether the product you are selling really is superior. All that matters is that you enthusiastically *believe* it is. Here's how to create that belief. Now go get 'em, tiger!

Happily, absolutely none of this applies to information professionals. Our services and our skills really *are* unique. With all due humility, there is probably no manager or professional on Earth whom we couldn't help in some way. They may not be willing to pay for what we can deliver. They may not even be aware that they need our assistance. But that in no way changes the fact that what we offer has a genuine value. It is very much the real thing.

Stop erosion now!

The problem is that you are out there trying to make a living offering this genuine jewel, and no one is buying. Meantime, your rent or mortgage payment is due. The kids need new clothes for school. And your teenager has just wrecked the car. You're desperate. You can't figure out what you're doing wrong. Is it you? Is it your sales material? Is there something you're missing?

Your confidence begins to erode. You no longer believe in yourself and what you're selling. And it shows. As a result, you sell even less. You become even more uncertain. Your business begins a downward spiral.

There's an old saying that banks are eager to lend you money only when it is clear that you don't really need it. If you need it, the coin purses snap shut. The same general principle applies to selling information services or any other product. If you feel desperate, your prospects will sense that fact, and you will get even less business. No one wants to hire a loser. If you're not confident in yourself, how can you expect a client to be confident in your ability to execute an assignment?

How we wish there were a mantra you could chant or a magic phrase you could utter to shield yourself from desperation like this. But, alas, none exists. Everyone encounters doubts and desperation. The difference is that if you work for a company, you can coast for a while until it passes. But if you are self-employed, it can affect your income.

Competence alone will suffice

On the positive side, after you have been in business for awhile, after you have learned your craft, you will eventually reach a point where you are absolutely confident in your ability to make a living, doing something, regardless of what else happens. Remember: Regardless of the business you are in, you don't have to be good to make a living. All you have to be is *competent*. That alone will set you apart from the vast majority of people. It may not make you rich, but you will always eat.

The best practical advice we can offer to ensure that you will remain confident is to suggest that you not put all your eggs in the information broker basket to start. If you have some other source of income, failing to make a sale of your information services may be a disappointment, but it will never be a tragedy. You can say to yourself, "Sorry, Ms. Anne Howe, Esquire, you will never know what you're missing out on," and mean it. End of story. Next case.

Ideally, your other source of income should be something that permits you to be in your office during normal business hours. Your clients are businesspeople, and you must be available when they need you. That means at least between the hours of 9 A.M. and 5 P.M. weekdays. In other words, make information brokering your main "real" job and, if necessary, do something else to earn money after normal business hours.

Now let's turn to the sales side of things. Let's assume that your follow-up phone call has resulted in an appointment. To make the most of this opportunity, it may pay to do a little research. See if you can get up to speed on the industry jargon. Find out what are the most widely read journals and magazines, the industry and trade associations, and the leading companies and competitors.

Basic sales technique

You might check to see if the person you will be meeting has published any articles. If the company has been in the news recently—winning a major suit or landing a new account—that can also be of interest. Don't go overboard. Don't spend a lot of money. (You are perfectly free to use Knowledge Index for this kind of research.) But anything you can find out about the prospect and his or her company can be useful.

If nothing else, these little items are good fodder for small talk. And slipping into the conversation a few well chosen phrases based on this information will impress the individual with how interested you are in the firm and/or its problems. It will set you apart from all the other salespeople who pass through the office's doors.

The key to success in any sales call is to *listen*. Offer your opinions and ideas as appropriate, but above all, listen to what the prospect is saying. What are her concerns? What is he really saying? Forget about your own agenda and about making a sale. What does the person really want?

The art of active listening

Alfred has always said that "the hardest part about being a freelance writer is not the writing. It's finding out what the client really wants." Sue readily agrees. "Determining what the client is trying to accomplish," she says, "rather than what he or she thinks you can do is a major aspect of the sales effort. But, you know, it's also an important part of the service that we offer. As information brokers, we can help clients develop a clearer idea of what they really want. And, we should consider the time spent doing this when making up our bill, for it is a very valuable service."

It is true that some clients will tell you what they want in no uncertain terms. But most prospects have only the vaguest notions. Like all of us when we were infants—or teenagers or adults, for that matter—they know they want *something*. But they don't know what. They may have a rough idea. They may be certain what it is *not*. But they are powerless to express their desires in words.

As an information broker, you will certainly face this problem. But it will be complicated by the prospect's lack of knowledge about what can be done. As Sue says, "People will only ask for what they think is possible. It's up to you to expose them to resources they never knew existed."

That's why you should never take the person's initial request as a precise description of what is needed. Always ask "What are you trying to accomplish?" That will open things up and get the person thinking about the true goal, not about the assumptions regarding what you can and cannot do to help accomplish it.

They've no idea what you can do

The best example is the one we told you about briefly at the beginning of this book. A client once asked Sue to produce a list of magazines on solar energy. That's a clearly defined request, and it is easy to satisfy. A less experienced broker might have said, "Be happy to," and left it at that.

But Sue said, "Sure, we can do that for you. But I'm curious. Why would you want such a list?"

"So I will know where to look for articles on how to build a solar greenhouse," the client said. "I like to grow tomatoes, you see."

Sue smiled. "Well, you know, we could get you the actual articles if you want. That could save you a lot of time, and I doubt that it would be too expensive."

The client was simply amazed. "Do you mean all I have to do is say, 'I'm interested in subject XYZ,' and you can get me the latest articles on that topic? That's simply incredible."

It's always fun to be seen as a wizard or a miracle worker. But as simple as it is, this kind of situation comes up all the time. And if you don't handle it right, it can actually hurt your business. People will ask for only what *they* think you can do, when in reality they don't have the slightest idea of the power you can place at their disposal.

Somehow you've got to convey to your clients that you are not being nosy and that their needs will be kept in the strictest confidence—but in order to be able to really help, you need to understand the ultimate goal. That's why we recommend that you always ask, "What are you trying to accomplish?"— or words to that effect.

Sympathize and suggest

You must convince your clients that you are there to help and that you have the power to be very helpful indeed. So listen to what they say. Suggest alternatives and possibilities and pay attention to the reaction. Then state what you think has been said in your own words: "So, if I understand things correctly, what you want is a comprehensive report on everything that has been published in leading trade journals on . . ." and so on.

We can offer endless scenarios, both hypothetical and drawn from real life. Ultimately, the only way to perfect this part of your skill repertoire is to practice. Get to your interview on time, but no more than about five minutes early (even if you have to drive around or sit in the car). Dress for the occasion. Bring any documents, reports, charts, or other materials that might help you make your case. Concentrate on projecting a professional, credible image.

Then have at it. Go into each interview with a song in your heart. Sure, that sounds hokey. What we mean is that you should approach each interview as if you were about to meet a witty, fascinating, comfortable person whom you just might be able to help with your skills and experience. If you can, great. If not, that's also fine. At the very least, you're going to have an enjoyable afternoon and will undoubtedly learn a great deal.

Human contact

Forget about selling. Forget about the bills at home. You're here to make contact with another human being, which is what life is really all about. Of course you'll talk business. It may be that you will be able to help the person you're meeting. If not, well, there's always the future. Truly, you never know when some contact you made a year ago will suddenly call with a major assignment.

That's the attitude you should take. We are not crazy about the phrase, "Have fun with it." As a denizen of the East Coast, Alfred, for one, feels it's "too California." But one must admit that it summarizes perfectly the way you should approach each and every sales call.

You will find that you get better and better with each interview. You will be able to anticipate the questions people will ask of you, and thus be well prepared to answer them. Strange as it may sound, your mouth will become comfortably familiar with the words and phrases you utter. With each interview you will refine your presentation and the words will flow with greater ease.

After the interview

It is wonderful if your sales call results in an assignment or a request that you bid on a project. We'll cover what happens next in a later chapter. But if you don't walk away with an assignment, don't give up on the prospect.

Assuming you had a good meeting, write the individual a note expressing your appreciation for the time spent with you. Say you're sorry that you could not get together this time, but that there is always the future.

You don't *have* to do this. And if you do, the elaborateness of your response may depend on how well you hit it off with the individual. The important thing is to keep in mind your goal.

You want to make yourself stand out from the crowd. You want to persuade the prospect that you are different. You are more than a name and address.

You are a flesh-and-blood personality in the prospect's mind, with something valuable to offer. You also want to keep your name before the person's eyes.

If the prospect receives an initial letter and brochure from you one week, meets with you the following week, and gets a thank-you note from you the week after that, you will have made yourself a presence in the person's life for the better part of a month. You will have made an impression.

If the interview went well but no business resulted, you may want to keep an eye out for articles or information your prospect might be interested in. It probably will not pay you to seek out such articles. But if you happen to spot something in a magazine or online search, make a photocopy and send it with a brief note to your prospective client. Again, this is a personal touch that just happens to keep your name before the client.

Conclusion

Mining personal contacts, mounting a personalized, highly targeted direct-mail campaign, making a sales call, keeping in touch on a regular basis—these are the major elements of a basic sales and marketing effort. You make contact, you explain your services and the benefits they can offer the prospect, and you get the job. If you don't get the job, and you feel the prospect is worth the effort, you keep in touch. When the next job comes up, you will be the first person to come to mind.

In the next chapter we're going to show you how to create variations on those themes. Once you have the basics firmly in hand, you can let your imagination run free into the realm of "power marketing."

21 Power marketing tips & techniques

The last chapter outlined the basic elements of any sales and marketing program. These are making contact, explaining how the benefits you offer match the prospect's needs, and getting the job. You could describe such a program as:

- Make contact.
- Make a good impression (by establishing rapport).
- Make the sale.
- Make sure you stay in touch.

Virtually every sales and marketing activity you can think of falls under one of those four headings.

These elements are not a secret. Everyone sends out brochures and letters. Everyone tries to get sales appointments. Everyone wants a prospect or client to remember them the next time a job comes up. And we mean *everyone* in nearly every industry.

But not everyone gets good results from a marketing campaign. There are lots of reasons for this. However, assuming you're a pleasant person who bathes regularly, assuming you're competent at what you do, the reason for less than stellar results may be that you are not using the techniques we call "power marketing." The difference between power marketing and ordinary, run-of-the mill marketing is the difference between a thin broth and a hearty stew. Let the others ladle the broth—you dish up a tasty ragout.

And how do you do that? With imagination. With creativity. With energy. It's not the ingredients. And it's not your advertising budget—everyone in this profession is basically in the same boat when it comes to marketing dollars. It's how you put the ingredients together, and the spices you add to make it interesting. It's also how much of yourself you put into the effort. If you're looking for a nice, comfortable, nine-to-five job that makes few demands, you don't belong in this profession!

Start by thinking abstractly. Don't think in terms of placing ads or sending out personalized mail pieces. Think instead of the four elements: Make contact, make a good impression, make the sale, and make sure you keep in touch. Write each one at the top of a page of paper, then find a quiet spot and *think*. Let your imagination run free. Don't stop any thought. There is plenty of time to edit your ideas later.

Thinking free: Making contact

For example, consider the element of making contact. Who do you think would be interested in your services? What kind of assignments and projects would you most like to have, and who can give them to you? Forget about what it would cost: How many different ways can you think of to reach these people? What's the wildest and craziest idea you can think of to make contact?

If you did not have a good imagination and if you were not blessed with a certain amount of creativity, you would not be an information broker. So put your innate talents to work for yourself. "Thinking free" or brainstorming is an exhilarating experience. Once you get started, you will find it difficult to stop.

Don't edit yourself. Don't worry about money or time or how outrageous an idea may be. You can never know when something that is clearly out of the question will suggest something else that is not only doable but devastatingly effective. Have fun with it. (There's that phrase again.)

We will discuss the other three elements in a moment. For the sake of continuity, let's follow this one through. Let's assume that you've got a page or more of scribbled notes. (Use a tape recorder if your hand cannot keep up with your brain.) We'll assume that this list contains every technique you can think of for making contact with the people who are likely to need your services.

A cardinal rule or two

Now we can edit. We can temporarily rule out anything that costs money. That will still leave some very effective options. For example, one of Sue's cardinal rules for making contact is: Whenever possible, try to talk to more than one person at a time. Sending out brochures and cover letters can be expensive. And it can be time-consuming if you follow our advice to personalize each letter. But that doesn't mean that it is not necessary. It is.

Joining your local Chamber of Commerce, however, is cheap. Attending Chamber meetings, luncheons, and other functions puts you in touch with businesspeople and professionals.

Another of Sue's rules is to join organizations that put you in contact with your clients—not just your colleagues. Otherwise, you're preaching to the choir. For example, check to see if there are local chapters of the American Marketing Association, the American Chemical Society, or the American Management Association (AMA) in your area. If there are, join them! You may not be a marketer, a chemist, or a manager, but your potential clients are, so make it easy for them to get to know you.

In any organization, you get to know people and they get to know you. Your activities may not lead directly to a project, and it is bad form to make overt sales pitches at meetings. But contacts and friendships evolve naturally, and you never know when someone you met through the Chamber or an AMA meeting will put you in touch with a friend who wants to hire you.

Similarly, it costs you nothing to speak before local organizations like Kiwanis, Rotary, Optimists, and other clubs. Church groups, adult education classes, the local YMCA/YWCA, professional associations, the list of organizations and groups needing luncheon or dinner speakers is nearly endless. And every one of them has a program chairman who is dying to hear from someone like yourself.

Kiwanis, Rotary, & others

It is true that you can burn up a lot of time this way talking to people who are not in a position to hire you. So pick your groups carefully. Alfred once gave three talks in a single day at various branches of the New York Public library. The topic was online information and the idea was to promote a new book on the subject. Only a handful of people showed up at each location, and most of them were retirees with nothing else to do. Those who wanted the book would simply borrow it from the library.

It is difficult to hear a song in your heart when your voice is raw and you're trudging to the subway station in the pouring rain. (It is a well-documented fact that taxicabs in New York change into fire hydrants, street lamps, and perform other shape-shifting tricks at the first few droplets of an oncoming storm.) But it was a very worthwhile experience.

Alfred didn't speak to a single person who had even the remotest intent of buying the book. But nothing teaches you how to explain a topic to a group of people like actually doing it. You may know exactly what it is you do for a living and the benefits you can offer. But have you ever stood up and tried to explain them?

Before opening on Broadway, many musicals and plays open first "out of town." Holding performances in Boston lets the production company work out the kinks and smooth over the rough spots before hitting the big time. That's what we suggest you do. Before volunteering to speak at the Chamber of Commerce, perfect your act by speaking at other groups. It doesn't matter that there may be no one in the audience who can buy your services. You're there for the practice; they're there to learn something.

THE SPEECH & how to use it

When you have quite literally gotten your act together, it's time to open on Broadway. Though you will never stop perfecting it, once you have given four or five talks about what you do, you will find that THE SPEECH has begun to emerge. You will know the points that should be covered, and you will have discovered the most effective language for doing so. You will have anecdotes, examples, possibly a laugh line or two, whatever.

Now you can use THE SPEECH as a real business development tool. Watch for conferences that come through your city. Renting exhibit space might be warranted if you have the money and the conference topic is particularly germane, especially if you have the opportunity to speak. Most conference organizers are happy to have someone else on their seminar/speech schedule. You might receive a very small honorarium, or they might pay your expenses. But don't count on it. Always remember that you are there for the audience of potential clients, not for the money.

Note that speaking at conferences involves a long lead time, six months at the very least. So check directories of conventions and exhibits and contact the organizers well in advance. There are several such directories, some organized geographically, some by topic. (See Appendix A.)

You might also ask the large hotels in your area for their convention schedules. And don't forget the convention and visitors bureaus.

Make the most of the opportunity

Now, here's a real insider's trick. If you do get the opportunity to speak at a convention or meeting of some sort, give serious consideration to signing up for an exhibit booth.

This reinforces your presence, and it gives potential clients an easy way to locate you. Stock the booth with plenty of copies of your brochure, business cards, and other relevant literature—and offer *free searches* to people who stop by.

Yes, that's what we said: free searches. DIALOG, DataTimes, Dow Jones, among others, will provide you with free passwords to demonstrate their services at conventions. Ziff-Davis's Information Access Company may be able to help you, too, even to the point of giving presentations to explain online business resources to your potential clients, free of charge. It goes without saying that you should find a way during your talk to let the audience know about the free searches available at your booth and invite them to stop by.

Whether someone asks you to speak or you ask them, you will have a great deal of control over the topic and title. So make it good. Organizations do not want to hear a librarian talking about how to use the library. Tell them instead that you'll be talking about new electronic ways to gather information, even if the techniques you plan to discuss are not all electronic.

Declaring your topic

The idea is to deliver enough information and examples to show your audience what's possible. If one or two of your examples has a little razzle-dazzle, so much the better. In effect, you want to say, "All *this* is available today in the Information Age." And you want your audience to be thinking, "Wow, there's so much. I'm really glad to know that these things exist. Probably I should hire this person to help me make the most of it."

Many times Sue has given a talk, returned to her office, and had a call from someone who was in the audience. "I really enjoyed your speech today at the meeting," he or she says. "It sounds like you might be the person who could help us with this problem." You can't count on results like that, and sometimes it takes months for an appearance to bear any fruit, if ever. But it happens too often to be accidental.

The basis of your talk will be THE SPEECH, but it is important to customize it with examples and databases that are relevant to your audience at the time. Try for five basic examples from the areas you know your audience is interested in. If possible, you might consider soliciting research questions before the meeting. Then pick one or two of them and incorporate them in your talk.

We can't overemphasize the importance of good examples. You can spend 15 minutes or more explaining the concept of online searching, and as soon as you say "For example, we were once asked to research the market for water-pumping windmills," they say, "Oh, do you do *that*?" It is as if a 1,000-watt light bulb went off in their heads. All of a sudden they understand.

Be sure to leave plenty of time for "Q&A" (questions and answers) at the end of your talk. A Q&A session lets you learn what people are interested in, something you can only guess at when preparing your speech. It can often provide your audience with more relevant information than your prepared remarks. For this reason, Sue typically leaves at least half of the allotted time for questions.

Leave time for Q&A

There's just one problem. Every audience is different, and some can be real duds. As Alfred says, "You have to try to sense the audience and adjust your presentation accordingly. Are they responding to what you are saying, or are they bored? If they are bored, and there is nothing you can think of to kindle their interest, then bring the speech in for a landing as soon as you can reasonably do so. Talk only long enough so that people don't feel cheated. Fifteen minutes is about right. Ask for questions, and if none are offered, smile, say your thank-yous, and get off the podium.

"On the other hand, if you look out on a sea of attentive faces, warm to your topic and let 'em have it. More than likely such an audience will produce a lively Q&A session that will probably extend beyond the time allotted for your speech, assuming there's no one else on the dais and no one else is scheduled to use the room.

"One other point. If at all possible, try to avoid getting scheduled either immediately before or immediately after lunch. Right before lunch, people are hungry and distracted. Right after lunch they're often sleepy."

Press releases

Now for some more power marketing. You've scheduled a speech called "Electronic Information: Productivity and Privacy" to be given at some fairly large convention that's coming to town. Don't stop there. What more can you do with what you've got?

You can send out press releases, for one thing. A press release has always got to have a "news peg" or other clear raison d'etre. Your scheduled speech is just the thing. Write the release as if you were a reporter. "The such-and-such organization announced today that Ms. Joan R. Questor will be speaking on the topic of electronic information at their upcoming convention to be held at the Hilton on June 6, 1995. According to Ms. Questor, 'Electronic information holds the greatest opportunity . . .'" and so on.

You may not be aware of it, but a great deal of the material you read in newspapers and magazines originated as a press release. Sometimes a release will be edited to fit, and sometimes it will even be rewritten. But Alfred and Sue have both sent out press releases that have been published *verbatim*.

Talk about free advertising!

You've got to write the release as a genuine news story. See your local paper and favorite magazines for examples. After a while you'll be able to spot a published press release a mile away. There is never any guarantee that a publication will pick up (print) your release. But sending out press releases is not very expensive. And sometimes a reporter will call you to do an interview as a result.

Master's tip: Use Business Wire & PR Newswire

Here's another hot insider's tip. The most productive and cost-effective way to send out a press release is via Business Wire and/or PR Newswire. You may be familiar with these two databases in their online form, but the databases are actually only a by-product of their real purpose. Their real purpose is to deliver press releases electronically to TV, radio, newspaper, and magazine newsrooms.

But you don't have to be a big company to put a release on the wire. For only $250, you can send a press release out to over 1,000 newspapers and trade journals. Your release is sent electronically, which means that upon receipt, the editors can "clip" it out and "paste" it right into their publications. (No need for retyping.)

As a bonus, your press release becomes part of the Business Wire or PR Newswire database. That means that it will appear again and again whenever anyone searches those databases for terms like "information broker." Sue uses Business Wire regularly to promote her seminars.

For more information and current prices and conditions, contact:

Business Wire
44 Montgomery Street, 39th Floor
San Francisco, CA 94104
(415) 986-4422

PR Newswire, Inc.
806 Plaza Three
Jersey City, NJ 07311
(800) 832-5522
(212) 832-9400

Television talk shows

Television talk shows? Surely you jest. Who's going to want me to appear on television to talk about "electronic information?"

You'd be surprised. One of the things that separates a power marketer from everyone else is an appreciation of the need for free editorial material. (The media considers anything that is not paid or public-service advertising "editorial," not just the opinion pieces from an editor or station manager.) The purpose of editorial material is to attract an audience so the advertisers who pay the bills can get a crack at them. This is as true for magazines and print publications as it is for television shows and radio programs.

Without good, interesting editorial matter, there is nothing to attract readers/viewers/listeners. So the need is *constant*. As a power marketer, your job is to figure out what you can offer that would be of interest to one of these audiences.

There is a long tradition of interviewing authors with a new book to promote. Alfred has done countless radio interviews, either by phone or in person, and made one or two local television appearances, for example, all of them pegged to the publication of a new book. It is always amazing how enthusiastic and helpful most interviewers are.

Sue has done many interviews as well, with similar results. The media, in short, is eager to help you tell your story because it helps them fill the time or the space between ads and it does not cost them a cent. Never think it is a waste of time to talk to a writer or reporter. Many times Sue has been featured in a story because she spent an hour or more educating the writer—

while other people were willing to give the person only a few minutes of their time.

You can't be too overt. You can't make a straight sales pitch. But the mere fact that you are there—a member of the Rugge Group or the author of a recently released book—talking about a subject makes the point.

There is only one rule: Whatever you say, you've got to be *interesting*. Your assignment is to hold the audience between ads. If you are boring or self-serving or if your appearance begins to sound like a sales pitch, you will not be asked back. As when preparing a talk before the Association of American Widget Manufacturers, take the time to put yourself in the shoes of your audience. Think of one or two interesting examples you can use before you go on the air. Or before the newspaper reporter calls to interview you. If you can, try to think in "sound bites"—short, catchy ways to express what you do.

Columns, articles, & trade journal pieces

So far we've talked about press releases, talk shows, and the like in connection with the promotion of a specific speech you have lined up at a convention. Obviously, all of these power marketing techniques are available to you at any time, for any purpose.

Sometimes even something as mundane as your getting a subscription to another online system could be sufficient cause for a press release. The media won't know that all you did was open a NEXIS account and maybe took a little training. This is one time when the general lack of knowledge of the online world can work in your favor. If you make it sound like a big deal, and if you include several on-target examples, there's a good chance that the media will pick it up.

More free publicity

There are many other opportunities to trade a little time and effort for free publicity. Without wishing to seem cynical, all of them are based on the unending need for free or low-cost editorial material. For example, have you considered asking a newspaper if you might do a column in which you would answer one or two questions each week? Readers would send you their questions. You would make a selection, do the search, and then publish the results.

If you get paid for this, it will be only a token amount. Perhaps $50. But since you are providing editorial copy in effect for free, make sure that the paper publishes your name, address, and business phone number at the bottom of the column: "Joan R. Questor is a professional information broker. She can be reached at . . ." You might consider a similar idea for a local radio program.

Trade magazines are another easy mark. Trade magazines have titles like *Ad Week*, *Progressive Grocer*, and *Plunge: The Monthly Magazine of Holistic Plumbers*, and they are unabashedly in the business of promoting products of interest to members of a given profession or "trade." To speak crudely, they are basically advertising rags with a desperate need for editorial copy. Many trade magazines will print *anything* you send them.

Why? Because U.S. Postal regulations state that in order to qualify for third-class mail status, a publication must maintain a certain ratio of ads to editorial. Alfred once did a regular column for a very fat computer magazine. When he asked the editor how long the columns should be, he was told, "As long as you can make them." The postal regulations were the reason why.

Trade journal articles

A trade journal article can be simply a written variation of THE SPEECH. It is in your own best interest to do a good job. Take the time to customize the opening and the examples so that both speak to the needs of the trade journal reader. But treat the piece as an extended, very subtle ad for you and your services. Also, ask if the magazine would like a photograph and see if you can have the piece copyrighted in your name, not that of the publication.

That way you can reuse it at will. If the journal won't give you the copyright, at least ask if you can get reprints and for how much and if you can have the right to distribute the article to your own clientele. All of this falls short of owning the copyright, but it's close enough that actually owning the rights may make no difference. The goal, after all, is promotion.

You might also consider magazines and newsletters published by associations. As we said in a previous chapter, there is an association for nearly everything. Almost all associations publish some kind of magazine or newsletter, if only to help members feel they are really getting something for the dues they pay. These, too, are hungry for copy. Which, thanks to your computer and word-processing program, you can assemble with relative ease.

How to place an article

If you have never had contact with an editor, you may be reluctant to tap into the goldmine of free publicity that is waiting for you. Don't be. Editors put their pants or pantyhose on one leg at a time, just like you. Most of them genuinely need what you can offer. If they reject your proposal, under no circumstances should you take it personally. Like you, editors have deadlines, commitments, and priorities.

When soliciting an editor he doesn't know, Alfred likes to send a query letter. The letter outlines the proposed piece, cites the reasons why readers would be interested, and generally does a written sales job. Typically, Alfred will follow up with a phone call about a week later.

Sue favors a more direct approach. She'll pick up the phone and call an editor at the drop of a hat. More than likely, she will talk about electronic access to information sources in the publication's subject area. The word *electronic* is still a hot-button. Use it to the fullest, even though we all know that there is much more to information retrieval than going online. There are so many specialized databases that it is relatively easy to find one or more dedicated to the editor's topic.

As Sue says, "I'm not often paid for a trade journal article. The editor usually says, 'If you'd like to get it into the next issue, we need it by such and such a date.' But they usually don't say they won't publish it. It's been my experience that trade journals are pretty hungry for material. But it's not a way to make a living."

Information industry journals like *Online*, *Database*, and *Information Today* are welcome exceptions. They do indeed pay for material. In any case, once you have published something, use it in your brochure. Many magazines will be able to sell you impressive-looking reprints at a reasonable cost. These are almost always preferable to your own laser printout, particularly if they include your photograph. There is nothing like a published article or two to help boost your credibility in the eyes of most clients.

Speaking at company staff meetings

There are many other opportunities to tell your story. One of them is the company staff meeting. You will need to contact someone within the company, of course. When you do, say, "If your company doesn't have any internal information-gathering facility, I can explain the resources that are available." It's always better to present it generically. Talk about the whole industry rather than just your own company and what it offers. Try to position what you propose to do as educational.

And whom should you try to contact to set up such an appearance? It depends. Often information is a stepchild to the rest of the company. Sometimes you have a president who is really information-oriented. Sometimes the president is someone who has come up the financial ladder and doesn't care about research. The Director of Research, the Chief Scientist, and the VP of Marketing are probably the three titles you should shoot for.

If you are good on the phone, simply give the individual a call. Or send a letter and follow up with a phone call. As Sue says, "I like to get through to the person, and then say, 'I'll send you some information,' because then they're ready to look at it. If you can't get through on the phone, send a letter, if you think the firm is a good prospect or if you know it does not already have an internal information center."

The local chapter directory of the Special Libraries Association (SLA) will often be able to tell you if a firm has some kind of information-gathering facility. The SLA is an organization of about 13,000 corporate librarians. You can join different divisions, like "business" or "federal" special libraries.

The SLA can be a valuable resource. As Sue says, "The Rugge Group has many special librarians as clients. They're very familiar with the needs of their companies, and they make wonderful clients because we can communicate in a common language. That's a luxury not available with most clients.

"If a company has an information center staffed by a special librarian, that's where you go. You do not try to contact management directly. These folks have a hard enough time selling themselves within their own companies due to the general lack of understanding of information resources. The last thing they need is some outside information broker complicating the process. Fortunately, there are times when, working with a company's special librarian, we can help."

Some local public libraries carry the newsletters of companies in their area, which might be a good way of getting insight into a firm's operations. And a lot of libraries clip newspaper articles. But it may be easiest to call the company and ask, "Do you have a library or information center?"

The best thing is to go after smaller companies that are less likely to have such facilities. Companies with 50 to 100 employees, for example, are usually good candidates. You can get that kind of information about companies in your area from the local Chamber of Commerce, or a Dun's directory, or trade directories.

Advertising

Advertising falls under the heading of "making contact," so let's spend just a moment on that subject as well. In general, advertising to the public at large does not work for information brokers. It is simply a waste of money. If you were selling shock absorbers, kitchen appliances, or lawn-care services, things would be different. There is a very large market for such items and services and the entire population fully understands what the product is and does.

Not so with information services. This is a one-on-one, person-to-person sale. It will never be a mass-market item. The best we can all hope for is that our profession eventually achieves the same status and recognition accorded attorneys and accountants. But that day is likely to be a long time coming.

On the other hand, taking an average size ad in a newsletter or bulletin put out by a trade association or other organization of people and businesses you count as prime prospects can be a good idea. Such ads can help to build your name recognition. It can help keep your name before your prospects. And, equally important, it is visible evidence that you are supporting the organization with your advertising dollars.

Also, if you plan to offer a specific database specialty to a client group whose members know what you are talking about, an ad may be effective. The best example we can offer is an ad in a local or state Bar Association publication promoting your ability to search LEXIS or WestLaw. Every litigator and almost every attorney today will know precisely what you mean.

Yellow Pages listings

Still, advertising may be thrust upon you. If you opt to have a business phone and business listing (which Sue strongly recommends), you may find that your phone company will give you a listing in the Yellow Pages free of charge. So what classification do you choose?

A few Yellow Page directories have begun to introduce an "information broker" category. In fact the profession recently got its own SIC code. But you have to be careful with Yellow Pages listings. If you specify "Information Bureaus" you may find yourself in with the Polish Tourist Society or the Gray Panthers.

The Rugge Group is listed under "Market Research," a category more people are familiar with. It is always useful to have a line in such a listing to inform potential customers that you do "secondary research." That way they will know you do not offer primary research services like interviewing passersby at shopping malls.

The Rugge Group can also be found under "Information Retrieval and Research Services" and under "Legal Research." In these listings it can be a good idea to indicate that you do database searching or to indicate your particular specialty or emphasis. That way you will not have to spend time dealing with calls from people who don't really know what you do.

Incidentally, there's a book called *Marketing Without Advertising*—$14.95 from Nolo Press—that offers an excellent treatment of this subject. Please see Appendix A for details.

Creating "credentials"

There are many other ways of "making contact," of course. And we hope we have stimulated your thinking in that direction. Not all of them are equally effective in bringing in new business. You will certainly have to decide which are worth your while.

Appearing on a television talk show may not generate a single sale, but it confers a certain status. Just as our parents' generation believed that anything they saw in print must be true, our generation accepts without question the idea that if you appear on television you must be an authority, a pundit, an expert, or otherwise know what you're talking about. As an independent information broker, you can use "credentials" like these to your benefit. So even if the appearance took a day of your time and produced no inquiries or sales, it can still be worthwhile.

Making a good impression

Now let's turn to "making a good impression," the second step in any marketing campaign. What we mean here is paying close, personal attention to your prospective client. Information services are the antithesis of soap, cottage cheese, potato chips, or any other mass-marketed product. People are going to buy from you (give you an assignment or project) on the basis of whether they like you, whether they feel that you can do the job, and whether you demonstrate that you are truly interested in *their* problems.

So once an initial contact has led to an inquiry and appointment, consider the ways you can demonstrate your "worthiness" for the job. Go to the library and ask to see clipping files of local newspapers. Then look for references to your target company. Who are its competitors? What trade associations and/or trade publications would they be interested in monitoring? What are the key buzz words and special terms in the industry?

Only you can determine how much time and effort you want to invest at this point. Just remember: Don't tell them what you *do*, tell them what you can do for *them*. As we have said before, the mistake many brokers make is to say "We search this and this database, we have document delivery from these 10 libraries." You need to stress the benefits of saving a prospective client time and money. The more industry- or company-specific you can be, the better.

One key to making a good impression is trying to put yourself into the prospect's shoes. This is true whether you are going to be appearing in person or plan to call the prospect on the phone. Personal appearances and sales calls can be time-intensive. You owe it to yourself and your business to make several face-to-face calls. These offer invaluable experience.

In person or on the phone

But at some point you may have to draw the line. A sales call that takes the better part of a day and holds only the possibility of one $500 assignment may not be worth your while. On the other hand, if you sense that there is more business to be had from this firm, you may well decide that making a personal call is worth the investment. Otherwise, try to make a good impression by phone.

Another key component of this step is what we said in the previous chapter: the fine art of listening. Try to "hear between the lines" what the prospect is really saying. Then put your brain, creativity, and imagination into gear to suggest alternatives, options, and possibilities.

Think of yourself as a consultant. By dint of your hard work, you have special knowledge about what can be found in the world of information. You know what's possible. The prospect does not. He or she is turning to you as an expert. So adopt that role. As we have said before, ask what the person is trying to accomplish, not what he or she wants to know. It is your job to educate the prospect on what can be done. And it is crucial that you do so, since people will not ask for things they think are impossible to obtain.

A good and respected friend who spent his entire career as a salesperson, district manager, and sales executive put his finger on it. "Selling," he said as he lit his pipe, "is teaching. A librarian or a teacher is in the business of communicating information and ideas. They help students grasp a certain idea.

"A salesperson's job is no different. It's the same skill. You communicate information to a prospective client and help the person see a particular idea.

You show how your product or your service can solve a problem or fill a need."

Teachers, librarians, lecturers, and anyone else whose job it is to communicate information and ideas *already* have the skills needed to sell effectively. They just aren't aware of the fact. Forget what you read in *Booklist* and *The New York Review of Books* when you see a title about sales technique. The media and the publishing industry have got it all wrong.

Sales is not some mystical profession where people learn to magically force the unsuspecting masses to do something against their will. *Selling is teaching.* So, if you have been teaching people to learn, to read, to use the library's resources, you already have all the skills you need to sell your services by teaching prospective clients what can be done and what you in particular can do for them.

You must believe us. All of this is to the good. The fact that you don't come from a "sales background" and are not considered to have a "sales personality" can be a real plus.

Prospective clients will not look at you and immediately say, "Ah, another saleswoman." Or "Will no one rid me of these troublesome salesmen?" Unlike the popular image of someone in sales, you've got a really good service to offer. You don't have to manufacture enthusiasm—you already know how good what you have to offer is. And your goal is not to make a quick hit and move on. You are interested in developing a long-term, service-oriented relationship. Your prospects will sense that. And they will buy from you.

No guarantees of success

For your part it is important to avoid any implications that you can somehow guarantee success. What you guarantee is to leave no stone unturned in your quest. Remember, you are not selling the answer. You are selling your expertise and your knowledge of the most productive ways to obtain the information we *hope* exists. In order to protect yourself, say that "the project has been done to the best of our ability within your budget limitations." That's perfect, because there's no recourse; if they'd given you more money, you could have done more research.

At The Rugge Group, Sue always tells people that "We don't take on a job unless we feel confident that we have at least a 50-50 chance of finding the information you need." It is up to you as an information professional to refuse jobs that you don't feel you have a reasonable chance of completing successfully. After all, you want repeat business, and you want to get paid, neither of which is likely to take place if you aren't at least partially successful.

If Sue or her associates suggest that a particular question is not a good search candidate and the client insists they go ahead and try, then she'll be sure to get a written agreement or contract. According to Sue, "If we feel at the outset that the client is going to be unhappy, we'll push for a contract.

The less knowledgeable the person is, the more trouble we're going to have. The person will assume the answer exists and expect miracles."

The hardest part of selling is making the sale. In one sense, everything we have talked about so far in this chapter is "selling." Making contact, doing your homework on a prospect, listening intently, offering alternatives and suggestions. But you'll never make a sale until you "ask for the order." The hardest part of selling, in other words, is asking for the order.

Make the sale

You've had a nice conversation with your prospect. You've explored many avenues together, and you yourself have developed a pretty good idea of what you can do for the person. A "project" has begun to take shape in your mind. Now it's time to ask for the order.

Some information brokers are uncomfortable with this, because making the request forces the prospect to make a decision. They are afraid that they will be seen as coming on too strong or being too aggressive. Or they are afraid that the answer will be "No," the pleasant atmosphere will evaporate, and they will be embarrassed. It would be so much nicer if the prospect would make the first move. If he or she would say, "Joan, we want to hire you to take care of this for us. How does $1,500 sound to start?"

Sometimes a prospect will do exactly that. But what if she doesn't? What if he is a man of strong indecision? Then what? You could wait until a year from next Friday and never hear the magic words. You have got to force the issue. Gently, artfully, but firmly. By asking for the order in such a situation, you are actually doing the person a favor. Some people are psychologically unable to decide what they want to do until you give them a choice.

Even if your prospects don't have this problem, they may hold back and wait for you to make the first move. Again, put yourself in their shoes. You are not offering a tangible, nuts-and-bolts product that they can look at and evaluate. You are offering something intangible which, by its very nature, must be customized to their needs. It is *your* responsibility to make the project real before the prospect's eyes. It is *your* responsibility to put a price on it.

Making the first move

Forget everything you may have heard about those sleazy salesperson tricks. Tricks like asking for the order by saying, "Well, Mr. Smith this has been most informative. Did you want this widget in red or blue?" Or "When would be convenient for us to deliver the widget, Tuesday or Wednesday?" The idea behind these approaches is to control the prospect's choices. It is not a question of whether you want to buy a widget or not—your choices are red or blue, Tuesday or Wednesday.

That is not the way for an information broker to ask for the order, even assuming that any of us could pull it off. The way you ask for the order is the same way you close a meeting. Meetings have a natural rhythm. They start

The right way to do it

with small talk as everyone gets comfortable. Participants then get down to business. At some point it becomes clear that all the major issues have been discussed and several possible plans of action have emerged. The meeting begins to wind down, and it is time for the leader to summarize what has been discussed and make clear everyone's assignments.

As an information broker, you ask for the order by summing up, by outlining the project that has developed in your mind as a result of the discussion, and by addressing the issues of deadlines and price.

For example:

"Well, Ms. Smith, I think I understand what you need. You'd like us to help you identify your firm's top three competitors and, with your approval, check to see what patents they have applied for in the past year. Let me tell you what I think we can do for you.

"We can start with a literature search and produce a report containing the competitor information, including a D&B search to give you their financials. Because patent searches can be so expensive, I think we should hold off on that part of the project for now. Let's see what develops in the initial phase.

"We can do this part of the job for between $450 and $650, depending on how much information there is. In any case, we will not exceed $650 without your approval. You said you were in something of a hurry. Would next Tuesday be soon enough?

"Good.

"Because this is the first time we have worked with you, we require a deposit equal to 50 percent of the authorized budget. In this case, that's $325. We can accept credit cards or checks. We will then bill you for the remainder after we are sure you are satisfied with our work.

"I'll fax you a letter of agreement today confirming these arrangements."

Now, was that so bad? Did you get any sense of high-pressure sales tactics? Of course not. You're not trying to force anyone to buy something. But you are bringing matters into focus. You are taking positive action to sum up the meeting and guide things to a decision point. To put it another way, as a teacher you have planted an idea in the prospect's mind. Now, like any good teacher, you are motivating the person to do something with it.

A few points on finances   If a new client chooses to pay the deposit by check and is in a hurry, make sure it's understood that you will not start the project until you have the check in hand. Of course what you really mean is "until your check has cleared," but there is no need to be that precise.

First-time clients do not know what to expect. They can build up false hopes, be disappointed with the results, and refuse to pay. With a deposit, however, you have a much better chance of getting paid for the whole job. The deposit helps commit the client to the project.

When mentioning a credit card, you can say that if the project is to start immediately, then you must bill the credit card now. It's important to be flexible—but it's even more important to get paid. You can accommodate a long-time client without much worry. But for someone new, the rule should be, "No payment, no project." Even experienced information brokers get taken sometimes. Your main hope should be that, when it happens to you, that you don't get too badly burned. And it will happen. Some plausible sounding person will call you up with a rush request and you'll want to help. You'll do the work and fax off the results. And never hear from the person again. But you will know better the next time!

In the vocabulary of professional salespeople, the phrase "overcoming objections" is as common as the phrase "bibcite" or "full-text record" is in ours. It refers to how one deals with questions, roadblocks, and concerns prospects raise at any time during a sales interview. "Does this car have a guarantee?" "Gee, I didn't think this watch would cost so much." "Can I bring this program back if I don't like it?"

"Overcoming objections"

Sales courses suggest all kinds of ways to overcome objections, not all of them savory. Distract the prospect, mumble, say you don't know and immediately highlight some other feature. But that's claptrap.

You're a professional, not a street hawker or carnival barker. You don't *overcome* objections. You answer them in a straightforward, scrupulously honest fashion. People aren't fools. They know when you're trying to snow them. And they know that no product or service is absolutely perfect. To pretend otherwise, to have a slick comeback for every objection they may raise, is to insult their intelligence.

It is extremely important that the client understand what the "product" will look like. If they expect a full-blown report, complete with recommendations and detailed analysis, and you send them a bibliography, you are likely to have a hard time collecting the balance due on your bill. Make absolutely sure you both agree on the format of the information "product." If possible, show the client a sample of a similar past project so that it's clear what you will be delivering.

So what happens in the case above if you just get finished saying "do the job for between $400 and $600," and the prospect holds up his hand and says, "Whoa, hold on there. I was thinking more in terms of $100 . . . $150, tops"? Your smoothly flowing closing has been derailed. Now what?

Don't cut your price

If you are inexperienced or lack confidence in what you're offering, your first instinct will be to cut your price. The perspiration will break out on your brow and you'll go all cold in the pit of your stomach. You've just made a terrible mistake by asking for too much money. And look, the guy's ready to buy at $100. He said so himself. Maybe I *could* do it for that amount.

Forget it! If there was ever a time to get a grip on yourself, this is it. If you've done your homework, you know that the price you have quoted is fair. So stick to it for the work you have said you will do for that amount. If you cut your price now, the prospect will not respect you. You will also find that you have set a dangerous precedent for the future. More important, you will never be able to work for this person—or anyone else at his company—for the fees you need to survive. Word will spread that Joan Questor is good, but be sure to ask her to cut her price. Again we say, forget it! You don't want business like that.

Instead, do what Sue does—improvise by thinking on your seat. The guy's willing to spend up to $150? That is not enough to do anything you will be proud of. Sue, for one, does not accept jobs for less than $250, and even then only in special circumstances.

So counter offer:

"I'm afraid we can't afford to do what I've described for that amount. But I'll tell you what we can do for $300. We can identify your top three competitors and tell you what they have been up to for the past year. We would not be able to do any patent searching or Dun & Bradstreet reports, however."

If the prospect objects to your counteroffer of a reduced project at a lower price, it is time to start packing your briefcase and getting ready to leave. The person obviously is not going to buy from you.

Of course he may say, "Wait a minute. Hold on there. I think my boss might be very interested in the competitor information you could develop. And I'm sure that if I explained it to her, I could get authorization to spend up to—what was it?— $500?"

At that point, you smile and say, "Great. I really think you'll be pleased with what we can do for you." What you do *not* do is continue with the closing presentation mentioned earlier. There is no question now of offering to forego getting an initial half-payment before starting work. Now you say: "Our terms are half in advance and half on delivery of the material, so we'll need $250 before we can start work. When do you think you can get approval for the budget?"

By posing this last question about budget approval you are again "asking for the order." Or you might say, "How would you like to handle it?" Or, "Do you suppose I could pick up a check tomorrow?" There are many, many other things you could say as well. But notice that all of them ask the person to make a commitment.

Get a commitment

That's the key to making the sale. Make it easy for the prospect to make a commitment to you of some sort. It doesn't have to be a direct order for your services or a direct agreement on your fee. But it should leave no doubt in either of your minds of how things stand between you.

Our retired salesman friend says, "In my business, our rule was never to walk out of an office without a signed piece of paper. An order, a letter of intent, sometimes even a sales contract. I know your business is different. But I also know that if you leave with the prospect shaking your hand and saying he'll definitely call you next week, your chances of doing any business with him are less than 50 percent."

The thing to avoid is a sales interview that flaps to a close without any agreement on a definite course of future action. As we said, some prospects will take the initiative. But ultimately it is *your* responsibility to sum things up, make a proposal, and suggest what should happen after the meeting.

That's what "sales" is really all about. That's how you ask for the order. And don't forget: In most cases the prospect/client is already on your side. The individual would not have agreed to see you without being at least partially convinced that the two of you have something to offer each other.

Two final points

Two final points on sales. First, we have used a face-to-face meeting as our example. But everything we've said applies equally well if you are discussing the project with the prospect on the phone.

Second, we will look at how to price your services in greater detail later in the book. For now, it is important to be aware that pricing works both ways. We've discussed reducing the scope of a proposed project and offering to do it at a lower price.

But if you sense that your quote of "$400 to $600" is accepted without the bat of an eyelash, you might say, "Now, of course, that's for a basic search. If the budget allows, we could also do profiles of the three top executives at each competing firm and assemble all the press releases the company has issued in the last two years. Adding that to the basic search would bring the price to around $800."

Again, this is one of the few times where the fundamental characteristics of the information industry actually work to your advantage. We've said it before: One of the things that makes information services so hard to sell is that information is so nebulous. It is not cut-and-dried.

The good news is that because of this, there really is no limit on what you can offer a prospective client. You might do a $750 project on a given industry or market, for example. But you can always go deeper, go back further in time, check additional databases, search from a different angle. The result might be a study of the same industry or market that you can charge $10,000 for. Truly, information is endless.

As a consultant, you do not want to suggest information likely to be of little value to the client based on what you have learned from your sales interview. Your job is to suggest the *right* information for the problem at hand. But there are always grey areas, things that may not be wholly relevant to the problem but are nonetheless nice to know. If you sense that the prospect would be willing to pay for them, offer them as part of a higher priced "deluxe" package.

Keep in touch

Keeping in touch means keeping your name in front of the prospect's or the client's eyes. It's like a free "current awareness" service for the client or prospect regarding your firm. This is a smart thing to do, for at least two reasons. In the language of finance, you might call it "protecting your investment" and "leveraging your assets." Here's what we mean.

Not every sales encounter (phone or in-person) results in a sale. The parties may be willing, but the budget may be weak. Or there could be a dozen other reasons. The point is that every prospect you talk to represents an investment on your part. You've spent time and money making contact and making a good impression. The prospect knows who you are and what you do. That makes the person infinitely more valuable to you than prospects you have yet to meet.

Protect your investment in this person by making sure that he or she continues to remember you. It takes a large amount of effort to get a wheel to spin, but once it's spinning—once you have overcome its inertia—it only takes a little effort every now and then to keep it in motion. That's why you want to keep in touch with prospects who have yet to buy from you.

The best source of additional business

Once a prospect pays you money, he or she becomes a client. Clients are even more valuable. They are absolutely the A-Number-One best source for additional business. Not only do they know you, they know your work firsthand. You don't have to sell them on anything. The next time there is an information need, they will hire you as a matter of course.

Maybe. If they remember your name. If they think to call you instead of someone else. If they think about information services at all. Clients are like movie stars in this respect. Lot's of people know who *they* are, but they cannot be expected to remember everyone they have done business with. They need to be reminded.

You had to be there

Alfred once worked with a former vice president of Merrill Lynch who found the corporate environment too confining. He left the firm, with a fat, two-year consulting contract and scores of contacts and friends in the financial industry. For several years he and Alfred made a good living producing all manner of corporate communications pieces.

The only problem was that business rarely came in over the transom. Friends, contacts, and satisfied clients did not automatically call with new work. It used to drive the guy crazy. Whenever he would go into New York, he would invariably come back with multiple assignments. Forget about low-hanging fruit, the stuff was lying on the ground waiting for someone to pick it up.

But you had to be there. No one, not even well-satisfied clients, was picking up the fruit and tossing it in the direction of Yardley, Pennsylvania. There was simply no way to get around the need to keep in touch. There was no way for this guy to avoid spending about one day a week going after new business in The City.

How to keep in touch

Keeping in touch is very much a part of power marketing. Where it differs from "making contact" activities is in the materials you use. You can only "keep in touch" with people you have already met, worked for, or otherwise dealt with. Thus you cannot send the same direct mail letter and brochure you would send to brand-new prospects.

So what can you send? Should you make a personal phone call? Send flowers or salted nuts? This is a great topic for thinking free and brainstorming. So pull out the page headed "Keeping In Touch" and give it a go.

We have a few suggestions to get you started, of course. You might consider sending out a newsletter on a regular basis. The purpose of a newsletter is to keep your name in front of someone's eyes. So make it as self-serving as possible without allowing it to turn into a total advertising rag.

What topics can you cover in such a piece? Say you have a new doc del runner somewhere, new databases that have become available, what's going on, how to use your firm's services more effectively, the "five most important things to tell us when you're ordering documents." You might even include an "Employee of the Month" feature, though when Sue did this in her newsletter for IOD it got to be a jinx—invariably whoever was selected would quit or be, er, "outplaced" the next month.

Chris Dobson of F1 Services in Dallas, Texas, even offers a newsletter service for information brokers. Ms. Dobson prepares a collection of informative articles each month which she sells to brokers who want a quick and easy way to produce a high-quality newsletter for their clients. For more information, call (214) 528-9895 or send a fax to (214) 528-9819.

You might do things that focus on the people at your firm. As Sue says, "At IOD we would send a Christmas card with all of us on it, faces and names. Ninety-five percent of the clients never met us. They knew us only over the phone. But sometimes they talked to the same person every day, especially if it was a big doc del client.

"My good friend Georgia Finnegan used to send out cards on Valentine's Day to promote her company, The Information Store, because it was a time of the year when businesses didn't get any cards. So hers really stood out. Some other holiday might serve as an excuse for you to do the same thing."

Personal notes are also good, particularly if they are attached to some article or other piece of information you have found that is likely to be of interest to the client or prospect. The note doesn't have to be elaborate. But it would be a natural thing to write it on your business note stationery.

How to get more business out of current clients

As we said earlier, it is much easier to get more business out of current clients than it is to get new clients. So as part of your "keeping in touch" activities, ask clients if you can come and talk to their staff. They already know you and thus can be certain you're not just wasting their time. Maybe there's some new database or approach to a database that's come out that would be useful. Ask for 15 minutes to describe it to the staff.

If you know they're interested in Japanese technology and a new database just came up that translates all Japanese patents into English within three weeks, you can say, "Now there's a really quick, efficient way to get at this literature." The client may never have thought to ask you to do Japanese patent searching because it's in Japanese, and six months behind. Now that's changed, and you're there to pass on the good news.

You will also find that if you can get one person on your side in a company, they'll do a lot to spread the word about you and your services. You might say, "We've been able to do this for your company in marketing. You may not realize that there are technical resources that would be of interest to your research people. Is there anyone I could call about this?" Ideally, you'll get somebody fairly close to the top. You want someone who can tell his or her people to call you if they need help.

Discipline yourself to do it

The final ingredient in power marketing is discipline. You may have the best technique and the best materials in the world, but if you do not continue to market—day after day—it will all go for naught. If you stop marketing when you get business, you're going to be on a roller coaster of too-busy-to-market, then no work coming in, so you have to market to get some. Don't allow your newsletter to become a periodic, for example. Make yourself keep it on a regular schedule.

It isn't easy. Most of us would far rather be online or throwing our minds against some fascinating problem than throwing ourselves into marketing. But it is essential.

For example, plan to spend one day a week or the first two hours of every day engaged in marketing activities. "I always like to do it in the morning," Sue says, "because I'm fresher and sharper. At IOD, I didn't start taking calls or listening to employee problems until 9:30 or 10:00. I'd get on the phone first thing. A couple of times I made calls from home to the East Coast before 8:00 California time, and just stay home until I'd finished them. When you send out a brochure, if you don't follow up within 10 days or so, you've lost the momentum."

Please see Fig. 21-1 for an example of how a typical marketing conversation might go as Sue follows up on a brochure she sent the previous week. Note how she handles the prospect's question about purchase orders.

Sue	Did you get our brochure?
Prospect	Yes it looks very interesting.
Sue	Do you understand what we do?
Prospect	Something to do with information. I guess you can save me money.
Sue	We can save you money, and we can save you time. Time is money as well. What kind of topics have you been dealing with lately?
Prospect	Packaging, in grocery stores. We have a new product, and we want an attractive color scheme. Is there anything you can do to help us?
Sue	Would knowing what psychologists say about color be of interest to you?
Prospect	Sure, if there's some research that indicates how people react to certain colors.
Sue	That's something we can do. We can't tell you what we think is the best color for you, but we can get you what psychologists say about it, and we can also check the business literature to see if anyone's reported on what seems to have worked for them, and why they've changed from one to another, if they have.
Prospect	Well, how much would this cost me?
Sue	Usually we can do a bibliographic search, if we're just checking the published literature, for around $500.
Prospect	A bibliographic search?
Sue	That means giving you a list of articles and an abstract, which is a description of the article, for everything that's been published in the last couple of years. Probably you don't want to go back much further than that in this case, since the research might be changing a lot.
Prospect	Suppose I needed it two days from now. Is there any cost for rush service?
Sue	It depends on where you are. We might have to charge you for Federal Express, but we can normally get a bibliographic search out to you within three days. If you'd like us to go beyond that—to call some of the authors, check libraries and see if any more extensive studies have been done, dissertations and so on—it would probably take another three or four days.
Prospect	And you can also get the articles for me?
Sue	Yes. We think it's better if you look at the abstracts and pick the ones you want. But if you're on a tight deadline, we can look at them and pick, say, the five that seem to be most useful. But if you've got a little bit of time, we think you'll be more satisfied with the documents you get if you pick them out yourself.
Prospect	It sounds reasonable. I think I'd like to take a chance on it. What do we do next?
Sue	Since you haven't used us before, we need a deposit equal to half the budget that you're authorizing. You can do it by credit card or send us a check.
Prospect	Since we're under time pressure, I'd like to do it by credit card. But our company doesn't issue them, and I don't want to put it on my own. Would a purchase order do?

21-1

A possible follow-up phone call conversation.

The only time The Rugge Group accepts a purchase order (PO) is from really major companies. "If a company I've never heard of wants to give me a PO," Sue says, "I don't consider it worth the paper it's printed on. So I'd say, 'Because we're a small company, and we have out-of-pocket expenses like phone and computer time, we do need the money up front.'"

Day in and day out

These are the kinds of calls you have to make day after day to keep an information business in the pink financially. You sit down at your desk and look through the letters you've sent out in the last week. It's just a stack in chronological order marked "for follow-up," so you start with the oldest one first. You pick up the phone and call.

If the prospect says, "We don't have any needs right now, but we're interested for sometime in the future," you put the letter into another folder with a Post-It note reminding you to follow up on June 1, or September 1, or whenever.

Keep those in chronological order, too. That way when the first day of a new month arrives, you can look through these long-range letters instead of the short-range weekly follow-up file. Keep notes on your calls. "I make a phone call, and I make a note of the date," says Sue, "along with what was discussed. Maybe the person said 'We won't know until the beginning of the fiscal year, and that's September 1, but we're really interested.' Or the response might be 'Sometime in the next year,' so I put that one on the bottom. It's just common sense."

When calling these long-range follow-up prospects, you say, "You asked me to give you a call in three months. Is anything happening?" Often the person you talk to really wants to hire you, but can't get the budget or permission from somebody else.

You don't want to keep calling somebody every couple of months if his or her answer the last time you talked to them was "If I need it I'll call you." But you might call them six months later and say "I was going through my files the other day. Should I keep you on my list?"

Ask in a nice way, "Is this ever going to be of interest to you?" Most people in business are cognizant of other businesspeople's time. They're not going to string you along if there's no interest. And if there is, maybe they'd like to be reminded every three months that you're still available.

When business was slow at IOD, Sue would sometimes suggest to the research staff that they think about who they hadn't talked to or done work for lately, and give them a call. "It wasn't very organized," Sue says. "But with all the new computer tickler files, it is now relatively easy to keep track of recent clients and instead of simply keeping in touch, call them and directly solicit new business.

"Never forget that your best clients are the people you've already done work for, because they're happy with you. For the most part they don't see your phone calls as a bother. In fact, in my experience, they genuinely appreciate your interest.

The essence of power marketing is simply making that extra effort. Use your brain, use your creativity and imagination. *Think* about what you might do in the areas of making contact, making a good impression, making the sale, and making sure you keep in touch.

Power marketers are not passive. They don't simply hang out their shingle and wait for people to walk in the door. They don't necessarily do the conventional, expected thing. They *engage*.

Power marketing takes a lot of energy. You've got to be committed, and you've got to be disciplined. To ensure the health of your enterprise, you must market every day.

There are no guarantees of success. But we can guarantee one thing: There is a market out there for the services an information broker can offer. And it's growing. There is no reason why a share of that market shouldn't go to you— if you're willing to seize it. The power marketing techniques outlined here, augmented by your own creative ideas, will help you do just that.

Conclusion

22 Executing the project
10 steps to follow

There's a famous scene at the end of the 1972 movie, *The Candidate*, in which Robert Redford, after fighting a campaign full of ideals and promise, unexpectedly wins the senate race in California. After the official announcement of his victory, after the smiles and the photo opportunities, Redford retires to a back room with his campaign manager. Then, as the camera moves in for a close-up, he turns to his campaign manager and says, "Now what?" Fade to black. Roll closing credits.

Well, you've got the job. Your incredible power marketing activities have paid off. The client has given you the go-ahead. You've got your first assignment. Maybe you have a glass of white wine or a milk shake to celebrate the occasion before returning to your office.

Now what?

It's a scary moment. You may have done searches before in your former life. But now someone has said, "Yes. I believe in you. Find this information for me. As agreed, I will pay you $1,000." Now what do you do? Where do you start?

We can't give you exact instructions. Every job and every situation is different, after all. But we can help you come to grips with the process of executing an assignment, regardless of the subject matter or the sources you plan to plumb. And we can offer what we hope will be insightful tips to help you along the way.

The 10 major components of any search assignment

The key to so many things in life is "divide and conquer," and search assignments are no different. For example, when you stop to think about it, a search assignment or project falls naturally into ten major phases. These are:

1. Confirmation of the assignment.
2. Think time & strategizing.
3. Assembling the tools & preparing for battle.
4. Making the first cut at the problem.
5. Following up on first-cut results.
6. Organizing & analyzing retrieved information.
7. Packaging & presenting your report.
8. Confirming client satisfaction.
9. Preparing & sending your invoice.
10. Following up if the invoice is not paid on time.

We'll cover the last two steps—preparing your invoice and making sure you get paid—in the next chapter. Here we'll discuss items 1 through 8. We will also offer some advice on nitty-gritty, but essential, details like search request sheets, search logs, and other prepared forms you will want to use to keep yourself organized.

Step 1: Confirmation of the assignment

We have spoken in previous chapters of the importance of "asking for the order." Confirming the assignment is the very next step. Once the client says "Yes, I'd like to have you do this for me," it is your responsibility to make sure that both you and the client clearly understand what you will do and deliver, and what the client will be charged.

This is in everyone's best interests, and it goes a long way toward preventing problems down the road. The last few sentences on the phone should be a summary of the "order":

Okay, my understanding is that you would like us to do . . ., and get the results to you by 10:30 tomorrow morning. You'll pay the Federal Express charges, and we will be sure not to exceed your budget of $500. As we discussed, because of the time constraints, we're limited in what we can do, but we'll do everything possible, starting with the approach we think is going to produce the most results.

The output will be a bibliography with abstracts and some full text.

Does that about cover it?

Notice four things here. First, the summary is followed by a direct question to the client. This gives the individual a chance to once again confirm the agreement and to interject any modifications or amplifications that might be necessary.

Second, nothing is said here about doing a "complete" search or preparing a "complete" report or anything of the sort. You should take care to guard against using the word "complete" or "all" or any other similarly comprehensive adjective. These are such elastic terms, and you don't want to set yourself up for being liable for anything you may have left out.

Third, notice that the form of the output is clearly stated ("a bibliography and some full text"). You might instead say that "Because of your time constraints, we will only print full text," or whatever else applies to the situation. Make absolutely sure that the client knows what you plan to deliver. Make sure that the client is not expecting a narrative report when you intend to send a bibliography.

Fourth, as is obvious, there is nothing in writing. No contract. No letter of agreement. Sue notes that this was typical at IOD because many clients were in a hurry. They always wanted it yesterday. It is also typical in Alfred's experience as a freelance writer. An editor calls; the assignment is discussed and agreed to; and the paperwork follows later, often after the piece has been written and submitted.

Both Sue and Alfred agree, however, that if you have time to prepare a written proposal, bid, or letter of agreement, you should do so. We have not researched the legal fine points, but it seems safe to assume that in the event of a disagreement, a piece of paper setting forth what you will do and what the client agrees to pay will carry much more weight than the parties' recollections of a phone conversation. Though, if someone is going to cheat you, they're going to cheat you, written agreement or no, which is the best reason to exercise great care in choosing your clients.

You must get something in writing. But there is nothing to be gained in being specific about the actual databases you will search at this point. Instead, make it clear that you will cover the published literature on the topic, plus the publicly available information via appropriate government agencies, trade associations, trade journal editors, and experts in the field.

Get it in writing, if possible

Better still, see if you can get the client to mail or fax you a letter summarizing your arrangement and acknowledging his or her acceptance of same. This puts the onus on the client to send the letter. And it gives you a written summary of the client's request. This isn't so important from a contractual standpoint, but it can be crucial in making sure that both parties fully understand what the job is, the deadline by which certain materials will be delivered, and so on.

If you find that you must generate the letter yourself, be sure to include sentences along the lines of: "The product will be a summary of our phone conversations, with a list of the sources we called, plus a bibliography and any key documents we find. As agreed, the cost will be $500, half payable in advance and the remainder on completion."

One way or another, it is important that both parties have as clear an understanding as possible of what the job consists of and what you will be paid. You don't have to write a legal contract, but it is in your best interests to make sure that all the bases have been covered and to strive to leave no grounds for misunderstanding.

The more you can make yourself clear in writing, the better. The problem is that clients tend to call at noon saying they need information at 8:00 A.M. tomorrow morning. Then you don't really have time to do a conventional letter of agreement. Usually you will have to rely on the good faith of the person who has hired you and upon your verbal agreement, though you might suggest that you fax the client a letter of agreement.

This is simply the nature of the business. You must be prepared to work on a verbal understanding. That doesn't mean you have to accept everyone who calls with such a request. If it's an established client, someone for whom you have worked before, there's no problem. But if it's a brand-new client, there is no point in taking a chance. Get a deposit! Have the person FedEx you a check or give you a personal credit card number before spending any of your own money. Clients who refuse are probably not people you want to do business with, since what you are asking is not at all unreasonable.

When to steer clear

There is no cut-and-dried formula we can give you for deciding when to take a chance and when to politely disengage. When you are just starting out, you assume that everyone is as upright and honorable as you are. After you get burned a few times—and you *will* get burned—you develop a sixth sense for people who, no matter how good they sound on the phone, would have no compunctions about leaving you holding the bag (and the bills).

If someone like that calls, someone who somehow just doesn't give off the right vibrations, our advice is to steer clear. If for some reason you feel you have to take the job, at least get half the fee up front. Don't forget that Federal Express works in both directions—a client who is really interested in hiring you can FedEx a check to you immediately.

In situations like these, you are also within your rights to ask for credit references. Never forget that the client is asking you to spend your time and your money doing a search. When the bill from DIALOG arrives, it will not be addressed to the client—it will be addressed to *you*. So if you have any doubts, either "cut 'em loose" or get your money up front.

Step 2: Think time & strategizing

You're off the phone. The assignment has been confirmed, and you are ready to start work. Again, "Now what?" The first thing to do is to focus on the final product you plan to create and submit. If you have done your marketing correctly, you should have a pretty clear idea of what the client wants (and is willing to pay for). It will be several pages of bibliography listing all the material published on a particular topic over the last five years. It will be a handful of pages on which you summarize your phone conversations with several key sources. It may simply be a report of the steps you take to run down the required information and the results (in your own words) of each step.

Or it may be something else. The point here is to ask yourself from the beginning, "What kind of report will best satisfy the client's needs? What elements will it contain?" The outline may change and grow as you get deeper and deeper into the topic, but you will still be working toward assembling the elements needed to meet your overall goal.

Eventually, this will become second nature. As you are selling the job, you will know without thinking the shape the final report should take and the elements it will have to include.

Keeping track: The project folder

At this point, there are two main things you have to worry about. First, you have to worry about keeping your search results, strategy, and notes for a given search in the same place. Second, you have to worry about keeping track of your time and the expenses associated with a given project. Fortunately, there's a single answer to both questions: the lowly manila folder.

You may choose to do things differently, but one way or another, you will have to arrange to keep the materials associated with each project separate. We have always found that manila folders do the trick efficiently and inexpensively.

The search request form

When you are on the phone with the client or meeting face-to-face, you will undoubtedly be making notes on what the client wants and ideas that occur to you on databases to search or sources to call.

You should have a "Search Request" form that you automatically reach for whenever you are discussing an assignment with a client. (You'll find a sample in Fig. 22-1 and the disk accompanying this book.)

The form becomes your "work ticket" or control sheet. In addition to offering space for you to describe the search subject, it should remind you to ask for the client's address, phone number, fax number, e-mail address, and so forth. Also the date the report is expected, credit card number and expiration date (if you are set up to accept credit cards), and the budget limit.

It should also have spaces for summarizing the costs you will incur in doing the project, and the sources already checked by the client, if any, to avoid duplicating efforts. The idea is to create a single-page form that makes it easy for you to see at a glance all the relevant pieces of information about a project.

Project reference or search numbers

The search request form/control sheet is the first and most important piece of the many pieces of paper you will probably collect in the course of executing an assignment. To prepare a folder for a job, use a pen or Magic Marker to

22-1
A sample search request form.

Here is a sample search request form. You will find a copy of this form on the accompanying disk, which you can use as a starting point in creating a search request form for your own operation.

The Rugge Group
Search Request

Name: _____

Company Name: _____

Address: _____

_____

_____

Phone:(___)_____ FAX:_____

E-mail:_____ FedEx:_____

Search Subject:

Sources already utilized/to utilize:

Referred by:_____

Finder's Fee Y/N:_____ Amount: $_____

Proj. Ref. No.:_____

Phone Code:_____

Date Rec.:_____

Date Due:_____

Date Sent:_____

Researcher:_____
(date)

Researcher:_____
(date)

Budget:_____

Deposit:_____

COSTS

Labor:_____

Online:_____

Postage:_____

Phone:_____

Photocopies:_____

Direct:_____

Other (specify):_____
_____

BILLING

Invoice No.:_____

Amount: $_____

Date:_____

CLIENT COMMENTS
===============

write a reference number or name on the folder's tab. One technique you might use is to simply write the name of the client or the company on the tab.

Or you might do what Sue Rugge and many other brokers do and simply give the search a *project reference number*. If you are in the month of July and the year is 1996, make the first four digits of the tab read *9607*. Then, if this is your first project in July of 1996, add *01*. If it is the second project, add *02* and so on. The last two digits refer to projects, not actual dates. The job numbers would then read *9607-01* and *9607-02*.

The type of folder you use is entirely up to you. You might choose "third cut" so that each folder has a tab measuring one third of the folder's length. Or you might use single cut, with tabs running the entire length of the folder.

Since you will probably want to recycle the folders, you may want to use Post-it Tape to cover the tab and then write on the tape. The nice thing about Post-it Tape is that it holds fast yet is easily removable. You will also find Post-it brand removable file-folder labels at your office supply store. (The 3M product number is 7770-6.) These are sized for third-cut folders.

Of course, you could also use paper clips and hand-written notes instead of folders. The point is not the mechanism but the results. You want to keep all the materials associated with a given project together.

The search log

At IOD, where many projects were being worked on at once, Sue found it imperative to maintain a *search log*. It is a practice she carried over to The Rugge Group and beyond. A search log is simply a few sheets of paper designed to provide an instant summary of all current projects. (Please see Fig. 22-2 and the accompanying disk.)

It lists the date the assignment was received, the name of the client, the subject, the due date, the person assigned to do the search, the search number, the date the invoice for the search was sent, and the phone code.

Using phone codes is a real master's tip. To keep track of phone expenses for project billing purposes, Sue uses MetroMedia phone codes. For about $10 per month, you can easily assign a two- to three-digit code to each call that you make. It works like this: You dial the phone number you want to reach. Then you hear a special sound on the line. At that point, you key in the phone code assigned to a particular project. Your call is then connected as usual.

The payoff comes when you get your bill, since all of your calls will be broken down by their codes. Needless to say, this makes things much easier than making a handwritten note of each call for each project. Contact your phone company to see if they have a similar program. You may find, for example, that Sprint and MCI offer a service like this.

The search log is a form designed to help you track the progress of your projects. It lets you know at a glance how all of your current projects stand—client name, due date, etc. And it tracks projects from inception ("Date Rec'd") through completion ("Invoiced Date"). Notice how the items on the search log correspond with those in the search request form.

There is no need to let your forms become overly complex. Indeed, we have typed in the information in the first line for clarity, but in actual practice, you will undoubtedly write them in by hand. See the accompanying disk for a copy of this form that you can customize for your own operation.

The Rugge Group Search Log

Date Rec'd	Client	Subject	Due Date	Searcher	Proj. Ref. Number	Invoiced Date	Phone Code
7/12/68	ABC Manuf.	Ultra Process	7/23/96	Jayson	9607-47	7/23/96	65
(etc.)							

Dealing with simultaneous projects

You will undoubtedly want to customize The Rugge Group form to your own needs. (Just load the copy on the accompanying disk into your word processor.) Our point is that it is extremely helpful to have not only a control sheet for each job, but also a summary sheet or log. The log will make it easy to keep track of the work status as well as the invoice status of all jobs, whether you are a one-person or multiperson operation.

But what do you do if you find yourself working on several projects at the same time? You're hard at work figuring out how to approach an assignment when the phone rings. It's a new assignment. Or it's someone calling you back with information for a different project. Now you've got to switch gears and talk about that project. When you hang up the phone, your tendency is to forget to note that you'd spent 15 minutes thinking about the first project. Before long, your work day starts oozing through the cracks.

The only answer is to discipline yourself. You make your stopwatch your friend and get in the habit of keeping track of how you spend your time. Of course, you don't have to become fixated on it. Everybody ends up *estimating* time, but the more accurate you can be, the better. You will find that you tend to undercut yourself rather than overestimate.

You'll say "I've been sitting here all afternoon, but I've probably just spent two hours on this project." When Pergamon bought IOD, the new management tried to get everyone to keep track in six-minute increments—tenths of an hour. It drove the research staff crazy. But 15-minute increments is a good target to shoot for. If you take a phone call related to a project, for example, mark down a 15-minute segment, because there are always going to be things you did that you didn't mark down for that project.

The word *battle* may seem a bit too strong to describe this phase of the operation—until you actually complete a few projects. Finding information, whether online, on the phone, or at the library, really *is* a battle. You may be confronting what is essentially a force of nature, but it is a contest and struggle nonetheless.

If you expect that a project is a candidate for online searching—which you should know, or sense, off the top of your head—you start by choosing the databases and checking the database catalogs for any you might not have thought of. We've mentioned printed database catalogues, but online versions are also available.

But electronic databases are only the starting point. There are also trade associations, newsletters, newspapers, and other sources. All of which should go into your search preparation.

Never block an idea

As you are thinking and preparing, you may also come up with ideas that are beyond the scope of the authorized budget. No matter—write them down. Never block or disregard an idea, no matter how off-the-wall it may seem at the time.

When you complete a project and are preparing a cover letter for your report, you may find it appropriate to say, "Additional avenues of inquiry include the following: . . ." It is here that you slug in your other ideas and possibly offer to pursue them for an additional fee. Be specific. Say "for another $300 we could track these down as well."

Sue always makes suggestions for further business. She might suggest more phone calls, mentioning a few additional sources that could be contacted. She might note the possibility of searching other databases that may have been too costly for the first budget. And, she usually offers the possibility of providing the full text of documents referenced in the bibliographic citations.

Everything depends on the client you're working with. But there is usually no reason not to include these kinds of suggestions. Doing so may or may not lead to an additional assignment. But even if nothing comes of it, including additional suggestions demonstrates that you have really committed your mental resources to the client's project.

As you complete this step of the process, you should have all your tools laid out. You have selected the databases you plan to search and confected a search strategy. You have a list of associations to call (or associations' numbers to look up at the library). Everything is in readiness to make a first cut at the problem.

Step 4: Making the first cut at the problem

Rarely will your initial foray against the information dragon prove decisive. It is in the nature of things that information retrieval is a developmental process. You may search a database and find some promising leads. You will spend some time selecting and thinking about these leads and then have at it again, either online or on the phone.

Retrieving information is like extricating a quarter that has fallen behind a counter. First you look at the situation with your flashlight. Then you select a tool—possibly a yardstick—and apply it to the problem. This succeeds in moving the target closer to a position from which you can grasp it. You might then reach for the flashlight again to check the current status. Then maybe you need a stick or a screwdriver or a pair of tongs or who knows what.

The example is a bit whimsical, but the concept is clear. Information retrieval is an iterative process most of the time. You will use a variety of tools as you repeatedly move the target, examine the current situation, and select a tool to move the target again, with each iteration bringing you closer to your goal.

Often the first cut at an information problem involves an online search. From this search, you learn the names and affiliations of people whom you can phone to get more specific information on the names of still other people to call, or books to read, articles to consult, or whatever. Eventually, you achieve your goal of dredging up the information the client needs and is paying you to retrieve.

What if you get more than you expect? Or less?

When doing a manual search, you should be able to tell within the first hour or so whether your quote was really wrong. If you are online, you can tell much sooner, due to the number of hits you find you're getting.

It is important during the reference interview stage, when you are trying to get a clear idea of what the client wants, to ask how much has been published on the topic in the last five years or so. How much are you expected to find? A good online search should not produce more than about 20 citations or records in most cases.

As many an information broker will tell you, our role is often to serve as a filter. Many times we screen out the noise so the client can hear the melody. Often, "less is more." It depends on the client and also on the degree of trust you develop over the years, but many clients appreciate distillations and summaries. They will be much happier if you give them five articles that you have selected because, in your professional judgment, they are the most relevant to the client's needs than if you deliver 50 articles that discuss the topic in general.

The exception would be if the client has asked—and agreed to pay—for "everything." If you plunge into the project, apply all of your search skills, and come up with several hundred hits, stop immediately.

Sign off the system and consult your notes about the client's sense of how much has been published on the topic in the last five years. If the client said "You'll be lucky to get two or three articles," and you've found 500, something is out of whack. The client could be way off base about the topic. Or you might have misunderstood the assignment.

Contact the client by phone and read him some representative titles. Ask if they are on the mark. Are they the kinds of things the client expected you to find? Also, make sure that you are spelling things correctly and using the correct industry terminology. Be sure to discuss date and language limits (English? or all languages? or what?) if you have not done so already.

From the client's response you may be able to narrow the search. Or you may decide to print only the last two years of material, instead of the last five.

On the other hand, if you try to find the information and come up empty, get back to the client and say, "The first four resources I tried did not produce what we were looking for. This is going to take longer than I thought." For example, Sue recalls a market study on the parking meter industry. It certainly sounded definitive. How complicated could it be? So Sue offered a low quote.

What if you come up empty?

"It turns out," Sue says, "that there are only two parking meter companies in the United States—and they're not about to talk to anybody else in the world. There were no articles. No trade associations. There was simply no way to get at the information. It hadn't occurred to me when I was quoting my fee on that job that this was going to be the case."

Sue called the client. "It looks like this is much more difficult than I'd anticipated," she said. "These are the things I've tried, and I've gotten no positive results. As you can see, I've done all the most logical things. So, if you want me to continue to press for this information, the budget is going to have to be increased. But I can already tell that this is going to be a difficult project because the most obvious, common-sensical resources haven't turned up anything so far. How important is this to you?"

If the client says yes, then fine. If the answer is, "No it's not that important. No big deal," just stop. You can bill the client for the time spent so far. After all, you had no way of knowing going in that this was a closed industry. Remember, you don't guarantee to any client that you will get the information requested. You only promise to leave no stone unturned, within the budget that has been authorized.

That's why it's important to stop early on. You don't want to run up the bill and charge more than necessary when you can see it is going to be a fruitless search. That can cause hard feelings and possibly close off the possibility of future business with the client.

You must deliver something!

At the same time, when you bill the client for the time you did spend, it's a good idea to send *something*. The more detailed, the better. Tell the client in writing what you tried to do and list the resources you consulted. Let the person see how your brain worked as you approached the problem and how you followed the leads that you generated.

Whenever you come to the end of the budget on a project, it is important to have something that you can send to the client as evidence of the amount of time, energy, and resources you have brought to bear. In plain language, it is important to show most clients what they have gotten for their money—even if the project did not turn up just what they had hoped for. Again, most clients do not really understand what you do. So you have to go the extra mile to help them understand that you have indeed given good value for money.

Interaction with a client is very important. The client usually appreciates it, and it shows that you are concerned and that you want to do what the client wants you to do. At the Rugge Group, Sue never hesitates to call the client in the middle of a search. "The only thing we don't do," Sue says, "is let the client come in and sit beside us while we are online. That invariably runs up the online costs, and it can be very frustrating and tense because the client doesn't understand the process. Otherwise, we're very big on client interaction."

If you're a new broker, you might worry about appearing unprofessional. Don't. No one expects you to know the information jungle inside and out. You've been hired to use your special skills to go into the jungle and report what you find. You're like Lewis and Clark sent forth into the Louisiana Purchase to report back what they have found. When he commissioned them for the job, Thomas Jefferson didn't expect Lewis and Clark to already know the territory.

The question of filenames

Now let's look at more of the nitty-gritty details. Every assignment is different. But let's assume that you have decided that an online search is the best first step. You have picked a database and entered a search. You will want to record the process and the information it yields on disk. So what filename do you use?

It's a nuts-and-bolts question. But it's important all the same. In general, you will find it most convenient to use the same date-based number you assigned to the project in the first place.

One broker we know, for example, uses file extensions to classify files on disk. A search for the project she might label 9805-03 would have the filename

9805-03.SRH. The cover letter she eventually prepares for this search might have the filename 9805-03.LTR, while the invoice would be given the name 9805-03.INV.

This has the advantage of keeping everything together. Using DOS, for example, the command dir 9805-03.* would pull up a list of all files named 9805-03, regardless of the file extension.

You will probably want to develop your own system. But this one, using the year and month followed by the project number, can be very convenient. Among other things, it is much easier to use filenames like 9805-03 than it is to struggle with creating an abbreviation for a client's name. What would you do with "Minnesota Agricultural and Manufacturing Council" for example? How would you distinguish "Exxon Consumer Products Division" from "Exxon Corporate Relations" (if such entities existed)?

It is common sense to try to keep all of the notes and materials associated with a given project together in some form, whether in a folder or on your hard disk. The same logic applies to costs. Most major-league databases, like DIALOG or BRS, will tell you what you will be billed for a given search as soon as you sign off. So write that amount down on a piece of paper you include in your job or project folder: "DIALOG ABI/INFORM—$37.42—5/4/98." The online services will send you an itemized bill at the end of each month, but apportioning costs to various projects can be as challenging as apportioning a phone bill.

Record search costs immediately

Phone interviews or other phone work components are less precise. But here's a tip: Instead of trying to keep precise track of every nickel and dime, adopt a policy of charging a flat amount for each minute you spend on the phone. Your charge should be somewhere between 50 cents and $1 a minute for domestic calls. It all evens out in the end, and this practice is far preferable to spending the time needed to track the cost of each individual phone call. (As noted earlier, for Sue and many other brokers, the phone code service provided by MetroMedia, MCI, Sprint, and others can virtually eliminate this problem.)

Use a kitchen timer or a stopwatch instead. Start the timer when your party answers and stop it when the call is finished. Then make a note of the person called, the date, and the time spent on a sheet in your project folder. Some phone sets—we know of models made by Panasonic, for example—have call duration timers built in.

If you spend money buying books or other materials for a project, make a note of them as well and keep it in your project folder. Again, the idea is to keep everything associated with a project—whether it is search results, phone notes, or expenses—in a single place or filed under the same general heading. Simply record your charges, along with the labor time you spend day by day on the back of the form.

Here's another master's tip: Take particular care to record Federal Express (or other overnight carrier) charges. If at all possible, get your client's FedEx account number and use it when sending material. Most clients are happy to provide this number when asked since they know you will mark up the charge if you have to use your own account number. Using a client's FedEx number can free you from the burden of keeping track of shipping charges on a project and preserve precious budget money.

Step 5: Following up on first-cut results

As we have said, your first run at a problem will probably not produce all the information you need to complete a project. An online search, for example, is often only the starting point.

Your search results may contain important facts and figures relating to your assignment, but the real gold is usually the sources and experts that are mentioned. These are the people you will want to call to get the latest, up-to-the-minute information about what's going on in a particular field.

The same thing applies when your first step is to make a few calls instead of going online. More than likely, each call will produce one or more *other* names or contacts. If your first step is to go to the library, you'll encounter the same phenomenon. One reference book will lead to several others.

At this point you must decide what to do next. That's what we mean by "following up on first-cut results," and often it is the most critical phase of the entire project. You've got to do something more to find the information your client seeks. But what should it be?

You've turned up a list of additional contacts and sources, but not every one of them will be equally productive. Which ones should you pursue? And when should you stop? In an earlier time, one might have said that this is where we separate the men from the boys, though separating the amateurs from the professionals is more to the point.

Who you gonna call?

Let us suppose, for example, that an online search has turned up five people whom you might call for more information. These include: a reporter who has done a particularly insightful article on your topic; a professor who has been quoted in another article; an author who has been quoted in yet another article, and the spokespersons for two companies or institutions that have been referenced or quoted in two other articles.

Who you gonna call? It's an important question because budgets are usually limited. If you had an infinite budget, you could call all five individuals—and the other people and authorities these five suggest in the course of your conversations. Sue has worked on any number of assignments for which cost was no object. But they are few and far between and, in any case, are not likely to come your way as a brand-new information broker.

Each call you make will take time. You will have to assume, for example, that you will not be able to reach the person on the first try. So you will have to leave a message. With a bit of luck, the person will call you back. Better still, if you have established a toll-free "800" number, you can suggest in your message that the person use that number to call you back. (There is no need to publish this number, by the way. You can use it solely for research purposes like these.)

If the person does not call you back, you will have to call again and leave another message. Or you may find yourself engaged in "telephone tag," where each of you calls when the other is not in or not available.

That's why we suggest that, if you have to leave a message, leave as detailed a message as possible regarding what you are looking for. You will have much better luck in getting a return call—either from the person you need to reach, from an assistant, or from someone else who has been designated as the person to call you back.

If you are calling from a different time zone, for heaven's sake mention the fact. Sue has lost count of the times the phone has started ringing at 5:30 A.M. because the East Coast caller has forgotten that The Rugge Group is based in California. Also, if you know you are going to be out of the office, suggest a time frame when it is best for someone to return your call. Or ask when would be the best time for you to try again.

In addition, whenever you are successful, you may find that the source gives you part of the information you need but refers you to several other people who are "better qualified" to answer your questions. After finally getting in touch with all five of the sources turned up by your initial search, you could find yourself with 10 new people to call. And the game will begin again.

Information, as we have said from the beginning of this book, is nebulous. Its retrieval can be as endless as the root system of a tree stump. Not for nothing is the word *ramifications* derived from the Latin word for *root*. Your challenge is to know which path to pursue and when to stop.

Unfortunately, there is no way we can tell you what to do. This challenge is at the very core of the *business* of information retrieval. Given an unlimited budget and an unlimited amount of time, any reasonably bright person can find the information a client needs. The trick is to be able to satisfy the client's request on a limited budget in a short period of time and make a profit in the process.

The existentialism of information brokering

Only experience can teach you how to decide which leads to follow. And no matter how much experience you accumulate, you will still not always guess right. That professor you think is going to be such a font of information and thus are pursuing through several iterations of telephone tag can turn out to be a real dud once you finally make contact. While that little book with the uninformative title you decided not to look at in the library might contain the very facts and figures your client needs.

All brokers make right and wrong decisions about which paths to follow. But, through experience, successful brokers have learned how to guess right more often than they guess wrong. The best advice we can give you is to be sensitive to the *texture* of information and to be aware that different sources typically produce different textures.

Reporters, authors, professors, corporate public information officials, and politicians may all have something valuable to say on a given topic. But the texture of the information you get from people in each of these groups will be different. It will also differ within each group as well—a Republican Congressman will have a different view than a Democrat, a professor at a university may have access to more hard data than a counterpart at a small liberal arts college, and so on.

As an information broker, you must *always* think about the source and the texture of the information he or she can be expected to produce. If you do this and if you learn from your mistakes, you will soon find you are guessing right more often than not about which paths to pursue.

Know when to quit

Step 5 of the execution process holds another trap for the unsuspecting information broker. Sometimes you can get so wrapped up in a project and your mind can be so thoroughly engaged in the quest that you forget to quit when you should.

It's ironic, but the same inquiring mind, imagination, and thrill of the chase that makes you such a good information broker can also destroy your chances of making a profit.

You simply have to face the fact that information is endless. There will always be other leads you can pursue. There will always be more you can do. The hard part is to discipline yourself *not* to pursue them or do them unless you're getting paid for it. You've got to know when to stop.

Sometimes it's easy. If the client's request was specific—say, the names, addresses, and annual sales of the five leading producers of peanut butter— you will know when you have the information you need.

But suppose the request is less well defined. Suppose it's something like, "What is the projected market for solar energy panels in the United States over the next five years?" Now, before accepting a job like that you would make very clear what you will do for the budget the client is willing to authorize. But suppose you get into it, do everything "right," and still don't have anything approaching a definitive market projection.

That's fine. You're still not in trouble. You have done what you said you would and can report to the client what you have done and what you have found. You didn't promise that you would *find* a market projection, only that you would use your best efforts and skills to *look* for one.

Now for the twist. Suppose that you have spent the authorized budget and at this point have made an acceptable profit for the time and effort you have expended. The trouble is, you're convinced that if you just do a little more—make one or two more calls, check one more database, or track down one more journal or magazine article—you will have the market projection the client wants.

What do you do? Do you spend more time and money pursuing this target and consequently agree to make little or no profit on the job? Do you phone the client and explain that you don't have a definitive answer but—with authorization for a larger budget—you're almost certain you can find it? Or do you say, "Temptation, get thee behind me!" and prepare your report with the material you have already collected?

A tough call   Depending on the situation, either of these three alternatives could be appropriate. If it is a new client with good prospects for future business, you might decide to go the extra mile, even if it means making no profit.

In such situations, your invoice should reflect the costs you have borne. Itemize your total costs, but then charge the fee you and your client agreed upon and add a note to the effect that "We always honor our budget limits. But for future reference, we wanted you to be aware of our actual costs on this project."

You be the judge   Each situation is different, and only you can be the judge. However, if at all possible, we strongly recommend avoiding the above approach. It sets a precedent that is hard to overcome in the future. Your audit trail of what you have done to try to find the information is your best defense. Write it up—in detail—and tell the client what other avenues you would pursue if you had an additional budget of $x. (Be specific.) Do not apologize! You followed the right strategy. The information just wasn't there. The client will appreciate the professionalism demonstrated by this approach.

If you have a long-standing relationship with the client, you might call and ask for a larger budget. The client knows your work and can be confident that you are not stringing him along. If the client indicated that money was tight, you might take the third option and submit what you have.

There are other considerations as well. How confident are you that the market projection actually exists and that you can find it quickly? Given what you knew at the time, did you mistakenly quote too low a figure when you agreed to do the job?

Despite your making it clear that there are no guarantees, if you don't produce the market projection, is there a likelihood that the client will not pay you?

All information brokers encounter dilemmas like these. As a new broker you will probably be inclined to feel that the problem is a lack of skill on your part. And some of the time you will be right. Some of the time you will either earn no profit or actually take a loss on a project. But that's how you learn.

As your experience and skill grow, so will your confidence and self-assurance. You will know whether to go the extra mile or not, and you will know when to call it quits.

Step 6: Organizing & analyzing retrieved information

One mistake new information brokers make is not leaving enough time for sorting, organizing, and generally preparing material for the client. In this industry, this is called *post-processing*, and it can be as time-consuming as retrieving the information in the first place. You might think of it as the first stage in preparing your report.

Most downloads contain a lot of garbage that can safely be removed from the file before the abstract is included in a report to the client. Though we should note that cleaned up records may be a luxury the client's budget cannot afford. If the budget is extremely tight, you may have to eliminate much of the post-processing. Just make sure that the client understands that what you will provide is a "raw" download. (Software packages do exist to automate the "garbage removal" process, but we have never tried them.)

Actually, you may find that some clients prefer you to leave in the codes. This is often the case with "sci-tech" (scientific and technical information) clients since they tend to be more used to dealing with bibcites than their managers are.

Watch your time!

Cleaning up online search results thus involves a lot of word processing. It isn't difficult work, but it can be very time-consuming. Fortunately, there are ways to automate large parts of the process if you have a full-powered word processing program that will allow you to program a single key to execute a number of steps. Please look again at Fig. 11-1 and imagine that you had a dozen records to clean up instead of just one.

You could tell your word processing program to search the file for the first occurrence of *JRNL CODE:*, turn on its block marking function, move down five lines, and delete the entire marked block. All of these various keystrokes would be assigned to a single key. From then on, each time you strike that key, the entire sequence will be repeated. In computerese, a series of keystrokes loaded into a single key is called a *macro*.

With the right series of macros, you could make short work of cleaning up the file. Indeed, files of records captured from an online database are often ideal candidates for macros because every record typically has the same standard components. If every record were different, macros would be of little use.

Magazines like *Online*, *Database*, and *Database Searcher* frequently carry articles by librarians and information brokers on how to use specific computer programs for information retrieval and post-processing. In fact, "tradecraft" pieces like this are one of the things many readers look forward to in each issue. So use your budding broker skills and track down back issues to see if there is something you can apply. (Hint: Call up any college libraries in your area to see if they carry these publications.) Please see Appendix A for subscription information.

If your project involved phone interviews, you will probably have to write them up as well. You may work from the notes you made while doing the interview or from a tape-recorded conversation. You may or may not want to produce a verbatim transcript. It all depends on the client. Sometimes clients want merely a cogent summary of your phone conversations. Sometimes they are extremely interested in every word that was said and every nuance. In any case, preparing phone notes also takes time. Sue's experience is that it takes as much time to write up the conversation as it did to conduct the interview in the first place.

Preparing nonelectronic results

You are also being paid to be selective. We have said many times that information brokers should leave analysis of results to the client and to experts in a particular subject. It is not our job to tell the client what the information we have found means.

Exercising selectivity

At the same time, most clients do not want to be swamped with information. Years ago, for example, Sue did a consulting assignment for *American Banker* magazine. "I was in New York for a week," she says, "and they were paying me $500 a day. So every night I'd come home and write until 1:00 in the morning.

"I showed the client all the stuff I'd written. And he said 'These are just your notes, aren't they? You're not going to make me wade through all this stuff, are you?' He helped me edit it down for his boss. In the end, I think I only gave him four pages for $2,000. It's a lesson I have never forgotten."

It's an important lesson for new information brokers too. Your tendency will be to "justify" your fee by pumping out all the information you can. If someone's paying you $500, by golly, you'll show her what you can do and produce 20 to 30 pages of beautifully printed and prepared text.

Wrong. You may well have to adjust your value system. This is not college or high school, where the number of pages you produced for a term paper somehow equated to the amount of time and effort you poured into the project. This is the business world. Your client usually doesn't want *tons* of information, but rather a succinct summary of the *right* information.

The client isn't interested in how hard you worked or how much time you lavished on the project. Clients are interested in answers and results. If you tell them that producing the information they need or checking to see what's out there on a particular topic will cost $500 and they agree, then that is what they are buying.

But they expect you to be professional. That means tuning yourself to their needs and not burdening them with irrelevant, though copious, information.

So you will have to be selective in many cases. Make sure you have a firm grasp of exactly what it is the client wants. Then act in the client's place as you review the information you have retrieved: Would the client want to see this record? That record is close but not on-target. These five records all say essentially the same thing—perhaps I should include the best record and write up a note that there were four more just like it?

As we have said throughout this book: Put yourself in the client's shoes. So, in a sense, you have to do some analysis. It is not analysis in terms of "I found this, therefore we can conclude that . . ." But it is analysis in terms of "I think the client would be interested in *this* information, but *that* information would be a waste of time."

Step 7: Packaging & presenting your report

The report you hand over to the client is but the tip of the iceberg. We all know the time and effort that went into it that does not show directly. But obviously the tip of this particular iceberg is crucial. The report is the product we have been striving toward from the beginning of the assignment. In every sense of the word, it is the payoff.

What form should it take? How should you bind it? How long should it be? Those are the kinds of questions that will go through your mind. Along with, "I can't believe it. They're paying me $500 for *this*. But it's only four or five pages. I'd better see if I can spruce it up."

As we said a moment ago, of course they're not paying you for the four or five pages. They're paying you for the rest of the iceberg—all the work and expense that went into producing those particular four or five pages. But the tip of the iceberg is important, so what should you do?

The answer is easy: Make it neat, make it clean, make it clear. From a mechanical standpoint, that means that you will need either a laser printer, or a 24-pin dot matrix printer capable of letter-quality output, or an ink-jet printer. In today's world, nothing less will do. The use of bold, italics, and even different fonts and point sizes now constitute the lowest common denominator in business documents.

If you use a printer like one of these and standard copier paper (no need for expensive letterhead second sheets), no one will fault you for neatness. We've already discussed the need to remove extraneous information from online downloads and other text, so that takes care of making it clean.

Clarity is the real challenge. In preparing your report, whether it is a collection of bibliographic citations and abstracts, phone interview transcripts or summaries, or anything else, you should take great pains to make sure that there is nothing for the client to puzzle over.

There is *no* set form for an information broker's report. So if you need to weave notes into the text to explain or amplify things, do so. Ditto if you need to add diagrams, illustrations, charts, photographs, reprints of magazine articles, or anything else. As long as it is within the budget, if it adds to the clarity of your presentation, it is fair game.

Once again—put yourself into the client's shoes. If you were sitting at his or her desk with the same concerns and questions, what would *you* want to see in a report? That's the key. Every report you do may be physically different, but if you keep this key foremost in your thoughts, every client will be satisfied.

As for packaging, there are a number of alternatives. You might consider using high-quality pocket folders, available from your local stationery store. At the same store, you will also be able to find a variety of acetate report covers and spine clips of the sort you may have used for papers in college.

However, in Sue's opinion, it is important to present the client with a *document*, not a bunch of loose sheets of paper. Your local copy shop can bind a report for you at a cost of between $2 and $3. For her part, Sue spiral binds everything—so it will lie flat—and uses acetate covers. Bound into the report, clients will find a cover sheet on letterhead that states the title of the search, the databases searched and time frames covered, the current date, and the client's name.

Indeed, as your business becomes established, you may decide to invest $350 to $500 in some kind of binding machine. You can get hand-operated machines that will punch a stack of papers and apply a comb to create a comb-bound booklet. Others are designed to mate two plastic rails at the spine of your "booklet." In our opinion, however, there is no need to purchase this kind of equipment when you are just starting out.

There are many less expensive ways to make it neat, clean, and clear. If you will just bear in mind that your report *is* you and your firm in the client's eyes, you will have no problem. In a very real sense, your report is your child, and you want it to look good.

The cover letter

Never send a report to a client without a bona fide cover letter. Unless you are on very familiar terms with the client, a Post-it Note saying, "Here's the report you asked for," simply will not do. The cover letter is the formal introduction of your "performance." It is to your report what Jay Leno or David Letterman is to a performer. It sets up the audience and tells them what to expect.

Your cover letter should say in effect, "Here it is—the information you asked for. This is what we did, how we approached the problem. Interestingly, much of the information we found pointed in this direction. But, while we found a lot of information on this, there was very little on that. It may be that exploring additional sources would yield more detail on that. If you are interested, a budget of $x would allow us to follow up these leads.

"If you would like copies of any of the documents referenced here, we can supply them for a small fee. We hope this information will be useful to you and that you will consider us again the next time you have an information need."

When you are writing your cover letter, put on your "consultant's hat." You're the search expert reporting back. The enclosed report consists of two sections. You found this, but did not find that. You feel it is curious that there were so many articles on Subject A. You want to draw the client's attention to Point 5. And so on.

Let your report carry the real weight, but prepare the client for what he or she is about to receive. You may also take the opportunity to do a little selling. You could note the promising avenues that you uncovered that might be worth further exploration. You could suggest setting up an alert or current awareness service for the client on this topic. Whatever seems appropriate.

Our point is that the cover letter should not be a perfunctory, "Well, here it is," message. You're about to go on stage, as the client turns to your report, so make the most of the opportunity.

Finally, make sure you get your report to the client *on time*. One of the benefits all information brokers have to offer is timeliness. You will find that many of your assignments come from people who have waited until the last minute to call you. And if they are really in a hurry, you are foolish if you don't charge them extra for "rush" service.

But whether it is a rush job or not, it is so much better to come in early than to come in late. If you think they need your report in three days, or you think you can do it in three days, tell them "five days." Then deliver the report on the third day! That kind of performance usually costs you nothing, due to the expectations you have set up, and it pays big dividends in the "miracle-worker" department.

However, note the key phrase, "If you think . . ." You must do your best to sense the client's needs. If you say "five days," they may say, "Forget it. I've got to give my presentation the day after tomorrow." So do your best to navigate this passage carefully.

Once you have delivered your report, don't make the mistake so many new brokers make and just drop the ball. You're in a service business, and client satisfaction is thus paramount. Send off the report, wait a day or two, then follow-up with a phone call.

Ask the client if the report was received and if it is what he or she wanted. Are there any problems or questions? Is there anything that is not clear?

This is simply good customer relations. The person has hired you to deliver a product. You have done so. Now you are calling to make sure that the client is happy with what you have delivered. It's a good, "old-fashioned" way of doing business. And, of course, it can offer some nice payoffs.

Your follow-up call will impress the client with your concern for his or her problems. But it also creates an opportunity for discussion of additional assignments—whether further explorations of the topic at hand or something else. It gives the client a chance to say, "That current awareness service you mentioned in your cover letter sounds interesting. About how much would that cost and what would we get?"

If there is a problem—if the client is not satisfied—the follow-up call gives you the chance to solve it immediately. No one expects you to be perfect, so problems can and will arise. The key thing is how you handle them. If you do not handle them or do so ungraciously, the "word of mouth" about you and your business will suffer.

If you express concern and do all you can (within reason) to make it right, your client will have nothing but good things to say about you. It's not the *problem*, in other words, that is the issue. It is how you handle it. If you do it right, the problem will be forgotten, while your courteousness and willingness to help will be remembered.

There's a very practical reason for taking this step as well. The most common reason why people tell you three months down the road that they're not going to pay you is that they were dissatisfied. If you have made a follow-up call shortly after delivering the report, you can say, "Well, I have it right here that our researcher talked to you three days after you got the report, and you said it was great. If you didn't like it, that was the time to tell us."

Sue Rugge values client feedback so much that she has taken the unusual step of including a single-page questionnaire in her reports. Were the people you were working with efficient? Did they make every effort to understand your request? Were you satisfied with the results? Is there anything we can do to improve our service? On average, Sue gets about 25 percent of these questionnaires back from clients. Sometimes people complain about something that Sue and her searchers had not thought would be a problem or didn't know had occurred. So Sue calls and says thank you for bringing it to our attention.

Step 8: Confirming client satisfaction

What if they're not happy?

It is certainly true that by taking these steps, you are laying yourself open for someone to say, "No. I'm not satisfied with your work." That's a chance you simply have to take.

If a client is not satisfied, do your best to understand why. Was the client hoping for a lot more information? Was the report you provided far off the mark? What are the concerns?

There is no question here of cutting your price or saying, "Then you don't have to pay us." Not at all. At most, you may have to say, "Well if this was not what you wanted, we'll do it again."

Of course, sometimes you just can't win. Sue remembers a client who wanted to open a video store. He wanted a floor plan, and Sue and her staff found exactly that. They called a magazine for video store owners and located an article that included the layouts the client had asked for. They sent it to the client. He was furious. "I wanted a *computer* search," he said.

Sue responded, "Didn't this article tell you what you wanted to know?" He said, "Yes, but I could have done this myself. I could have gone to the library. I didn't need you guys to go to the library."

Sue tried to explain that it is the information broker's job to get the information in the format best suited to the client's needs. It didn't do any good. The client never paid the balance of his bill.

Conclusion

We've covered steps 1 through 8 of the execution process. In the next chapter we'll look at the last two steps—the "money" steps. From the client's standpoint, the report you produce may be the most important step. But we all know that nothing happens without money. So let's look at preparing and sending your invoice, and dealing with clients who are slow to pay.

23 Pricing, contracts, & billing

This chapter is about a subject dear to all of our hearts: getting paid! But not just getting paid. Getting paid *enough* to make sure that you have more money coming in than going out. If you don't do this, you'll be the one going out—of business. We'll look at the fine art of quoting on a job and presenting that quote to the client. We'll look at the kinds of written agreements you may want to have to protect both yourself and the client. And we'll discuss how to prepare and present your bill.

Calculating costs and coming up with a quote on a project is the hardest thing a new broker must do. There are so many things running through your head. With little or no experience under your belt, you really don't know how much time you will have to spend conducting phone interviews or what your expenses will amount to for searching online databases. So you don't know what your costs are going to be.

The toughest part of the job

But you have to come up with a price. And here, you're afraid that if you quote too high, you won't get the job. But if you quote too low, you won't make any money. Which means you will actually lose money—since even if the quote covers all of your costs, with enough left over to pay yourself $5 an hour, the overhead expenses of running your business will not be covered.

Looking them in the eye

Then there's that scary moment of actually telling someone what they will have to pay you. It can help to use the corporate "we," as in "We charge . . ." or "Our fee for this project will be . . ." But that doesn't change the fact that you are going to have to look someone in the eye, either literally or figuratively, and ask for money.

Western society in general tries to avoid such situations. We put price tags on store merchandise and post set charges for services on charts. So much for a tune-up, so much for a haircut, so much more if you want a blow-dry, and so on. It's convenient, of course. But it also eliminates the need for someone to peer under the hood and say to you directly, "This car . . . hmm, lemme see . . . I'll charge you $85, plus materials, to tune it up."

No one likes confrontations, and telling clients what they are going to have to pay you has the potential of leading to one. What if they say, "That's outrageous! You can't really mean you're going to charge me $500 for this!" What if they say, "That sounds a little steep to me. Are you sure you can't do better?" Or, "Oh, I'm sorry. I'm afraid that's out of the question. Thanks for your time. I appreciate your coming in."

On the other hand, you may encounter a client who has already decided that the price should be thus and so and you come in way below expectations. Such clients tend to automatically assume that you can't possibly serve their needs because your price is too low. So, you really never know what you will encounter. Just keep in mind that you almost certainly know as much about your field as the client does about his or her field. Therefore, you meet as experts of equal rank.

Other concerns

You're also worried about results. What if the client doesn't like what you produce? What if she refuses to pay? What if it's your fault, you think, because you weren't skilled enough to do the job? What will your friends, associates, and significant other or spouse say when it turns out that you've failed in your first assignment?

There are worries and concerns aplenty to go around. Each of them is significant—not because they represent truly serious, insurmountable problems, but because you are worried about them. We're certainly not going to tell you to stop worrying and be happy, though you could do worse than to adopt that philosophy. Instead, we're going to tell you how to deal with each of these problems in a professional and competent manner.

How to calculate your costs

Let's start with the matter of coming up with an actual quote on a job. As a new broker, you don't know what your costs are going to be. Established brokers don't always know either. But experience is the best teacher. Every project is a custom product with its own unique requirements. Every assignment holds the potential of involving significantly more work than is initially apparent. The difference is that experienced brokers have done enough projects to have a pretty good idea of what's likely to be involved in most new projects.

They don't know the costs to the penny, but they know enough to quote a *pricing range*. They also know enough not to take a job unless they are 50 to 65 percent sure that they can find what the client needs. (More on this later.) That means that they can often come up with a quote on the spot, while they are on the phone or in a face-to-face meeting with the client.

This is not something a new broker should even think about doing. There is no shame in saying, "Yes, Mr. Jones. I believe I understand what you need. Let me check a few sources (or check with my research staff) and get back to you later today with a quote." Most clients *expect* you to handle things this way. If the client were to call up a supplier to place an order, he might be pleasantly surprised if the transaction could be handled in a single call. But he would not expect most suppliers to be able to give a firm quote right away. Prices change. Items go in and out of stock. Shipping charges have to be calculated and delivery dates determined.

The one thing the client would definitely expect, however, is for the supplier to get back with a quote as soon as possible. As an information broker, you can do no less. If it's morning, strive to have the quote by mid-afternoon. If it's late in the day, be ready to present it first thing next morning. If you're running into problems, call the client and explain the delay.

Sharpen your pencil

You would think that, while not necessarily easy, the setting of prices of all sorts in our economy would be simple. Calculate the costs to the best of your ability and add a certain amount or percentage for your profit. But there's more to it than that. If there weren't, professors wouldn't be able to write thick tomes on price theory and teach entire courses on the subject.

What complicates the process, indeed what makes pricing an art, is the perfectly human desire to make as much money as possible for the time and effort expended. You may not feel that way yourself just now, but wait until you've begun expending time and effort on a project before you reach your conclusion. More than likely, you will agree with us when we suggest that it is just plain stupid to charge any less than the market will bear.

That sounds like advice from a nineteenth-century robber baron. And perhaps the shoe would fit if there were any wealthy information brokers or if anyone had ever gotten rich in this profession. As it happens, it's a very socialistic policy, with the "rich" subsidizing the "poor." Yes, charging what the market will bear is the best way to maximize your profits. Make the most you can on every job. But be aware that jobs can differ in their payoff.

Please note that we are not advocating that you provide the same level of service for different prices. But the larger the budget you can persuade the client to authorize—"what the market will bear"—the more work you can do. And the more work you do, the more money you will make.

As the budget goes up, the percentage you spend on outside expenses goes down. For example, with a $500 budget, about 50 percent ($250) might go to pay for online time and telephone work. Yet your out-of-pocket expenses may not be much more than that on a $2,500 project. The difference is that on the $2,500 project, your $250 in expenses amounts to only 10 percent of the total. Not 50 percent. A large portion of the remaining 90 percent is money in your pocket for work you perform.

The larger the budget, the more value-added service you can provide. Thus, the more profit you will make. One good example is the process of preparing raw online search data before sending it off to the client. You may be able to obtain the data for $450 in outside expenses. But if you have a budget of $650 to work with, you can probably afford to spend the time necessary to clean up the results, add bold and italic highlights, and possibly prepare an "executive summary"—some introductory text followed by bulleted quotes that point out the most significant results.

We want to make sure you understand that we are not suggesting that you charge $2,500 and spend a mere $250 doing the work. For $2,500, you provide a package that will knock the client's socks off. It is not a question of whether the work gets done. It's a question of who gets the money, you or DIALOG and other online systems? Many times, for instance, if Sue feels that she knows where to call to get the needed information, she will make those calls instead of using DIALOG or some other online system—even though she knows that the information is available online.

There should be no doubt that the resulting report will be "worth $2,500." If you are a good information broker, you will make sure that the client is satisfied. The crucial point is who gets the lion's share of the money the client has authorized to produce this wonderful report—you or DIALOG or someone else?

Base price & quoted price

Pricing is thus a two-stage process. The first step is to come up with as accurate a cost and profit figure as you can. That's your base price. The second step is to ask yourself, "Would the client be willing to pay more than the base price for the kind of value-added work you can do? If so, how much more?" The answer to that question determines the price you actually quote to the client.

Let's look at how to calculate your base price first. There is no cut-and-dried formula, since there are really no cut-and-dried projects. Each one is different, as we keep saying. Nor is it a matter of precise figures. You'll drive yourself crazy if you try to predict everything down to the penny. And your prediction will always be wrong. Calculate in round numbers, and always round up.

Start by analyzing the steps you will have to take to execute the job. How many databases will you have to search and how many records will you have to have displayed? How long will it take you, and what are the connect-time and display charges in each case?

For example, an efficient searcher can get in and out of the appropriate databases for about $150 to $200. That range is a good yardstick for a typical subject search. But there are exceptions. With a patent or chemical search, the "yardstick" costs will be much higher. But then, you probably should not be doing those kinds of expensive, specialized searches in the first place. Unless you have been trained in chemical or patent searching, you will often be best off calling upon your information broker colleagues who have had experience in these areas.

How many phone calls will you have to make and how long are they likely to be? Short ones for quick address and contact information? Or relatively long interviews? Multiply the time you estimate you will spend on the phone by $1 a minute to come up with an estimate of long distance charges.

Will there be document delivery charges involved? If you can estimate the number and type of documents you will have to order, you can check with a document supply house and come up with an estimate for this component.

Will you have to purchase special materials, either for delivery to the client or to enable you to perform a component of the job? You might need to buy a mailing list, a directory, or some piece of database documentation, for example. Will you have to travel anywhere, and if so, what will your expenses be? And don't forget those little expenses like charges for photocopies, postage, and the like.

In short, *think through the job*! On the first few jobs you may find it especially helpful to sit down in a quiet room and visualize each step you plan to take. Write the steps down in order, or use a base-price job estimating form like the one shown in Fig. 23-1. (You will find a copy of this form on the accompanying disk as well.) But wait before you try to come up with estimates for each cost.

If you are a real novice at searching, you may want to check DialIndex to get an indication of the volume of material you are going to encounter and which databases are likely to contain it. As Sue says, "You want to watch for two conditions here, both of which should raise red flags. The first condition is finding too much information, and the second is finding too little. In other words, finding only three or four citations is as bad as finding 5,000. Either way, it is a signal that the job is likely to be more difficult and time-consuming than you may have anticipated. Ideally, you would hope to find 50 to 100 citations that you could expect to whittle down to a handful that were right on target.

23-1

A sample base-price job-estimating form.

Here's a form you may want to adapt and use when working up a preliminary base-price figure. Notice that the Project Element column consists of each of the steps you feel will be necessary in completing the job. Use the entry labelled "Allowance for direct expenses" to factor in any books, journals, or other special materials you may have to buy and deliver to the client with your report.

Please remember that, as formal as it may look, this form is intended merely to help you organize your thinking. There is no single "correct" way to bid a job. You may not want to add the same percentage markup to all of your costs, for example. Or there may be costs you feel you should simply pass through and not mark up at all.

This form will get you started. But you will want to use the copy supplied on the accompanying disk to create and print out your own customized version.

Project Element	Est. Hours	Est. Costs
Reference interview (labor)	_____	_____
Strategizing (labor)	_____	_____
Online search preparation (labor)	_____	_____
Online search execution (labor)	_____	_____
Online search execution (costs)		_____
Analysis of results (labor)	_____	_____
Library research (labor)	_____	_____
Library expenses (costs)		_____
Phone research (labor)	_____	_____
Long distance charges (costs)		_____
FAX long distance charges (costs)	_____	_____
Postage (costs)	_____	_____
Document delivery (costs)	_____	_____
Report preparation (labor)	_____	_____
Allowance for direct expenses (books, reports, etc.)	_____	_____
Estimate totals:	_____	_____
Total charge for labor (Estimated hours times $85):	a. _____	
Markup to be added to costs:		_____
Total charge for costs (Sum of costs and markup):		b. _____
Estimated base price (Add lines a. and b.):	$ _____	

"Also, if you are a beginner, don't rule out the possibility of using an established broker to do the online research. After all, the client doesn't care who does the research. The client cares about the results.

"The Rugge Group is happy to give free price quotes. But you may also want to consider using a *house broker*. A house broker is basically an online searcher employed by one of the big online information systems. For a fee, these people will search their system for you. DIALOG calls the service DialSearch. On NEXIS, it is NEXIS Express. And so on." In short, there are lots of ways to get an online search done without necessarily doing it yourself.

As we have said before, if you do not come from an information resources background, you will learn faster and be better able to satisfy your clients if you use an experienced broker on your first few jobs. New brokers should never forget that establishing a client base must be the number-one priority and goal during the first year.

With the list in front of you, continue your visualization to include estimates of the time you will have to spend on each step. Estimated costs are one component of a quote, estimated labor charges are another. And it is here that we so often cheat ourselves. Not necessarily by failing to charge enough per hour, though that is a problem for some brokers. But through neglecting to charge for all the hours we spend.

Counting the time

As a new broker, you may forget to count the time you spend with the client conducting a reference interview. This is the time you may have to spend finding out exactly what the client wants after you have been given the job. But you should also consider the time you spend selling the client on your services, since this often amounts to educating the client on what's possible, the resources available, and so on. All of which is valuable information.

Most brokers would not forget to charge for the time they spend searching online, but many fail to count the time spent preparing and planning a search before turning on the modem.

You will also spend time printing out, reviewing, and, budget permitting, cleaning up search results. You'll spend time analyzing and selecting data, whether it is from an online system or books and magazines at your library. And speaking of the library, if you visit its hallowed halls, don't forget to start your meter the moment you start your car to make the trip. (If it's a long drive, count your mileage and include it in your costs at 26 cents or more per mile.)

More time will be involved in writing your final report, and more time printing it, packaging it, and sending it off. You might include a time allowance for making a follow-up phone call once the report has arrived. This is a nice personal touch, but it can be an important opportunity to discuss the results with the client.

Estimate your time in minutes or hours as appropriate. Then convert everything to hours or fractions of an hour. What's the smallest fraction you should use? As we said before, when Maxwell Communications bought IOD, it tried to get searchers to record their time in six-minute segments, one tenth of an hour. It used to drive us all crazy. A more workable approach is to follow the lead of many attorneys, CPAs and other professionals and bill in 15-minute, quarter-of-an-hour segments.

Adding everything up

When you think you've got a pretty good handle on the elements that are going to cost you money and the number of hours you expect to spend, you will be ready to calculate a preliminary base-price number. Again, see Fig. 23-1.

If you are a novice or are otherwise inexperienced in using information resources, this approach can be a big help. However, if you are an experienced reference librarian, you probably will not need to go through each step. Sue tries to find out what the information is *worth* to the client. If they are basing major decisions—such as a decision to acquire a company, enter a new market, or move a plant site—then a four-figure budget is not unreasonable. But if they are just looking for a little background information on a prospective client, then $500 may seem a bit high. The key point is that Sue has had enough experience to be confident of what she and The Rugge Group can do for either budget.

Again, when we speak of "what the market will bear," we mean how much the client is willing to spend on a project. We are not suggesting that you should charge one client more than you would another for the identical amount of work. Whatever you charge, you will earn your money.

But, all things being equal, we would rather have a few clients willing to authorize relatively large budgets than a clutch of clients who are primarily interested in doing things on the cheap. The total dollar figure taken in may be the same, but the amount of nonbillable, non-information-related time and effort involved (sales calls, client contact, even hand-holding) will differ considerably.

As you review the form in Fig. 23-1, two points may leap out at you: the markup added to the estimated costs and the price of $85 per hour for labor. Let's discuss both items, starting with the markup.

Marking up your expenses ensures that the figures you quote will more closely reflect your *actual* cost for each item. Let's assume that you have just completed a job that involved doing a telephone interview and downloading a file from a corporate presence on the Internet.

Mark up your costs

You could not have done that job if you didn't own a computer, printer, and a modem—equipment that probably cost you $2,000 or more. These components tend to be very reliable, but sometimes they need service. And sometime in the future you will eventually want to replace them. There are also your expenses for the documentation and training sessions you buy from online systems like DIALOG. And there is the fact that the company that provides you with Internet access expects to be paid regularly each month—regardless of whether you yourself have been paid by your clients. So at the very least, you are losing the interest you could have earned on that money. That too is a very real cost.

The question then is: Where does the money come from to compensate you for the interest lost or to pay to repair and replace the equipment you need to do online searches or to pay for the seminars and training you need?

If you bill clients for just your exact costs and your labor, there's only one place the money can come from. It has to come out of your labor charges. But your labor charges, as we'll see in a moment, already cover office overhead and other expenses. Thus, if you aren't adding a markup to your costs, and your modem suddenly stops working, the money to replace it will ultimately come out of your profit.

Protect your profit!

Of course, most of this is simply a matter of how you choose to account for things. You could pass online and other costs directly through to the client and just raise your hourly rate to cover equipment repair and replacement costs. Or you could leave your hourly rate the same and add a line item to the costs column labelled "Equipment repair and replacement contingency fund."

Clearly, neither of these two other approaches is likely to look good to the client. So most brokers keep it simple. They estimate their costs and then add a markup of between 25 and 50 percent in each case. The marked-up figures are the ones that appear on the final client bill or statement.

Sue marks up most costs by 15 to 30 percent. Generally, the lower the cost, the higher the markup. The higher the actual cost, the lower the markup.

For example, buying a book for a client costs you much more than the actual price you pay for the book. You have to order it, follow up on the order, have it delivered, and deliver it to the client. Then you have to process the invoice for payment. All of this takes *time*, and time is really the only commodity you have to sell. So don't feel that you are "gouging" the client by adding your markup. You are providing a service—if you didn't spend the time, the client would have to do so—and you are entitled to make a profit on that time.

The key point is to be aware of your *true* costs in every instance and to make sure that you account for them. There is no information broker's guild rule forcing you to charge a client for all of your true costs. But there is an iron law of business that if you do not know what your true costs are, you cannot know whether you are actually making any money or not. And if you are not making any money, eventually you will go out of business.

If all of this is strange to you, seek professional help. Ask your accountant for guidance. If you don't have an accountant, get one. Your time is best spent finding new clients and executing searches, not preparing tax returns or analyzing costs.

How much per hour?

Now we get to it. As an information broker in the 1990s, you should be charging between $85 and $125 an hour for your labor. (If you are an expert in patent or chemical searching, biotechnology, or the like, $175 to $200 is not unreasonable.)

That sounds like a princely sum, doesn't it? Why, at 40 hours a week for 52 weeks a year, it amounts to 2,080 hours or between $176,800 and $260,000. Won't the folks back home be proud!

Right. As they say, it's nice work if you can get it. And by the way, why 52 weeks? Aren't you going to take any vacation? Okay, okay, so we take two weeks off and shave the yearly total by a few thousand dollars. While you're at it, since, when you work for yourself, there are no paid holidays, you'd better deduct another thousand dollars or so. That still leaves some impressive figures.

But what happens if you get sick? Say you're unable to work for a week. And what happens if, God forbid, you develop a serious medical problem? Better shave off some more for your health insurance premiums and your disability insurance (if you can get disability coverage at all as a self-employed individual).

And, by the way, who says that all of the 2,080 hours or less you are available for work are going to be billable? Fat chance! The truth is that you will be lucky to be able to bill 25 to 50 percent of your time once you are established. When you are just starting out, the figure is more likely to be even lower than 20 percent.

Deciding what you're going to charge for anything is an imperfect science at best. Our point here is to help you realize that, while thinking in terms of $85 to $125 an hour may *sound* like a lot of money, it is not at all out of line when you consider the expenses you have and the fact that you have to pay for all your own benefits, including vacations and health insurance.

Ultimately, an hourly rate is merely a rough yardstick. Even an experienced information broker can't tell you precisely how many minutes will be required to execute a given assignment. But an experienced broker will not undervalue his or her time. And that is the point we want to drive home here.

Quote your prices any way you wish. But if you cannot sell, bill, and execute a project at an effective rate of around at least $85 an hour, then you should stop to consider whether you can make a living in this profession.

Naturally the optimal or minimum rate will vary somewhat with your location. The cost of searching DIALOG or NEXIS is the same, regardless of where you live. But other expenses may be less. Or they may be more.

The main point we want to make here is that you should be aware of all of your expenses and of the fact that a corporate worker typically receives vacation and other benefits that equal or exceed one third of the nominal salary. When you're thinking of what you plan to charge per hour or any other way, don't sell yourself short!

Finally, of course, the lofty annual income we cited assumes that the jobs and assignments are continuous throughout the year, every year. We all know that's not going to happen. So if you think of your time as worth $85 an hour, you're not really making the corporate equivalent of $176,800. With skill, luck, and experience, you might be able to line up enough work to actually earn the equivalent of $30,000 to $50,000, less nonbillable expenses and operating overhead.

You are charging for being available

Far from being unreasonable, given all the expenses and self-funded benefits you must deduct from what you receive, you can't afford to charge much less than $85 to $125 an hour.

Or consider things another way. Have you ever stopped to figure out the hourly rate you are paying the people you buy services from? Alfred pays Tony, his barber, $12 (including tip) for a haircut that takes, at most, 20 minutes. That's a rate of $60 an hour. And it's cheap. The cost of a haircut at a fancier place down the road, with tip, is more than double.

Yes, the barber has expenses. He has to pay rent on his shop. He has equipment to maintain. There are advertising expenses. He has to attend conferences to keep up with the latest techniques and styles.

And, while Tony has plenty of work, not every 20-minute segment of his day is always booked. As with an information broker, or anyone else in a service profession, part of what Alfred and the other customers are paying for is Tony's *availability*. If he couldn't make enough when he was busy to carry him through the periods when he is not, Tony would close up shop and seek another line of work. His barbering skills would then not be available to anyone.

Of course not every time component of a job should be rebilled at your professional rate. The time you spend performing clerical tasks (filing, photocopying, etc.) should be billed at clerical rates. The reason is simple. If two brokers are bidding on a job, one charging clerical rates for clerical chores and the other charging the full professional rate, the first broker will come in with a more competitive bid.

Differing rates for differing job components

It is simply a fact of the marketplace. Since clerical help can be hired at clerical rates, whether you actually hire someone or perform a task yourself, you pretty much have to charge clerical rates for clerical chores. If you don't, someone else will.

But don't cheat yourself! Don't assume, for example, that your post-processing work qualifies as a clerical function. As you read over the results of an online search, getting it ready to send to the client, you are looking for false drops (records that match your search criteria but are actually unrelated to the subject at hand). You may be adding printer codes for boldface type or italics to highlight information you know the client will want to zero in on. You might even be adding comments and call-outs to further add value or otherwise enhance the product.

Post-processing often requires skills and a depth of knowledge no clerk can be expected to bring to bear. Therefore it simply does not make good sense— nor is it fair to you—to charge clerical rates for this kind of work.

The second stage of preparing your price

Let's assume that at this point you have calculated a marked-up figure for your costs and a figure for the labor involved (both clerical and professional). Add them together to come up with a preliminary figure, then add something more as a fudge factor. This should be at least 10 to 15 percent, depending on the size of the project. The idea is to build in a little bit of leeway in case things don't go according to plan.

You might discover that you have to do a quick online search that you had not planned on. It might cost you only $20. But if you haven't built in a fudge factor, that's $20 right out of your pocket, since you can hardly ask the client to pay $20 more if you have agreed to a fixed price. There are also small costs that you may forget to pick up or quarter-hour segments that you didn't count on.

Add everything up—costs, labor, and fudge factor—and you will have what we call the base price for the job. This is the price for which you feel you could do the job and both cover your expenses and make a profit. It is, in effect, your minimum. But it does not have to be the price you quote to the client.

In preparing the quoted price, consider what the market will bear. How badly does the client need the information? How badly do you want the job? Is someone else likely to be bidding against you? Is the client likely to become a regular customer once you do this project?

When you've sifted and assessed considerations like these, ask yourself how much more you feel you could charge. It could be $100 more, or $500 more, or some other figure. It is completely up to you. As you gain more experience, you will not only develop a better idea of what a proposed project will cost, you will also get a feeling for how much the market will bear. Remember, the greater the budget you can persuade the client to authorize, the more you can do for that client and the more profit you will make.

Also, if the client has asked for rush service, then you must charge extra. How much extra is a function of how much you will be inconvenienced. If you have your week scheduled in a way to let you make all your deadlines without working 19-hour days, and someone calls with a rush request, the inconvenience will be considerable. You will have to put your other projects on hold and possibly risk missing their deadlines. You will have to instantly shift gears and swing into action. At times like that, you may well be within your rights to charge double your normal labor fee.

Charge extra for rush service

Even if you do not have anything else scheduled, consider charging extra for a rush job. Clients expect to pay more for this kind of attention. And you certainly don't want to say, "Sure, I can get it to you tomorrow. I wasn't doing anything else anyhow." Rush service is almost universally viewed as an extra for which there is always an extra charge.

For example, Sue added a surcharge of 25 percent of the labor costs for rush service at IOD. So far The Rugge Group has been able to accommodate client deadlines. The group approach makes it possible to avoid putting anyone out when a fast turnaround is required. If one member is busy, Sue gets another member to do it. However, if yours is a one-person operation, you should definitely charge extra for rush service.

Experience will also introduce you to an entirely different frame of reference. To us, $500 is a lot of money. There are very few things the average person purchases for $500. But in the corporate world—including advertising agencies and law firms—where you will undoubtedly find many of your clients, $500 is just "noise." It is insignificant. If they want the information and that's what you say it costs, that's what it costs. Now, when can you deliver it?

The corporate frame of reference

We are by no means suggesting that every job will be $500 or more. We merely want you to be aware that your clients will very likely be operating with a different frame of reference than you are accustomed to, particularly if you came to this profession from a public library, college, or other institution.

If you quote $250 on a job the client is expecting to pay $500 for, you will thus do yourself more harm than good. Instead of jumping at the chance to get your services for half the expected cost, your client is likely to wonder what's wrong with you. Maybe you're not confident enough in your abilities to actually do the job. Maybe you're desperate. Or worst of all, maybe you're an amateur. In any case, the client may not respect you or your abilities, however good you may actually be. Sue has found through her consulting that the most prevalent problem for novice information brokers is their inability to charge what they are worth.

Quote a pricing range

Now, before you contact the client and quote the price you have just calculated, stop and consider the wisdom of quoting a pricing range. Instead of saying, "I can do it for $300," say, "We can do this project for between $400 and $500, with a guarantee not to exceed $500." As you are well aware by now, even experienced brokers cannot be sure what they'll run into once they start a project. Remember how nebulous information is and remember that you have made that point with your client.

Given the nature of information and its retrieval, there is no reason why you should be forced to submit a single, firm price quote for most projects. To do so is to make yourself vulnerable to the unexpected and to risk losing money on a project. By the same token, the client should not be expected to give you an open checkbook.

Quoting a project as a range of prices, with a not-to-exceed guarantee, answers both of these concerns. It protects you both from unexpected expenses. If the project comes in at only $300, you might consider charging the client $400 if it seems appropriate. If it comes in at $450, at least you are protected. Imagine how you would feel if you quoted a firm price of $300 in such a case.

Plus expenses?

You may not be able to get a client to agree to "$400 to $500, plus expenses," though it may be worth a try. Most clients want an outside limit, and "plus expenses" can be too vague. Still, there are certain costs you should definitely strive to get outside the search budget.

The Federal Express charges on a rush job are a good example. If you quote $350 to $400, and the client says, "Okay, but don't go over $400," you might say, "All right. We'll keep it at $400, but then we'll add the FedEx costs on top of that." The client will almost always agree because Federal Express is a specific item. (Better still, ask if you can use your client's Federal Express or other overnight delivery service number.)

It was not uncommon at IOD for Sue and Company to spend $50 shipping materials off to a client. If there was a not-to-exceed limit of $400, and the job cost $350 to execute, that $50 could be all that's left of the profit. If FedEx charges are in the budget, then you'll be sending your profit directly to the company's Memphis headquarters. If the client has agreed that FedEx charges are to be billed *in addition* to the budget, that $50 will stay put in your pocket.

In general, if there is a cost that is a straight pass-through—where you accept money from the client with one hand and pass it to a supplier or service provider with the other—try to get the client to agree to pay for it, over and above the project cost. And don't forget to mark most costs up by at least ten percent to compensate your business for the hassle.

When Sue was running IOD, she established an hourly charge of $75, with a two-hour minimum per job. Even if the job took only one hour, the client had to pay for two. At the Rugge Group, where overhead is much lower, a more flexible policy is possible. But Sue still will not consider doing a job of any sort for less than $250, and certainly not less than $450 if any online searching is required. "You can't possibly talk to the client, understand what he wants, execute a job, and prepare a bill for anything less than $250," Sue says, "and that's not very much."

What about a minimum charge?

You should definitely set a minimum of at least $250. Whether you decided to make that point with a new client or not depends on the circumstances. If the person calling you is a private individual interested in hiring you for a personal project, you should probably find a moment early in the conversation to quote your minimum charge. Individuals may not be aware of how expensive it is to be in business and may be expecting you to charge, say, $25 or $30.

If the prospect is seeking to hire you for a corporate project, use your own best judgment. The chances are that the person will be expecting to pay much more than $250, so stating your minimum can seem amateurish.

On the other hand, depending on how the conversation has gone, when the prospect asks you what it's going to cost, you might say, "Well, our minimum fee is $250 per project. Based on what you've told me, it doesn't sound like the total charge will be much more than that. Let me check a few resources and get back to you later today with a more accurate estimate."

We should note here that $250 is at the absolute bottom of an acceptable minimum. Sue's average project runs between $500 and $650. But you will have to find your own level. Just remember what we said about not charging too little.

Bucking up your confidence

You might as well admit it. The first few times you prepare a bid and present it to the client, you're going to be nervous. It's like learning to ride a bicycle. You can't help being wobbly at first. But before long you master the knack, and from then on going for a spin is simply not an issue.

So what about those first few times? Well, at base you have to accept the fact that you have got to master this part of the job if you want to become an information broker. Either that, or you'll have to find a partner who can go out and sell your search services. And that partner had better be able to present a price quote with confidence or neither one of you will be in business very long.

Fortunately, there are a number of things you can do to help ease yourself over this initial hump. Call them training wheels, if you like.

Start with your self-image. You are not a librarian forced to smile and be nice to anyone who happens to walk in the door. You are not a back-office research drudge at some company forced to spend your days doing every boring assignment company managers throw at you.

You're a professional. You've got the personality, special skills, and talents required to do what so very few others can do. And you're good at it. With a little luck and hard work, those talents and skills will let you be your own boss and run your own company. As much as anyone can ever be, you are in charge of your own life. Unlike your friends and former co-workers, you have elected *not* to trade independence and freedom for the security of a corporate job.

"What budget did you have in mind?"

You're more like a lawyer opening his own office or a doctor hanging out her shingle. You're good at what you do. You may feel a bit uncertain about this phase of the job right now, but you've got it where it counts. Besides, you don't *need* this particular job, even if it's the first one you've had a shot at. Another one will come along directly. Don't be afraid that your quote will be too high. If you've done your best to calculate your costs and labor accurately and fairly, and the client says that's too much, then the client simply can't afford the service.

If anyone should be embarrassed, it should be the client, not you. The client is in over his head. He had no business asking you to spend the time and effort coming up with a quote if he wasn't willing to pay a fair price.

You can guard against this outcome by trying to get your clients to tell you what type of budget they have in mind. If they are coy about the figure and won't answer this query, then be sure that within the first three or four minutes of the conversation you manage to work in the fact that an average search runs around $450 to $650. If you fail to do this, you can easily end up spending 20 minutes or more discussing the project—only to find at the end that the client does not have more than $150 to spend. As Sue says, "This is most likely to happen with individuals and with corporate people who have little authority."

In situations like this, more than likely, the client will not say no. He or she will probably try to appear to be thinking it over and then say, "Yes. That will be fine." If the client has some other reaction, you've got things covered. Following Sue Rugge's advice, you're prepared with alternatives: If the client reacts negatively to your quote, you suggest doing a less extensive search for less money. If the client indicates that your price is lower than expected, you say, "Now, that's for the basic project we discussed. With a larger budget we could also do thus and so."

You might try practicing your presentation on your friends. Do your best to make it real. Seat the friend at a desk and yourself at a chair in front of it and do a little role-playing. Encourage your friend to give you a really hard time, raising all kinds of questions, reacting to the price, and so on. Try to get into the spirit of it and improvise your responses. Think of it as your workout before the big event. And have fun with it. (That phrase just will not die.)

There is no substitute for working through the process of preparing an estimate of your costs and labor. However, when you are just starting out, you could consider calling an established information broker or one of the "house brokers" at DIALOG, NEXIS, DataTimes, or some other online system and ask that person to give you a quote on the job. That should certainly give you a better idea of what the job should cost and whether your own estimate is way off.

Call a broker

Then go a step further. Add a markup of $100 or so to the quote and take it to the client. When you get the job, hire the broker to do the actual work. Then use a low-cost system like Knowledge Index to do the same search yourself, if possible, and keep track of your time and costs. Comparing your approach and costs with those of the broker you hired will be most instructive. (Remember, though, that you may not use Knowledge Index to actually complete an assignment. So don't forget to adjust for the cost difference.)

It is the nature of the information brokering profession that the time between the placement of an order and its execution and delivery is usually very short. In most cases, there simply isn't time to spend drawing up and exchanging signed contracts. The client calls and needs it *now*. But you've done work for this particular firm before and you know they're good for it. Though, as you will see in a moment, we do suggest you prepare a letter of agreement. (For your convenience, should a contract be necessary, you will find a sample contract on the disk accompanying this book.)

Contracts & agreements

If someone you don't know calls up, you may not be quite so willing to take the job. If the person has been referred by somebody you know and trust, that will usually come out in the first 30 seconds of the call. That may be completely satisfactory. If it isn't, you can always call your mutual friend to check the new client out.

Talking to strangers on the phone

If someone calls you out of the blue, perhaps because they heard you speak or saw your ad, you will have to be more cautious. If it's to be a rush job, provide your quote and explain that with all new clients your firm's policy is to request half payment in advance and half on delivery of the final report.

If the person makes remarks to the effect of "What's the matter? Don't you trust me?", you might consider turning the question around. On the contrary, you trust the person completely. Just as you expect to be trusted with half the fee in advance.

"Okay, but how can I get it there in time?" Easy. We accept MasterCard, Visa, or American Express. Or you can send us a check via Federal Express and I'll have it by 10:30 tomorrow morning. No access to Federal Express? No problem. Have your bank wire the funds into my account. Here's my account number and the other information you need. The money will be there within a couple of hours.

If none of this is possible, you should give serious thought to turning down the job. Someone you don't know is asking you to spend your money and time and to accept on faith that you will be paid. Should you believe the person? It's a tough call. We might as well say that everything depends on the "vibes" you get from the phone conversation. Is this person for real or out to take you?

Clients in person If it is not a rush job, and the person seems a plausible fellow, you might consider preparing a quote and faxing it along with a letter of agreement. The letter of agreement should stipulate half payment in advance and half on completion. When the client sends you confirmation of acceptance and a check, you can pretty much assume it's safe to begin work. Please see Fig. 23-2 for a sample letter of agreement. (You will also find a copy of this sample letter on the accompanying disk.)

Letters of agreement can also be useful when you are meeting a client face-to-face. Suppose that a month or two after your sales call on the Ajax company, the vice president you spoke with calls. You arrange to go in to meet with her to get a clearer idea of her needs. The meeting goes well. It concludes with your saying something like, "Good. I'll get back to you today with a quote. Our terms are half in advance and half on completion. Does that pose any problems?"

The point is to politely make it clear that you cannot begin the work until you receive the initial payment. Don't wait until you spend the time preparing your quote to make your terms clear to the client.

If your terms do pose a problem, you will have to decide what to do. The person might say, "That's fine. But we're a big company and it takes at least a week to cut a check. Do you suppose you could get started anyway? I'll do my best to get you a check by next Wednesday." In that case, you may feel that it is safe to start the job. If the person says, "No. I'm sorry, but we never do business that way," you may have to respond, "I'm sorry too, but I can't afford to do business any *other* way."

Don't argue about it. Just bear in mind that attorneys often ask for an initial payment before starting to work. So do advertising agencies. So do management, marketing, and other corporate consultants. Consequently, your request for half in advance should not throw anybody for a loop.

Now let's assume that you have returned to your office. Your terms are acceptable and you can now begin to prepare your quote. Next you call the vice president to present your numbers. If she approves, you say, fine, I'll send

Shown below is a bare-bones letter of agreement. It is quite utilitarian and limits itself to just the essential facts. Depending on the situation, you may wish to make your letters more warm and friendly. But do not lose sight of the letter's purpose: to state the project, the deadline, and the fee and payment terms in writing.

If you have business letterhead stationery, there is obviously no need to include your firm's address as we have done here with Questor, Inc.

Questor, Inc.
246 Aedile Acres
Praetor, CA 12354

15 July 1996

Mr. Jasper Jones
ABC Manufacturing Company
54321 Bowvista
Summit, AZ 67893

Dear Mr. Jones:

After our conversation on Friday, I would like to summarize the project as follows:

Project: A bibliography of articles and books that address the subject of Information Brokering.

Deadline: Tuesday, July 23, 1996, close of business.

Budget: Not to exceed $600. $300 payable in advance, balance on satisfactory completion. Our terms are net 30 days.

Thank you for your business.

Sincerely,

Joan R. Questor
President

---

you a letter of agreement confirming the details of the project. One of those details, of course, is payment of half the fee in advance and the balance on completion.

Once you develop a working relationship with a client, you may feel that you no longer need a letter of agreement. That may turn out to be a safe thing to do with some clients. But in these days of fax machines and e-mail, it is very easy to get a written agreement into someone's hands almost instantly.

And, no matter how good the client, a letter of agreement still raises the comfort level on both sides. That's because a letter of agreement clearly states what you will do, what the client will pay you, and how the payments will be made. (Some brokers we know actually have the client prepare the

Letters of agreement

letter of agreement because this gives the person the chance to state in his or her own words what they expect you to do.)

The contents of a letter of agreement are derived from the details of your conversations with the client. Once you've spelled these details out in writing, and the client has reviewed and agreed with your description of the project, there is no excuse for any misunderstanding about what will be done and what will be paid. This is much better than both parties relying on what they think they remember of the conversations.

Better than a contract

A letter of agreement may carry less legal weight than an official contract that has been signed, witnessed, and countersigned. But it is still a contract of sorts and it has several advantages over the "official" kind. First of all, it's simple. It is designed to cover broad issues, not every little nuance and possibility. "I agree to do this. You agree to pay me that." End of story. The idea behind a letter of agreement is to obligate you to do the work and the client to pay for it, so it's mutual.

Second, if you haul out an official contract with its party-of-the-first-parts, whereases, and supplemental terms and conditions, you cause people to draw back. Wait a minute, this looks more serious than I thought. What am I getting into here? They're not getting into anything, but you've inadvertently made them think they are by laying a full-blown contract on the desk.

Third, aside from the presidents of small companies, we can't think of anyone in the business world who is likely to be in a position to sign a contract on the spot. "Oh, a contract. Better put this through Legal." If you have ever dealt with a company and you think the accounting department is slow to pay your bill, wait till you see how long it takes for the legal department to go over a contract.

And, of course, the legal department will be billing for every hour the newest, greenest attorney in the department spends going over your contract for a $350 project. The legal billing may even be charged against your client's division, which isn't likely to go over very well.

Games not worth the candle

Finally, take a moment to consider the amounts of money involved here. You may *think* that a full-blown contract gives you more protection than a letter of agreement, but you may be surprised. A client who isn't going to pay, isn't going to pay. It makes not a whit of difference whether you have a contract, a letter of agreement, or a verbal understanding.

But if you have a contract, you could take the matter to court, couldn't you? Sure you could. In fact, you can take it to Small Claims court without a full-blown contract. Sue Rugge has done exactly that a number of times. And she has always won. But you know what? None of the chiselers ever paid.

Getting a judgment against someone and actually collecting are two different stories. It is up to you, the recipient of the favorable judgment, for example, to find a client's bank account and get it attached.

Even if you have a duly executed contract and even if the amount in question is unusually high by information broker standards, say $2,500, you probably would not sue a nonpaying client. The reason? Legal fees, of course. Filing costs. Plus the hours of lost work time you will have to spend in the lawyer's office and in court.

The majority of the time, it simply is not worth it to sue a client, whether you have a legal contract or not. Given this fact of life and given the difficulties and delays contracts can cause, why bother? In the vast majority of cases a clear letter of agreement is simpler, quicker, and just as effective.

When it's crucial!

It's true that in the past Sue has been known to operate without a letter of agreement. "But that was years ago, before I had a fax machine," she says. "Today, it is so easy to get a letter of agreement to a client, or have the client get one to you, that I can't think of a situation in which I would consider being without one.

"And certainly there are times when a letter of agreement is absolutely crucial. Even when you're dealing with an established client."

If it's a big job, say, several thousand dollars big, or if it is an especially difficult job, *prepare a letter of agreement*. Sue's rule of thumb has always been that "If I don't think I have a really good crack at producing what the client wants—at least 50 percent, and maybe more like 65 percent, I just don't want to take on a job.

"Doing so invites all kinds of negative responses from the client. But sometimes the client will say, 'I just don't know what else to do, and I really want you to try. If you don't find anything for me, that's okay. I agree to pay.'"

"In those cases, I say, 'Because that's not the way we usually function, I'd really appreciate having that in writing.'"

Sue then writes a letter clearly stating their understanding. The letter closes with the line: "If the above reflects your understanding of our agreement, please so indicate by signing below." At the bottom of the letter there will be a line with the person's name and date. Sue then signs the letter and sends it off. The client signs it and sends a copy back to Sue.

Nowadays, this can all be done by fax, so timing is not a big problem. Still, it can be a crucial step to take when the client insists you take on a project for which you feel your chances of success are low. Or when the size of the fee is quite large.

What about retainer agreements?

Information On Demand used to offer a retainer package to clients. For a fee of $500 a month, the client was entitled to up to 10 hours of research a month (IOD was charging $75 an hour at the time), no per-project labor minimums, and volume discounts on document delivery services. Retainer clients also were assured VIP service, which meant IOD would do rush work for them without charging a rush surcharge.

It was unquestionably a very good deal. But it was a very tough sell. In all, IOD never had more than two retainer clients at a time during the years the program was offered.

Anytime someone has to sign off on a purchase order that says "I'm going to be paying out $500 a month, and I'm not sure if I can use it, and I'm not sure what I'm going to get back for it," they're very reluctant. That's why, with the exception of the large New York-based firm Find/SVP, nearly every information broker who has tried retainer arrangements has had similarly poor results.

As one broker we know told us, "Hell, it's hard enough to sell most clients on a single $350 project every two months or so. There's no way they're going to pay me $500 every month as a retainer. And a retainer's got to be something like that to even be worth fooling with."

The bottom line seems to be that retainers look like a good deal for both the broker and the client. The broker gets an assured income and flow of business. The client gets guaranteed discounts and preferential treatment. The problem is the same one that affects the entire information brokering industry—a general lack of awareness and insufficient demand.

Hopefully this will change someday. But the time is not yet. Until things do change, you will probably be better off developing new business and offering excellent service to your current clients rather than designing retainer agreements and programs.

Offering a deposit account plan is much more feasible, however. If the client puts up, say, $1,500 in advance, you will offer the above advantages. You only charge the account when you actually do the work, so the client doesn't lose anything. You get the advantage of cash flow. In short, everybody wins.

Preparing your bill

Once you have completed a project, it's time to prepare your bill. As discussed previously, there is no need to purchase a special form. Indeed, it is déclassé to do so. Use your business letterhead stationery. Type in the date and inside address (the client's name, title, company, etc.), just as if you were preparing a business letter. Skip a few blank lines and do two underlines from margin to margin.

If you have quoted by the project, then you should bill that way. For example: "Floor covering market study . . . $600.00." (See Fig. 23-3.) It's very important,

Here is an example of the kind of invoice you may wish to present to your clients. Notice that the invoice does not itemize expenses and that it includes the total project cost, the amount paid in advance, and the balance due.

23-3

A sample "project" invoice.

Questor, Inc.
246 Aedile Acres
Praetor, CA 12354

23 July 1996

Mr. Jasper Jones
ABC Manufacturing Company
54321 Bowvista
Summit, AZ 67893

INVOICE

Invoice No.:90054
Proj. Ref.: 9607-47

Floor covering market study $600.00
Less advance (paid 7/18/96) . . . . (300.00)
_____

Balance due $300.00

If you have quoted by the project, then you should bill that way. For example: "Floor covering market study . . . $600.00." (See Fig. 23-3.) It's very important, particularly for brand-new information brokers, to resist the temptation to itemize expenses and hours of labor. You will want to do this for your own records, of course. But not on the bill you present the client. Think *project*, not *hours*.

Naturally, some clients will ask for a breakdown of labor and expenses. (See Fig. 23-4.) But Sue never starts out that way. As she says, "When you are forced to itemize, you run the risk of questions about costs. Not that this is bad in and of itself. It's just that most clients really don't understand your business. And certainly most have no point of reference for evaluating online and database costs."

Still, some clients feel more comfortable with an "itemized" invoice. We put the word *itemized* in quotes because we do not want you to think that this means you must itemize each and every expense, cost, and markup that goes

23-4
A sample itemized invoice.

Shown below is a sample itemized. Notice the blanks for "Invoice No." and "Proj. Ref" number. These items track with the search request form shown in Figure 22-1.

Questor, Inc.
246 Aedile Acres
Praetor, CA 12354

21 July 1996

Mr. Jasper Jones
ABC Manufacturing Company
54321 Bowvista
Summit, AZ 67893

Invoice No.:90054
Proj. Ref.: 9607-47

Project: Rent Control Case Law search

Labor:

Attorney's fees:	350.00
Online research:	297.50
Online costs:	459.80

Postage:

Federal Express	35.00
	25.00
Phone charges:	11.40
TOTAL:	$1,178.70

into preparing your bill. Instead, offer the clients who require it a rough breakdown of the sort shown in Fig. 23-4.

Project & purchase order numbers

Notice that in both types of invoices we refer to the project by subject and number. The subject is important for communication between you and the client, particularly if you are doing several projects for the same client. But you should also refer to the project by some kind of number. Most service organizations (law firms, consultants, ad agencies, etc.) have file numbers for their projects as well. It is important to the smooth flow of payables to use project numbers of some sort.

If you are dealing with a large company, you will need to include a purchase order (PO) number. (Add a line like this to your invoice: "Purchase Order:

X-101-576.") Theoretically a PO is a promise by a company that it will pay you for what you are going to deliver upon receipt of your invoice.

By controlling who can sign off on POs, companies can control purchases made for the firm by employees. So when you are dealing with a big company, make sure that you get a PO number before you agree to do the job. This ensures that the person who is hiring you has the authority to do so, and that your bill will be processed by the accounting department with minimum difficulty and delay.

Sometimes, however, the delay in getting paid via PO can be longer than you'd like. Or the client may simply suggest that a check request will be put through as soon as you submit your invoice. If you know the client and have done other jobs this way, theoretically there's nothing wrong with this. On the other hand, people who work for companies do get transferred or fired. Or they take extended leaves.

Your invoices can easily fall through the cracks. Or, as Sue learned at the cost of close to $10,000, your copies can get burned up in a fire, while the copies you sent the client end up gathering dust in the bottom of some employee's desk drawer. Without a purchase order for each project, there's no way for you to prove—or even remember—what work you did for whom at a given company. So, even though taking the PO route requires more effort, and even though you may not get paid quite as quickly, it is definitely the safest approach.

The bean counters

Generally, you can expect to encounter two types of, well, of "bean counters." There are those who feel that computer time is expensive, so they expect to pay a lot for it—but not very much for labor. Then there are those who feel computers are so fast that computer time should not be a large part of the bill. But this group agrees that computers are complicated, so they expect to pay more for labor and less for connect time.

Look at how long it has taken us to explain the information brokering business in this book. There is no way you can hope to ever convey the details of the business to a client. Therefore, as we have said, billing with a single fee is often the best course. After all, attorneys and physicians do it. So why not you?

However, as we said, if you are forced to itemize, there is no need to go into elaborate detail. You should definitely include a line for labor. And *call* it that. The figure may actually be derived by multiplying the number of hours you spent by your professional rate, but there is no need to say so. Call it "labor."

You should also include a line for your online database charges. You should have a line for direct expenses as well. It is up to you whether you lump everything into a single figure or break it out to include clerical support, photocopies, copyright clearance fees, postage, long distance telephone, fax, travel, and so on.

Anything you had to buy for the client should also be given a line. Mailing lists, document delivery charges, books, tapes, maps—whatever. The client does not need to know everything, so use your own best judgment on how much billing detail you'll provide when submitting an itemized bill.

Creating an impression

As you can imagine, it is possible to have an invoice with only three lump-sum line items or one with a dozen smaller line items. Both will add up to the same total, but the impressions they create will be quite different. In most cases it is probably best to be moderately specific. Don't go into too much detail. But use enough to help your client understand all that was involved in executing the project. Unless the project is extremely complex, under no circumstances should your invoice run more than a single page.

It is also a good idea to leave room for a line reading "Please make check payable to . . ." followed by your name and your social security number. If you do not include your social security number, the accounting department may have to phone you to get it, and your check will be delayed.

Be sure to state your terms as well. Sue uses "Net 30 days," and recommends that you do likewise. Though you may be tempted to try "Net 15 days" or "Payable upon receipt."

Sue feels that asking for terms like that is a little pushy. "You have to remember that most of the work you do will be for clients, like attorneys and advertising agencies, who pass your results on to *their* clients. So you are part of a 'food chain' that sometimes can be very, very long. And all along that chain 'net 30 days' is usually the standard. By insisting on 'net 15' or 'payment on receipt,' you are in effect squeezing your client because he or she probably gets paid 'net 30.' So, in my opinion, asking for something other than 'net 30' really isn't fair.

"Some manufacturers will say, '2 percent 10 days, Net 30,' meaning that if you pay within 10 days, you can take a two-percent discount. But we have never found that to work in our business. Customers will take the two percent, but pay within 30 days—not 10—and that wreaks havoc with your accounting system."

How to present your bill

There are at least two schools of thought on the best way to convey your invoice to the client. Whenever Alfred completes a writing assignment, he sends his invoice along with the finished piece. But he includes a cover letter introducing the package and assuring the client that he will do the single revision that was agreed to. Whether a revision was part of the deal or not, the letter concludes with "Please don't hesitate to call if there are any questions," or words to that effect. Many information brokers follow a similar practice.

Sue, on the other hand, likes to make sure the client is completely satisfied before submitting her bill. Within four or five days of the time she sends off a search, she calls the client to make sure the package arrived and to ask if it was satisfactory. If everything is fine, then an invoice is prepared and sent. If there are problems, Sue does her best to resolve them, even to the point of having the search done over again.

This is good customer relations, to be sure. But Sue is also careful to make notes on when she made the call and what the client said. "The easiest excuse a client can give 90 days later for not paying you is that they were not satisfied," Sue says. That's why you want to be able to say, "There must be some misunderstanding. We talked to you three days after you received the materials and you said. 'Fantastic. This looks like exactly what I wanted.'"

There isn't much a deadbeat client can say to that without looking extremely foolish. Ideally, the person will be embarrassed enough to expedite payment—especially since the client knows you're going to call again if you are not paid.

How to dun a client

It is one of those curiosities of language that the word *dun* is the first word in the name of the credit reporting agency Dun & Bradstreet, as well as the verb that describes the process of going after deadbeat customers. No one likes to dun a customer. But it is naive to believe that you will never have to do so. The best policy is to follow Sue's advice and make sure the client is satisfied with your services.

Whether you send your invoice with the project or later, *always* make a follow-up call to the client a few days after the materials have been received. This is a very natural thing to do, since as a professional you will be sincerely interested in whether you delivered what was wanted. You want to provide superb service.

But the follow-up phone call is also the ideal time to uncover any dissatisfactions or problems. Unless you have made a serious error in judgment in taking on a client in the first place, you can assume that the client is not out to deliberately stiff you. If you are not paid on time, it may be because the client is dissatisfied. So find out early and correct the problem quickly.

In other cases, the client may simply be too busy (or somehow think so) to deal with the necessary paperwork to put through your invoice. By calling, and continuing to call, you move your request higher and higher on the client's "must-do" list. Office politics may also play a role. Your client may be having a problem with a superior whose signature is required. Or the superior may simply be out of the office on vacation.

It may be that the client has overstepped his authority. He may be able to sign for expenditures of $500, but not the $750 on your invoice. And he may be too embarrassed to tell you that what he really needs are two invoices of $375 each. Be sure to ask in the beginning if there will be a problem like this.

Obviously, there may be all kinds of other reasons as well. The fact remains that you have done the work the client contracted with you to do and you must be paid. The most effective technique is to make noise. Start with a gentle, inquiring phone call after the invoice is 45 days old if your stated terms are "30 days."

If asking for the money directly is uncomfortable for you, consider saying something like, "I'm planning my cash flow for the next month, and I'd like to make sure I know when I can expect to receive your check. I'm sure you know that I'm a small company and really need to be paid on time."

Some giant companies like IBM and Hewlett-Packard have established policies that are designed to make sure small businesses get paid quickly. Your contact at such a company may or may not be familiar with this fact or with the procedure for getting yourself on record as a small business. But he or she can probably give you the phone number of someone in the accounts payable department. Needless to say, it's a good idea to get this in train before you do the work and submit your invoice.

Turning up the volume

If your first call does not yield results, call back two weeks later to turn up the volume. Be aware that, in contrast to the IBMs of the world, some companies as a matter of policy don't pay small vendors like you for 90 days. It's outrageous, but there is not much you can do but wait for your money. (Alfred remembers one large company that took about 90 days to pay and then did so with a check drawn on a bank clear across the country.)

At 45 days overdue, it is time to crank up the campaign. Be polite. But be persistent. Call every week, or even every three days if appropriate. If the deadbeat is always out of the office when you call and never calls you back, consider sending a registered letter. In the letter, inform the deadbeat that if you do not receive your check in seven days, you will escalate to a higher level in the company. At this point you have nothing to lose—you're never going to accept an assignment from this person again and probably not from anyone else at the company.

There are other things you can do, short of taking legal action. You can contact the president of the company with your complaint. You can file a complaint with the Better Business Bureau. It might even be worthwhile to send a complaint to Dun & Bradstreet and other corporate credit reporting agencies. But before you take these actions, make sure that the deadbeat knows you plan to take them if your invoice is not paid.

No one likes to be thought of as a pest. Dunning is not pleasant work and hopefully you will never have to take it to this level. But if you do, remember that someone who claims to be satisfied with your work and still refuses to pay you the amount agreed upon is no better than a common thief. That person's opinion of you for being so persistent is of no significance whatever. You're the one who was robbed.

As we said, big companies won't process an invoice without a purchase order number. But that's not where you are likely to have problems. Where you get into trouble is when you're working with a little company, and you think having a PO means everything's going to be fine. You tend to get stung by small companies—5 or 10 people—more often than you do by individuals or by large corporations. Individuals tend to be more honorable. Small companies tend to be undercapitalized and often have trouble paying their bills. They tend to think, "I'm a small company too, and if this information broker goes bankrupt, well, I've gone bankrupt too. I've got more important bills to pay."

Watch out for small companies

Of course you can get burned by the big firms too. IOD once had a client who worked for a large company and said he needed the information in a hurry. "Don't worry, I'll get you a purchase order next week. But I need the information right now." Of course he never did, and when IOD went to collect, the person no longer worked there. On further investigation, it turned out that the subject area he needed information on was probably for personal use. The company would not authorize payment, and IOD was left holding the bag.

There is no way to make sure that you are never left holding the bag. In industry in general, the rule of thumb is to assume that two percent of your customers will turn out to be deadbeats. So you may want to allow two percent for bad debt. You may be able to deduct it on Schedule C of your tax return, but always be sure to check with your accountant on tax matters first. Still, it would be better to have the money in hand.

We have covered a lot of ground in this chapter. Everything from how much to charge to how to charge what the market will bear to matters of contracts, letters of agreement, and presenting (and collecting) your bill. Excuse us, "invoice." We have tried to give you the outlines and as many relevant tips and tricks as possible in each case.

Conclusion

But ultimately, you can't really learn these parts of the information broker's job until you've actually performed them. As you gain experience, you will develop your own tips and tricks. You'll discover the things that work for you.

Just remember that you must never be shy or at all embarrassed about asking to be paid the money a client owes you. If you have followed our advice and made sure that you have a letter of agreement, a purchase order (if applicable), and a satisfied client, the client has no excuse for not paying you as agreed.

One way or another, you've got to get paid. And get paid enough to cover your expenses and make a living. If you don't, you won't be an information broker for very long.

Conclusion
Welcome Aboard!

Well, you made it. If you have read this far, you are well on your way to becoming a practicing information broker. But don't stop here. There's lots of excellent information in the appendices that follow and on the accompanying disk.

In closing, we have two final bits of advice for all aspiring information brokers. First: Take it slow. Do not try to set up your office, your business, or your information brokerage all at once with every detail in place. Neither Rome nor anything else was ever built in a day.

Second: Do it! If you are truly interested in the information brokering profession, if we have not succeeded in scaring you out of a passing fancy, then, by all means, take the plunge. We have presented the profession and the field in the fairest, most honest way we know how. Indeed, we have gone out of our way to show you the downside and to disabuse you of any lingering notion that there is easy money to be made as an information broker.

If you are still fascinated by information and information gathering, if you have been bewitched by the power and by the thrill of the hunt—if you simply cannot get it out of your mind—then, you might as well face it: You're as hooked as we are.

We can't promise you that you will be able to make a living at this trade, regardless of your enthusiasm and hard work. But we can definitely promise that you will be in excellent company. Professional information brokers are among the most fascinating people you will ever meet. And they're good friends as well.

We cannot emphasize strongly enough what a collegial profession this is. It is probably not accurate to say that everybody knows everybody else, but that's not far off the mark. Certainly we all rely on each other. That's why Sue can be so firm in stating that you should never say "No" to a project. "No one who has gotten the phone to ring should ever turn down a project. Regardless of your own personal schedule, you can always find a fellow broker who can serve as a subcontractor.

"You don't have to say that to the prospective customer on the other end of the phone. Say instead, 'I'll have to check with my researcher.' The prospect doesn't have to know that you plan to call a fellow information broker located thousands of miles away.

"The client doesn't care where the work comes from or who does it, as long as you yourself stand behind it. This is one of the main thoughts I want to leave with you. There are many people who go into this profession thinking that they have to do everything. But that's completely wrong.

"It's not a question of whether you have the *skills* to do well at marketing and searching and bill collecting and everything else. There simply isn't enough time in the day for you or any other one individual to do everything. If you are a good marketer, you will generate more research assignments than you can possibly handle on your own. And while you are handling those assignments, you're not out there selling the *next* job.

"So, as I have said before, remember that this is a *business*. Do what you do best, and hire the rest."

That not only makes good practical sense, it is the only way to make decent money. Only by concentrating on what you do best can you leverage your particular talents.

If you're good at searching, concentrating in that area will make you *very* good at searching. That means you'll be able to execute assignments faster and cheaper than others, but you can still charge about the same. The result is more profit for you from a given assignment.

If you're good at marketing and at dealing with clients, concentrating in that area will generate lots of assignments—most of which you can subcontract to other brokers. Since you always make a percentage on each such job, the more jobs and assignments you can generate, the more money you'll make.

Of course, as Sue says, "We'd all like to make more money than we do. Maybe someday that will happen. Thanks to the popularity of the Internet and other online systems and to the 'Information Superhighway' idea, more and more people are finding out about information brokers and what we can do.

"Meantime, it's a wonderful profession filled with both monetary and nonmonetary rewards, as well as lots of interesting people and colleagues. All of whom are pleased to meet hard-working, enthusiastic, new members. So, welcome aboard!"

The Sue Rugge Forum on IPN

The Information Professionals Network is a worldwide network of information and investigative professionals who share information gathering tips, contacts, and opportunities online. IPN subscribers tend to be intensive information gatherers, and include information brokers, private investigators, public record researchers, business intelligence analysts, online searchers, due diligence consultants, and law and corporate business librarians. Known for its high caliber interdisciplinary and international membership, IPN supports professional networking with online conferencing, public and private message forums, e-mail, digital libraries, and electronic newsletter publishing services to information industry associations, including their Boards of Directors and members.

Extraordinarily powerful search options are available to IPN members. Unlike CompuServe and other commercial online services, the full text of messages in Discussion Forums, file archives, and other content is wholly and collectively searchable with a powerful, one-sweep, system-wide, Boolean supported search engine. For example, a single search for a Florida private investigator may turn up a list of online PI resumes in the Membership Directory, and a discussion of Florida's PI licensing authorities in the Legislative Affairs discussion forum.

The Sue Rugge Forum on IPN is available for prospective information brokers to learn more about Sue's educational, training, and consulting services. You can obtain and read free information about these services, and also participate in her retainer-based consulting forum—in which she goes into depth on a one-on-one and small-group basis, answering individual questions ranging from business plans to pricing issues.

Visit the forum for further details by using your Internet telnet capability. Telnet to ipn.net, login as rugge, and key in the password rugge. Here's an example of what you'll find there:

- Navigating the Sue Rugge Forum
- Introduction to the Sue Rugge Forum
- The Sue Rugge Story
- The market for information
- What is an information broker?
- Pros and cons of the information business
- The crucial question, is it for you?
- How to get started
- Services to sell

- Private Consulting Services ($)

IPN was founded by James S. Cook of Menlo Park, California. For more information, send an e-mail message to ipninfo@ipn.net, or call or write to him at:

415-364-6121 (voice)
415-364-5945 (fax)
Internet: jcook@ipn.net, jcook@netcom.com

The information broker's bookshelf
Crucial resources & reference works

This appendix is designed to pull together and present in a single place a selective list of the premier business and information resources available to information professionals, consultants, and brokers. As you can see from skimming lightly over the titles and the publishers cited here, many of these books are not the kind that you are likely to find on the shelves of the Waldenbooks or Dalton's at your local shopping mall. Indeed, you'll have a hard time finding some of them at local libraries.

That's why we've included publishers and ISBN numbers along with the description of each publication. In addition, a number of titles are available for purchase directly from the Information Professionals Institute. These titles are marked with a ☆, and an order form is provided at the end of the appendix for your convenience.

To make it easy for you to prepare your own customized list of titles, we have placed a copy of this appendix on the accompanying disk. Simply copy the file APPEND-A.TXT to your hard drive. Then use your word processing program to edit the list to your liking and print it out.

The reference works presented here are categorized by topic. Topics include:

- Books and Other Guides to Information Brokering
- Online Information Resources

Arrangement of the appendix

- Online Information Directories
- Business Information
- Useful Directories
- Guides to Reference Materials
- Small Business Management
- The Internet
- Public Records
- Government Information
- Continuing Education
- CD-ROM
- Software Products
- Magazines and Newsletters

It is important to emphasize that the ultimate value of this appendix is making you aware that certain reference works exist. In some cases, if you live near a good library, you may not need to buy any of these books at all. On the other hand, if you find that you're using, say, *The Encyclopedia of Associations* for every third project, then it simply makes good sense to buy your own printed copy or the CD-ROM version.

Many of the titles cited here carry hefty price tags. Yet, as an information broker, you must never forget that your time has *value*. Even if a reference work costs several hundred dollars, buying your own copy can still be a very cost-effective solution.

And, speaking of costs, the prices and publication dates quoted here are current at this writing. But of course, they are subject to change. For an annually updated list, use the order form at the end of this appendix to order a copy of *The Information Broker's Resource Kit* ($10 from the Information Professionals Institute). Or contact the publishers directly for current information and prices.

Books & other guides to information brokering

☆ **The Information Broker's Seminar on Audiotape**   A live recording on six hours of audiocassettes. An excellent opportunity for those unable to attend the seminar in person, as well as a refresher for our "graduates." Includes full documentation and a half-hour telephone consultation with Sue Rugge. $175. (See Appendix D for a complete description of the seminar.)

☆ **The Information Broker's Handbook, Second Edition**   No list of books and resources about information brokering would be complete without Rugge and Glossbrenner's best-selling guide. If you like the book you are now reading and would like to order additional copies, contact the Information Professionals Institute. As we hope you can attest, it's indispensable for those new to the field, as well as established brokers. Windcrest/McGraw-Hill, 1995. ISBN 0-07-911878-X. $34.95 (paperback).

☆ Information for Sale: How to Start & Operate Your Own Data Research Service Authors John H. Everett and Elizabeth Powell Crowe have completely updated their popular how-to manual on becoming a successful information broker. Management, marketing, legal considerations, fees and charges, technology, and resources are all included. McGraw-Hill, 1994. ISBN 0-07-019951-5. $16.95.

Mind Your Own Business: A Guide for the Information Entrepreneur This guide from Alice Sizer Warner offers highly practical, straight-forward financial advice for the aspiring or newly established information entrepreneur—guidance that will also prove useful for the already well-established businessperson. This book is exceptionally thorough in the area of business plans. Neal Schuman, 1987. ISBN 1-55570-014-4. $24.95. (212) 925-8650.

Making Money: Fees for Library Services Also from Alice Sizer Warner. Based on the first-hand experiences of those who have set up fee-based services, as well as the author's nationwide workshops, this book deals with both the ethics and the practicalities of charging back to other individuals or departments inside the organization, or charging fees to users. If you're even considering charging fees, you must have this definitive guide. Neal Schuman, 1989. ISBN 1-55570-053-5. $39.50. (212) 925-8650.

☆ Managing the Economics of Owning, Leasing, & Contracting Out Information Services Authors Anne Woodsworth and James F. Williams II help managers determine whether contracting out or outsourcing of information services will benefit them. Serious support is given to contracting out to information brokers. Issues of costing, pricing, and internal chargebacks are discussed. They also take a look at future trends. Ashgate Publishing, 1993. ISBN 185-7420187. $49.95. (800) 535-9544.

Insights on Information Brokering This publication lists a selection of articles and supplemental references describing the field of information brokering. Special Libraries Association, 1991. ISBN 0-87111-376-7. $20 ($15 for members). (202) 234-4700.

☆ Burwell's Bibliography on Information Brokering The publication will lead you to current and retrospective books, articles, and tapes on information brokering. Burwell Enterprises. Semiannual, $25. New from Burwell is their *Document Delivery Bibliography*, also $25.

☆ The Burwell Directory of Information Brokers This annual directory from Burwell Enterprises is your one source for complete, accurate information on who has the answers—or knows where to get them. An excellent resource for information on who's out there and what they do. Use it for competitive intelligence, subcontracting, and networking. There simply is no other source for the information in this directory. Burwell Enterprises. Annual. $85.00. (Also available on diskette $150, book and diskette $195.)

☆ **Burwell's Survey of Independent Information Professionals**
Get an inside look at the industry. Topics include average company size, location, gross income from research, market sectors served, and economic impact of information entrepreneurs. Burwell Enterprises. Biennial, $150.

☆ **Selected Aspects of Potential Legal Liabilities of Independent Information Professionals**   Attorney/information broker T.R. Halvorson explores how you might protect yourself from the liability issues that make all of us "a little nervous." From Burwell Enterprises, 1993. $40.

☆ **Infopreneurs: Turning Data into Dollars**   H. Skip Weitzen's book is a primer for people who want to take advantage of today's information movement and management technologies, a down-to-earth, logical, plain-language approach with a steady stream of examples. John Wiley, 1988. ISBN 0-471-63371-2. $24.95.

The EIRENE Directory (European Information Researchers' Network)   This is an excellent source for locating European information brokers. It gives full contact information, areas of specialization, costs and working languages. EIRENE. Annual. 55 pounds sterling. First Contact Ltd., UK. Phone: 44(0) 71 490 5519 (voice); 44(0)71 490 4610 (fax).

Fiscal Directory of Fee-Based Research & Information Services
Compiled by Steve Coffman, this directory is invaluable for locating fee-based providers, including libraries and commercial sources, in the U.S. and internationally. Detailed information is provided on services offered, rates and specialties of the collection or research service. ALA, 1993. ISBN 0-8389-2161-2. $65. (800) 545-2433.

Opening New Doors: Alternative Careers for Librarians   Edited by Ellis Mount. Read first-hand accounts of librarians who've gone into entrepreneurial ventures as independents or employees. Inspiring! Special Libraries Association. ISBN 0-87111-408-9. $36 ($29 member price). (202) 234-4700.

Online information resources

☆ **Secrets of the Super Searchers: The accumulated wisdom of 23 of the world's top online searchers**   Super searcher Reva Basch probed the minds of some of the top online searchers and reveals their secrets for successful, cost-effective database searching. Online, Inc., 1993. ISBN 0-91096512-9. $39.95.

☆ **Online Information Hunting**   Despite downplaying the importance of search intermediaries, author Nahum Goldman offers practical advice for cost-effective searching. Windcrest/McGraw-Hill, 1992. ISBN 0-8306-3944-6. $19.95.

☆ **The Electronic Traveller: Exploring Alternative Online Systems**
Information for Sale co-author Elizabeth Powell Crowe profiles some of the

lesser-known online/bulletin board systems such as BitNet, FidoNet and The Well. Windcrest/McGraw-Hill, 1992. ISBN 0-8306-4016-9. $16.95.

☆ **Find it Online** New from *Find it Fast* author Robert Berkman, this is a consumer's guide to doing research on such systems as America Online, Prodigy, CompuServe, the Internet, and CD-ROMs. Databases and services are indexed by subject. Windcrest/McGraw-Hill, 1994. ISBN 0-07-005102X. $29.95.

☆ **The Complete Guide to CompuServe** Brad and Debra Schepp's book speaks to new and experienced users alike. The accompanying disk will easily enable you to take advantage of all of CompuServe's features. Osborne/McGraw-Hill, 1992. ISBN 0-07-881632-7. $34.95.

☆ **Fulltext Databases** From Carol Tenopir and Jung Soon Ro, this is a comprehensive treatment of full-text databases highlighting DIALOG, LEXIS and NEXIS, WestLaw, STN International, and BRS. Greenwood Press, 1990. ISBN 0-313-26303-5. $49.95.

How to Look it Up Online: Get the Information Edge with Your Personal Computer Alfred Glossbrenner has written a unique and much-needed book that unlocks and uncomplicates the research potential of today's information technologies. St. Martin's Press, 1987. ISBN 0-312-001320-0. $15.95. To order, call Glossbrenner's Choice at (215) 736-1213 or use the order form in Appendix F.

The Little Online Book Alfred Glossbrenner's latest treatment of the electronic universe shows readers what's available in the information marketplace, how to tap in, and how to take maximum advantage of this incredible resource. Peachpit Press, 1995. ISBN 1-56609-130-6. $17.95. To order, call Glossbrenner's Choice at (215) 736-1213 or use the order form in Appendix F.

Online information directories

The Gale Directory of Databases This is the most comprehensive guide available to aid you in selecting databases worldwide. Gale Research. ISBN 0-8103-5747-X. 4 parts per year, $300. (800) 877-4253.

Books & Periodicals Online This publication has been greatly expanded to include over 43,000 newspapers, newswires, magazines, directories, and conference proceedings currently online or on CD-ROM. Library Alliance, 1993. ISBN 0-9630277-1-9. $199. (800) 845-4768.

The Online Manual (Second Edition) Edited by Jill Cousins and Lesley Robinson, the latest edition of this manual has been greatly expanded to include over 2,000 databases and 60,000 sources covered in the databases. Blackwell Publishers, 1992. ISBN 0-631-18931-9. $195. (800) 488-2665 or (802) 878-0315.

☆ **The Business Database Finder**   *Find it Fast* author Robert Berkman's guide lists and compares hundreds of features and specific data elements for a selected group of the most popular business databases. $129.

Also recently updated and revised: *Business Researchers' 1992 EuroGuide*, which identifies key sources of information on the unified European market. Online expert Reva Basch wrote a special section on the best databases for researching the European market. $129. Published by Information Advisory Services.

☆ **Fulltext Sources Online**   Your guide to finding full-text periodicals online. This comprehensive directory covers all subjects and all major database services such as Dialog, NEXIS, Dow Jones, and NewsNet. Periodicals are listed along with dates of coverage, database codes, degree of coverage, and subject/geographic indexes. BiblioData. ISBN 1-879258-09-9. Semiannual. $95.

☆ **Newspapers Online: A Directory to North American Daily Newspapers whose Articles are Online in Full Text**   Edited by Susanne Bjorner, this comprehensive guide to newspapers online contains geographic indexes as well as details on what's included and excluded online. BiblioData. Annual. ISBN 1-879258-04-8. $120 (loose-leaf binder with two updates annually).

☆ **CompuServe Companion: Finding Newspapers & Magazines Online**   This new directory lists full-text periodicals available on the CompuServe service. When publications are included in multiple databases, the user is guided to the most cost-effective source. Includes geographic and subject indexes and a section on how to search. BiblioData, 1994. ISBN 1-879258-10-2. $29.95.

OPAC Directory   This directory provides access information to hundreds of library Online Public Access Catalogs internationally, including over 700 that are accessible on the Internet. Mecklermedia. Annual. ISBN 0-88736-962-6. $70. (203) 226-6967.

Business information

Business Information: How to Find It, How to Use It (Second Edition)   The new edition expands and updates this highly popular resource by Michael R. Lavin. Lavin provides good comparisons of similar resources (online and print sources) and extensive references at the end of each chapter. Oryx Press, 1992. ISBN (paper) 8-89774-643-0. $38.50. (800) 279-6799.

International Business Information: How to Find It, How to Use It   Authors Ruth Pagell and Michael Halperin bring together a wealth of information, from electronic and print sources to major business environments outside of the U.S. Special coverage of the most recent sources on Eastern Europe, the former Soviet Union, and Asia. Oryx Press, 1994. ISBN 0-89774-736-4. $74.50 (800) 279-6799.

Business Information Sources (Third Edition)   This classic by Lorna Daniells has been completely revised to include new sections on competitive intelligence, economic and financial measures, and health care marketing. University of California Press, 1993. ISBN 0520-081-803. $35. (800) 822-6657.

Encyclopedia of Business Information Sources   Information sources on over 1,000 business topics in an easy-to-use format. Gale, Annual. ISBN 0-8103-7489-7. $275. (800) 877-4253.

☆ **Competitor Intelligence: How to Get It, How to Use It (Second Edition)**   This classic reference book from Leonard M. Fuld is an essential resource for conducting basic competitor intelligence. John Wiley, 1994. ISBN 0-471-585-09-2. $24.95.

Outsmarting the Competition: Practical Approaches to Finding and Using Competitive Information   Authors John McGonagle, Jr. and Carolyn Vella provide insight into the public domain sources of competitor information. Sourcebooks, 1990. ISBN (paper) 0-942061-04-7. $17.95. (800) 727-8866.

The Competitive Intelligence Handbook   Richard Combs and John Moorhead offer advice from their many years of experience in the CI field. A nice mix of theoretical and practical information. Scarecrow Press, 1992. ISBN 0-8108-2602-2. $25. (800) 537-7107.

The Desktop Business Intelligence Sourcebook   Designed to provide general research guidance to anyone seeking business information. Author Kent Frantze covers the best and most current sources available in this compact volume. Hyde Park Marketing Group, 1992. ISBN 1-880186-00-4. $16.95. (800) 444-2524 (ext. 244).

Find It Fast: How to Uncover Expert Information on Any Subject (Third Edition)   This popular and recently revised book by Robert I. Berkman discusses how to find and interview experts in any field. HarperCollins, 1994. ISBN 006 0964863. $12. (212) 207-7000.

Who Knows What: The Essential Business Resource Book   This 1,200-page volume by Daniel Starer is sure to point you in the direction of a publication, association, agency, or expert that can provide a jumping off point for your research into even the most obscure topics. Henry Holt & Company, 1993. ISBN 0-8050-1853-0. $45. (212) 886-9200.

How to Find Information About Companies   This book from Washington Researchers is well-known in the CI field. Its three volumes are broken down by sources, techniques and case studies ($395 for each volume). Call Washington Researchers at (202) 333-3499 for a catalog of all their books and seminars.

The National Book of Lists   How many times are you asked for the top companies in certain industries? Well, here are the top 40 companies in 50 U.S. industries, from banks and biotech to golf courses and travel agencies. Kevin Cronin, Editor. Local Knowledge, 1992. $29.95. (800) 792-2665.

Hoover's Handbook of American Business   Here you'll find one-page profiles of 500 major U.S. companies, including private companies. At $34.95, it's a bargain. The Reference Press, Annual. ISBN 1-878753-03-7. (800) 486-8666. Ask about their other international handbooks, too.

The Art of Being Well Informed: What you need to know to gain the winning edge in business   As president of one of the first information brokering firms, FIND/SVP, Andrew Garvin brings his years of experience to focus on raising your information consciousness and reveals how a lack of information and knowledge of information tools can be costly in business and personal decisions. Avery Publishing Group, 1993. ISBN 0-89529-576-8. $12.95. Available from FIND/SVP, (800) 346-3787.

Analyzing your Competition   Also from FIND/SVP, this book reveals simple, cost-effective techniques for intelligence gathering and analysis. FIND/SVP, 1993. ISBN 1-562-410-62-8. $95. (800) 346-3787.

Useful directories

The following directories are of a general nature and are worth considering for your own collection. Most libraries carry these titles as well. For subject-specific directories and reference books, contact Gale Research at (800) 877-4253 and ask for a catalog.

The Librarian's Yellow Pages   Provides access to a wide variety of information companies. Also a good place to list and advertise your service. Garance, Inc., Annual. Free. (800) 235-9723.

Encyclopedia of Associations   Describes over 22,600 associations of all types nationwide. An indispensable resource for many research projects. Also available in regional and international editions. Gale, Annual. ISBN 0-81-3-7619-9. $375. (800) 877-4253.

Directories in Print   Contains over 13,000 listings arranged in 26 subject chapters. Gale, Annual. ISBN 0-8103-7627-X. $290.

National Trade & Professional Associations of the U.S. (NTPA)
Lists 7,000 associations with national membership. Narrower in scope than Gale's directory, but more affordable! State and Regional Associations of the U.S. (SRA) is also available. Columbia Books, Inc., Annual. NTPA, $75. SRA, $60. (202) 898-0662.

Standard Rate & Data Service (SRDS)   We use their Business Publication Rates & Data for locating trade publications in almost every industry. They also publish advertising rates for a variety of publications, TV, radio, and other media. Monthly. Call (800) 323-4601 for prices.

Burrelle's Media Directory   In three volumes, this directory contains contact information for thousands of newspapers, trade and professional magazines, newsletters, and radio and TV stations. Burrelle's Information Services, 1994. $500 for 3 vols. plus 3 quarterly supplements. (800) 631-1160.

Ulrich's International Periodicals Directory   This is the source for locating all types of "recurring" publications. R.R. Bowker, Annual with quarterly updates. ISBN 0-835232-64-6. $450. (800) 521-8110.

Standard Periodicals Directory   Lists 75,000 U.S. and Canadian periodicals. Gale, Annual. ISBN 0-917460499. $495. (800) 877-4253.

National Directory of Addresses and Telephone Numbers   Lists over 230,000 phone and fax numbers for the most frequently called businesses and government agencies in the country. A must! Omnigraphics, Annual. ISBN 1-55888-140-9. $85.00. (800) 234-1340.

National Fax Directory   This directory from Gale lists over 160,000 U.S. fax numbers for top institutions and companies. Gale, 1993. 0-8103-5636-8. $89. (800) 877-4253.

Guide to Reference Books (10th edition)   Annotates 14,000 reference works worldwide. Eugene Sheehy, Editor. American Library Association, 1986. $80. (800) 545-2433.

Guides to reference materials

New York Public Library Book of How & Where to Look it Up
This book by Sherwood Harris is another one-volume resource for places to turn for more information on a variety of topics. McMillan General References. 1991. ISBN 0-13-614728-3. $30. (800) 223-2336.

The Book of Answers   This book is subtitled *The New York Public Library Telephone Reference Service's Most Unusual and Entertaining Questions.* From Barbara Berliner, Melinda Corey, and George Ochoa, it's a treasure trove of fascinating and useful information is probably more fun than utilitarian, but "all work and no play . . ." Prentice Hall, 1990. ISBN 0-13-406554-9. $10. (800) 223-2336.

Lesko's Info-Power II   Another of Matthew Lesko's one-of-a-kind information bibles with over 10,000 free and low-cost sources of information for investors, job seekers, teachers, students, artists, travelers, businesses, consumers, homeowners, techies, communities, and more. Information USA, 1993. ISBN 1-878346-17-2. $39.95. Also available on CD-ROM or DOS disk, $69.95. (800) 545-3888.

Legal Research: How to Find & Understand the Law   Excellent for paralegals, legal secretaries, social workers, police, and journalists, this book by attorneys Stephen Elias and Susan Levinkind gives clear step-by-step instructions on how to find legal information. It's so good that although written for nonlawyers, a number of law schools have adopted it as a text. Nolo Press, 1993. ISBN 0-87337-144-5. $19.95. (800) 992-6656.

Nolo's Legal Research Made Easy (Video)   Taught by legal research authority Robert C. Berring, this video takes you on a tour of a major law library with detailed explanations of the tools and resources you will find there. Includes a 40-page booklet. Nolo Press, 1993. ISBN 0-87337-138-0. $89.95. (800) 992-6656.

Small business management

The Legal Guide for Starting & Running a Small Business   Author Fred S. Steingold lays out everything you need to know as a small-business owner, whether you are just starting out or already established. Nolo Press, 1993. ISBN 0-87337-174-7. $22.95. (800) 992-6656.

How to Start Your Own Business: Small Business Law (Audiotape) This 60-minute tape by attorney Ralph Warner covers the most important legal questions facing the small-business owner. Nolo Press, 1993. ISBN 0-87337-210-7. $14.95. (800) 992-6656.

How to Write a Business Plan   Author, consultant, teacher, and financial manager Mike McKeever pushes you to ask some hard questions and to dig for some solid answers. With your answers in hand, he shows you how to write the business plan and loan application package necessary to finance your business and to make it work. Nolo Press, 1993. ISBN 0-87337-184-4. $19.95. (800) 992-6656.

The Partnership Book   This book by attorneys Denis Clifford and Ralph Warner shows you, step by step, how to write an agreement that covers evaluation of partner assets, disputes, buy-outs, and the death of a partner. There is also a good introduction covering the problems of getting started in business and an overview of partnership taxation laws. Nolo Press, 1991. ISBN 0-87337-141-0. $24.95. (800) 992-6656.

Trademark: How to Name your Business & Product   This book by Stephen Elias and Kate McGrath is a friendly guide to the laws that govern commercial names. Includes sources of trademark research. Nolo Press, 1992. ISBN 0-87337-157-7. $29.95. (800) 992-6656.

The Copyright Handbook: How to Protect & Use Written Works Everything you need to copyright your works, by Steve Fishman. Nolo Press, 1992. ISBN 0-87337-130-5. $24.95. (800) 992-6656.

Small Time Operator   From Bernard Kamoroff, CPA, this is the classic, informative, humorous guide to starting a business and staying out of trouble. Nothing comes close to its explanation of bookkeeping, business licenses, and taxes. Includes all of the ledgers and worksheets you'll need for one year. Bell Springs, 1993. ISBN 0-917510-10-0. $14.95.

Marketing Without Advertising   Michael Phillips and Salli Rasberry demolish the myth of advertising effectiveness and outline practical steps for marketing your small business. Even better, they show you how to increase personal recommendations and customer loyalty without spending a lot of money. Probably the last $14 you'll ever spend on advertising. Nolo Press, 1992. ISBN 0-87337-019-8. $14. (800) 992-6656.

☆ The Contract & Fee-Setting Guide for Consultants & Professionals   Howard Shenson presents lots of practical advice on running a consulting business. John Wiley, 1990. ISBN 0-471-51538-8. $22.95.

☆ Shenson on Consulting: Successful Strategies from the Consultant's Consultant   Another worthwhile offering from Howard Shenson. John Wiley, 1990. ISBN 0-471-50661-3. $29.95.

Take the Money & Strut!   Subtitled *A private eye's guide to collecting a bad debt.* Need we say more? Creighton-Morgan, 1988. ISBN 0-96200960-1. $10. (415) 922-6684.

Working From Home: Everything You Need to Know About Living & Working Under the Same Roof   This book by Paul and Sarah Edwards includes advice for setting up your home office and practical methods for managing your work at home, including legal aspects, how to get yourself to work, and how to avoid disruptions, isolation, and overwork. Jeremy P. Tarcher, Inc., 1991. ISBN 0-87477-582-5. $15.95. (800) 788-6262.

Making Money With Your Computer at Home   New from working-from-home experts Paul and Sarah Edwards, this book provides inspiration and practical ideas for choosing and setting up a computer-based enterprise at home. Jeremy P. Tarcher, 1993. $11.95 ISBN 0-87477-736-4. (800) 788-6262

Making It On Your Own: Surviving & Thriving the Ups & Downs of Being Self-Employed   Also by Paul and Sarah Edwards. Jeremy P. Tarcher, 1992. ISBN 0-87477-636-8. $11.95. (800) 788-6262.

Getting Business to Come to You   This book by Paul and Sarah Edwards and Laura Clampitt Douglas is chock full of great information on what you need to know to do your own advertising, public relations, and sales promotion. Jeremy P. Tarcher, 1991. ISBN 0-87477-629-5. $11.95. (800) 788-6262.

The Best Home Businesses for the 90s   The inside information you need to know to select a home-based business that's right for you. Jeremy P. Tarcher, 1991. ISBN 0-87477-633-3. $11.95. (800) 788-6262.

The Internet

New books about the Internet are being published at an amazing rate. The books included here are those that have received positive endorsements from our information broker colleagues. For a comprehensive and frequently updated list of Internet titles, look for Kevin Savetz's *Unofficial Internet Book List*, which is widely available on the Internet. You can also order the list from Glossbrenner's Choice. (See the Internet 1 disk in Appendix F.)

General guides & references

Internet Slick Tricks   An entertaining and informative introduction to the Internet by Alfred and Emily Glossbrenner. Random House, 1994. ISBN 0-679-75611-6. $16. Available from Glossbrenner's Choice. (See Appendix F.)

Zen & the Art of the Internet: A Beginner's Guide (Third Edition)
This book by Brendan Kehoe is a practical and highly readable introduction to the Internet, though geared to those already somewhat familiar with the system. Kehoe provides a good behind-the-scenes look at why the Internet is the way it is. Prentice Hall, 1994. ISBN 0-13-121492-6. $23.95. (800) 223-1360.

The Internet Companion: A Beginner's Guide to Global Networking   Tracey LaQuey and Jeanne Ryer's book is another good choice for Internet novices. If you are already a frequent Internet user, the book may be a bit basic; however, this easy-to-read guide offers a good discussion of how people use the Internet in their daily activities. Addison-Wesley, 1993. ISBN 0-201-62224-6. $10.95. (800) 447-2226.

☆ **The Whole Internet User's Guide & Catalog**   This book by Ed Krol remains one of the most popular on the topic. It provides clear (and humorous!) explanations for navigating the Net without burdening the reader with technical jargon. O'Reilly & Associates, 1994. ISBN 1-56592-063-5. $24.95.

☆ **The Internet Complete Reference**   Harley Hahn and Rick Stout's book comes highly recommended by a number of our broker colleagues, one of whom uses it as a text in her beginning Internet course. Osborne McGraw-Hill, 1994. ISBN 0-07-881980-6. $29.95.

☆ **The Internet Guide for New Users**   Daniel P. Dern's book covers both the nuts and bolts of logging on as well as responsible use of the system. McGraw-Hill, 1993. ISBN 0-07-016511-4. $27.95.

Doing Business on the Internet   Mary E. Cronin offers practical ways business executives can take advantage of new opportunities on the Internet. Van Nostrand Reinhold, 1994. ISBN 0-442-01770-7. $29.95. (800) 544-0550.

The Canadian Internet Handbook   This book by John A. Carroll describes how to tap into numerous Canadian information sources. Prentice Hall Canada, 1994. ISBN 0-13-304-395-9. $16.95.

Internet for Dummies   From IDG's series of "Dummies" guides. Authors John R. Levine and Carol Baroudi provide a fun and easy-to-follow look at the Internet. IDG, 1993. ISBN 1-56884-024-1. $19.95. (800) 762-2974.

The Internet at a Glance   Information broker Susan E. Feldman's book is a quick reference guide to Internet commands. $7 prepaid from Datasearch, 170 Lexington Dr., Ithaca, NY 14850, (607) 257-0937.

Internet Connections: A Librarian's Guide to Dial-up Access and Use   This book by Mary E. Engle et al. is very strong in providing detailed listings of service providers, but unfortunately a bit out of date in its resources information. American Library Association, 1993. ISBN 0-8389-7648-4. $22.

☆ **Connecting to the Internet: A Buyer's Guide**   Susan Estrada offers a thorough discussion of how to get an Internet connection and how to choose the service options and technical support you need. O'Reilly & Associates, 1993. ISBN 1-56592-061-9. $15.95.

An Internet Primer for Information Professionals: A Basic Guide to Networking Technology   Authors Elizabeth Lane and Craig Summerhill help the novice user get connected. Meckler, 1993. ISBN 0-88736-831-X. $37.50. (203) 226-6967.

Internet Access Providers: An International Resource Directory This directory by Greg R. Notess is aimed at those with no current access as well as those looking for home access. Mecklermedia, 1994. ISBN 0-88736-933-2. $30. (203) 226-6967.

☆ **Internet: Getting Started**   April Marine's book is the one to get if you are looking for an Internet connection, especially outside of the U.S. SRI International, 1994. ISBN 0-13-328959-6X. $28.

Getting connected

☆ **The Internet Yellow Pages**   Harley Hahn and Rick Stout have put together a comprehensive and humorous guide to what's out there. Osborne McGraw-Hill, 1994. ISBN 0-07-882023-5. $27.95.

Netguide   Peter Rutten et al. covers a number of commercial systems in addition to the Internet, making it more comprehensive than the Yellow Pages described above. But it's more serious and not as much fun to browse. Random House, 1994. ISBN 0-679-75106-8. $19.

New Riders' Official Internet Yellow Pages   Christine Maxwell and Czeslaw (Chet) Jan Grycz have put together a massive reference guide to the actual content of the Internet. With over 10,000 entries, this 836-page reference book helps eliminate the frustration of finding information on the Internet. Unlike previous directories, it organizes resources by subject, rather than computer address (newsgroup, mailing list, etc.). New Riders Publishing, 1994. ISBN 1-56205-306-X. $29.95.

The Legal Researcher's Internet Directory   Josh Blackman, Esq., catalogs all the documents, databases, and communication resources available on the Internet of interest to legal researchers. For those who want immediate and (usually) free access to government documents, laws, court

Guides to What's Out on the Internet

opinions, and other legal materials, plus mailing lists and newsgroups relevant to practicing and researching law, this is a must. $49.95. (718) 399-6136.

The Internet Directory   Eric Braun lists over 1,500 mailing lists, 2,200 Usenet newsgroups, 1,000 OPACS, and more! Fawcett Columbine, 1994. ISBN 0-449-908984. $25.00.

☆ **The Internet: Mailing Lists**   The 1993 edition from SRI explores the diversity of discussion groups on the Internet, with descriptions of more than 800. Topics include how to join a mailing list, as well as how to start your own. Prentice Hall, 1994. ISBN 0-13-289661-3. $29.

Directory of Directories on the Internet: A Guide to Information Sources   Written by Gregory B. Newby. Mecklermedia, 1993. ISBN 0-88736-768-2. $29.50. (203) 226-6967.

Public records

You, Too, Can Find Anybody: A Reference Manual   Though we don't like its misleading title, Joseph J. Culligan presents an excellent overview of public records on the national, state, and local levels. He provides contact information for such diverse records sources as the National Archives and the bankruptcy courts in every state. Hallmark Press, Inc., 1991. ISBN 0-9630621-0-7. $19.95. (800) 831-8900.

Get the Facts on Anyone: How you can use public sources to check the background of any person or organization   Dennis King's 216-page book has gotten positive reviews from several of our public records colleagues. Prentice Hall, 1992. ISBN 0-671-86470-X. $15.00. (800) 223-1360.

The Reporter's Handbook   Study the same "nuts-and-bolts" guide that shows reporters how to research and document their investigative stories with information available from the public record. Locating and describing more than 500 specific documents, *The Reporter's Handbook* also shows you how to investigate individuals and institutions. St. Martin's Press, 1990. ISBN 0-312-004354. $17. (212) 674-5151.

☆ **A Public Records Primer & Investigator's Handbook: California Edition**   The sources revealed in Don Ray's handbook will help streamline any investigation. It includes explanations of the various types of public records available from government offices, and instructions on how you can get the most cooperation from the curators of the records. A special feature is the comprehensive list of telephone numbers for public record offices throughout the state of California. The News, 1994. ISBN 0-938717-05-9. $18.95.

Paper Trails: A Guide to Public Records in California   Like Don Ray's *Primer* above, Barbara Newcombe's guide to California's public records is a popular resource for uncovering this state's vast sources of public records. Center for Investigative Reporting and the California Newspaper Association, 1990. ISBN 0-962-1793-1-0. $14.95. (415) 543-1200.

☆ **The Guide to Background Investigations: A Comprehensive Source Directory for Employee Screening**   This 936-page directory will take you step-by-step through the process of conducting a background investigation with publicly available records. You'll learn how to obtain and use five major types of records: Criminal Records, Federal Court Reports, Workers' Compensation Records, Educational Records, and Driving Records. National Employment Screening Services, 1993. $124.95

The Instant National Locator Guide   Area codes, ZIP codes, and locations of 8,000 U.S. cities and towns are provided in this directory and atlas. Creighton-Morgan, 1991. ISBN 0-9620096-6-0. $15.95. (415) 922-6684.

Business Intelligence Investigations   This publication by Ralph D. Thomas is just one of the numerous offerings from Thomas Publications. Contact them for a variety of public records, investigative, and business intelligence books and videos: (512) 928-8190.

Audio- & videotapes

☆ **A Public Records Odyssey Seminar**   This is a live recording of ENG Productions' day-long seminar—a very lively and informative seminar for anyone interested in accessing public sources of information to investigate people, companies, nonprofits, and government agencies. Includes handouts. ENG Press, 1993. Audiotapes: $60; VHS videotape: $80.

How to Locate & Investigate People   An edited recording of this day-long seminar on finding and profiling people. Includes handouts. ENG Press, 1993. Audiotapes: $60; VHS videotape: $80.

BRB Public Record Research Library

The Public Record Research Library (PRRL) is a leading authority on location, access, and retrieval of public records. These highly accurate, annual, easy-to-read sourcebooks detail how to find/read documents and access the best retrieval firms. The PRRL received the Information Industry Association's First Place Product Achievement Award in 1993. Their publications are a must for those specializing in public records.

☆ **The Sourcebook of Public Records Providers**   A 288-page directory of over 500 companies that furnish public records searches and investigative information. Includes online services, proprietary databases, and CD-ROM products. 1994. $29.

☆ **Federal Courts**   This is a 672-page guide to more than 500 U.S. Court locations and 13 Federal Records Centers. $33.

☆ **The County Locator—LOCUS**   The ultimate in searching, with other 95,000 "places" indexed to counties and ZIP codes. Identifies the more than 10,000 ZIP codes that cross county lines and shows more than 10,000 ZIP codes that are not actual locators but are PO boxes, APOs, FBOs, etc. $25.

☆ **Local Court and County Record Retrievers**   This is a 432-page county-by-county directory of over 2,100 firms and individuals who do hands-on retrieval of files and documents from U.S., state, and local courts and county offices. $45.

☆ **State Public Records**   A 304-page state-by-state guide for all kinds of state-level public records. Includes availability, contact information, pricing, restrictions and more. $29.

☆ **County Court Records**   Lists over 5,300 local courts with details on how to obtain information on civil and criminal cases, probate, liens, UCC, vital statistic records. 544 pages. $33.

☆ **The MVR Book & Decoder Digest**   An annual national reference detailing and summarizing in practical terms the descriptions, access procedures, regulations, and privacy restrictions of driver and vehicle records in all states. 256 pages. $17.

☆ **License Plate Book**   Over 1,000 color illustrations of license plates used by each state and Canadian province. An important new reference source for professionals dealing with motor vehicle information. 128 pages. $12.95.

☆ **County Asset/Lien Records**   A national directory with in-depth profiles for all 4,252 county/city-level jurisdictions where UCC, federal, and state liens are filed on real and personal property. 460+ pages. $29.

Government information

Government Giveaways for Entrepreneurs II   Matthew Lesko reveals over 9,000 sources of loans, grants, venture capital, franchises, auctions, experts, free market studies, and home-based business information from the federal government. Information USA, 1994. ISBN 1-878346-19-9. $37.95. (Also available on Search and Retrieval Software, audiocassettes and videotape.) (800) 545-3888.

Tapping the Government Grapevine: The User-friendly Guide to U.S. Government Information Sources   This updated edition explores how new technologies affect your ability to locate information from the world's largest information publisher: the U.S. government. Oryx 1993. ISBN 0-89774-712-7. $34.50. (800) 279-6799.

US Government Books for Business Professionals   Free from the US GPO. Write to: Business Books Catalog, U.S. Government Printing Office, Stop SM, Room 3103, Washington, DC 20401.

How to Locate Anyone Who Is or Has Been in the Military   By Lt. Col. Richard S. Johnson, 241 pages, 1993. $19.95. Write to: Military Information Enterprises, PO Box 340081, Fort Sam Houston, TX 78234.

SIGCAT CD-ROM Compendium   Describes 300 CD-ROMs of federal government information provided by the GPO. GPO stock number 021-000-00158-9. $11. Send check, MO or Visa/MC number to: Superintendent of Documents, POB 37194, Pittsburgh, PA 15250-7954.

The Virtual Community: Homesteading on the Electronic Frontier
Author Howard Rheingold explores a new definition of community and shares his concerns about the commercialism and control of this new media. Addison-Wesley, 1993. ISBN 0-201608-70-7. $22.07. (800) 447-2226.

Information Anxiety   From Richard Saul Wurman, a fascinating look at our data-rich and information-poor society, with creative ways to harness the information we need. Doubleday, 1989. ISBN 0-385-24394-4. $14.95. (800) 223-6834.

The Now Realities: In Government & Politics; In Economics & Business; In Society & World View   Peter Drucker, considered to be the "founding father of the science of management," discusses his analysis of changes in America and the world. The chapter on "The Shifting Knowledge Base" is of particular interest. Harper & Row, 1990. ISBN 0-06-091699-0. $12. (800) 331-3761.

PowerShift: Knowledge, Wealth, & Violence at the Edge of the 21st Century   Alvin Toffler, author of *Future Shock*, writes about the fast-arriving civilization of the twenty-first century, citing knowledge as the key to creating wealth in the future. Bantam, 1990. ISBN 0553-29215-3. $6.99 paper. (800) 223-6834.

CD-ROMs in Print: An International Guide to CD-ROM, CD-I, CDTV, Multimedia, & Electronic Book Products   Compiled by Regina Rega, this edition includes new multimedia formats. Listings include compatible disk drives, necessary software, pricing and update frequency. Macintosh CD-ROMs are listed separately. Meckler, 1993. ISBN 0887368816. $95. (203) 226-6967.

CD-ROM Finder   Compiled & edited by James Shelton. This newly expanded fifth edition contains over 1,400 titles in a variety of subject areas. Learned Information, 1993. ISBN 0-938734-70-9. $69.50. New edition in Fall 1994. (609) 654-6266.

SIGCAT CD-ROM Compendium   Descriptions of 300 CD-ROMs of federal government information provided by the GPO. GPO stock number 021-000-00158-9. $11. Send check, MO or Visa/MC number to: Superintendent of Documents, POB 37194, Pittsburgh, PA 15250-7954.

Continuing education

CD-ROM

Software products

Online Log by Et Cetera, Inc.　Designed to help the online searcher track online costs and keep permanent records of online sessions with ease. It works with most DOS-based communications packages and just about any online service. Et Cetera, Inc. $79. PO Box 312, Dover, DE 19903, (302) 736-5110.

Personal Bibliographic Software　Pro-Cite and Bibliolink Products. Write to PO Box 4250, Ann Arbor MI 48106-4250, (313) 996-1580.

DB Direct　This is a post-processor program that easily converts your online search results from the major vendor systems into several database programs, including Paradox, Access, and DBase. $99. IMS Software, 3585 Lexington Ave. N, Suite 140, Arden Hills, MN 55126. (612) 484-4923.

Olson's Book of Library Clip Art　Several hundred images of information and library themes available for DOS and Mac formats. Pricing varies by collection. Chris Olson & Associates, 857 Twin Harbor Drive, Arnold, MD 21012-1027, (410) 647-6708 (voice), (410) 647-0415 (fax), olson@access.digex.net (e-mail).

Post Search Series　Software to automate clean-up and editing of online searches from all of the major vendor systems. Free demo disk and literature available from Pastel Programming Co., HC56, Box 6038, Sydney, MT 59270, (406) 482-4180.

Magazines & newsletters

Note: Prices shown are for personal subscriptions.

Business Information Alert $142 (10 issues)
Legal Information Alert $149 (10 issues)
Alert Publications
399 West Fullerton Parkway
Chicago, IL 60614
(312) 525-7594

CD-ROM Today
$20.95 (6 issues)
GP Publications
23-00 Route 208
Fair Lawn, NJ 07410
(201) 703-9500

Competitive Intelligence Review
$98/year (issued quarterly)
John Wiley & Sons (published in conjunction with SCIP)
605 Third Avenue
New York, NY 10158
(212) 850-6645

Computers in Libraries $39 (10) issues
Internet World $29 monthly
Internet Research $115 quarterly
Meckler Publishing
11 Ferry Lane West
Westport, CT 06880
(800) 632-5537

Corporate Library Update
$69 (bi-monthly)
PO Box 1983
Danbury, CT 06813
(800) 722-2346

DATABASE $49.50
ONLINE $49.50
The CD-ROM Professional $53.40
(All bi-monthly)
Online, Inc.
Pemberton Press Inc.
462 Danbury Road
Wilton, CT 06897-2126
(800) 248-8466
(203) 761-1444

Fee for Service
$85 (quarterly)
Whitmell & Associates
PO Box 213
RR No. 1
Huntsville, Ontario, Canada P0A 1K0
(416) 978-1924
(705) 789-3671 (fax)

Fortune Business Reports
Avenue Technologies
425 California Street
San Francisco, CA 94104
(415) 705-6960

Information Gatherer Newsletter
$20 (quarterly) by e-mail or regular mail
Mike James, CIS 74361,2017
Worldwide Consultants
2421 W. Pratt Blvd., Suite 971
Chicago, IL 60645

Information Today $43.95 (11 issues)
LINK-UP $26.75 (6 issues)
Searcher $49.50 (9 issues)
Learned Information
143 Old Marlton Pike
Medford, NJ 08055
(609) 654-6266
(609) 654-4309 (fax)
Ask for their publications catalog.

Information Broker (newsletter)
$40 (bi-monthly)
Burwell Enterprises
3724 FM 1960 West, Suite 214
Houston, TX 77068
(713) 537-9051

Information Technologies and Libraries $50 (quarterly)
LITA Newsletter $25 (quarterly)
Library Systems Newsletter $40 (monthly)
American Library Association
434 W. Downer
Aurora, IL 60506
(708) 892-7465
Ask ALA for their publications catalog.

Information Advisor
$99.50 (monthly)
Robert Berkman
Information Advisory Services, Inc.
47 Wilmer Street
Rochester, NY 14607
(406) 728-1171

Information Retrieval & Library Automation
$66 (monthly)
Lomond Publications
PO Box 88
Mt. Airy, MD 21711
(301) 829-1496

Information Times
(free to members only)
Information Industry Association
555 New Jersey Avenue NW, Suite 800
Washington, DC 20001
(202) 639-8262

The Informed Librarian
$99 (monthly)
Infosources Publishing
140 Norma Road
Teaneck, NJ 07666
(201) 836-7072

Lesko's Info-Power Newsletter
$128 (monthly)
Information USA
PO Box E
Kensington, MD 20895
(800) 545-3888

Library High-Tech News $70 (10 issues)
Library High Tech Journal $45 (4 issues)
Serials Review $45 (4 issues)
Reference Services Review $45 (4 issues)
Pierian Press
PO Box 1808
Ann Arbor, MI 48106
(800) 678-2435

Marketing Treasures
$59 (6 issues)
Chris Olson & Associates
Editor/Publisher
857 Twin Arbor Drive
Arnold, MD 21012
(410) 647-6708

MLS: Marketing Library Services
$65 (8 issues)
Learned Information
143 Old Marlton Pike
Medford, NJ 08055
(609) 654-6266
(609) 654-4309 (fax)

Online Access
$29.79 (monthly plus quarterly supplements)
Chicago Fine Print, Inc.
900 N. Franklin, Suite 310
Chicago, IL 60610-3119
(800) 36-MODEM
(312) 573-1700
(312) 573-0520 (fax)

Special Libraries & Specialist
Members free. $60 non-members (quarterly)
Special Libraries Association
1700 18th Street NW
Washington, DC 20009
(202) 234-4700

Wired
$39.95 (monthly)
Wired Ventures Ltd.
544 2nd Street
San Francisco, CA 94107
(800) SO-WIRED
E-mail: subscriptions@wired.com

Information Professionals Institute Order Form

Please mark the number of copies you wish to order in the space to the left of each title. Then complete the order information and fax or mail this form (or a photocopy) to the **Information Professionals Institute, 46 Hiller Drive, Oakland, CA 94618. Phone: (510) 649-9743. Fax: (510) 704-8646**.

Enclose check (U.S. dollars only) payable to **Information Professionals Institute** or provide complete credit card information. We recommend credit cards for all non-U.S. orders. Books will be shipped within 10 days.

Books and Other Guides
___ The Information Broker's Resource Kit ($10)
___ The Information Broker's Seminar on audiotape ($175)
___ The Information Broker's Handbook—2nd Edition ($34.95)
___ Information for Sale ($16.95)
___ Managing the Economics of Owning, Leasing, and Contracting
    Out Information Services ($49.95)
___ Burwell's Bibliography on Information Brokering—semiannual ($25)
___ Burwell Directory of Information Brokers
    Annual ($85)
    Diskette ($150)
    Book and Diskette ($195)
___ Burwell's Survey of Independent Information Professionals ($150)
___ Selected Aspects of Potential Legal Liabilities of
    Independent Information Professionals ($40)
___ Infopreneurs: Turning Data into Dollars ($24.95)

Online Information Resources
___ Secrets of the Super Searchers ($39.95)
___ Online Information Hunting ($19.95)
___ The Electronic Traveller ($16.95)
___ Find it Online ($29.95)
___ The Complete Guide to CompuServe ($34.95)
___ Fulltext Databases ($49.95)

Online Information Directories
___ The Business Database Finder ($129)
___ Fulltext Sources Online ($95)
___ Newspapers Online: North American Daily Newspapers Online in
    Full Text—annual ($120)
___ CompuServe Companion ($29.95)

Business Information
___ Competitor Intelligence ($24.95)

Small Business Management
___ The Contract and Fee-Setting Guide for Consultants and
    Professionals ($22.95)
___ Shenson on Consulting ($29.95)

The Internet
___ The Whole Internet User's Guide & Catalog ($24.95)
___ The Internet Complete Reference ($29.95)

___ The Internet Guide for New Users ($27.95)
___ Connecting to the Internet: A Buyer's Guide ($15.95)
___ Internet: Getting Started ($28)
___ The Internet Yellow Pages ($27.95)
___ The Internet: Mailing Lists ($29)

Public Records
___ A Public Records Primer and Investigator's Handbook:
    California Edition ($18.95)
___ The Guide to Background Investigations ($124.95)

Audio- and Videotapes
___ A Public Records Odyssey Seminar ($60 Audio/$80 VHS)
___ How to Locate and Investigate People ($60 Audio/$80 VHS)

BRB Public Record Research Library
___ The Sourcebook of Public Records Providers ($29)
___ Federal Courts ($33)
___ The County Locator—LOCUS ($25)
___ Local Court and County Record Retrievers ($45)
___ State Public Records ($29)
___ County Court Records ($33)
___ The MVR Book & Decoder Digest ($17)
___ License Plate Book ($12.95)
___ County Asset/Lien Records ($29)

Name_____

Mailing Address_____

City/State/ZIP/Country_____

Daytime
Phone_____

Amex/Visa/MC
Number_____

Signature_____Exp_____/_____

Multiply the number of copies times the price of each
title and enter the total here: $_____

California residents add 8.5% sales tax: $_____

Use the following chart to determine shipping charge: $_____

US Postage:
    First Class $6 for first book + $2.50 for each add'l book
    Fourth Class $4 for first book + $2 for each add'l book
Canada/Mexico: $8 for first book + $3 for each add'l book
Rest of World: $5 + $1 for each add'l PLUS actual postage

TOTAL $_____

B Contact points
Online systems, organizations, associations, & trade shows

This appendix is designed to be used as a quick reference. It makes no attempt to be comprehensive but instead concentrates on the names, addresses, and phone numbers most information brokers need most of the time. There are, for example, over 5,000 databases and over 800 online systems. But the 30 or so shown here are the ones you will use for most of your projects and electronic mail communications.

Similarly, most brokers will want to join one or more of the information-related organizations and associations listed here. If you can possibly manage it, we also strongly suggest that you try to attend one of the two leading trade shows in our industry. There is no better way to gain an instant appreciation of the depth and scope of the information industry than to attend National Online and/or the Online/CD-ROM conference.

If you can't attend one of the trade shows, consider contacting each of the addresses given below and requesting more information. We have put a copy of this appendix on the accompanying disk to make it easy for you to print out letters and labels.

America Online
8619 Westwood Center Dr.
Vienna, VA 22182-2285
(800) 227-6364

Database vendors, e-mail, & online services

BRS (Division of CD Plus Technologies)
333 7th Ave., 6th Floor
New York, NY 10001
(800) 950-2035
(212) 563-3006

Burrelle's Broadcast Database
75 E. Northfield Rd.
Livingston, NJ 07039-9873
(800) 631-1160
(201) 992-6600

CARL/The UnCover Company
3801 E. Florida Ave.
Building D, Suite 300
Denver, CO 80210
(303) 758-3030

CQ's Washington Alert Service
Congressional Quarterly, Inc.
1414 22nd St., NW
Washington, DC 20037
(202) 887-6353

CERFnet
Susan Estrada
PO Box 85608
San Diego, CA 92186
(800) 876-2373

CompuServe and **Knowledge Index**
CompuServe Information Service, Inc.
PO Box 20212
Columbus, OH 43220
(800) 848-8199 in Ohio
(800) 848-8990 or (614) 457-8600

DRI/McGraw-Hill
Data Products Division
24 Hartwell Ave.
Lexington, MA 02173
(617) 863-5100

Data-Star
Radio Suisse Services
1 Commerce Squ.
2005 Market St., Suite 1010
Philadelphia, PA 19103
(800) 221-7754
(215) 587-2147 (fax)

DataTimes Corporation
14000 Quail Springs Pkwy.
Suite 450
Oklahoma City, OK 73134
(800) 642-2525
(405) 751-6400
(405) 755-8028 (fax)

DELPHI
General Videotex Corporation/DELPHI
3 Blackstone St.
Cambridge, MA 02139
(800) 544-4005
(617) 491-3393

DIALOG and DIALMAIL
DIALOG Information Services
3460 Hillview Ave.
Palo Alto, CA 94304
(800) 334-2564
(415) 858-3719
(800) 387-2689 in Canada

Dow Jones News/Retrieval Service
PO Box 300
Princeton, NJ 08540-0300
(800) 522-3567
(609) 520-4000

EasyLink (AT&T)
One Lake St.
Upper Saddle River, NJ 07458
(800) 527-5184
(201) 818-5000 (fax)

EasyNet
Telebase Systems, Inc.
435 Devon Park Dr., Suite 300
Wayne, PA 19087
(800) 220-7616
(610) 293-4700

GEnie
General Electric Information Services
401 N. Washington St.
Rockville, MD 20850
(800) 638-9636

Infomart/Dialog Ltd.
1450 Don Mills Rd.
Don Mills, Ontario, Canada M3B 2X7
(800) 668-9215
(416) 442-2198
(416) 442-2126 (fax)

Information Access Corp./Predicasts
362 Lakeside Dr.
Foster City, CA 98404
(800) 227-8431

Knowledge Express Data Systems
Cathi Stahlbaum
900 W. Valley Rd., Suite 401
Wayne, PA 19087
(215) 293-9712

Legi-Tech
1029 J St., Suite 450
Sacramento, CA 95814
(916) 447-1886
(916) 447-1109 (fax)

LEXIS and NEXIS
Reed Elsevier, Inc.
PO Box 933
Dayton, OH 45041
(800) 227-4908

MCI Mail
1133 19th St. NW
Washington, DC 20036
(800) 444-6245
(202) 833-8484

MEDLARS
U.S. National Library of Medicine
8600 Rockville Pike
Bethesda, MD 20894
(301) 496-6193
(800) 638-8480
(301) 496-0822 (fax)

NewsNet
945 Haverford Rd.
Bryn Mawr, PA 19010
(800) 952-0122
(610) 527-8030
(610) 527-0338 (fax)

Online Computer Library Center (OCLC)
6565 Frantz Rd.
Dublin, OH 43017
(614) 764-6000
(800) 848-5800

ORBIT Online Products
8000 Westpark Dr.
McClean, VA 22102
(800) 290-9587

QUESTEL
8000 Westpark Dr.
McClean, VA 22102
(800) 424-9600

Reuters America, Inc.
1700 Broadway
New York, NY 10019
(800) 435-0101

STN International
c/o Chemical Abstracts Service
Customer Service
PO Box 3012
Columbus, OH 43210
(800) 753-4227

WESTLAW
West Publishing Co.
620 Opperman Dr.
Eagan, MN 55123
(800) 328-9352

Wilsonline
H.W. Wilson Co.
950 University Ave.
Bronx, NY 10452
(800) 367-6770
(718) 588-8400
(718) 590-1617 (fax)

VerdictSearch
128 Carleton Ave.
East Islip, NY 11730
(800) 832-1900
(516) 581-1930
(516) 581-8937 (fax)

Public records available electronically

CBD Infotech
6 Hutton Center Dr.
Santa Ana, CA 92707
(800) 427-3747

Equifax
PO Box 740245
Atlanta, GA 30374-0245
(800) 766-3708

Information America
600 W. Peachtree St. NW
Atlanta, GA 30308
(800) 235-4008 or (404) 892-1800
(404) 881-0278 (fax)

Mead Data Central
PO Box 933
Dayton, OH 45401
(800) 543-6862

Metronet
360 E. 22nd St.
Lombard, IL 60148-4924
(800) 456-6638

Prentice Hall Online
15 Columbus Circle
New York, NY 10023
(800) 333-8356

Transunion
555 W. Adams St.
Chicago, IL 60661
(312) 258-1717

TRW
2000 S. Anaheim Blvd.
Anaheim,CA
(800) 682-7654
(714) 385-7000

Organizations & associations

American Association of Law Libraries (AALL)
53 W. Jackson Blvd., Suite 940
Chicago, IL 60604
(312) 939-4764
(312) 431-1097 (fax)

American Library Association (ALA)
50 E. Huron St.
Chicago, IL 60611
(312) 944-6780

American Society for Information Science (ASIS)
8720 Georgia Ave., Suite 501
Silver Spring, MD 20910-3602
(301) 495-0900
(301) 495-0810 (fax)

Association of Independent Information Professionals (AIIP)
Robert Purcell
245 5th Ave., Suite 2103
New York, NY 10016
(212) 779-1855
(212) 481-3071 (fax)

Association of Information & Dissemination Centers (ASIDIC)
PO Box 8105
Athens, GA 30603
(706) 542-6820

Copyright Clearance Center
222 Rosewood Dr.
Danvers, MA 01923
(508) 750-8400
(508) 750-4470 (fax)

Electronic Frontier Foundation
c/o On Technology
155 2nd St.
Cambridge, MA 02141
(617) 864-0665

EUSIDIC
Berry Mahon, Exec. Director
PO Box 1416
L-1014
Luxembourg, Belgium
011 352-250-750-220
011 352-252-750-222 (fax)

Information Industry Association (IIA)
555 New Jersey Ave. NW
Suite 800
Washington, DC 20001
(202) 639-8262
(202) 638-4403 (fax)

Investigators Open Network
Investigators Anywhere Resource Line
ION, Inc.
Leroy Cook, President
2111 E. Baseline Rd., Suite F-7
Tempe, AZ 85283
(800) 338-3463
(602) 730-8088
(602) 730-8103 (fax)

Medical Library Association (MLA)
6 N. Michigan Ave., Suite 300
Chicago, IL 60602
(312) 419-9094
(312) 419-8950 (fax)

National Association of Screening Agencies
Don Baker
c/o Index Companies
14232 Marsh Ln. #331
Dallas, TX 75234
(214) 247-7878

National Commission on Libraries and Information Science (NCLIS)
1110 Vermont Ave. NW, #820
Washington, DC 20005
(202) 606-9200
(202) 606-9203 (fax)

National Federation of Abstracting and Information Science (NFAIS)
1518 Walnut St.
Philadelphia, PA 19102
(215) 563-2406

National Federation of Paralegal Association, Inc.
PO Box 33108
Kansas City, MO 64114
(816) 941-4000

National Public Records Research Association
PO Box 10329
Tallahassee, FL 32302
(800) 637-8605

Society of Competitive Intelligence Professionals (SCIP)
1700 Diagonal Rd.
Alexandria, VA 23314
(703) 739-0696
(703) 739-2524 (fax)

Special Libraries Association (SLA)

1700 18th St. NW
Washington, DC 20009
(202) 234-4700
(202) 265-9317 (fax)

Online/CD-ROM

Online Inc.
11 Tannery Ln.
Weston, CT 06883
(800) 248-8466
Annual conference in the fall. Location varies.

National Online Conference

Learned Information
143 Old Marlton Pike
Medford, NJ 08055
(609) 654-6266
(609) 654-4309 (fax)
Annual conference each spring in New York City.

International Online Conference

Learned Information (Europe) Ltd.
Woodside, Hinksey Hill
Oxford OX1 5AU, UK
011-44-865-730-275
011-44-865-736-354 (fax)
Annual conference held each December in London.

Association of Independent Information Professionals (AIIP)

245 5th Ave., Suite 2103
New York, NY 10016
(212) 779-1855
(212) 481-3071 (fax)
Annual conference held each spring. Location varies.

Internet World and Internet World International

Mecklermedia
11 Ferry Ln. W.
Westport, CT 06880
     or
Mecklermedia, Limited
Artillery House
Artillery Row
London SW1P 1RT, UK
44 071 976 0405
44 071 976 0506 (fax)

Conferences & seminars

Society of Competitive Intelligence Professionals (SCIP)

1700 Diagonal Rd.
Alexandria, VA 23314
(703) 739-0696
(703) 739-2524 (fax)
Annual conference held each spring. Location varies.

Open Source Solutions International Symposium

Robert D. Steele, Pres.
Open Source Solutions, Inc.
11005 Langton Arms Ct.
Oakton, VA 22124-1807
(703 242-1700
(703) 242-1711 (fax)
Annual conference held in the fall in Washington, DC.

Competitive Intelligence Seminars

Fuld & Company, Inc.
Leonard M. Fuld, President
80 Trowbridge St.
Cambridge, MA 02138
(617) 492-5000
(617) 492-7108 (fax)

The Information Professionals Institute (IPI) offers **The Information Broker's Seminar**, **Comparative Online Searching**, **The Public Records Seminar**, **Intermediate/Advanced Patent Searching**, and several **Internet** courses in a variety of cities. For more information, see Appendix D or call (713) 537-8344 for a current schedule.

Dialog offers their annual **Dialog Update** every 18 months. Call (800) 334-2564 for current information.

C Association of Independent Information Professionals

Once you become an information broker, you'll want to give serious consideration to joining the AIIP, the Association of Independent Information Professionals. Indeed, we feel that membership is virtually essential. The AIIP is quite simply *the* society of independent information professionals recognized by information providers and users worldwide. In this appendix, we'll give you an overview of AIIP, describe the types of memberships that are available and the benefits associated with each, and tell you how to send for your membership application.

AIIP was founded in 1987 by Dr. Marilyn Levine of Information Express in Milwaukee, Wisconsin, along with 26 other information professionals. They recognized that their success as individuals would be enhanced by an organization bringing together the experience and ideas of independent information professionals such as consultants, researchers, brokers, writers, document delivery providers, and freelance librarians. To that end, the AIIP founders set forth these three goals:

What is the AIIP?

1. To provide a forum for the discussion of issues and concerns shared by independent information professionals.
2. To promote high professional and ethical standards among members.
3. To advance knowledge and understanding of the information profession in general and the independent information professional in particular.

Since its formation, AIIP has attracted more than 600 members. They are innovative, independent small-business owners who provide fee-based information services such as database searching, manual research, document delivery, database design, library support, consulting, writing, and publishing.

AIIP also welcomes, as Associate Members, information experts who do not own their own firms, as well as professionals in affiliated fields.

Work smarter with an AIIP membership!

An AIIP membership can make your work as an information professional easier and more productive, and possibly even more profitable. The association provides its members with timely information, outstanding networking and professional development opportunities, and a variety of special product and service offerings designed exclusively for AIIP members. Benefits enjoyed by all members include:

- Annual Meeting—Each spring, members gather to meet colleagues, participate in panel discussions, and learn from guest speakers. The location rotates among major cities throughout the United States.
- Membership Directory—Each member receives a free copy of the annual membership directory, which lists names, addresses, services offered, and areas of expertise. AIIP also distributes directories to database vendors and other organizations to give members exposure to potential clients and referral sources.
- Quarterly Newsletter—The AIIP newsletter provides you with association and industry news, an events calendar, highlights from the electronic bulletin board, and advertising opportunities.
- Advocacy—AIIP has led the fight to end contractual barriers to the use of information products by independent research companies.
- Electronic Bulletin Board—A private bulletin board lets you communicate with other members for networking, subcontracting, and problem-solving. The bulletin board is part of the Working From Home Forum on CompuServe (key in go work).

The AIIP Vendor Program

AIIP also acts on behalf of members in negotiating special discount programs with vendors of print and online products and services.

In the fall of 1990, the first AIIP Vendor Program was established with LEXIS/NEXIS. Since then, more than 20 additional vendors (including DIALOG Information Services, Dow Jones News/Retrieval, NewsNet, DataTimes, and Burrelle's Broadcast Database) have recognized the increasing role of the independent information professional by negotiating special programs with AIIP. These programs include features such as additional training and special pricing designed to meet the operational needs of the Association and its members.

What type of membership is right for you?

Membership in the AIIP is open to any individual or organization which supports the objectives of the Association. Prospective members must complete a membership application and submit it to the Membership Committee. The AIIP offers three types of membership: Regular, Associate, and Supporting.

Regular Membership

Regular Membership in AIIP is open to any individual who is the principal of a business which provides information services to more than one client, supports the goals of the Association, and accepts its Code of Ethical Business Practice. In plain language, this means you've got to be a "real," practicing information broker—someone who makes a living at it.

Although it is not required, when applying for Regular Membership, it is a good idea to include a business card, your brochure, and any other appropriate supporting material with your membership application. Also, pay your membership fee ($160 at this writing) with a check drawn on a business bank account.

There are two reasons why the AIIP has to be so stringent in its requirements for Regular Membership. First, unlike many other associations, the AIIP Membership Committee must rely almost exclusively on the material you submit to verify that you do indeed qualify. There is no employer to phone and no practical, independent way to confirm that you really are a practicing information broker. This is important because Regular Members can vote and run for office.

Second, there is the matter of the Special Vendor Programs. As a Regular Member, you will enjoy preferential treatment from information suppliers, database vendors, and online services through programs designed especially for the AIIP. Discounts on connect time, elimination of annual or monthly subscription fees or minimums, and special marketing advice and services are just a few of the special benefits you will receive.

The Association has been tireless in proposing, negotiating, and implementing these special deals. And it continues to do so. Vendors have responded because they realize that information brokers are among their best customers and most important "resellers." Understandably, however, no vendor wants to find itself granting these accommodations to people who aren't "real" information brokers. Vendors trust the AIIP to make sure that all of its Regular Members do indeed qualify.

The AIIP Code of Ethical Business Practice

An independent information professional is an information entrepreneur who has demonstrated continuing expertise in the art of finding and organizing information. The independent information professional provides information services on a contractual basis to more than one client. Information professionals serve as objective intermediaries between the client and the information world.

They bear the following responsibilities:

1. To uphold the profession's reputation for honesty, competence, and confidentiality.
2. To give clients the most current and accurate information possible.
3. To help a client understand the sources of information used, and the degree of reliability which can be expected of them.

4. To accept only those projects which are legal and are not detrimental to our profession.
5. To respect client confidentiality.
6. To honor intellectual property rights, and to explain to clients what their obligations may be.
7. To maintain a professional relationship with libraries, and comply with all their rules of access.
8. To assume responsibility for employees' compliance with this code.

Associate Membership

Associate Membership is open to those individuals who support both the objectives and the principles of AIIP, but who are not themselves currently engaged in an active, independent information business. This includes applicants who are currently employed full- or part-time by someone else, and who plan to become "real" information brokers in the future. The current annual fee for Associate Membership is $85.

As an Associate, you cannot vote, run for office, or take advantage of Special Vendor Programs. But you may be invited to serve on committees, and, of course, you will receive the newsletter and gain access to the AIIP bulletin board on CompuServe.

The AIIP generally assumes that Associate Members will eventually take the plunge and become full-time information brokers in the future. As an Associate Member, you may apply to change your status to Regular Membership at any time it becomes appropriate to do so. In the meantime, Associate Membership offers a great way to get to know everybody and seek the advice and counsel you will need in setting up your own firm.

We cannot emphasize strongly enough that information brokering is a collegial, not a competitive, profession. Brokers help each other, hire each other, and generally march shoulder-to-shoulder in bringing the pure light of information to the outside world. Of course, we all try to make a living while doing so. But information brokers as a group are vastly underpaid for the gold they provide. And that, too, is a source of camaraderie.

Supporting Membership

This third category of membership is primarily designed for organizations and corporations that wish to show their financial support for the objectives of the AIIP. Individuals may also be Supporting Members. At this writing, dues for a Supporting Membership are $500 a year. Each Supporting Member organization may designate one representative to serve as a principle contact. That person receives all of the benefits of Associate Membership. Supporting Members are publicly recognized for their contribution to the goals of the AIIP.

For a complete AIIP membership application package, contact:

AIIP Headquarters Office
245 Fifth Ave., Suite 2103
New York, NY 10016
(212) 779-1855 (voice)
(212) 481-3071 (fax)
CompuServe: 73263,34

1986–1987	Dr. Marilyn Levine (AIIP Founder), Information Express
1987–1988	Helen P. Burwell, Burwell Enterprises
1988–1989	Sue Rugge, Information Professionals Institute
1989–1990	Susanne Bjorner, Bjorner & Associates
1990–1991	Linda Cooper, Cooper Heller Research
1991–1992	Reva Basch, Aubergine Information Services
1992–1993	Janet Gotkin, InfoLink
1993–1994	Susan Feldman, Datasearch
1994–1995	Stephanie C. Ardito, Ardito Information & Research, Inc.
1995–1996	Susan Detwiler, S. M. Detwiler & Associates

Seminars offered by the Information Professionals Institute

No single book can ever cover all there is to know about a given subject. Nor can the printed word—at least not the *paper* printed word—ever be interactive. You can ask all the questions you want of this book, and we guarantee you it will never answer back. That's why, for those who want to know more, there are the seminars offered by the Information Professionals Institute (IPI).

Founded in 1992 by Sue Rugge, Helen Burwell, and Ruth Orenstein, IPI offers seminars that are distinctly different from the vendor- or database-specific seminars that are the industry norm. IPI seminars are designed to offer objective, subject-specific courses which cut across these commercial lines. Continuing education seminars for staff and independent information professionals are offered in major cities throughout the U.S. each year.

The specific lineup of seminars may vary each year depending on industry developments and the popularity and demand for information on specific topics. But IPI will always offer the latest edition of Sue Rugge's Information Broker's Seminar and Helen Burwell's Public Records Seminar, both of which are summarized in this appendix.

For a copy of the current IPI brochure and seminar prices and schedule, contact:

The Information Professionals Institute
3724 F.M. 1960 W., Suite 214
Houston, TX 77068
(713) 537-8344 (voice)
(713) 537-8332 (fax)
CompuServe: 75120,50

The Information Broker's Seminar

Sue Rugge has been preparing and presenting her Information Broker's Seminar for the better part of a decade. A one-day course, this program offers a unique opportunity to profit from the experience of one of the pioneers of the information brokering field—and to learn first-hand how to start and operate a successful information brokering service. Seminar topics include:

- Small Business Management
  - Small business resources
  - Choosing a business structure
  - Merchant status—Visa, MasterCard, American Express
  - Managing your cash flow
  - The 10 biggest mistakes in business
- The Business Plan
  - Purpose of a business plan
  - Creating the business plan
  - How do you define your business
  - Determining how much capital you will need
  - Questions your business plan should answer
- Product and Service Definition
  - Whether to specialize
  - Identifying your competition
  - Defining your product
- Marketing and Advertising
- Identifying your target market
- Getting clients/keeping clients
- What your advertising should say
- Marketing without advertising
- The most effective marketing techniques
- Fees and Charges
  - Determining your costs
  - Setting your fees
  - The art of quoting on a job
  - Credit and collections
- Technological Considerations
  - Equipment
  - Software
  - Database vendors and gateways

- Legal Considerations
  - Copyright issues
  - Using contracts
  - Errors and omissions insurance
  - Confidentiality
- Professional Resources
  - Publications
  - Professional associations
  - Conferences
- Training
  - Do you need to be a librarian?
  - Traits of a good database searcher
  - Traits of a good information broker
  - Traits of successful entrepreneurs

The Information Broker's Seminar runs from 9 A.M. to 5 P.M., with lunch included. At this writing, the cost is $225 with advance registration ($250 at the door). The price includes an extensive set of course materials. For more information on upcoming seminar dates and locations, contact IPI at the Houston address given above.

Seminar on Audiotape

Sue Rugge's seminar is also available on six hours of audiocassette tapes for $175. To order the tapes, use the order form provided in Appendix A. Or contact Sue Rugge at (510) 649-9743 (voice) or (510) 704-8646 (fax).

The Public Records Seminar

Public records: What's available and how to get it! That's what this seminar by Helen Burwell is all about. A past president of AIIP, Helen is president of Burwell Enterprises, Inc., publisher of the invaluable *Burwell Directory of Information Brokers*, *The Information Broker* newsletter, and regularly updated bibliographies on both information brokering and document delivery.

In addition, through long experience, Helen has some very special expertise in legal and business research. All of which she brings to her seminar on public records searching. Topics covered in the seminar include:

- Sources of Information
  - Courthouse records
  - Licensing board records
  - Motor vehicle records
  - Real estate records
  - Tax records
  - Uniform Commercial Code filings
  - Voter registration records
- Information on People
  - Asset searches
  - Background checks
  - Financials

- Pre-employment
- Skip trace
- What's Legal and What's Not
- The Fair Credit Reporting Act
- The Privacy Act
- Other laws
  - Obtaining the Records
    - Free versus fee
    - Who has what
    - Canadian records
    - European records
  - Database Producers and Vendors
    - Information America
    - LEXIS
    - CDB Infotek
    - Other online services
    - Superbureaus
    - Gateways versus direct
    - How to choose and necessary trade-offs
    - Cost considerations
  - Putting the Pieces Together
    - Hints and shortcuts
    - Following the data trail
  - Uses for Public Record Information
    - Business decisions
    - Competitor intelligence
    - Genealogy
    - Locating people
    - Private investigation
    - Other types of research
  - Other Resources
    - Publications
    - Professional associations
    - Conferences

The Public Records Seminar runs from 9 A.M. to 5 P.M., with lunch included. At this writing, the cost is $225 with advance registration ($250 at the door). The price includes an extensive set of course materials. For more information on upcoming seminar dates and locations, contact IPI at the Houston address given on page 416.

Other IPI seminars

Naturally, you will want to send for the latest brochure and information. But it is worth knowing that in the past, the Information Professionals Institute has offered the following seminars:

Conducted by Helen Burwell, this seminar is designed to answer questions like the following:

- What to look at when comparing and evaluating various online services.
- How to compare sources of online information.
- Feature-by-feature comparisons of the major online systems.
- How to take advantage of special services.
- What about systems like CompuServe, AOL, Prodigy, and the rest?
- Online services for specific professions.
- Online versus CD-ROM searching.
- The easiest way to get online: scripts, vendor products, software packages, telecommunications networks, and more.

IPI also offers seminars focusing on the Internet. We cannot promise that the following courses will be available at all times, but in the past, IPI has offered these Internet-related seminars:

The Internet—An Introduction   This is a half-day *hands-on* practical introduction to accessing and using the Internet. Students learn how to get on the Net, how to use e-mail, how to read and participate in newsgroups, how to use Telnet, how to transfer files with FTP, and more. The course is held at Columbia University in New York City.

Internet 1: A Beginner's Guide to the Internet   This is a one-day seminar designed to make you "Internet literate." It covers using newsgroups and listservers, Gopher, Archie, WAIS, Mosaic and other front-end programs, plus tips on getting free software, locating news articles, as well as obtaining magazines and files.

Internet 2: Mining the Internet for Business & Research Information   Here's a one-day seminar designed to show you how to use the Internet as a vehicle for business and information research. It includes topics like: the Researcher's Internet Toolkit; The Community and Culture of the Internet; Locating Government Information (free and for-fee); Business Research on the Internet (science, medicine, high-tech, trade, economics, global market research, and more); and Tracking the Future Internet, a look at future developments.

Many of the leading online systems (DIALOG, Dow Jones, NEXIS, and so on) offer seminars at various locations around the country. Numerous databases or information providers do the same. All of which is to the good. The prices are usually reasonable, and the instructors are always talented, dedicated people.

Such seminars are always aimed at selling you on using a particular online system or database. There's nothing wrong with that, and no one pretends to be offering you an unbiased view. Certainly current and prospective information brokers should take advantage of such seminars.

The Information Professionals Institute was formed, however, to offer valuable seminars that are completely unbiased. The IPI faculty have nothing to lose or gain if you opt to use one system or database over another. Sue Rugge, Helen Burwell, and the rest are free to tell you the unvarnished truth. And they do so with charm and grace and with an assurance that's rooted in deep experience in their respective fields.

How to use the accompanying disk

The most important thing to know about the disk you will find at the back of this book is this:

It is a 3.5-inch disk that can be read and used by DOS, Windows, and Macintosh users alike!

The files the disk contains are plain, pure ASCII text. No special codes, no strange formatting, nothing to make your life difficult. If you are a DOS or Windows user, you have only to put the disk into the drive and use the DOS DIR command, Windows File Manager, or whatever other program you use to copy, move, and manipulate files.

Since floppy drives tend to be much slower than hard disks, we suggest you make a directory on your hard drive called BROKER or some such and simply copy all of the files on this disk into it. You can then use your favorite word processor or text editor to look at each file, print it out, search it for a keyword of your choosing, or whatever.

If you have an Apple Macintosh

If you are a Macintosh user, you will need to take an additional step or two. If you are an absolute computer novice, the first of these steps may be contacting a Mac-using friend who has had more experience. Neither of your co-authors knows enough about the Mac to be able to answer your questions. We do know that the procedure discussed here works, because, under the guidance of our Mac-using friends, we have tried it.

There is also the fact that as the PC and Mac worlds converge and as both the PowerPC chip and the Macintosh operating system become more widely available, the differences between the two platforms may fade into nonexistence. In any case, at this writing you should know that all Macintoshes manufactured after 1989 are equipped with a SuperDrive—a disk drive capable of reading and writing high-density (1.44 megabyte) DOS-formatted floppy disks.

These computers also include a program called Apple File Exchange to tell the Mac how to handle DOS disks. Apple File Exchange (AFE) is on one of the Utility disks supplied with System 6 and System 7. Apple's System 7.5, in contrast, offers an even more powerful program called PC Exchange 2.0. Call Apple for details on getting an upgrade at (800) 769-2775.

You will want to see one of the appendices of your Macintosh manual for details on using AFE or PC Exchange. However, you can basically put the Utility disk containing Apple File Exchange into your drive and double click on its icon when it appears. Use the Open, Drive, and Eject buttons, if necessary, to display the names of files you want to copy onto your Mac hard drive and the destination disk or folder where you want to store the files.

Open the Translation menu for the kind of file translation you want by pointing to its title and holding down the mouse key. When translating DOS into Mac files, open the MS-DOS to Mac menu. At the appropriate point, opt for *text* translation. Since the files on this disk are plain ASCII text, you won't need any kind of fancy translator module. That's just about all there is to it. The Mac's famed ease of use will see you through.

Once you get the files on the accompanying disk copied onto your Macintosh hard drive, use your favorite word processor to look at, edit, search, and print out the files.

What's on the disk?

Here are the files you'll find on the disk:

100-BBS.TXT — The top 100 Bulletin Board Systems (BBSs) as ranked by readers of *Boardwatch* magazine. Phone numbers, speeds, and one-line descriptions.

AGREE.TXT — The sample letter of agreement from Chapter 23. (Fig. 23-1)

APPEND-A.TXT — The electronic version of Appendix A—The Information Broker's Bookshelf: Crucial Resources and Reference Works.

APPEND-B.TXT — Appendix B—Contact Points: Online Systems, Organizations, Associations, and Trade Shows

APPEND-C.TXT	Appendix C—The Association of Independent Information Professionals (AIIP)
APPEND-D.TXT	Appendix D—Seminars Offered by the Information Professionals Institute
APPEND-E.TXT	Appendix E—How to Use the Accompanying Disk (the text you are reading right now)
APPEND-F.TXT	Appendix F—The Internet Toolkit and Glossbrenner's Choice
CIS-SIGS.TXT	An alphabetical list of the names of all CompuServe forums (SIGs), and the "GO" command word you need to move to each one.
CONTRACT.TXT	We recommend using a letter of agreement to outline the assignment, what you'll deliver, what you will be paid, etc. But if you find that you must use a contract, this file can serve as your model.
COVER.TXT	The generalized cover letter discussed in Chapter 19 (Fig. 19-1).
ENVIRON.TXT	Just one of the more than 150 files prepared by the Clearinghouse for Subject-Oriented Internet Resource Guides. Prepared by Carol Briggs-Erickson and Toni Murphy, this particular file alerts you to just about every Gopher, FTP site, or Telnet location offering information about environmental issues. (The current list of all available Clearinghouse files can be found on the Glossbrenner's Choice disk, Internet 1.)
ESTIMATE.TXT	Here is a form you may want to use to help estimate your costs on a job. As we said in Chapter 23, this is not the kind of thing you want to share with your client, but it can be helpful internally (Fig. 23-1).
FOINFO.TXT	The full text of *A Citizen's Guide or Using the Freedom of Information Act and the Privacy Act of 1974 to Request Government Records*.
GOVTBBS.TXT	This file contains a list of the bulletin board systems operated by U.S. Government

agencies that you can reach by direct dial or by connecting with the NTIS FedWorld BBS system described in Chapter 8.

INVOICE.TXT	A sample invoice from Chapter 23 (Fig. 23-3).
IPN.TXT	Additional information on the *Information Professionals Network*.
ITEMIZE.TXT	Generally, we recommend against using an itemized invoice. But if you find you have no choice, here is the one shown in Fig. 23-4 of Chapter 4.
KEEPERS.TXT	The *Boardwatch* magazine list of BBS list keepers. Each of the systems cited here maintains a list of other BBS systems of some sort.
LETTERS.TXT	Letters prepared by actual information brokers and sent to their clients. Reading this correspondence is like looking over the shoulder of a working broker. All names and revealing details have been changed, of course. We think you will find it an education.
LOG.TXT	The Search Log form from Chapter 22 (Fig. 22-2).
REPORT.TXT	An actual information broker report prepared for a client by Sue Rugge's The Rugge Group. Again, names and details have been changed. But that doesn't matter. Concentrate on the format, organization, and overall presentation of the information.
REQUEST.TXT	The Search Request form from Chapter 22 (Fig. 22-1).
SIGS.TXT	The rest of the SIG story. Which is to say, a list of all the SIGs, Clubs, Bulletin Boards, and Forums on every consumer system except CompuServe (America Online, Delphi, GEnie, and Prodigy). The CompuServe SIGs are listed in the file CIS-SIGS.TXT.
SLICK.TXT	A really neat excerpt from a really neat book called *Internet Slick Tricks* by Alfred

and Emily Glossbrenner. The two tricks included here deal with movies and Seinfeld. (See the file for more information!)

SUCCESS.TXT   Internet Success Stories—22 of them—in which real librarians tell you how they used the Internet to answer patron queries. Some are super; some are mundane. But all are instructive.

WORKING.TXT   Here's a great introduction to the Working from Home Forum on CompuServe: the message board topics, the names of the file libraries, and the names and descriptions of the files you'll find in the Information Professionals library. All that's missing is the famous "Section 0," to which only AIIP members are admitted.

Where can I get the disk?

If you're reading a library copy of *The Information Broker's Handbook*, the disk we've just described may no longer be at the back of this book. Or perhaps you bought the book but have misplaced or accidentally damaged the disk that came with it.

In either case, you'll be happy to know that additional copies of the disk are available from Glossbrenner's Choice for a nominal cost ($5 for the disk, plus $3 for shipping to U.S. addresses and $5 outside the U.S.). You can use the order form provided in Appendix F, or send your request along with payment to:

Glossbrenner's Choice
699 River Rd.
Yardley, PA 19067-1965
(215) 736-1213 (voice)
(215) 736-1031 (fax)

In the unlikely event that the disk supplied with your book is defective and you don't wish to pay for a replacement, you will need to contact the publisher, Windcrest/McGraw-Hill at (800) 233-1128. Glossbrenner's Choice is not in a position to bear responsibility for replacing defective disks for free.

Conclusion

Clearly, there is no magic wand we can wave to automatically make every reader a bona fide information broker. With this disk, however, we have tried to make it as easy as possible for you to get *started*. We urge you to print out all of the non-appendix text files. If you don't yet own a computer yourself, ask a friend to print them for you.

Every client, and every report, is different. But the collection of cover letters and the sample report provided here will give you a much better idea of the kind of material a successful information broker delivers to a client. Since the letters are derived from actual letters, we have substituted names ("Ms. Jones," "Mr. Roe," etc.) and changed things around to protect the confidentiality of the real-life client.

The specific names, places, and subjects, however, are not the point. Concentrate on the tone of the letters, how they detail the work that has been done, and how they suggest (if appropriate) additional research possibilities. To provide a well-rounded picture, we have included letters sent when a research project was unsuccessful, as well as ones for which the client did indeed receive what he or she was hoping for.

Finally, we strongly suggest that you contact the organizations and online services cited in Appendix B. Ask for an information packet, and when it arrives, put it in a file. That's why we've included these appendices on the accompanying disk. With these addresses and a word processing program, you can quickly generate the query letters you need.

The Internet Toolkit & Glossbrenner's Choice

Computers, the Internet, and commercial online services aren't really all that difficult to use, provided you've got two things—the right information and the right software. Throughout this book, we have done our best to give you the right information. This appendix addresses the other need—the right software.

Through years of experience, Alfred has become something of an expert in public domain and shareware software for DOS/Windows machines. (He has even written several books on the subject.) He knows exactly what utilities and tools you need to make it easier than you've ever imagined to go online, and as a convenience to readers, he has long made them available on disk as part of a collection called Glossbrenner's Choice.

In addition to the software, however, Glossbrenner's Choice also offers a series of disks called the Internet Toolkit. These disks contain the FAQ (Frequently Asked Questions) files, the best guides to resources, and other information you'll need if you want to make the most of the Internet. With just two exceptions (Internet Disks 3 and 6), the disks in the Internet Toolkit contain plain, pure ASCII text files and so can be used by both DOS/Windows users and by Macintosh users.

If you have a Macintosh . . .

The PowerPC chip notwithstanding, it is likely to be a while before Macintoshes and PCs can share the same software. But the two systems have long been able to share *text* files, thanks to Apple's SuperDrive 3.5-inch disk-drive technology. If your Mac was manufactured after August1989, it is almost certainly equipped with one or more SuperDrives and thus has the ability to read 1.44MB Mac- and DOS-formatted disks.

Check your Reference manual for an appendix titled "Exchanging Disks and Files with MS-DOS Computers," or words to that effect. As you will discover, the necessary Apple File Exchange software is supplied on one of the Utility disks provided with your Mac system software. If you are using System 7.5, check your disks for a program called PC Exchange.

Follow the Apple File Exchange or PC Exchange instructions, and you will be able to copy the files on the Internet Toolkit disks onto your hard drive. Since the files are all plain ASCII text files, you can read and search them with your favorite word processor as easily as if you had created them yourself. There is no need to worry with any of the "translator" modules supplied with the Apple File Exchange software.

Glossbrenner's Choice disks

Here's a list of the disks described in this appendix:

The Internet Toolkit
Internet 1 Internet Must-Have Files
Internet 2 FTP Essentials
Internet 3 Telnet Essentials (DOS/Windows only)
Internet 4 Newsgroup Essentials
Internet 5 Mailing List Essentials
Internet 6 Compression Tools (DOS/Windows only)
Internet 7 Just the FAQs

DOS/Windows Tools and Utilities
Communicator's Toolchest
CommWin Communications Package
Encryption Tools
Idea Processing
Information Broker Disk
Instant File Management: QFILER, QEDIT, and Associates
Qmodem Communications Program
System Configuration Tools
TAPCIS for CompuServe
Text Search
Text Treaters

The disks in the Internet Toolkit collection contain key FAQs, directories, guides, lists, and other information about using various features of the Internet. Any word processing program can be used to view, print, and search the files for keywords.

All of the disks are 3.5-inch, high-density (1.44MB). Most computer users today have at least one drive in their systems that can read high-density disks. If you don't, you really should consider getting one. A high-density drive these days sells for about $40 at local computer stores. The only reason not to upgrade is if you've got a very old system that's not worth putting more money into. In which case, it's probably time to get a new computer.

This disk includes the latest versions of the key text files which, as we said in Chapter 15, every Internet user should have. All of these files are available on the Net, but you may find it more convenient to get them in one neat package:

- *The Internet Services FAQ* by Kevin Savetz
- *Special Internet Connections* by Scott Yanoff
- The List of Subject-Oriented Internet Resource Guides
- John December's *Internet-CMC List*
- John December's *Internet Tools Summary*

The disk also includes *The Beginner's Guide to the Internet*, an excellent tutorial for DOS and Windows users by Patrick J. Suarez.

Before you start using the Internet's file transfer protocol (FTP), you'll want to read Internaut Perry Rovers's excellent FAQ on the subject. And you'll want a copy of Mr. Rovers's comprehensive list of FTP sites, which provides detailed information on FTP locations throughout the world. Both are provided on this disk.

This disk is for DOS and Windows users only. It contains Peter Scott's remarkable Hytelnet package. Hytelnet provides a gigantic database of Telnet locations, with at least one screen per location describing what you'll find there. It's like a huge, computerized directory of Telnet sites, organized as a hypertext-style menu system to make it easy to use.

Also on this disk is Bruce Clouette's optional Subject Guide for the main Hytelnet menu, as well as WINHytelnet, a Windows front-end program.

There are close to 10,000 newsgroups on the Internet, and groups come and go all the time. To help you locate the ones that might be of interest to you, this disk contains two periodically updated lists of Internet newsgroups, organized by category (alternative, business, computer, recreation, science, etc.).

The lists include the name of the group and an often witty one-line description. The search function of your favorite word processor will make it

The Internet Toolkit

Internet 1— Internet Must-Have Files

Internet 2— FTP Essentials

Internet 3— Telnet Essentials

Internet 4— Newsgroup Essentials

very easy to locate all the Internet newsgroups devoted to a given topic. Here are the lists on this disk:

- The List of Active Newsgroups (Parts 1 and 2)—This list includes newsgroups for all categories except ALT (alternative), which has its own list.
- The List of Alternative Newsgroups (Parts 1 and 2)—This list includes *only* newsgroups in the ALT category.

As an added bonus, you'll also find the DOS version of the Rot-13 program, which you'll need if you want to be able to decode the coded jokes and messages posted in some newsgroups. You can use the same program to encode text in the Rot-13 format.

Internet 5—Mailing List Essentials

As with newsgroups, it helps to have a comprehensive, updated source of mailing lists available on the Internet. This disk includes two such lists:

- The SRI List of Lists—Covers both Internet and Bitnet lists.
- Publicly Accessible Mailing Lists—Mainly Internet lists, with about a dozen or so Bitnet lists.

For each mailing list, you'll find a paragraph or more describing the list's purpose, intended audience, and subscription information. You can use your word processor to search for topics of interest, or to simply browse.

Internet 6— Compression and Conversion Tools

This disk is for DOS/Windows users only. It contains all of the programs you will need to uncompress or unarchive or decode the various files you will find at FTP sites around the Net. Plus a Glossbrenner-written quick-start manual to show you how to use each one. Most of these programs come with on-disk manuals as well, but you probably won't need to read them. Here are the programs:

File extension	Name of required DOS program
.arc	ARCE.EXE
.arj	ARJ241A.EXE
.btoa	ATOB11.ZIP
.cpio	PAX2EXE.ZIP
.gz or .z	GZIP124.ZIP
.hqx	XBIN23.ZIP
.lzh	LHA.EXE
.pak	PAK251.EXE
.pit	UnPackIt
.shar	TOADSHR1.ARC
.sit	UNSIT30.ZIP
.tar	TAR.ZIP
.uue	UUEXE (Richard Marks)
.Z	U16.ZIP
.zip	PK204G.EXE (PKZIP)
.zoo	ZOO210.EXE

As its name implies, this disk is devoted exclusively to Internet FAQs (Frequently Asked Questions files). It includes the gigantic 100-plus page FAQ Index listing all of the FAQs currently available on the Internet. In addition, you'll find some of the best FAQ files dealing with topics ranging from finding addresses on the Internet to performing Veronica searches. Here's a partial list of what's included:

- Addresses FAQ—How to find e-mail addresses and locate people on the Internet.
- Gopher FAQ—Questions and answers about using Internet Gophers.
- IRC and MUD FAQs—All about the Internet's IRC (Internet Relay Chat) and MUD (Multi-User Dungeons) features, in case you're so inclined.
- Pictures FAQ—Information on graphics images on the Internet, newsgroups devoted to graphics, decoding and encoding images, image formats, and so forth.
- Veronica FAQ—Answers to frequently asked questions about using the Veronica search utility on the Internet.

Internet 7—Just the FAQs

It's been our experience over the years that, whatever computing task you want to accomplish, there's almost always a program that can easily do it. In fact, there are often several programs that fill the bill. The trick is to find the programs and pick the very best ones. That's what the Glossbrenner's Choice collection is all about.

DOS/Windows tools and utilities

The disks in this collection are for DOS and Windows users. All of the programs are fully functional, and most are extensively documented in ready-to-print manuals. The software itself is either *public domain* (PD) or *shareware*. Public domain programs are yours to do with as you please. But if you like and regularly use a *shareware* program, you are honor-bound to send the programmer the requested registration fee, typically $15 to $25. No one can force you to do this, of course. But when you see a really good piece of software, supporting its creator's efforts is something you will sincerely want to do.

If the comm program you use doesn't have the ZMODEM protocol, you can use the tools provided on this disk to add it. ZMODEM is quite simply the best download protocol, and every online communicator should have access to it.

Communicator's Toolchest

The disk also includes a program for adding support for CompuServe's QB (Quick B) protocol to virtually any comm program. This is by far the best protocol to use when you are downloading files from the data libraries of CompuServe's forums. Like ZMODEM, this protocol has the ability to resume an interrupted download at a later time. Just sign on and start the download again, and it will pick up right where it left off.

The disk also contains several other extremely useful utility programs to make life online easier.

CommWin Communications Program

Our current favorite comm program for Windows users is Gerard E. Bernor's CommWin program. It's quick, clean, intuitive, and beats the Windows terminal program all hollow.

Encryption Tools

You have to assume that if your e-mail *can* be read it *will* be. Thus, it is always a good idea to encrypt sensitive information before sending it electronically. The programs on this disk can so thoroughly encrypt a binary or text file that cipher experts from the National Security Agency or CIA would have a tough time decoding the results. If you have the key, however, you can decrypt files in an instant.

Among other things, this disk includes Philip Zimmermann's famous *Pretty Good Privacy* (PGP) public key RSA encryption program. For more on Mr. Zimmermann, see the Steven Levy cover story "The Cypherpunks vs. Uncle Sam" in the June 12, 1994, issue of the *New York Times Sunday Magazine*.

Idea Processing

PC-Outline is an incredible clone of the commercial idea outlining program, Thinktank. Indeed, many former Thinktank users prefer this shareware product. PC-Outline lets you randomly enter information of almost any type (thoughts, plans, ideas, etc.) and then organize it into a hierarchial structure.

You can then go from viewing the lowest level of detail to a view that shows you only the highest, most important topics. You can also print the outline, copy it into another outline, or paste it directly into your word processor. Ideal for organizing projects, reports, books, and lists—or just organizing your thoughts!

Information Broker Disk

This is the disk described in detail in Appendix E and bound into each copy of *The Information Broker's Handbook*. It includes plain ASCII text files of all the appendices in the book, as well as sample forms, contracts, agreements, and other valuable resources to help you get started as an information broker.

Instant File Management: QFILER, QEDIT, & Associates

QFILER (Quick Filer) by Kenn Flee gives you *complete* control over your files and disk directories. You can tag a group of dissimilar files for deletion or for copying to another disk or directory. You can easily move up and down your directory trees, altering the date and time stamps of files, changing their attributes, compressing, uncompressing, and peering into archives. You can also look at any file on the screen, copy it to your printer, and more. You will find QFILER much easier to use than the Windows 3.1 File Manager or similar DOS-based products.

Also on this disk is WHEREIS, a lightning fast Archie-like file finder. And QEDIT, the famous DOS text-editing program. QEDIT specializes in creating plain text of the sort you must use on the Internet and in most e-mail letters on other systems. Yet it gives you many of the convenience features of a full-blown word processor.

Here's what a recent issue of *Computer Shopper* had to say about Qmodem from Mustang Software: "This is simply the best DOS-based shareware communications package you can find . . . simple to set up and use, and it features about every bell and whistle you expect from a communications package . . . a true powerhouse . . .."

The article goes on to note that Qmodem "bears a great deal of similarity to the ever-popular shareware program Procomm, right down to the key commands . . .. This shareware program is superior to the shareware version of Procomm, however, because when Procomm went commercial, Datastorm stopped developing the shareware version. Mustang, on the other hand, has continually updated the free version of Qmodem, and will continue to do so. It's hard to beat the power, and you can't beat the price."

We heartily agree. If you don't have a first-class comm program yet, try Qmodem.

Qmodem Communications Program

This disk includes the UARTTOOLS package (UARTID.EXE) mentioned in Chapter 12. It allows you to find out whether any of your COM ports have the 16550A National Semiconductor UART and if so, what interrupts they are using. Also on the disk are such intriguing DOS tools as BAT2EXEC (converts a batch program to an .EXE file), PopDOS (lets you shell out to DOS from any program), and UMBFILES (a hands-on memory management tool).

System Configuration Tools (Utilities 9)

TAPCIS makes it easy to handle electronic mail and get the most out of CompuServe forums. It will automatically sign on, pick up your e-mail, and check forums you have specified for messages addressed to you. Then you can sign off, review the information TAPCIS has gathered, and draft replies using the built-in editor. TAPCIS will then sign on again and automatically upload your e-mail and forum message replies. The whole idea is to make using CompuServe as easy and inexpensive as possible.

TAPCIS for CompuServe

TAPCIS can do the same thing when it comes to uploading and downloading files. Just tell it what to do offline, then stand back and let it sign on and zip around the system.

This disk contains the programs AnyWord, LOOKFOR, and FGREP. AnyWord by Eric Balkan can parse any text file, build its own index of keywords, and make it easy to search the file using sophisticated search logic. LOOKFOR works even faster. It lets you do AND, OR, wildcard, and proximity searches of text files—with no prior indexing. You can then print (to disk or printer) relevant file excerpts. FGREP by Chris Dunford operates in a similar way, though it is more UNIX-like and not quite so user-friendly.

Text Search

This disk contains some 45 programs to manipulate, filter, and prepare a text file in virtually any way you can imagine. These programs are particularly convenient when you're dealing with text you get from e-mail correspondents and Internet sites.

Text Treaters

For example, a program called TEXT lets you remove all leading white space on each line of a file, remove all trailing blanks, or convert all white space into the number of spaces you specify. CHOP, will cut a file into the number of pieces you specify. CRLF makes sure that every line in a text file ends with a carriage return and a linefeed so it can be displayed and edited properly. There's also a package by Peter Norton to create an index for a report, document, book, or whatever.

Order Form

You can use the order form on the next page (or a photocopy) to order Glossbrenner's Choice disks. Or you may simply write your request on a piece of paper and send it to us.

We accept Visa and MasterCard, as well as checks or money orders made payable to Glossbrenner's Choice. (U.S. funds drawn on a U.S. bank or international money orders only.) Please allow one to two weeks for delivery. For additional information, please write or call:

Glossbrenner's Choice
699 River Road
Yardley, PA 19067-1965
(215) 736-1213 (voice)
(215) 736-1031 (fax)
alfred@delphi.com

For the latest information or current and forthcoming Glossbrenner books, send a blank e-mail message to *books @ infomat. com.*

Glossbrenner's Choice Order Form
for Readers of *The Information Broker's Handbook*

Name_____

Address_____

City_____State_____ZIP_____

Province/Country_____Phone_____

Payment [ ] Check or Money Order payable to **Glossbrenner's Choice**

       [ ] Visa/MC_____Exp___/___

Signature_____

Mail to:

Glossbrenner's Choice
699 River Rd.
Yardley, PA 19067-1965

The Internet Toolkit
____ Internet 1 Internet Must-Have Files
____ Internet 2 FTP Essentials
____ Internet 3 Telnet Essentials
____ Internet 4 Newsgroup Essentials
____ Internet 5 Mailing List Essentials
____ Internet 6 Compression Tools
____ Internet 7 Just the FAQs

Other Glossbrenner's Choice Disks
____ Communicator's Toolchest
____ CommWin Communications Program
____ Encryption Tools
____ Idea Processing
____ Information Broker Disk
____ Instant File Management: QFILER, QEDIT, & Associates
____ Qmodem Communications Program
____ System Configuration Tools—Utilities 9
____ TAPCIS for CompuServe
____ Text Search
____ Text Treaters

____ Total number of disks, 3.5-inch HD ($5 per disk)   _____

Glossbrenner Books (Book prices include $3 for Book Rate shipping.)
____ The Little Online Book ($21)   _____
____ How to Look It Up Online ($19)   _____
____ Internet Slick Tricks ($19)   _____
____ Internet 101: A College Student's Guide ($23)   _____
____ Glossbrenner's Master Guide to GEnie ($28)   _____
                                          TOTAL   _____

Pennsylvania residents, please add 6% Sales Tax.   _____
Shipping Charge ($3.00 for shipment to U.S. addresses
and $5.00 for shipment outside the U.S.)   _____
                         GRAND TOTAL ENCLOSED   _____

Index

***Boldface** page numbers refer to art

I

IBM-to-Mac file exchanges, 155-156

inaccurate data, 39-40

income potential (*see also* pricing your services), xviii-xix, 7-8, 43-44, 45-46, 51, 53-54, 349-350, 371-373

indexers/abstracters for databases, 152

indexing terms, database, 150, 152, 200

Info USA Inc, 99

InFocus Research Services document delivery service, 93-94

Infomart/Dialog Ltd., 402

Infopreneurs: Turning Data into Dollars, 378

Information Access Company (IAC), 16, 41, 81, 152, 183, 257, 402

Information America, 109, 123, 404

Information Anxiety, 391

information broker disk, 432

Information Broker's Newsletter, 122, 417

Information Broker's Resource Kit, 83, 376

Information Broker's Seminar, 20, 26, 415, 376, 416-417

Information Express, 257, 259, 260

Information for Sale, 377

Information Industry Association (IIA), 405

Information on Demand (IOD), 11, 14, 17, 79, 258, 259, 354, 369

information organization services, 20

Information Professionals Institute (IPI), 123, 415, 420

  order form for literature, 397-398

Information Professionals Network (IPN), 373-374

information providers (IP), 147

Information Today, 42

Information USA Inc., 88

InfoTrak, 71, 81

InfoWorld, 247

Insights on Information Brokering, 377

Inspec, 68

Instant National Locator Guide, 389

insurance companies as clients, 9-10

intelligence required by information broker, 56

International Business Information, 380

International Pharmaceutical Abstracts, 68

International Standards Serial Number (ISSN), 150

Internet, 146, 156, 217-234, 424

  accessing Internet, 221

  ALT newsgroups, 223

  America Online interface, 221, 222, 226

  Archie, 224, 419

  ARPAnet predecessor of Internet, 219

  basic concept of Internet, 218

  Beginner's Guide to the Internet, 429

  BIZ newsgroups, 223

  bulletin board systems (BBS), 223

  Canadian Internet Handbook, 386

  COMP newsgroups, 223

  Compression and Conversion Tools, 233, 430

  CompuServe interface, 222, 226-227

  conferences and seminars, 407-408, 415-420

  connecting to Internet, 221-222

  Connecting to the Internet, 387

  cross-system connections via Internet, 155, 226-228

  Delphi interface, 221, 222, 227

  Directory of Directories on the Internet, 388

  Doing Business on the Internet, 386

  e-mail, 223, 226-228

  features of Internet, 222-225

  "free" use of Internet, 219-220

  frequently asked questions (FAQs), 229

  FTP Essentials, 232, 429

  FTP sites, 217, 222, 225

  GEnie interface, 221, 227

  Gopher, 217, 224-225, 233, 431

  Hytelnet, 232, 429

  information available on Internet, 220-221

information sources, 385-388

Internet 101: A College Student's Guide, 146, 220

Internet Access Providers, 387

Internet at a Glance, 387

Internet Companion, 386

Internet Complete Reference, 386

Internet Connections, 387

Internet Directory, 388

Internet for Dummies, 386

Internet Guide for New Users, 386

Internet Primer for Information Professionals, 387

Internet Relay Chat (IRC), 431

Internet Services FAQ, 230, 429

Internet Slick Tricks, 26, 220, 386

Internet Toolkit, 230, 429

Internet Tools Summary, 230, 231, 429

Internet Yellow Pages, 387

Internet-CMC List, 230, 231, 429

Internet: Getting Started, 387

Internet: Mailing Lists, 388

Just the FAQs, 233, 431

Legal Researcher's Internet Directory, 387

List of Subject-Oriented Internet Resource Guide, 230, 231

Mailing List Essentials, 232, 430

mailing lists, 223, 228-229

MCI Mail interface, 227

Mosaic, Delphi Internet interface, 222

Multi-User Dungeons (MUD), 431

Must-Have Files, 230, 429

NetCom, 222

Netguide, 387

networks included in Internet, 218

New Riders' Official Internet Yellow Pages, 387

NEWS newsgroups, 223

Newsgroup Essentials, 232, 429-430

newsgroups, 223, 228

Pipeline, 222

PPP connections, 171, 221-222

Prodigy interface, 221, 227-228

SCI newsgroups, 223

searching for Internet resources, 220

S

60 Minutes, 116
sales (*see* advertising and marketing)
San Francisco Chronicle, 69
San Jose Mercury News, 69
Sankey, Mike, 111
Savetz, Kevin, 230, 429
scanners, 159
SCI newsgroups, 223
Sci Search document delivery services, 256
Scientific American, 193
Scott, Peter, 232, 429
search log, 323, **324**, 325
search numbers, 321, 323
search-request forms, 321, **322**
  REQUEST.TXT, 424
search statements, 207
search techniques (*see also* databases and database searching), 28-31, 43, 69-70, 318-340
  AND searches, 202
  Archie on Internet, 224, 419
  assembling tools, 325-326
  Boolean logic, 201-202
  confirming customer satisfaction, 339-340
  confirming the assignment, 318-320
  contracts or letters of agreement, 319-320
  cost of search, recording costs, 329-330
  cover letter for reports, 337-338
  databases (*see* databases and database searching)
  day-to-day activity of information broker, 31-34
  differences in databases, 40-42
  duplication of data, 37-38
  EXPAND command, DIALOG, 40
  failed searches, 327-328
  filenames, 328-329
  five rules of search success, 191-196, 203-204
  follow-up on promising information, 330-332
  Gopher on Internet, 224
  government information, 85-101
  inaccurate data, 39-40
  information available, 192
  Knowledge Index, 68-69
  libraries (*see* libraries as sources)
  logbook, search log, 323, **324**, 325
  macros to speed searches, 334-335
  magazines, newspapers, and periodicals, 194
  narrowing the search, 29-30, 30-31, 192, 207, 288, 326-327
  National Technical Information Service (NTIS), 90-92
  needs determination, 28-29
  NOT searches, 202
  options to going online, 193-195
  OR searches, 202
  organizing and analyzing retrieved information, 334-336
  planning the search, 320-325
  practice search, 72-74
  problem clients, 340
  project folders, 321
  project reference numbers, 321, 323
  proximity operators, 201-202
  public records, 103-123
  quitting, knowing when to quit, 332-334
  reference interview, 28-29, 31
  reports
    nonelectric reports, 335
    packaging and presentation, 336-338
  search numbers, 321, 323
  search statements, 207
  search-request forms, 321, **322**
  selectivity in presenting information, 335-336
  source material considerations, 192-193
  syndicated articles, 37-38
  telephone-based research, 19, 69
  testing search techniques, 189-190
  tools and techniques, 196-203, 325-326
  trade journals, 194
  Veronica on Internet, 225
Searcher, 42
Sears online catalog, 162

Secrets of the Super Searchers, 183, 378
Selected Aspects of Potential Legal Liabilities..., 378
selective dissemination of information (SDI), 20, 260
self-employment guidelines, 50
seminars, 407-408, 415-420
serial ports and cards, 167-168
Serials Supplement, 90
services online, shopping services, etc., 161-162
Shannon, Larry, 37
shareware, 237, 431
  communications (comm) programs, 173-174
Shenson on Consulting, 385
SIGCAT CD-ROM Compendium, 390-391
sign off, 206, 208
sign on, 206
SIGS.TXT, 424
Silent Spring, 8
SilverPlatter Information Inc., 90
skills required by information broker, 59-60
SLICK.TXT, 424
SLIP connections, 171, 221-222
Small Time Operator, 384
small-business management, 384-385
SNN Version 5.2 software package, 112
Social Science Search document delivery services, 256
Social Security number verification, 116
Social Security taxes, 50
Society of Competitive Intelligence Professionals (SCIP), 406
software products, 391-392
Software Ventures Corp., 173
Sourcebook of Public Records Providers, 109, 389
special interest groups (SIGs), 160-161, 209-215, 223
  basic structure of SIG, 210-211
  CompuServe, 212, 214
  DIALOG, 214
  downloading files, 215

telex communications, 157-158
Telix, 242
Telnet, 222-223, 225-226, 419
testimonials, 272
testing search techniques, 189-190
text mode operations, 166-167
TEXT program, 434
text search, 433
text treaters, 433-434
TFPL Publishing, 253
thesaurus, databases, 152
Time magazine, 1, 147, 148
Trade and Industry Index, 68, 204, 257
trade associations, 129-130
trade journals, 69, 194
Trademark, 384
training programs, 190
training required by information broker, 58-59, 64
transcripts of SIGs, 161
Transunion, 404
TRW, 195, 404
TWX communications, 157-158
"type" or display charge, 187
types of information needed, 17-19, 21-22
  unusual needs, 18-19
typing skills, 60

U

UARTTOOLS, 433
Ulrich's International Periodicals Directory, 383
UMBFILES, 433
UMI/Data Courier, 183
Uniform Commercial Code (UCC) filings, 117

union lists of periodicals, 83
UNitek Research, 237
Universal Asynchronous Receiver/ Transmitter (UART), 172
Unofficial Internet Book List, 230-231, 386
uploading files, 156
US Government Books for Business Professionals, 390
USA Today, 69

V

V.34 modems, 171
"valuelessness" of information, 36-37
Vault BBS, 236
vendors, 147, 205
VerdictSearch, 403
Veronica, 233
Virtual Community, 391
vital records, 117
voice mail, 128
voter registration, public records, 118
Vu/Text, 41, 183

W

WAIS, 419
Waldenbooks online bookstore, 162
Wall Street Journal, 80, 122, 144
Walters, Barbara, 140
Washington Post, 37, 38, 69
WESTLAW, 403
WHEREIS, 432
White Knight 12, 173
Who Knows What, 381
Who's Who, 81
Whole Internet User's Guide and Catalog, 386

Wilsonline, 403
Windows, tools and utilities, *Glossbrenner's Choice*, 431
WINHytelnet, 232, 429
Work at Home Forum, CompuServe, 30, 60, 67, 161, 183, 188, 212
workers' compensation information, 115
Working From Home, 385
WORKING.TXT, 425
writing articles and columns, as marketing tool, 298-300
writing capture buffer to disk, 208
writing out the search statement, 205-206

X

X.400 gateways, 155
XMODEM, 156

Y

Yanoff, Scott, 230, 429
Yellow Pages ads, 302
yellowsheets, 256
You, Too, Can Find Anybody, 388
Your Internet Consultant, 230

Z

Zen and the Art of the Internet, 386
Ziff-Davis Publishing Company, 4, 239, 247, 248
Zimmermann, Philip, 432
ZIP compression, 233
ZMODEM, 156, 242, 431
Zoom Telephonics, 170
Zterm, 174

DISK WARRANTY

This software is protected by both United States copyright law and international copyright treaty provision. You must treat this software just like a book, except that you may copy it into a computer in order to be used and you may make archival copies of the software for the sole purpose of backing up our software and protecting your investment from loss.

By saying "just like a book," McGraw-Hill means, for example, that this software may be used by any number of people and may be freely moved from one computer location to another, so long as there is no possibility of its being used at one location or on one computer while it also is being used at another. Just as a book cannot be read by two different people in two different places at the same time, neither can the software be used by two different people in two different places at the same time (unless, of course, McGraw-Hill's copyright is being violated).

LIMITED WARRANTY

Windcrest/McGraw-Hill takes great care to provide you with top-quality software, thoroughly checked to prevent virus infections. McGraw-Hill warrants the physical diskette(s) contained herein to be free of defects in materials and workmanship for a period of sixty days from the purchase date. If McGraw-Hill receives written notification within the warranty period of defects in materials or workmanship, and such notification is determined by McGraw-Hill to be correct, McGraw-Hill will replace the defective diskette(s). Send requests to:

> McGraw-Hill, Inc.
> Customer Services
> P.O.Box 544
> Blacklick, OH 43004-0545

The entire and exclusive liability and remedy for breach of this Limited Warranty shall be limited to replacement of defective diskette(s) and shall not include or extend to any claim for or right to cover any other damages, including but not limited to, loss of profit, data, or use of the software, or special, incidental, or consequential damages or other similar claims, even if McGraw-Hill has been specifically advised of the possibility of such damages. In no event will McGraw-Hill's liability for any damages to you or any other person ever exceed the lower of suggested list price or actual price paid for the license to use the software, regardless of any form of the claim.

McGRAW-HILL, INC. SPECIFICALLY DISCLAIMS ALL OTHER WARRANTIES, EXPRESS OR IMPLIED, INCLUDING, BUT NOT LIMITED TO, ANY IMPLIED WARRANTY OF MERCHANTABILITY OR FITNESS FOR A PARTICULAR PURPOSE.

Specifically, McGraw-Hill makes no representation or warranty that the software is fit for any particular purpose and any implied warranty of merchantability is limited to the sixty-day duration of the Limited Warranty covering the physical diskette(s) only (and not the software) and is otherwise expressly and specifically disclaimed.

This limited warranty gives you specific legal rights; you may have others which may vary from state to state. Some states do not allow the exclusion of incidental or consequential damages, or the limitation on how long an implied warranty lasts, so some of the above may not apply to you.